HELPING
SKILLS
AND
STRATEGIES

Thomas M. Skovholt and David A. Rivers
University of Minnesota

LOVE PUBLISHING COMPANY®
Denver • London • Sydney

To my grandchildren, Hanna, Danny,
Julius, and Abby, with love
Tom Skovholt

To my parents, James and Julie,
and my brother, Art
David Rivers

Published by Love Publishing Company
P.O. Box 22353
Denver, Colorado 80222
www.lovepublishing.com

Library of Congress Catalog Card Number 2006920937

Copyright © 2007 by Love Publishing Company
Printed in the United States of America
ISBN 0-89108-327-8

Contents

Preface

This book focuses on professional helping, which is a process in which a trained helper assists a person in managing or resolving personal problems and becoming more skilled at meeting challenges in life. Professional helping can be a powerful and effective way to help people lead more productive and satisfying lives.

Although the concept of helping is not new, *professional* helping—encompassing research and theories, training programs, ethical guidelines, and licensure—has developed largely within the past 100 years. The number of helpers and clients continues to rise, and people increasingly are viewing professional helping as a credible and effective form of assistance.

What is professional helping? How does it work? What are its components? What skills, strategies, and procedures do helpers use? Our primary aim in this book is to address these questions and provide a basic understanding of professional helping by describing helping skills, strategies, and procedures that are used across various types of helping settings and helpers.

Our intended audience is broad. This book is written for students and helpers in the human service professions, such as counseling, psychology, and social work. This book also may be useful for individuals in such fields as nursing, teaching, and human resources because helping is often an aspect of the work these individuals do. The basic helping skills, strategies, and procedures that we discuss in this book are relevant to, and applicable in, many settings and circumstances.

We describe the helping process as consisting of four major activities:

1. *Exploring client concerns*, which involves learning about and developing an understanding of the client's life and problems
2. *Promoting client understanding*, which involves helping clients develop useful and productive understandings of their problems
3. *Charting a new course*, which involves setting goals for positive change and identifying actions to achieve the goals
4. *Working for positive change*, which involves taking action toward goal achievement and evaluating client progress.

These activities all occur within the helping relationship. Most of this book is devoted to describing the helping relationship, the four major activities, and the helping skills and strategies associated with each activity. Many chapters of this book contain hypothetical dialogues and practice exercises to facilitate understanding of the activities, skills, strategies, and procedures discussed.

Our discussion of the helping process is supplemented with chapters on important topics, including diversity and culture in helping and ethical and legal issues in helping. We also discuss aspects of the helper's professional journey as a helper, such as helper development and challenges that helpers face in their work.

Our View of Helping: Influences and Acknowledgments

Our view of helping has been greatly influenced by the work of Carl Rogers (1942, 1951, 1961), Robert Carkhuff (1969, 1984, 2000), and Allen Ivey (e.g., Ivey & Authier, 1978). Rogers stressed the importance of a positive, supportive helping relationship in facilitating change. He also emphasized the need to understand the world of the client from the client's perspective. In his 1942 work *Counseling and Psychotherapy,* Rogers described the characteristic steps in the therapeutic process: (1) The client comes for help; (2) the helping situation is defined; (3) the counselor encourages free expression of feelings; (4) the counselor accepts, recognizes, and clarifies negative feelings; (5) the client gradually expresses positive feelings; (6) the counselor accepts and recognizes the positive feelings; (7) the client develops insight, understanding, and acceptance of him- or herself; (8) choices and possible courses of action are clarified; (9) positive actions are initiated; (10) further insight is developed; (11) the client becomes more confident, self-directed, and independent; and (12) the client experiences a decreasing need for help.

Carkhuff has been instrumental in identifying particular skills (e.g., responding to the content, feeling, and meaning in client expressions) that helpers use to facilitate client progress through the "phases" of helping. In *The Art of Helping,* first published in 1971, Carkhuff (2000) described the phases of helping as follows: Helping begins with a pre-helping attending phase in which clients become physically, emotionally, and intellectually involved in the helping process and helpers communicate their attentiveness to clients. This phase serves as preparation for the three main phases: (1) responding, or facilitating client exploring; (2) personalizing, or facilitating client understanding; and (3) initiating, or facilitating client acting. A review of Rogers's (1942) 12 steps, listed earlier in this section, shows that the helping process, as Rogers described it, generally moves from exploring to understanding (insight) to acting, as does Carkhuff's model. As part of their models of the helping process, many other authors have subsequently described, in some form, the importance of these major components of helping (see, e.g., Hill & O'Brien, 1999; Kottler & Brown, 2000).

Many of the skills described in helping skills books, including this book, were identified by or derived from the early work of Rogers and the subsequent research of Carkhuff. Allen Ivey has been influential in organizing and describing helping skills, which he referred to as "microcounseling skills" or "microskills" (Ivey & Authier, 1978). He organized the skills into a hierarchy, or pyramid, that summarizes the steps of the interviewing, or helping, process (Ivey & Ivey, 1999). The foundation of the pyramid includes such skills as attending, asking questions, and client observation. More advanced skills, such as confrontation, are farther up the pyramid.

Ivey also described a model of helping that contains the same basic elements identified by Rogers and Carkhuff. Ivey's model involves (1) listening to client stories; (2) discovering client strengths and assets; (3) helping clients "restory," or find new ways to view their lives and experiences; and (4) helping clients act on their new ways of thinking and being. As noted in Ivey and Ivey (1999), "Listening to the story, finding positive strengths in that story or another life dimension, and rewriting a new narrative for action are what interviewing and counseling are about. In short: *story—positive asset—restory—action*" (p. 12).

Many helping skills books discuss stages (or phases) of helping and the skills associated with each stage. Carkhuff, for example, used this format. In our book, we discuss major "activities" rather than stages, and we address the major skills that go along with each activity. In many ways, our format is similar to the "stages and skills" format.

We are conscious of the European American and male origins of much of the research, theories, skills, and procedures that underlie helping and helper training in the United States. Such a perspective on helping may not fit for all helpers or clients. Skills and techniques cannot be applied in the same way with everyone. They need to be modified—or new ones need to be developed—to account for cultural variables. Indeed, new theories, models, and strategies have been developed for work with culturally diverse clients. Throughout this book, we attend to cultural issues in helping. We discuss and integrate our own observations as well as the research and work of numerous multicultural researchers and authors.

Thomas M. Skovholt
David A. Rivers

Special Thanks

We want to thank our reviewers, each of whom provided helpful, insightful, and constructive comments on the manuscript:

John C. Dagley, Auburn University
Lisa Y. Flores, University of Missouri
Mark S. Kiselica, The College of New Jersey
Susan A. Neufeldt, University of California, Santa Barbara

And we want to thank our editor, Beverly Rokes, for her diligent and skillful editing.

We extend our gratitude and appreciation to Stan Love for his patience, support, and encouragement throughout the process of writing this book.

Finally, we thank our teachers, students, and clients, who have helped in many ways to shape our understanding of the helping process.

Introduction

CHAPTER 1

Introduction to Professional Helping

CHAPTER OVERVIEW

In this chapter, we introduce professional helping, a form of assistance for people struggling with difficult personal problems. We begin by defining professional helping and by distinguishing it from more informal kinds of assistance. We continue with a discussion of problems and needs and how people cope with problems and unmet needs. We conclude this chapter by discussing how people identify and locate helpers once they have decided to seek help.

What do we live for, if it is not to make life less difficult to each other?

—character from George Eliot's *Middlemarch* (1871–1872/ 1956, p. 537)

What Is Helping?

The word helping is often used to describe assistance provided by one person to another. Whether the issue is personal, academic, financial, legal, spiritual, or something else, one could say that "helping" occurs almost anytime a person provides advice, support, counsel, comfort, information, or guidance to another person. Thus, doctors, lawyers, teachers, financial advisors, psychologists, friends, spiritual leaders, and village elders, to name a few, are all helpers in a general sense.

In this book, we focus on a particular form of helping: the process of assisting people who are struggling with personal problems of everyday living. More specifically, we focus on "professional" helping, in which a trained helper, such as a counselor, therapist, social worker, psychologist, or psychiatrist, assists a person (often referred to as a client, helpee, or patient) in the process of learning to effectively cope with problems that interfere with daily living, healthy development, and well-being. These problems are addressed in a developmental, remedial, and/or preventative way. Thus, helpers assist clients in doing one or more of the following: (1) learning new, more functional skills, attitudes, and behaviors (development); (2) managing or resolving current problems (remediation); or (3) minimizing the chances that particular problems will occur in the future (prevention). The word "professional" distinguishes help provided by a trained helper from more informal, "nonprofessional" kinds of help, such as family support, friendships, and mentor relationships.

Professional helpers do not merely provide advice, consultation, or guidance. They address the deeper, more personal component of problems and help individuals understand and accept responsibility for their feelings, thoughts, and behaviors. They also facilitate awareness of how people's attitudes and behaviors, as well as external forces, such as discrimination and oppression, impact the ability to satisfy needs. Through this process, helpers enable individuals to resolve difficulties, change unproductive attitudes and behaviors, relate to other people in a more satisfying way, more effectively confront everyday challenges, learn how to address future problems, and enhance their quality of life.

Three major models of helping used by professional helpers are the "medical model," the "developmental model," and the "systemic model." The model used depends on the helper's training and theoretical orientation. The medical model of helping involves making specific diagnoses of problems—for example, by using the *Diagnostic and Statistical Manual of Mental Disorders*, 4th Edition (*DSM-IV,* American Psychiatric Association, 1994)—and, sometimes, prescribing medication or hospitalization. The developmental model, which we largely focus on in this book, involves promoting positive growth, assisting in problem management, helping clients change ineffective attitudes and behaviors, and helping clients learn functional skills to deal with everyday challenges and problems. The emphasis is typically on what people can do, not on what is wrong with them. In short, the medical model tends to focus more on pathology or illness—what is "wrong" with the person—whereas the developmental model focuses more on strengths, abilities, and skill development—what is "right" with the person. The systemic model focuses on examining systems, such as families, and helping clients understand how individuals affect and are affected by those systems. The emphasis is on helping people function better in the systems by developing healthy relationships, managing conflict, and understanding how to use resources.

Professional helping is often referred to as "counseling" or "psychotherapy." These two terms are sometimes used to refer to distinct helping processes, and different types of helpers may prefer one term or the other (Young, 2001). Historically, psychotherapy has referred to the process of helping people who demonstrate serious mental disturbances, such as schizophrenia and severe depression, for which specific diagnostic criteria exist (Young, 2001). Psychotherapy has often been viewed as a long-term process that relies heavily on the medical model. Counseling, in contrast, has been viewed as a helping process for more "normal" individuals struggling with problems of everyday living. "Normal" individuals may be defined as people who are basically functioning in life but who experience temporary stresses and difficulties related to life circumstances or developmental transitions, such as leaving home for college, losing a romantic partner, or losing a job. Counseling is typically more short-term than psychotherapy. It places less emphasis on impersonal diagnostic criteria and more emphasis on building good helping relationships that will promote positive change and the acquisition of functional skills— a developmental focus.

The distinction between counseling and psychotherapy has been minimized over time, and today the terms are often used interchangeably (Young, 2001). It is not unusual to see helpers who call themselves "psychotherapists" helping "normal" people work through everyday problems, such as work stress or marital difficulties. Moreover, helpers who describe their work as "counseling" sometimes assist more seriously disturbed individuals, and they may use the *DSM-IV*, especially because many insurance companies require specific diagnoses and treatment plans before they will pay (Young, 2001). The term that a particular helper uses—counseling or psychotherapy—largely depends on the helper's training and preference.

Types of Problems Addressed in Helping

People who seek professional help typically do so because they are struggling in their efforts to manage or resolve personal problems. Problems affect how people feel, think, behave, and interact with other people. Here are some types of problems (along with examples of each type) that motivate individuals to seek help:

- Anger (e.g., abusive behavior toward family, friends, and coworkers)
- Anxiety (e.g., fear of social situations)
- Depression (e.g., social isolation)
- Loss (e.g., end of a romantic relationship)
- Everyday stress (e.g., facing deadlines at work or school)
- Traumatic stress (e.g., being involved in or witnessing a serious accident)
- Adjustment difficulties (e.g., moving to a new city)
- Relationship conflict (e.g., marital discord)
- Health concerns (e.g., insomnia; learning that one has a serious illness)
- Substance abuse (e.g., alcoholism; drug abuse)

- Vocational concerns (e.g., identifying career interests)
- Academic concerns (e.g., poor grades; inability to select a major)
- Existential concerns (e.g., boredom; feelings of meaninglessness in life)

As this list shows, people seek help for a wide range of problems. Sometimes, people need assistance in coping with a recent troubling event, such as a traumatic incident at work or school. Sometimes, they want support as they grieve the loss of a family member or friend. People may seek help as a way to increase their self-awareness and understanding of life. In many cases, however, people seek help in dealing with problems that have worsened over time—perhaps over a span of many years. Their coping strategies have not worked well, and they realize that they need professional assistance.

Problems may derive from many possible sources. For example, ineffective attitudes and behaviors, such as negative self-talk and aggressiveness, can cause (or exacerbate) problems. External, environmental factors, such as discrimination, oppression, or domestic violence, may also be important, as may biological or genetic factors. In most cases, numerous variables combine to cause problems. Depression, for example, may be the result of social isolation, low self-esteem, and chemical imbalances in the brain.

Problems and Needs

Problems and needs are often connected. In many cases, problems reflect unmet needs. People often seek help because their attempts to satisfy needs have largely failed.

Everyone has needs. People's needs affect how they feel, think, behave, interact with others, and view the world. Needs can provide direction and motivation in life, and satisfying them is key to a sense of well-being. There are many needs that are widely viewed as basic to all people, such as shelter, food, and affection. Numerous authors and theorists (e.g., Maslow, 1954) have discussed and ordered basic human needs. For example, Doyle (1998) identified two kinds of needs: physiological needs (drives) and psychological needs (motives). Physiological needs include, for example, food, water, and shelter. Psychological needs include

- the need for safety, security, and self-preservation;
- the need for structure and order;
- the need for attention, contact, and positive regard;
- the need for affection, belonging, and love;
- the need to feel unique and for positive self-regard; and
- the need to influence and control one's environment (Doyle, 1998, pp. 20–22).

When people experience failure in satisfying needs, they may decide to seek help (Cormier & Hackney, 1999). The unsatisfied needs are the problem they need to address, or at least part of it. For example, a college student may seek assistance because he is having trouble meeting people and making friends. He is having difficulty satisfying his need for attention, belonging, contact, and perhaps affection. Cormier and Hackney (1999) observed that people do not always recognize or understand their needs or possess the skills required to meet their needs once they do recognize them. These individuals know that something is wrong or missing in their lives, but many times they require the assistance of helpers to articulate exactly what need is unmet and to learn how to meet it.

Most people who seek help have tried to satisfy their needs, but they have done so in ways that are maladaptive and largely ineffective. Take, for instance, the example of the college student who is having difficulty meeting people and making friends. "Mark" wants a better social life, but he is apprehensive about initiating conversations, so he sits in public places, such as the university library, waiting and hoping that someone will approach and talk to him. With this passive effort to socialize, Mark makes other people responsible for creating his social life. As a result, he may have difficulty developing the satisfying relationships that he would like to have, and his need to meet people and make new friends will probably continue to go unmet.

When needs are unmet, they may be blocked or stifled, but they do not go away (Teyber, 2000). Unmet needs that continue to go unsatisfied ultimately manifest themselves, often through various physiological and psychological behaviors, such as anxiety, anger, stress, sadness, and weight loss or gain. All of these behaviors may worsen the longer the needs go unmet.

To deal with unmet needs, people develop various coping strategies. Effectively functioning people tend to cope with difficulties proactively by realistically assessing their problems, developing appropriate problem-solving skills, and learning how to express emotions in a mature, healthy manner (Doyle, 1998). People who function less effectively tend to utilize more reactive, maladaptive strategies, such as aggression, defensiveness, self-blaming, and withdrawal (Doyle, 1998). The longer needs go unsatisfied, the more deeply ingrained ineffective coping strategies may become. Often, the ineffective strategies only make matters worse. Individuals feel increasingly hopeless as they become "stuck" in patterns of ineffective attitudes and behaviors.

Efforts to Deal With Problems and Unmet Needs

Professional help is usually not an individual's first choice in dealing with problems and unmet needs. Here are some reasons why people may not seek help initially:

- Denial that problems exist or that they need help
- Insistence that they can address problems and needs on their own
- Embarrassment about acknowledging the need for help
- The stigma attached to seeking professional help for personal problems
- The feeling that seeking help means one is weak, defective, or "crazy"
- Lack of knowledge about whom to contact or where to go
- Previous negative helping experiences
- Cultural values and beliefs (e.g., personal problems should be handled within the family)
- Misconceptions or negative stereotypes about helpers and/or the helping process
- Financial cost

Individuals who seek professional help usually do so after having pursued other options. Often, they first attempt to resolve problems and satisfy needs using the largely ineffective strategies that they have learned—for example, by passively waiting for others to approach and initiate conversation. When they recognize the ineffectiveness of these methods, they may acknowledge the need for some kind of assistance and turn to friends or family or pursue other options, such as reading self-help books. Pedersen and Ivey (1993) noted that, as a way to address problems, clients in many cultures turn to inner resources and think about proverbs or basic truths taught to them when they were young.

Professional help is often the last resort, a step taken when previous actions have failed and people feel overwhelmed and confused. Their discouragement and hopelessness can make their problems seem impossible to manage, and demoralization is common (Frank & Frank, 1991). For many individuals, failed attempts to address problems and satisfy needs combined with the desire to alleviate the pain and discouragement caused by the problems and unmet needs can create the distressing, confusing sense of having unsolvable problems that must be solved. At this point, levels of stress and unpleasant emotions such as anger, frustration, anxiety, and sadness are high enough that individuals are motivated to seek professional help. Family members and friends may also persuade individuals to seek help. In some cases, problems reach the point where individuals get themselves into legal trouble (e.g., by committing violent acts). In these cases, a court may order such individuals to seek professional help.

With the exception of instances in which a court order is issued, whether and when a person seeks professional help is largely a function of readiness (see Prochaska, DiClemente, & Norcross, 1992). The concept of readiness generally refers to an individual's awareness of a problem and his or her willingness to address it. A person who is ready to participate in the helping process is typically more motivated to acknowledge and address problems than one who is not ready. People who lack awareness of problems or believe they can handle problems on their own probably are not ready to seek professional help. It may take greater awareness of problems or numerous frustrating experiences in trying to resolve problems before they will be ready to turn to professional helpers.

What to Do, Where to Go, and Whom to See

Deciding to seek professional help is a significant step. Once a person has made this decision, what to do, where to go, and whom to see become issues. How do I find professional helpers? Where do they work? Should I go to a counselor or a psychiatrist? What is the difference between the two? Not knowing what to do, where to go, or whom to see is sometimes a significant hindrance to seeking help.

When people are ready to seek help, they may use one or more methods to try to locate helpers. They may look in the telephone book. They may get referrals from friends or family members. Sometimes, they turn to referral services such as those offered by employee assistance programs and health insurance plans for suggestions of appropriate professionals. Social services agencies and family doctors can also suggest referrals. In fact, some people go first to their doctor to address problems, especially when the problems are manifested physically (e.g., through headaches or insomnia). It is not unusual for clients from cultures that value emotional control to present and describe their concerns in terms of physical symptoms. If it appears that there may be a psychological component to the problem, the doctor may offer a referral to a helper. Finally, schools, universities, religious institutions, and employers often have access to appropriate referrals or have professional helpers on staff.

A significant amount of research has been conducted on helper-client "matching," which has been described as "the process of asking clients who they would prefer to see if given a choice between culturally congruent (e.g., same race or gender) or incongruent (e.g., different race or gender) [helpers]" (Pope-Davis et al., 2002, p. 357). The assumption is that if the helper and the client are similar on one or more of these dimensions (e.g., race), the client may feel more comfortable working with the helper and the helper may better understand the sociopolitical context of the client (Pope-Davis et al., 2002). Although the research findings on helper-client matching have been mixed and research processes used in these studies have been criticized for methodological problems, it appears that, in general, clients prefer helpers who are similar to them in terms of values and worldview (Coleman, Wampold, & Casali, 1995; Fischer, Jome, & Atkinson, 1998; Pope-Davis et al., 2002). "Worldview" essentially refers to the way a person sees, interprets, understands, and relates to the world (see chapter 5). Pope-Davis et al. (2002) suggested that in the absence of a "guarantee" of similarity in values and worldview, clients may select helpers based on visible demographic criteria, such as race, in the hopes of obtaining a helper who shares some similar elements of values and worldview. The significance of particular cultural characteristics or constructs in a client's life and problems may also influence his or her preferences. In their study, Pope-Davis et al. (2002) found that clients who defined themselves and their problems using cultural constructs seemed to prefer racially or gender similar helpers.

Sometimes, individuals have to keep searching until they find professional helpers that suit them. Their first choice may not work out. The helper may believe that another helper would be more appropriate to address the individual's particular problem. The client may feel that the helper does not understand his or her problems. Or the helper and the client may not be a good fit in terms of their personalities or worldviews.

In any case, seeking help can be an uncomfortable process. A good deal of inner strength and a willingness to take risks are often required for individuals to admit the need for help and then actively seek out professional helpers that suit them.

Summary and Concluding Remarks

This chapter serves as a brief introduction to professional helping, which is generally defined as a process in which a trained helper assists a person in effectively coping with personal problems. Professional helping has become increasingly popular over the past several decades as people have recognized its value and importance in working through difficulties and achieving a sense of well-being.

Although there are many different kinds of professional helpers, a number of similarities can be seen among them. For example, all professional helpers work to develop good relationships with their clients, and helpers in different professions use many of the same skills. These similarities reflect some of the basic elements of professional helping. It is these elements that we focus on throughout this book.

In this chapter, we also discussed types of client problems and human needs. Most people attempt to address problems and needs on their own before going to helpers. Whether and when they seek professional help often depends on the success of their efforts in managing or resolving their problems, their readiness to acknowledge the need for help, and their ability to locate suitable helpers.

Deciding to seek professional help and then doing the work to address problems and unmet needs reflect a recognition of the need for change. Many people who seek help recognize the need for change, but then they resist change—for example, by becoming defensive or blaming other people for their problems. Change is difficult and involves risk because it forces people to expend effort; take responsibility; confront issues, feelings, and obstacles that they would rather avoid; abandon ineffective but familiar attitudes and behaviors; and learn new skills.

For some people, change is so scary that they never seek help. They choose instead to endure the long-term pain and consequences of their problems. Seeking help and working to manage or resolve problems often require a lot of patience, effort, and courage. Those who persist, brave the discomfort, and work hard are often rewarded for their efforts.

Questions for Thought

1. How would you describe professional helping?

2. In this chapter, we discussed several basic human needs. How would you categorize human needs? Can you identify any needs that were not described in this chapter?

3. If you were struggling with a difficult personal problem, what steps would you take to manage or resolve it? Whom, if anyone, would you talk to? How willing would you be to seek professional help, and at what point would you do so? How would you locate a professional helper suitable to you?

CHAPTER 2

Diversity, Culture, and Helping

CHAPTER OVERVIEW

Cultural content is integrated throughout this book, reflecting the fact that diversity and culture are pervasive influences in helping, not merely special topics. Nevertheless, as we begin our discussion of professional helping, we feel it is important to specifically address a number of cultural issues, topics, and concepts to highlight the cultural context within which helping occurs. We begin this chapter with a discussion of cultural diversity in the United States and the increasing attention given to diversity. We then describe several important terms and topics in multicultural helping, such as culture, multiculturalism, individualism, and collectivism. Next, we discuss cultural encapsulation, bias, prejudice, discrimination, and oppression. Our focus then shifts to culturally skilled helping, with a discussion of multicultural competencies and characteristics of culturally skilled helpers. Suggestions on how to become a culturally skilled helper are also provided. Much of this chapter focuses on diversity, but we also discuss the importance of recognizing how people are similar. Finally, we discuss two challenges associated with studying cultural issues in helping.

Racist, sexist and homophobic thoughts cannot, alas, be abolished by fiat but only by the time-honored methods of persuasion, education and exposure to the other guy's— or, excuse me, woman's— point of view.

—Barbara Ehrenreich (1991, p. 84)

Cultural Diversity

The United States is a culturally rich and diverse society. However, professional helping in the United States has largely been based on White, male, middle-class, heterosexual culture. The values of this culture, including verbal expression, individuality, material success, and self-sufficiency, have influenced the helping process and have often been used as indicators of mental health, normality, and success in helping. However, in a diverse society, all people do not share the same values. Despite the popularity of the metaphor, the United States is not really a "melting pot" where various cultures assimilate and blend together to create one "American culture." Rather, it is a pluralistic society in which "members of diverse ethnic, racial, religious and social groups maintain participation in and development of their traditions and special interests while cooperatively working toward the interdependence needed for a nation's unity" (England, 1992, cited in Hansen, 1997, p. 157).

Over the past few decades, especially since the civil rights movement in the 1960s, the helping professions have been challenged to pay more attention to diversity, to respect the values and traditions of all cultures, and to accommodate the needs of a greater range of clients. Indeed, culturally skilled helpers are in demand. The helping professions have worked in recent years to improve the multicultural competence of their practitioners so clients of diverse backgrounds can be served effectively. This effort can be seen in the following developments:

- Research on multicultural issues has flourished, with an increasing number of books and journal articles being published on multicultural topics.
- Various psychological tests and diagnostic tools have been broadened or revised so they can be used with many populations.
- Helpers are encouraged to apply helping theories with more flexibility, taking into account cultural variables. Also, new helping theories and models have been created, such as D. W. Sue, Ivey, and Pedersen's (1996) theory of multicultural counseling and therapy (MCT).
- Muticultural issues, topics, skills, and helping strategies are increasingly integrated into course work in helper training and degree programs.
- Multicultural workshops, seminars, and training programs are commonplace.
- Numerous organizations, divisions, and groups that focus on multicultural helping, such as the Association for Multicultural Counseling and Development (a division of the American Counseling Association), have been founded in the past few decades.
- Professional organizations, such as the American Counseling Association, the American Psychological Association, and the National Association of Social Workers, have adopted ethical guidelines that direct their members to respect the diversity of clients. (See, for example, the ACA (1995) *Code of Ethics and Standards of Practice,* Section A.2; the APA (2002) *Ethical Principles of Psychologists and Code of Conduct,* Principle E and Section 2.01(b); and the NASW (1999) *Code of Ethics,* Section 1.05.)

Even with these efforts, there is still much work to be done. For example, the helping professions in the United States need to do a better job of serving racial and ethnic minority groups. D. W. Sue and Sue (2003) have discussed research showing that the drop-out rate after only one helping session is higher for racial and ethnic minority clients than for White clients. Many racial and ethnic minorities see helping, especially by White helpers, as a way to get them to conform to a system of White values. These problems and concerns may be partially alleviated by increasing the diversity of helpers. More racial and ethnic minority helpers are needed to assist minority clients. Although helping can be done effectively when helpers and clients are of different cultures, some clients feel more comfortable with helpers from their own cultural group.

Important Terms and Topics: Definitions and Discussion

As we begin to address culture in the helping process, it is important to define some terms and discuss topics that are significant in multicultural helping. In the following sections, we describe culture, multiculturalism, multicultural helping, etic and emic approaches to helping, and individualism and collectivism.

Culture

You have heard the term "culture" and probably have a basic idea of what it means. However, precisely defining the term has been more challenging for the helping professions than one might think. When many people see the word "culture" or a variant of that word, such as "multicultural," they think of race or ethnicity. Hansen (1997), S. D. Johnson (1990), and Ponterotto and Pedersen (1993) noted that some authors and researchers have limited or narrowly defined the term culture and its variants in this way (see also Lee, 1991). Indeed, an argument for defining culture narrowly is that doing so helps the term retain integrity and meaning. When, in contrast, large numbers of variables are subsumed under terms such as culture and multicultural, the terms become overly inclusive and lose meaning (see Lee & Richardson, 1991). Then, any characteristic or difference can take on cultural significance.

We agree with a broader—though not overly broad—definition of culture that includes such variables as age, occupation, race, ideology, gender, social class, spirituality, disability status, and sexual orientation, among others (see Pedersen, 1991, 1997). A broad definition appears to be more accepted than a narrow definition in the helping professions today, and such a definition recognizes that there are many facets to one's identity—not just race or ethnicity. Here is a sample of how authors have broadly defined the term culture:

> Institutions, languages, values, religions, genders, sexual orientations, thinking, artistic expressions, and social and interpersonal relationships. (Baruth & Manning, 1999, p. 7)

> Shared constraints that limit the behavior repertoire available to members of a certain sociocultural group in a way different from individuals belonging to some other group. (Poortinga, 1990, p. 6)

> A convenient label for knowledge, skills, and attitudes that are learned and passed on from one generation to the next. Accordingly, this transmission of culture occurs in a physical environment in which certain places, times, and stimuli have acquired special meanings. (Segall, 1979, p. 91)

> Demographic (age, gender, place of residence, etc.), status (social, educational, economic, etc.), and affiliation (formal and informal) variables along with ethnographic variables (nationality, ethnicity, language, religion, etc.). (Pedersen, 1997, p. 5)

Axelson (1999) used a broad definition of culture, defining a cultural group as "any group of people who identify or associate with one another on the basis of some common purpose, need, or similarity of background" (p. 3). We offer the following as another broad definition of culture: the values, attitudes, customs, beliefs, characteristics, and behaviors of a group of individuals at a given point in time.

It is evident from these definitions that a person is a member of more than one culture. Pedersen and Ivey (1993) noted that "each of us . . . 'belongs to' a thousand or more cultures, any one of which might become salient or most relevant depending on the time, the place, and the situation" (p. 1). A person may tend to identify closely with one or two cultures, but one can imagine the vast number of cultural groups to which a person can belong. As just one example, think of a 21-year-old, middle-class, heterosexual, Indian, Buddhist, vegetarian, undergraduate, female mathematics major with a physical disability.

Cultures vary considerably in size. Some are very large (e.g., men); others are rather small (e.g., Ph.D. candidates in Counseling Psychology at the University of Minnesota). Cultures also tend to change over time as values, attitudes, and technology change. In addition, differences exist *within* cultural groups, and thus care must be taken to not stereotype people based on cultural characteristics. Clearly, not all people in a particular cultural group are the same: Not all men are the same. Not all people with disabilities are the same. Not all African Americans are the same (Pedersen, 1991). Indeed, differences within a particular group can be more significant and important than differences between groups (Pedersen, 1996).

As an example of differences within a group, Americans of Korean extraction, like members of other racial and ethnic groups, possess varying levels of "acculturation," which is defined as the extent to which they have modified their cultural patterns by adapting to the cultural patterns of the larger society (Axelson, 1999). As the children of Korean immigrants grow older, they may demonstrate more acculturation than their parents. For example, they may speak English more fluently and may be more fond of American popular music, while their parents may adhere to the more traditional values and customs of their homeland. Helpers need to recognize such differences in acculturation and avoid assuming that all Korean Americans, or members of other cultural groups, share the same attitudes and values.

People of all cultures deal with problems and stresses, but how they respond behaviorally to these challenges is often influenced by culture (see Das, 1995). Indeed, as Pedersen (1997) observed: "Behavior is not meaningful data until and unless the behavior is understood in the context of the person's culturally learned expectations" (p. 9). For example, when a man faces a setback, he may try to "suck it up" or "take it like a man." In contrast, a woman may be inclined to express her feelings. As another example, people from cultures that value verbal expression may be encouraged to show emotions and talk about problems as a way to work through them. However, people from cultures that value emotional control and privacy with regard to problems may keep more to themselves and manifest problems and psychological distress somatically, such as by having an upset stomach or a headache.

Each culture is unique. Recognizing and respecting cultural variables are necessary for helpers to relate to their clients and help them effectively. As noted by Pedersen (1997), "Culture is part of the environment, and all behavior is shaped by culture, so that it is rare (perhaps even impossible) for any human being ever to behave without responding to some aspect of culture" (p. 8).

Multiculturalism

Because there is no precise definition of culture, it is also hard to define "multiculturalism" with precision. Axelson (1999) described multiculturalism as "the involvement and inclusion of multiple groups of people with varied cultural backgrounds" (p. 14). One might also define the term as the existence and recognition of diverse groups and their unique needs, values, and experiences.

Multiculturalism is a particularly important concept for helpers because of all the different client cultures they encounter in their work. Helpers need to be culturally knowledgeable and culturally skilled to effectively assist diverse clients. Multiculturalism has had such a great impact on the helping professions in recent years that it has been referred to as the "fourth force" in helping (Pedersen, 1991). That is, it joins the three traditional forces—psychodynamic, humanistic/existential, and behavioral—as an important way to understand human behavior.

Multicultural Helping

"Multicultural helping" is a term used to describe a helping relationship in which the helper and the client belong to different cultural groups and have different worldviews (Das, 1995). "Worldview" refers to the way a person sees, interprets, understands, and relates to the world (see chapter 5). Under a broad definition of culture, multicultural helping occurs, for example, when a heterosexual helper assists a gay client, when a female helper assists a male client, or when a European American helper works with an African American client. With so many different cultures in the United States, it is hard to imagine a helping relationship that is not impacted by culture. Some authors have even noted that in such a culturally diverse society, all helping must be multicultural (Das, 1995; Gama, 1991).

Etic and Emic Approaches to Helping

A significant issue in multicultural helping relates to how helpers (as well as researchers and theorists) approach the helping process. There are two major approaches, the "etic" approach and the "emic" approach. These terms are derived from "phon*etic*" (language-general) and "phon*emic*" (language-specific) analysis, which are terms that linguists use to describe the rules of language (Pedersen, 1999). The "etic" approach attempts to identify universal aspects of human behavior across cultures (e.g., existential anxiety, desire for self-knowledge) and asserts that the same basic helping concepts, theories, and processes can be used anywhere in the world (Draguns, 2002; Fischer et al., 1998; D. Sue, 1997). This approach is often referred to as a "culture-general" approach. Fischer et al. (1998) observed that proponents of etic approaches have typically embraced Western-based helping theory and associated helping strategies that they believe are cross-culturally effective.

The "emic" approach asserts that helping strategies that are indigenous and unique to the client's culture are needed to effectively serve clients (Draguns, 2002; Fischer et al., 1998). This approach, which is often referred to as a "culture-specific" approach, does not reflect a mere modification of current theories; rather, it takes the cultural characteristics of clients into account and asserts that goals and processes need to be culture specific (e.g., utilizing culturally unique problem-solving methods) (D. Sue, 1997).

The etic approach has been criticized for not giving enough attention to cultural differences. Further, as D. Sue (1997) noted, it is difficult to demonstrate that certain constructs, such as "existential anxiety" and "self-knowledge," are truly universal. The emic approach also has limitations. Helpers must learn about the characteristics of each culture and must learn helping strategies and methods for each culture (D. Sue, 1997), which are daunting tasks. Also, because the focus in emic approaches is on cultural differences, individual differences receive less attention (D. Sue, 1997).

Some authors have suggested that combining both approaches, as opposed to using one or the other, may be the most effective approach to helping (Baruth & Manning, 1999; Das, 1995; Draguns, 2002). Fischer et al. (1998) suggested a method for bridging the gap between etic and emic approaches that involves looking at various common factors in helping.

Individualism and Collectivism

As noted earlier, professional helping in the United States has been based largely on White male culture, which tends to emphasize individualism. Many clients, however, come from cultures that place more emphasis on collectivism. In the United States, people of color, more so than White individuals, tend to have a collectivist perspective (Greenfield, 1994). The following is a comparison of the defining features of individualism and collectivism as described by Hall, Lopez, and Bansal (2001) and Triandis (1995, 1996):

Individualism

- The self is defined as independent and autonomous from collectives (e.g., families or tribes).
- Personal goals take priority over collective goals.
- Social behavior is shaped by attitudes and by consequences that are perceived as enjoyable.
- If costs of relationships exceed the advantages, the relationships are dropped.
- A dualist perspective is taken: The mind and body are separate.
- Independence and self-reliance are important.
- Competition is valued.
- Verbal expressiveness and assertiveness are important.
- An internal locus of control exists.

Collectivism

- The self is defined as an aspect of a collective (e.g., a family or tribe).
- Personal goals are subordinate to the collective's goals.
- Norms, duties, and obligations regulate social behavior.
- The needs of others in the collective are important determinants of social behavior.
- People are interdependent; cooperation is important.
- Respect for authority is important.
- Harmony with nature and the universe is valued.

The tendency of Western-oriented helpers to promote values and goals that are consistent with the individualist orientation can be problematic and inappropriate for clients who have a collectivist orientation. Schneider, Karcher, and Schlapkohl (1999) observed that in many Native North American and Asian cultures, the pursuit and fulfillment of personal desires and needs regardless of the effect on family or societal harmony might be seen as a sign of selfishness, isolation, and dysfunction rather than health. Non-Western clients may not be looking for a way to express individual desires but rather for a way to reach family or community goals, achieve or promote harmony in the group, or deal with rejection from the group (Schneider et al., 1999).

Helpers need to be careful, however, not to stereotype clients and assume, based on the client's culture, that the client possesses a particular perspective. Helpers can ascertain the client's perspective as they explore the client's concerns. For example, a helper might ask questions about the client's family, the importance of family to the client, and the involvement of family in the client's life.

Clients may possess or desire aspects of both individualist and collectivist perspectives. Indeed, Draguns (2002) states: "Perhaps the challenge to the helping professions is how to help individuals to attain equilibrium and integration of their strivings for autonomy and for belonging. Pronouncedly individualist clients might be encouraged to become aware of their latent or suppressed affiliative strivings, whereas lifelong collectivists might be helped to promote the realization of their private, yet habitually overlooked, aspirations" (p. 35).

Ignoring Culture in Helping: Cultural Encapsulation

Many helper training programs have been criticized for ignoring or paying very little attention to cultural variables in the helping process (see, e.g., Hall et al., 2001; D. Sue, 1997). Helpers trained in programs that basically ignore culture learn to help using a Western-oriented model of helping, but they receive little if any training on how to adapt their techniques or how to utilize new ones to accommodate cultural variations among clients. These helpers may assume that the procedures, skills, interventions, strategies, and concepts that they have learned can be applied in the same way to all clients regardless of culture. The result is a rigid helping style that may be unhelpful, irrelevant, or even harmful to clients of different cultures.

This failure to consider cultural variations reflects "cultural encapsulation," which can be defined as a rigid adherence to a narrow model of helping that disregards cultural variables and offers a universal concept of what constitutes health and normality (D. W. Sue & Sue, 2003; Wrenn, 1962). Cultural encapsulation may occur due to poor training or rigid personal beliefs. Regardless of the cause, culturally encapsulated helpers may hurt their culturally different clients more than help them. The following are some ways in which culturally encapsulated helpers can cause harm.

Disregard for Clients. Culturally encapsulated helpers may, deliberately or inadvertently, disregard their clients' perspectives and values. They may also disregard helping systems, sources, and processes that are important in their clients' cultures, such as mentors or respected elders. This behavior by helpers devalues their clients' cultural characteristics and suggests that the helping processes the helpers ascribe to are superior to those in the clients' cultures. Clients may feel ignored, disrespected, and imposed upon and may perceive the helping process as irrelevant to their lives and problems.

Rigid Application of Procedures, Skills, Interventions, and Strategies. A particular technique or helping approach will not work equally well with all clients. For example, clients from some cultures may be offended, scared, or confused by the confrontational interventions used in Gestalt therapy. If clients do not participate in or respond to particular interventions, culturally encapsulated helpers may perceive the clients as uncooperative or resistant when, in fact, the interventions were inappropriate.

Negative Assessments and Diagnoses. Because of their limited, culturally biased definitions of what is normal and healthy, culturally encapsulated helpers may incorrectly interpret some attitudes and behaviors of clients from other cultural groups. Behaviors and attitudes these helpers view as abnormal or pathological may be quite normal or adaptive, especially considering that many of these cultural groups have been subjected to discrimination and oppression (D. W. Sue & Sue, 2003).

Throughout their education and practice, helpers need to be aware of how their values, attitudes, and training affect their approach to helping. They must avoid cultural encapsulation and strive to increase their multicultural competence. Doing so improves their ability to work effectively with a diverse range of clients.

Bias, Prejudice, Discrimination, and Oppression

A thorough understanding of cultural issues in helping requires an awareness of how bias, prejudice, discrimination, and oppression may affect clients and the helping process. These attitudes and behaviors often stem from fear, intolerance, lack of empathy, and lack of respect for differences. They affect how people are viewed and treated. Not only must helpers recognize the extent to which bias, prejudice, discrimination, and oppression have impacted their clients' lives, they also need to become aware of the extent to which *they themselves* may demonstrate these attitudes and behaviors.

Bias

Bias is a preference, tendency, or inclination toward particular ideas, values, people, or groups. For example, an employer who prefers to hire only White males is demonstrating bias. Bias can narrow one's worldview, prevent the consideration of multiple perspectives and options, and lead to discrimination and oppression.

Prejudice

Prejudice is a negative, overgeneralized belief or judgment about the nature and characteristics of a person or group of people (Allport, 1954; Ponterotto, 1991; Ponterotto & Pedersen, 1993). Prejudice is based on faulty, inflexible generalizations and unsubstantiated data, and it is held regardless of evidence or facts that contradict it (Allport, 1954; Ponterotto, 1991; Ponterotto & Pedersen, 1993). An example of prejudice is a person's belief that all people not of his or her race are inferior. As with bias, prejudice can narrow one's worldview, prevent the consideration of multiple perspectives and options, and lead to discrimination and oppression.

Discrimination

Borrowing from and paraphrasing Ridley's (1989) definition of racism and expanding it to include other cultural dimensions besides race, we define discrimination as behavior or patterns of behavior that systematically tend to deny a person or group access to opportunities or privileges while perpetuating opportunities or privileges for another person or group. A key component of discrimination is power (Ridley, 1989). The discriminatory behavior is carried out by a person or a group that has power over others. Discrimination includes, for example, racism, sexism, ageism, and homophobia. As mentioned earlier, biases and prejudices may lead to discrimination.

The experience of discrimination is a common theme among many groups in the United States, including racial and ethnic minority groups, women, gays and lesbians, and persons with disabilities (see Atkinson & Hackett, 1998). Discrimination can be a significant factor in the identity development of members of these groups. By educating themselves about various groups and by exploring their clients' concerns (see Part Four), helpers can learn how discrimination affects their clients and factors into their problems. Helpers also need to take steps to avoid demonstrating discrimination themselves, lest they perpetuate the discrimination that their clients have suffered. Suggestions of ways to avoid discrimination are offered in the section of this chapter entitled "Becoming a Culturally Skilled Helper."

Discrimination can be expressed even by individuals who do not possess biased or prejudicial attitudes. As Ridley (1989, 1995) observed, intent to discriminate is not necessary for an action to be discriminatory. In his discussion of racism, Ridley described "unintentional racism" as the behavior of people who are well intentioned and relatively free of racial prejudice but who inadvertently engage in racist behavior (Ponterotto & Pedersen, 1993; Ridley, 1989, 1995). An example is a helper who views an Asian American client's silence and lack of eye contact as disinterest and resistance to the helping process when, in fact, such behavior may signal respect and deference to the helper (Ponterotto & Pedersen, 1993; Ridley, 1989). Such misinterpretations often occur due to lack of knowledge about cultural differences. Ridley's concept can easily be extended to other areas besides race. For example, one can engage in "unintentional sexism" or "unintentional homophobia."

Unintentional discrimination, such as unintentional racism, is an insidious and particularly damaging influence in helping because helpers who engage in it do not know they are doing so (see Ridley, 1995). It can, therefore, be very difficult to detect—and admit. It is important for helpers to continuously monitor their attitudes and behaviors, learn as much as they can about other cultures, and solicit feedback from supervisors and colleagues. Doing so helps them maximize their competence and avoid discrimination when working with culturally different clients.

An interesting perspective on the issue of discrimination—specifically on the issue of racism—was offered by McIntosh (1989) in her article "White Privilege: Unpacking the Invisible Knapsack." McIntosh observed: "As a white person, I realized I had been taught about racism as something which puts others at a disadvantage, but had been taught not to see one of its corollary aspects, white privilege, which puts me at an advantage" (p. 10). She then listed more than two dozen everyday privileges that she believes she has received simply because she is White. Among them are

- being able to turn on the television and see people of her race widely represented;
- knowing that when a police officer pulls her over, it is not because of race;
- feeling sure that if she needs legal or medical help, her race will not work against her;
- accepting a job offer without having coworkers suspect that she was hired because of affirmative action; and
- feeling that if she wishes to see the "person in charge," she will more than likely be dealing with someone of her own race.

McIntosh's article provides an informative description of the process of honestly confronting and examining one's biases, prejudices, discriminatory behaviors, and cultural beliefs. For helpers, this process continues throughout their careers.

Oppression

Oppression often overlaps with discrimination. It refers to abuse, harm, or mistreatment that leads to psychological distress, emotional pain, and suffering (Hanna, Talley, & Guindon, 2000). Power is a major aspect of oppression. A person or a group with power misuses that power and mistreats another person or group, who is expected to conform to the wishes of the oppressor (Hanna et al., 2000). Oppression can be obvious or more subtle, and it can occur by force (e.g., physical abuse) or by depriving a person or group of objects, experiences, or a set of living conditions (e.g., through neglect or withholding food or property) (Hanna et al., 2000).

As with discrimination, the experience of oppression is a common theme among many cultural groups in the United States, including racial and ethnic minority groups, women, gays and lesbians, and persons with disabilities (see Atkinson & Hackett, 1998). Oppression can significantly affect worldviews, mental health, and ways of interacting with other people and groups. Hanna et al. (2000) stated that "oppression, either by force or deprivation, is clearly a major source of psychological problems and issues, in general, and leads to depression, anxiety, and some personality disorders (see Jacobs, 1994)." They continued by stating that oppression "is related in some way or another to most of the problems presented to counselors" (p. 432). Helpers need to develop awareness of ways in which they might be engaging in oppression and strive to remove oppression from the helping process. Oppressive actions may include, for example, imposing Western values on non-Western clients or failing to consider cultural variables when diagnosing clients.

Hanna et al. (2000), citing Miller (1986), noted that oppressed individuals tend to be more perceptive than those who hold power. Their perceptive abilities help them cope, survive, and avoid negative consequences (e.g., violence). An important task for helpers is to encourage the expression of this perception, which can strengthen helping relationships and help clients become more "genuine" (Hanna et al., 2000). Helpers can do this by using exploration skills (see Part Four) and also by avoiding oppressive behaviors themselves. Perception has been identified as one of the significant and powerful factors in therapeutic change (Hanna & Ritchie, 1995).

It is important to note that clients may be victims of discrimination and oppression, perpetrators of discrimination and oppression, or both. Those who are victims might be helped to recognize and understand discrimination and oppression, dispute harmful beliefs, and effectively manage powerful emotions, such as rage. Those who are perpetrators might be helped to develop greater perception and empathy for the people they are hurting (Hanna et al., 2000).

Culturally Skilled Helping: Multicultural Competencies and Helper Characteristics

This section focuses on some important aspects of culturally skilled helping. First, we describe multicultural competencies that have been developed for working with culturally diverse clients. Then, we list numerous characteristics of culturally skilled helpers.

Multicultural Competencies

Over the past few decades, a significant contribution to multicultural helping practice has been the development of multicultural competencies. These competencies are concepts, principles, and guidelines that have been established for working effectively with culturally diverse clients (see, e.g., Arredondo et al., 1996; D. W. Sue, Arredondo, & McDavis, 1992; D. W. Sue et al., 1982; D. W. Sue et al., 1998).

Categories and Domains of Multicultural Competencies

One of the most frequently cited sets of multicultural competencies was described by D. W. Sue et al. (1992) and expanded and described comprehensively in D. W. Sue et al. (1998). The competencies that these authors described have been endorsed by various divisions of the American Counseling Association and the American Psychological Association. The competencies are divided into three major categories: (1) counselor awareness of own cultural values and biases; (2) counselor awareness of client's worldview; and (3) culturally appropriate intervention strategies (D. W. Sue et al., 1992). Each category is further organized into three domains—attitudes and beliefs (awareness), knowledge, and skills. Altogether, 31 competencies are described.

"Awareness" refers to helpers being conscious of their values, attitudes, assumptions, and biases. Helpers must develop the ability to recognize and compare their viewpoints with other points of view. They also must learn to recognize their own resources, skills, and limitations. "Knowledge" refers to helpers possessing correct and sufficient information about their own and other cultures. Helpers may acquire knowledge of other cultures from research literature and from members of those cultures. "Skills" refers to putting awareness and knowledge into action and using appropriate helping techniques, methods, and interventions (Pedersen, 2000; Pedersen & Ivey, 1993; Pope-Davis & Coleman, 1997; D. W. Sue et al., 1992; D. W. Sue et al., 1998). Developing awareness, knowledge, and skills is seen as a three-stage process. Students and helpers first develop awareness, then gain knowledge, and finally learn skills (Pedersen, 2002).

Arredondo et al. (1996) expanded on the Sue et al. (1992) model, clarifying and refining the domains of awareness, knowledge, and skills by providing explanatory statements to operationalize the competencies. The following description, excerpted from Arredondo et al. (1996, pp. 66–73), provides an example of competencies in the third major category, "culturally appropriate intervention strategies." One competency from each domain (awareness, knowledge, and skills) is listed along with some of the explanatory statements. See Arredondo et al. (1996) for a complete list of all 31 competencies and 119 explanatory statements.

III. Culturally Appropriate Intervention Strategies

A. Beliefs and Attitudes (Awareness)

Competency: Culturally skilled counselors respect indigenous helping practices and respect help-giving networks among communities of color.

Explanatory Statements

- Can describe concrete examples of how they may integrate and cooperate with indigenous helpers when appropriate.
- Can describe concrete examples of how they may use intrinsic help-giving networks from a variety of client communities.

B. Knowledge

Competency: Culturally skilled counselors have a clear and explicit knowledge and understanding of the generic characteristics of counseling and therapy (culture bound, class bound, and monolingual) and how they may clash with the cultural values of various cultural groups.

Explanatory Statements

- Can articulate the historical, cultural, and racial context in which traditional theories and interventions have been developed.
- Can identify, within various theories, the cultural values, beliefs, and assumptions made about individuals and contrast these with values, beliefs, and assumptions of different racial and cultural groups.

C. Skills

Competency: Culturally skilled counselors take responsibility for educating their clients to the processes of psychological intervention, such as goals, expectations, legal rights, and the counselor's orientation.

Explanatory Statements

- Assess the client's understanding of and familiarity with counseling and mental health services and provide accurate information regarding the process, limitations, and function of the services into which the client is entering.
- Ensure that the client understands client rights, issues, and definitions of confidentiality, and the expectations placed on that client. In this educational process, counselors adapt information to ensure that all concepts are clearly understood by the client. This may include defining and discussing these concepts.

Multicultural training ideally incorporates balanced treatment of all three domains—awareness, knowledge, and skills. Pedersen (2002) described a four-step process in the development of multicultural competence. The first step is needs assessment, which involves assessing the trainees' level of awareness, knowledge, and skills. Consideration is made of the awareness, knowledge, and skills that trainees already possess and of the ways that trainees need to develop in these areas. The second step is definition of objectives, which involves identifying specific objectives or goals in the three domains. Consideration is made of what trainees want or need to accomplish. The third step is design of training techniques, which involves determining how the identified objectives will be carried out. Techniques are matched with each of the domains to foster development (e.g., role-playing to stimulate awareness). The fourth step is evaluation, which involves determining whether trainees have met their stated objectives (e.g., through discussions or supervisor assessments). D. W. Sue and Sue (2003) observed that, in addition to training individuals, developing cultural competence should involve working with organizations, systems, and society (e.g., becoming a change agent to combat discriminatory or oppressive institutional policies).

Measuring and Evaluating Multicultural Competencies

Several instruments have been developed to measure and evaluate multicultural competencies in the areas of awareness, knowledge, and skills. These instruments are based on the D. W. Sue et al. (1982, 1992) competencies and include the following:

- Multicultural Awareness—Knowledge—Skills Survey (MAKSS) (D'Andrea, Daniels, & Heck, 1991)
- Cross-Cultural Counseling Inventory—Revised (CCCI-R) (LaFromboise, Coleman, & Hernandez, 1991)
- Multicultural Counseling Inventory (MCI) (Sodowsky, Taffe, Gutkin, & Wise, 1994)
- Multicultural Counseling Awareness Scale—B (MCAS-B) (Ponterotto, Rieger, Barrett, & Sparks, 1994)

The CCCI-R requires supervisors to rate helpers, whereas the other three instruments are self-report measures that direct helpers to respond to the various items in the instrument. Self-report measures allow helpers to carefully consider their own abilities and competence, but they have drawbacks as well. For example, helpers may overestimate their abilities.

It is beyond the scope of this discussion to describe each of these instruments in detail. For more information, we invite readers to examine the instruments (see the citation after each one) and to look at such resources as Pope-Davis and Dings (1995), in which the various instruments are reviewed.

More research is needed on the multicultural competencies and the competency instruments. For example, it is not yet known whether helpers who score high on the competency measures demonstrate more success in helping. Gelso and Fretz (2001) stated: "None of the measures has had extensive use in assessing actual performance of counselors with culturally diverse clients. Yet to be determined is whether counselors who are rated higher on the scales have more effective counseling outcomes with culturally diverse clients than do counselors who rate lower on these scales" (pp. 180-181; see also Ponterotto, Fuertes, & Chen, 2000).

Client Perspectives on the Multicultural Competence of Helpers

Multicultural competence has been evaluated from the perspective of supervisors and helpers, but what about the client's perspective? Pope-Davis et al. (2002) examined this issue with a qualitative study about clients' experiences with culturally different helpers. The model that emerged from this study postulates that client perceptions of multicultural helping competence and of the overall experience in helping result from the interaction of many factors, including (1) client needs and how well helpers meet them, (2) client characteristics, (3) the helper-client relationship, (4) client processes (how clients make meaning of the helping interaction and the actions clients take to deal with the helper), and (5) client appraisals of helping. The findings of the study support assertions that helpers who demonstrate an interest in the client's culture are perceived as being more culturally competent than those who do not.

The importance of multicultural competence varied for the clients in the study. For some clients, multicultural competence was pivotal. For others, it was less critical, contingent upon other needs being met and the experience of a positive therapeutic relationship. Clients who did not believe that culture impacted their interpersonal relationships tended to place less importance on the helper's cultural competence. The researchers asserted that even though some clients found multicultural competence to be less important, this does not mean that it was irrelevant. Rather, "the cultural competence of the counselors provided an environment within which the client gauged the extent to which his or her choices and options for a full range of interventions and opportunities could be reached" (Pope-Davis et al., 2002, p. 385). All of the clients in the study indicated that they wanted the helper to behave in ways that communicated caring, attentiveness, and general competence.

Characteristics of Culturally Skilled Helpers

The following list identifies many of the characteristics of culturally skilled helpers. The list is derived from Arredondo et al. (1996), D. W. Sue et al. (1992), and our own observations. Many of these characteristics have their basis in the multicultural competencies.

Culturally skilled helpers

- engage in self-exploration and constantly strive to increase their self-awareness;
- understand their own cultural characteristics and values and how these factors impact their work with clients;
- understand their own perspectives on helping—their style, theoretical orientation, and definition of helping—and how their cultural characteristics have shaped their perspectives;
- honestly confront their own biases, prejudices, and discriminatory or oppressive behaviors and work to keep them out of the helping process;
- possess a wide range of skills, interventions, and strategies and apply them in a flexible manner consistent with the cultural characteristics and needs of their clients;
- possess knowledge of the cultural characteristics and needs of the client populations they serve;
- understand that not all problems are internally created—they recognize the extent to which discrimination and oppression affect clients' lives and contribute to their problems;

- acknowledge cultural differences between themselves and their clients and address client concerns and discomfort about these differences while still communicating their willingness and desire to help;
- value diversity and demonstrate an openness to exploring and learning about other cultures outside of their own;
- constantly work to expand their cultural awareness, knowledge, and skills (e.g., through workshops and reading books and articles);
- recognize the limitations of their awareness, knowledge, skills, and competence—they seek supervision and consultation and refer clients to other helpers when necessary; and
- facilitate access to helping services for individuals and groups that have experienced discrimination and oppression. (Culturally skilled helpers are aware of institutional barriers that prevent such individuals from using helping services and try to remove these obstacles.)

Becoming a Culturally Skilled Helper

For those who wish to become helpers, understanding and reflecting on the topics discussed in this chapter are important. However, to become culturally skilled, one must do more than passively recognize cultural differences, learn multicultural concepts, and think about personal attitudes and values. It is important to become actively involved in the learning process. Here are some suggestions for students and helpers.

Engage in Cultural Immersion. This concept was described by Hansen (1997) and Pedersen and Ivey (1993). Cultural immersion involves personally experiencing other cultures. People have a natural tendency to associate with others who have cultural characteristics that are similar to their own—"birds of a feather flock together." However, as Ponterotto and Pedersen (1993) noted, "This preference to associate primarily with 'like-minded' individuals leads to a form of cultural ignorance among many people" (p. 28). Cultural ignorance can lead to bias, prejudice, discrimination, oppression, cultural encapsulation, and culture-centric thinking, which involves valuing one's own culture while devaluing others. These phenomena hurt helping relationships. Cultural immersion, in contrast, promotes tolerance and greater knowledge of various cultures. Examples of cultural immersion include living and working in another country for some time or attending spiritual/religious services of a cultural group different from one's own (see Pedersen & Ivey, 1993).

Exposing oneself to the behaviors, customs, values, and experiences of other cultures increases the chance of developing a deeper understanding of and respect for those cultures. Also, for many people, prejudices, misconceptions, and fears about other cultures begin to disappear with increased contact. Cultural immersion is perhaps the best way to learn about different groups of people. There is no substitute for personal experience and interaction.

Become a Change Agent. In the helping professions, change agents serve many functions. One important function is promoting social change and justice. When engaged in this function, change agents "take active roles in bringing about political and institutional changes to combat discrimination and inequality" (Okun, 2002, p. 288). Change agentry has become increasingly important in the helping professions as helpers have become more sensitive to the needs and problems of various populations and "more cognizant of the role that social influences play in psychological discomfort" (Okun, 2002, p. 288). Change agentry is a way for helpers to "practice what they preach." As change agents, helpers are encouraged not merely to condemn racism, sexism, ageism, homophobia, political persecution, and other forms of discrimination and oppression, but to work to stop them through such efforts as promoting policy changes, providing public education, writing to legislators, and organizing support groups (Okun, 2002).

Engage in Self-Exploration and Increase Self-Awareness. Helpers need to honestly examine and understand their own cultures, attitudes, behaviors, biases, prejudices, and views about other cultures. They should also challenge their assumptions about people and the world around them. In the process, they may become more familiar with their own "worldviews" as well as those of their clients.

Take Advantage of Multicultural Learning Opportunities. Culturally skilled helpers develop and refine their multicultural skills by taking courses, working under supervision, and attending workshops and seminars. They also actively consume multicultural helping literature. These activities allow helpers—and students—to interact with specialists in multicultural helping and stay current on important research. Ponterotto et al. (2000) discussed research showing that multicultural course work, clinical supervision of cases involving minority clients, multicultural workshops and seminars attended, number of client contact hours with minority clients, and multicultural research experience contribute to higher competency scores across many instruments and subscales used to measure multicultural competencies.

Becoming a culturally skilled helper is part of professional development and continues throughout the helper's career. It is important for students and helpers to take the process seriously and constantly work to improve their awareness, knowledge, and skills.

Different But Also Similar

So far in this chapter, we have focused on differences between people. It is important to recognize differences and to not make the mistake of believing that all people are alike. However, people also have similarities that should not be overlooked (Pedersen, 1996, 1997). Everyone has basic survival needs—food, water, and shelter. Everyone has the need for dignity, respect, and security. Everyone encounters struggles in life. Many behavioral responses are similar as well. For example, happiness is often marked with certain facial expressions, such as smiling. This response is remarkably consistent across cultures (Mesquita & Frijda, 1992). If similarities could not be observed and generalizations could not be made, research on human behavior would have limited meaning. It would have no general applicability beyond the people under study, and from it researchers and helpers would have difficulty deriving helping procedures, skills, interventions, and strategies.

When working with clients, helpers need to consider (1) the unique experiences, characteristics, and needs of the clients' cultural groups; (2) clients' individual experiences, characteristics, and needs; and (3) basic human needs—those that are common to all people (e.g., food, shelter, dignity, respect) (see Leong, 1996; Leong & Bhagwat, 2001). Awareness of cultural differences is important, but helpers must be careful not to ignore similarities and basic human needs. Also, they need to recognize the individuality of their clients and avoid stereotyping them because of culture (see Pedersen, 1996, 1997).

Challenges Associated With Studying Cultural Issues in Helping

Two challenges to studying cultural issues in helping are worth noting. First, students sometimes feel overwhelmed and frustrated when studying cultural issues in helping. The ambiguous, imprecise nature of helping is confusing enough (e.g., how to earn the trust of clients, when to use particular helping skills). How can one also become familiar with the unique characteristics, experiences, and needs of people from so many different cultures? Becoming a culturally skilled helper typically takes much time, study, practice, and effort. The suggestions offered in the section of this chapter entitled "Becoming a Culturally Skilled Helper" are some ways to become familiar with other cultures. In addition, helpers learn about culture from their culturally different clients. Consulting with experts or members of particular cultures can be helpful when questions arise. Also, many helpers work with particular populations, so through their education, training, and experience, they develop cultural awareness, knowledge, and skills that are relevant to their work. Finally, helpers have to accept that they do not know everything and that they will not "connect" with every single client. Sometimes, helpers acknowledge that clients probably would be better served by other helpers, and referrals are provided.

Second, some students feel defensive about studying cultural issues in helping. They feel as if they are being indoctrinated or told how to think, speak, and treat other people. Perhaps this is a consequence of poor multicultural training. In any event, students must choose for themselves how to view cultural issues. However one views these issues, the reality is that cultural differences exist. Effective helping is about aiding clients in making some kind of improvement, change, or adjustment in their lives, not about molding them into what helpers want them to be. What would you, as a client, expect if you were to see a culturally different helper? Isn't the helper there for you? Aren't you the focus of helping? It is very difficult, if not impossible, for helpers to provide effective assistance to people whose cultural characteristics they do not understand or respect. To do their jobs ethically and effectively, helpers must learn about, accept, and respect cultural differences. With the existence of so much human diversity, how could helpers function well if they were not culturally competent?

Summary and Concluding Remarks

In this chapter, we focused on diversity, culture, and helping. We described several important terms and topics, including culture, multiculturalism, individualism, and collectivism. We discussed harmful attitudes and behaviors, namely cultural encapsulation, bias, prejudice, discrimination, and oppression. We then described culturally skilled helping and discussed multicultural competencies and characteristics of culturally skilled helpers. We provided suggestions on how to become a culturally skilled helper. While diversity is important, we discussed that similarities should not be overlooked. Finally, we described two challenges associated with studying cultural issues in helping.

Studying cultural issues in helping can be challenging and difficult. It can evoke resistance, defensiveness, and strong emotions, but it is a necessary and an important step in becoming a culturally skilled helper. Culturally skilled helpers are in demand as the unique needs and perspectives of various groups are increasingly being recognized. Effective, ethical practice requires helpers to develop multicultural competence.

Questions for Thought

1. Think for a few minutes about the cultural characteristics that define you. Consider characteristics such as age, educational status, ethnicity, race, nationality, residence, disabilities, gender, sexual orientation, occupation, social class, ideology, language, and spirituality/religion. Which of these are most important in defining who you are? What other cultural characteristics are important to you? What influences, people, or experiences in your life have caused these characteristics to be important to you? How do these characteristics affect your worldview and the way in which you relate to other people?

2. Think about any biases or prejudices that you have. What are they, and in what ways have you acted on them? Have you ever engaged in discriminatory or oppressive behavior? Do you tend to confront or ignore these issues?

3. Assume that you are a helper. What are the cultural characteristics of the clients you feel *most* comfortable helping? What are the cultural characteristics of the clients you feel *least* comfortable helping? Why do you feel comfortable or uncomfortable with the particular characteristics that you identified? How do biases and prejudices factor into your responses?

4. On your own or in a small group, identify a particular cultural group, such as African Americans, gays and lesbians, or persons with disabilities, and describe some of the unique concerns and needs of this cultural group and its members. How might culturally skilled helpers address the concerns and needs of members of this cultural group?

5. Helper competence can be measured from the perspectives of supervisors, helpers, and clients. What are the advantages and disadvantages of measuring competence from each perspective?

PART TWO

The Helping Process

**3. From Start to Finish:
Beginning, Maintaining, and
Ending the Helping Process**

CHAPTER 3

From Start to Finish: Beginning, Maintaining, and Ending the Helping Process

CHAPTER OVERVIEW

This chapter describes the helping process and shows how the helping relationship and the major activities of helping fit into it. The discussion sets the stage for more thorough coverage of the helping relationship and the major activities of helping in the chapters that follow. In this chapter, the helping process is described from the first session through the middle sessions to termination and follow-up. The first session is usually fairly structured and largely consists of building the relationship and gathering information. During the middle sessions, most of the work in helping occurs. The end of helping is known as termination and involves evaluating helping and wrapping up the process. Follow-up, when conducted, is a post-helping evaluation process. This chapter concludes with a discussion of helping outcomes—the positive changes that clients may experience when helping works as intended.

It is not enough to do good; one must do it in a good way.

—John Morley (1910, p. 58)

Variability in the Helping Process

There is much variability in helping. The following are some of the reasons for this variability: Each client and helper possesses a unique personality, and how clients and helpers interact differs from one relationship to another. In addition, helping occurs in many settings, such as schools, clinics, and hospitals, and is provided by different types of helpers, including psychologists, counselors, and social workers, among others. Further, the length of the helping process varies from one relationship to another. Many helpers and clients meet for only one session, either by design or because the clients choose not to return. Other helping processes continue for several, or even dozens, of sessions spread out over weeks, months, or years. The length of the helping process depends on a number of factors, including the nature and complexity of client problems and goals, policies of the helping setting, time constraints, insurance coverage, and the quality of the helping relationship.

With all of this variability, it can be challenging to describe the helping process. There is no formula or precise method that applies to all situations. However, we can make some general statements and provide guidance about the helping process across various settings. What follows is a basic outline describing how helping may proceed from the first session to the end of the helping process. This outline assumes that the helping process will last for more than one session.

The First Session

From the moment a helper and client meet, the helper strives to create a safe, trusting environment and build a good helping relationship. In doing so, he or she helps the client feel comfortable and promotes open discussion and the exploration of problems. Thus, the first session often consists of the following.

Opening the Helping Process: Beginning to Build a Good Relationship

One of the first things clients encounter in the helping process is the physical environment within which helping occurs. It is important for this environment to be conducive to helping. A quiet, clean, fairly small, private room with soft lighting and comfortable chairs helps to create a warm, inviting, accepting atmosphere in which clients can feel safe and comfortable. During the initial session (and all subsequent sessions), there should be no interruptions, such as telephones ringing, pagers beeping, or people knocking on the door. Such distractions disrupt the flow of the session and may cause clients to believe that their helpers have more important things to do.

The first session often begins with greetings and introductions. If the meeting was initiated by the client, the helper and client may briefly engage in some initial small talk to help put the client at ease. If, however, the meeting was initiated by the helper (e.g., a school counselor requesting a meeting with a student), the helper should avoid small talk and begin by explaining the purpose of the meeting. In such situations, initial small talk often exacerbates the worry, anxiety, and anticipation the client may already be feeling. The first meeting may be somewhat uncomfortable for clients, who enter helping feeling perhaps hopeful and fearful at the same time—hopeful about change but fearful about what helping involves. They often look to helpers for initial cues about what to do.

Relationship building occurs throughout the helping process, but it begins with the first session. In chapter 4, we discuss characteristics of the helping relationship and helper factors that promote the development of the relationship, including empathy, unconditional positive regard, and genuineness. From the moment helpers and clients meet, helpers strive to nurture the relationship, which serves as the foundation for all of the work that is done in helping. Research has consistently shown that a good relationship is a significant factor in the success of helping (see, e.g., Bachelor & Horvath, 1999; Sexton & Whiston, 1994). Building the helping relationship is not always easy, of course. Many clients seek help because they have difficulty developing and maintaining healthy relationships with people. Some clients do not want to be in helping in the first place; others are afraid to explore their concerns, express feelings, and make changes; still others do not trust helpers. Helpers often must deal with this reluctance and resistance when building relationships.

In the first session, addressing cultural issues, differences, and mistrust may be important for clients who are culturally different from their helpers (e.g., race, ethnicity, gender). The clients may want to know how well their helpers respect and understand their experiences and perspectives. They may want to know how sensitive and responsive their helpers are to cultural issues. They may have questions such as, "What do you know about discrimination and oppression?" and "Why should I trust you?" It is noteworthy that the drop-out rate for racial and ethnic minorities is higher than that for European American clients (Prieto et al., 2001; D. W. Sue & Sue, 2003). This may be due, in part, to a failure on the part of helpers to recognize, address, and respect cultural differences. Bringing these issues and questions out into the open and addressing them upfront (e.g., through dialogue and/or helper self-disclosure) can promote the development of trust and increase the chances that these clients will not drop out of helping (Atkinson & Lowe, 1995; see also D. Sue, 1997). Indeed, Atkinson and Lowe (1995) discussed cultural responsiveness, which they described as helper responses that "acknowledge the existence of, show interest in, demonstrate knowledge of, and express appreciation for the client's ethnicity and culture and that place the client's problem in a cultural context" (p. 402). Based on their review of research, Atkinson and Lowe asserted that cultural responsiveness can enhance helpers' credibility with their clients. According to these authors, there is "evidence that culturally responsive counseling results in greater client willingness to return for counseling, satisfaction with counseling, and depth of self-disclosure" (p. 403).

In some helping settings, the first professional that a client sees is an intake specialist, not the person who will ultimately be helping the client. The intake specialist assesses client needs and problems and gathers information for the helper who eventually will be assisting the client. In other words, the intake specialist conducts intake interviews and, as the client's first contact in the helping setting, plays an important role in introducing the client to the helping process. He or she may, for example, assess client expectations and describe how the helping process works. At the outset, the client should be informed of the intake specialist's role so he or she knows what to expect. Clients who believe that intake specialists will be their helpers may feel upset—sometimes even betrayed or abandoned—when they are told that in future sessions they will be meeting with someone else.

Structuring the Helping Process

Brammer and MacDonald (2003) described structuring as the way that helpers define the nature, limits, and goals of helping as well as helper and client roles and responsibilities. Structuring is an important part of the helping process because so many clients enter helping not knowing what to expect. The following are some of the many purposes structuring serves: (1) It allows clients to see what they are "getting into" when they enter helping; (2) it relieves apprehension and helps clients feel more comfortable by providing them with information about the helping process; (3) it helps to establish realistic, appropriate expectations about the helping process and each participant's role and responsibilities; (4) it helps to prevent misunderstandings and misconceptions that can undermine helping; (5) it establishes boundaries; and (6) it demonstrates an open, honest, upfront, and straightforward style of interaction.

Through the structuring process, helpers also address many of the questions that clients want answered when they seek help. Consider the following questions that clients often have about the helping process. Note that some of the questions reflect concerns that clients may be afraid to articulate. They want answers but may not ask the questions.

Questions Clients Often Feel Comfortable Asking:

- How long will each session be?
- How long does helping take?
- Can I ask questions?
- Can I come back?
- How often can I come for sessions?
- How much money will I have to pay?
- What will my insurance cover?

Questions Clients May Feel Somewhat Uncomfortable Asking:

- How does helping work?
- What do you, as a helper, do in the helping process?
- What kind of training do you have?
- What am I going to get out of helping?
- What am I supposed to do?
- Will the process be painful?
- Who will see my records or know about our sessions?
- Will you tell my friends, relatives, or employer what we say?
- How much do I have to reveal?

Questions Clients Often Have But May Choose Not to Ask:

- How can you solve my problems and improve my life?
- Will you judge me?
- Why do you care about my problems?
- Why should I trust you?
- What if I don't like you?
- What problems have you dealt with in your own life?

These questions reflect uncertainty, concern, and even fear about the helping process. Through structuring, helpers anticipate and answer many of these questions. In doing so, they help clients begin to trust them as people who will respond to their needs and concerns. Described next are some key components of structuring. Note how helpers, in carrying out these components, address many of the client questions listed earlier.

Describing the Helping Process

Describing the helping process at the beginning of the first session helps clients develop accurate, realistic perceptions about helping. Helper descriptions of the helping process often address the following items in some way:

- Helping is a process in which helpers assist clients in managing or resolving problems and making desirable changes. The process can be rewarding, though it may be uncomfortable and challenging at times.
- The role of helpers is to provide guidance, support, and feedback and to help clients increase self-awareness, express feelings in a healthy manner, set goals, confront problems, recognize ineffective attitudes and behaviors, and develop more effective attitudes and behaviors.
- Personal growth and change occur gradually through understanding problems and working with helpers to learn new attitudes and behaviors.

Helpers may convey this information through a written document known as an informed consent statement (discussed later in this chapter) and then verbally elaborate on items that they choose or that elicit questions from clients. The extent to which helpers describe the helping process depends on their own style and work setting as well as on a number of client factors, including age, culture, level of comfort with helping, and familiarity with the helping process.

Discussing Credentials and Training

At the beginning of the helping process, either on their own initiative or at the request of clients, helpers may describe their credentials and training. They may describe their educational background, theoretical orientation, experience, and licensure. Providing this information can affirm helper credibility, knowledgeability, and expertness in the eyes of clients. When helpers are seen as credible, knowledgeable, and expert, they are more likely to earn the trust and respect of their clients.

Exploring Client Expectations

Clients often enter helping with some ideas and expectations about how the helping process works, such as what they will get out of the process and what helpers do. Some of their expectations are realistic, and some are not. To facilitate good relationship development, helpers need to pay attention to their clients' statements and questions about the helping process and ensure that client expectations are realistic. Managing expectations is often a significant part of helpers' work.

Helpers need to pay particular attention to any unrealistic expectations expressed by their clients (e.g., an expectation that the helper's role is to make important decisions for the client or an expectation that the helper and the client can socialize together outside of helping sessions). It is important for helpers to dispel unrealistic expectations at the outset of helping. Unrealistic expectations lead to dissatisfaction with the helping process and hinder the development of relationships. If these expectations go unchallenged for some time, clients may feel angry and frustrated when they realize that helping is not what they expected. Describing the helping process is one of the ways that helpers dispel unrealistic expectations and promote realistic ones.

Discussing Confidentiality

Helpers need to address confidentiality and its limitations in the first session. Client confidentiality refers to the obligation of helpers to not reveal client information and statements to other people (although helpers are typically permitted to discuss client cases with colleagues and supervisors, who are also bound by confidentiality). This obligation to keep information private can be found in laws, ethical guidelines, and policies of the helping setting. Confidentiality is a significant aspect of helping. Clients seek help to address very personal issues. Many clients are concerned initially about how the information they disclose will be handled. Will notes or records be kept? Will anyone else have access to the information? If helpers were free to reveal client information to anyone, clients would probably choose not to discuss issues at all. Thus, confidentiality encourages candor, open expression, and the development of trusting relationships.

Confidentiality is qualified, not absolute. There are numerous limitations and exceptions defined by laws and ethical guidelines. For example, helpers are typically permitted to disclose client information when discussing client cases with supervisors or when defending themselves against ethical complaints or lawsuits filed by clients (Welfel, 2002; Woodworth, 2000). In certain cases, however, helpers are required, not merely permitted, to breach confidentiality and relay information to authorities or potential victims. For example, in general, helpers are required to breach confidentiality, with or without client permission, when (1) clients state that they seriously intend to harm themselves or others, or (2) clients report abuse or neglect of children or vulnerable adults. These exceptions reflect that some interests, such as protecting people from physical harm, supersede the privacy afforded by confidentiality. Regarding confidentiality and its exceptions, it is wise for helpers to review the ethical guidelines of their profession and the laws of their state. With respect to the law, exceptions to confidentiality are not uniform among the 50 states (Woodworth, 2000).

Specifically discussing confidentiality and its limits is important because clients typically enter helping expecting that the information they provide and the statements they make will be held in confidence. Many clients do not know that limitations and exceptions to confidentiality exist (Hillerbrand & Claiborn, 1988; Rubanowitz, 1987). Indeed, research has shown that most clients (more than two-thirds in one study) believe that virtually all, if not all, of the information that they provide to helpers will be held in confidence (D. J. Miller & Thelen, 1986; VandeCreek, Miars, & Herzog, 1987). Thus, part of promoting realistic client expectations—and avoiding ethical complaints and lawsuits—involves being very clear at the outset of helping about the nature of confidentiality and its limits.

Students sometimes ask, "Won't clients be reluctant to talk about issues that fall within one of the exceptions to confidentiality, knowing that the police and the legal system might become involved?" The answer is that they may be. It is clear, however, that helpers have an obligation to inform clients about the limitations of confidentiality and to breach confidentiality when required by ethical guidelines and laws (e.g., reporting child abuse to law enforcement authorities or child protective services when the helper learns of abuse). The "silencing effect" that these responsibilities may have on clients with respect to certain issues may simply be unavoidable. When issues are raised that require breach of confidentiality, some helpers may delay breaching or choose not to breach at all, depending on the seriousness of the issues, how long ago they occurred, personal values, and the consequences that breaching or not breaching may have for themselves and their clients (see Pope & Bajt, 1988). However, helpers who choose this course may incur serious ethical and legal consequences, such as lawsuits or suspension or revocation of their licenses to practice. Helpers need to consult ethical guidelines and laws and use their professional judgment in determining whether and when to breach confidentiality. It is also wise to consult with supervisors or colleagues.

Some helpers believe that, throughout the helping process, it is prudent to occasionally remind clients about confidentiality and its limitations. Doing so helps to reaffirm the commitment to a trusting, professional relationship.

Addressing Administrative Matters

Helpers also structure helping by addressing various administrative matters—that is, the established policies and procedures that govern and define the helping process. These administrative matters typically cover client responsibilities, rights, and options. They include, for example, fees, how to get insurance reimbursement, the need to pay bills when due, length of sessions, limits on number of sessions, the need to be on time for sessions, how to cancel sessions, client access to records, the requirement of not coming to sessions under the influence of drugs or alcohol, and whom clients should contact if they have concerns, questions, or complaints about the helping services received. These issues are addressed by helpers in the first session either through an informed consent statement (described in the next section) or verbally.

The Informed Consent Statement

At the beginning of the first session or shortly before, most helpers give their clients an informed consent statement, which is a one- to two-page written document that describes such issues as the nature of the helping process, confidentiality, and administrative matters. In a concise manner, the informed consent statement lets clients know what they can expect from the helping process and their helpers, and it outlines client rights and responsibilities. The client reads it, asks any questions, and in many cases, signs it to indicate that he or she understands it. Reading and signing the statement helps to clarify and solidify the commitment that helpers and clients make to each other.

Not all informed consent statements are the same. Each is tailored to meet the unique needs of the helping setting and the population with which it is designed to be used. Thus, a statement used in an alcohol treatment center may read differently from one used in a university counseling center. Despite these differences, informed consent statements typically address the same basic topics. An example of an informed consent statement that is appropriate for adult clients in a community counseling clinic is provided in Figure 3.1.

A limitation of written consent forms is that some clients may not be able to read them due to illiteracy, the use of language and terminology that is beyond their reading ability, or their being non-native English speakers (Kitchener & Anderson, 2000). Using simple language in the forms, providing information verbally, and asking clients whether they understand or have any questions can mitigate some of the problems. Indeed, Kitchener and Anderson (2000) asserted that a combination of written and verbal informed consent procedures might be useful. They cited research (Sullivan, Martin, & Handelsman, 1993) showing that helpers who used informed consent procedures that contained both written and verbal components were rated as more trustworthy and expert than those who did not. Whatever procedures are used, helpers must know that informed consent is not ethically or legally valid unless clients understand the information provided (Kitchener & Anderson, 2000).

Providing information about helping must be regarded as a continuous process, not as a one-time event at the beginning of helping. An informed consent form may be read, discussed, and signed in the first session, but throughout the helping process, helpers strive to ensure that their clients understand the helping process. Clients are entitled to know about the services that are being provided to them, to know the purposes, risks, and benefits of the interventions they are asked to participate in, and to have their questions answered. These are all aspects of informed consent.

Beginning to Explore Client Concerns

As the first session gets under way, helpers begin to explore and strive to understand their clients' lives and problems. Part Four of this book describes this exploration process in detail. Skills such as listening, asking questions, and reflecting feelings are useful for exploration. Exploration tools such as intake interviews and tests may also be used in the first session to gather information. If, after gaining

Community Counseling Center
Information Sheet and Consent Form

Welcome to the Community Counseling Center! The following information will help you understand more about counseling and may answer many of your questions.

The Counseling Process: Counseling is a process that can help you better understand yourself. It can help you make changes in your life by increasing your awareness of how you feel, think, behave, and relate to other people. Counseling also helps you focus on your strengths and assets and can help you change attitudes and behaviors that are not working for you. Personal growth and change often occur gradually by working with your counselor to learn new, more productive attitudes and behaviors.

The Counseling Experience: The counseling process can be comforting, but it can also be difficult. You may feel good knowing that you are not alone in your problems. However, confronting problems, recognizing feelings, and changing old behaviors can be uncomfortable. Your experience in counseling and what you get out of the process depend largely on you and how well you and your counselor work together. If you decide that you would rather work with a different counselor, or if you and your counselor decide that you require specialized services that we do not offer, we will gladly suggest and refer you to alternative services.

Confidentiality: With some exceptions, information about you and your counseling sessions is confidential. In other words, your counselor and the Center are not permitted to share this information with anyone, except other counselors at the Center for purposes of supervision and consultation. To ensure quality service and to comply with state licensing requirements, your counselor may talk with a supervisor or colleague about your counseling. Like your counselor, these individuals are required to maintain confidentiality.

By law, there are some exceptions to confidentiality. Certain topics that you might mention in counseling require that your counselor report that information, *with or without your permission,* to the proper authorities or individuals. We are required to report if:

- you state that you seriously intend to harm yourself or someone else;
- you report or describe physical abuse, neglect, or sexual abuse of children, dependent elders, or vulnerable adults; or
- a court of law orders us to turn over your counseling records.

You may waive your right to confidentiality by signing a written release form that authorizes your counselor or the Center to release information about you and your counseling sessions to third parties, such as your insurance provider or another mental health professional.

Missed Appointments: If you cannot keep an appointment, please give us 24 hours notice so we can use the time for other clients. If you miss two or more appointments in a row, we reserve the right to contact you to determine whether you wish to continue counseling.

Questions/Concerns: If you have any questions or concerns about the information on this sheet or about the counseling that you are receiving, feel free to talk to your counselor or contact the Executive Director of the Center.

I have read the information above and understand what it means.

Client's Signature   Date   Counselor's Signature   Date

Permission for Audio/Video Recording and Observation: I give permission for my counseling sessions to be taped or to be observed by my counselor's supervisors and/or colleagues. Such taping or observation will be used only for purposes of supervision and consultation and will be considered confidential. Only my counselor and my counselor's supervisors will have access to identifying information about me. All tapes will be erased or destroyed within three months of the taping. I understand that I have the right to refuse to be taped or observed (if refusing, do not sign below).

Client's Signature   Date   Counselor's Signature   Date

FIGURE 3.1   Sample Informed Consent Statement

some understanding, a helper believes that another helper would be better suited or more qualified to assist the client, a referral may be made.

Helpers may move beyond exploration in the first session, depending on the nature of the concerns that clients present and the duration of the helping process. For example, after some exploration, a helper might assist the client in seeing the connection between the client's excessive socializing and his or her poor grades—the client does not study enough. In addition, helpers and clients may discuss client goals. Some goals may be immediate, such as reducing anxiety. Long-range goals, if clients want to set any, may be fairly general at this point, but a basic sense of what clients want may be discussed. Role plays may also be conducted to help clients prepare for taking action to achieve goals.

Developing Norms

Both helpers and clients bring unique personalities to the helping process. As the first session begins, helpers and clients develop ways of communicating and interacting that set the tone and boundaries of their relationship (see Cormier & Hackney, 1999; Kottler & Brown, 2000). These "rules of engagement" are known as norms. They help define the relationship and the roles of each individual. For example, where do the helper and the client sit with respect to each other—a few feet apart or several feet apart? Who talks the most? Where and how frequently do they meet for helping sessions? Both helpers and clients develop norms. Helpers set some of them, but others depend on clients. Thus, many norms are not predetermined or the same for all helping relationships. It is important, however, that all norms facilitate good helping relationships. Problematic norms, such as helpers or clients consistently arriving late for sessions, need to be challenged before they damage the helping process.

Many of the norms developed initially will change over time. In fact, altering them may be an intervention used by helpers. For example, a helper may be working with a very passive client who waits for the helper to speak and determine the topic of discussion at the beginning of each session. This style of interaction is one of the norms of their relationship. If one of the client's goals is to become more assertive, after several sessions the helper might say, "I've noticed that you always wait for me to begin each session. Why don't you go first today and tell me what you'd like to talk about."

Instilling Hope

It is important for helpers to convey confidence in both the helping process and the ability of clients to make positive changes. Doing so helps clients develop faith that they can manage or resolve their problems and improve the quality of their lives. When clients expect that the helping process will be beneficial (i.e., when they have hope for positive change), the chances of a successful outcome in helping are greater (see Frank & Frank, 1991; C. R. Snyder, Ilardi, Michael, & Cheavens, 2000). Some ways in which helpers instill hope include

■ telling clients that seeking help is an important step in managing or resolving problems and that it took courage for them to admit the need for help;

- stating that helping is a process that often requires hard work but that it can reduce painful feelings and produce desirable attitude and behavior changes;
- telling clients that they are not alone in facing their problems, that the helper will be there to support them;
- pointing out client strengths, assets, and abilities; and
- describing research findings relevant to clients and their problems, if clients are interested.

This reassurance and information can put clients at ease. It can help them feel positive about the work they will do by showing that their helpers believe in the value and effectiveness of the process and will be there to provide guidance. Instilling hope also helps to reduce the feelings of discouragement, hopelessness, and demoralization that are often high at the outset of helping (Frank & Frank, 1991). People who have hope tend to be more motivated and less likely to succumb to anxiety and defeatist attitudes in the face of challenges or setbacks (Goleman, 1995).

Instilling hope is an ongoing feature of helping. It is important for clients to consistently maintain confidence that they can make positive changes in their lives. If hope fades, they may end helping and choose not to seek further assistance.

However, there are some noteworthy cautions about instilling hope. Helpers need to avoid instilling hope that unreasonable or unrealistic client wishes can be fulfilled. Not all client expectations, desires, or goals can be realized (e.g., "I want to develop good people skills so everyone will like me."). Helpers also need to be careful not to make promises that they may be unable to keep (e.g., "You will see great positive changes within the next few months."). Such guarantees can make clients suspicious—"How can she say that? She doesn't even know me yet!" Unfulfilled promises can anger and frustrate clients and even lead to litigation. Thus, although helpers should be positive and confident, they must also be realistic about the benefits of helping and the changes it can facilitate.

Giving Clients "Permission" to Share Their Concerns and Feelings

For some clients, discussing concerns and expressing feelings are fairly easy. They are empowering experiences that create a refreshing, cathartic sense of relief and liberation, as if an enormous weight is being lifted. Many other clients, however, come from environments where open discussion of concerns and expression of feelings are discouraged. Thus, they may feel shame, guilt, embarrassment, and discomfort when sharing their lives with helpers. Clients may even resist sharing concerns and feelings altogether.

If clients who feel discomfort about sharing concerns or feelings do express themselves and then experience guilt or shame that helpers fail to acknowledge, their belief that it is shameful or inappropriate to express themselves and talk about their problems may be reinforced. Helpers may need to acknowledge their clients' discomfort and the courage that it took to express feelings and discuss concerns. They need to reassure clients that they will listen and that it is okay to express feelings and share problems. This reassurance can be a powerful gesture that goes a long way toward gaining client trust and fostering open, honest communication. Moreover, clients will more likely return for future sessions if they feel comfortable expressing themselves and talking about their problems than if they leave a session feeling anxious, guilty, or ashamed.

However, helpers must also recognize cultural differences in the expression of emotions. Some clients (e.g., many Asian clients) may feel uncomfortable about expressing emotions because their culture tends to value emotional control. If these clients express emotions at the urging of their helpers, they may feel guilt or shame about having violated their cultural values. Helpers should not force or pressure clients to express themselves. Doing so would probably result in clients not returning for additional sessions.

Checking Out What Clients Think and How They Feel About Helping

As helpers work to build relationships, it is important for them to check out what clients think and how they feel about the helping process: How comfortable are they? How do they feel about discussing their problems? What would be helpful to them? Do they have any concerns about the process? If clients seem reluctant to communicate their concerns, helpers may need to elicit this information by inquiring. Expressing thoughts, feelings, and concerns can help clients alleviate some of their anxiety about the helping process and enable them to look forward to future sessions. It also gives helpers and clients the opportunity to correct any problems that may be developing in their relationships. It is more likely that clients will return for future sessions if they have a chance to express their thoughts, feelings, and concerns about helping.

Skillfully Managing Time and Ending the Session

A typical helping session lasts from 30 minutes to an hour. It is important to begin on time and move quickly to important aspects of the helping process, such as structuring and the intake interview. As the session draws to a close, perhaps 5 to 10 minutes before the end, helpers should let clients know that the meeting is almost over. That way, helpers and clients have a chance to wrap up their discussion and close the meeting. Simply saying at the end, "We have to stop now," may leave clients hanging, prevent a sense of closure, and increase feelings of stress and anxiety about sharing personal problems—feelings that are probably already strong during the first session. Helpers sometimes extend the session beyond the allotted time if clients are expressing powerful feelings or addressing very difficult issues, but helpers need to manage time effectively to prevent this from becoming an established norm in session after session.

To announce that the end of the session is near, helpers may say, "We're nearing the end of our time today. Do you have any last thoughts or feelings about what we discussed today?" or "We need to finish up in a few minutes. Why don't we review what we've covered today." Clients often feel some anxiety about the end of the session and may feel that many issues were not covered adequately, if at all (Belkin, 1988); however, if helpers end the session skillfully, some of these negative feelings may be mitigated.

To prepare for the end of the meeting, helpers and clients may review the session and express their thoughts and feelings about how it went. In addition, they may decide to address particular issues in the next meeting. This gives clients something to look forward to, helps to establish continuity between sessions, and lets clients know that important issues will not be left unaddressed. If plans are made to address certain topics in the next session, the plans typically should not be too definite. A lot can happen between meetings, and clients may wish to discuss other issues next time.

Because sharing concerns with helpers can be a new and profound experience, many clients leave the first helping session and "percolate"; that is, they spend a good amount of time thinking about their problems and what transpired in the session—what they said, how they felt, and how their helper responded. They may even begin to see their problems from a new perspective now that they have discussed them with a helper and are no longer alone in their experience. When clients leave this helping session feeling good about it and where the session left off, they are more likely to develop positive perceptions about helping. Sometimes, the session can be difficult for clients (e.g., they may express a lot of negative feelings). In such instances, helpers can take time at the end of the session to invite clients to discuss their feelings and can talk with them about how they plan to take care of themselves in the near future. Doing so can help clients leave with more positive perceptions of the helping process (S. Neufeldt, personal communication, May 6, 2002). Positive perceptions increase the chance that clients will return for more sessions (Belkin, 1988).

Middle Sessions

If the first session seems to go well, clients may return. A significant percentage of helping relationships never make it to the second session, so it is no small accomplishment to get to this point. Some degree of rapport has been established, and the young relationship has a chance to develop further. In the middle sessions, helpers and clients continue to build upon what they began in the first session.

The time between sessions varies from one relationship to another, but it is often 1 week. How many sessions will occur depends on factors such as the nature and complexity of the client's problems and goals, the policies of the helping setting, time constraints, insurance coverage, and the quality of the helping relationship.

Structure and Focus

Compared to the first session, the middle sessions in the helping process tend to have less structure and less certainty. In any given helping situation, the unique interaction of the helper and the client sets the course of the relationship. Indeed, the middle phase of the helping process—the time between the first session and the last—can be difficult to describe with precision because it "can go in any number of directions" (Nugent, 2000, p. 207; see also Moursund & Kenny, 2002). Whereas intake interviews and structuring activities often involve specific, precise procedures, "one of the signals of middle-phase work may be a sense of confusion, of muddleness, of not really knowing what is going on" (Moursund & Kenny, 2002, p. 75). During these sessions, clients need to be able to work at their own pace and address the issues that they need to discuss; however, helpers try to maintain some sense of direction and keep clients focused if they wander across topics (Moursund & Kenny, 2002; Nugent, 2000). If helpers and clients know that they will have only a limited number of sessions, the helping process is usually more structured and focused so client needs can be addressed efficiently.

Continuing the Helping Relationship

In the middle sessions, helpers and clients may begin each session with a summary of what was discussed last time. Helpers may also invite clients to speak about what they want to address during the current session. Gradually, the helper and client settle into what they will discuss in their meeting. This is part of continuing to build a good relationship. Some relationships develop in a fairly smooth manner. A good "fit" exists, and clients are motivated to work. Other relationships, however, may be more challenging to develop and maintain. Clients may distrust helpers, they may possess very poor relationship-building skills, or a poor helper-client match may exist. These relationships may end prematurely, or they may develop gradually, becoming healthy and productive through hard work.

Assuming that clients do not end helping early, relationships typically grow and strengthen over time as clients become more comfortable with their helpers. Communication becomes more candid and open. Clients develop greater trust in their helpers.

Over the course of helping, the helper-client relationship may be tested as the helper challenges the client to develop understanding of his or her problems, set goals, and work for positive change. Slow progress, boredom, resistance, loss of motivation, and lapses into old, ineffective attitudes and behaviors may occur. These challenges can be frustrating and may cause the helping relationship to seem stagnant and in danger of ending. At these times, it is often beneficial for the helper to initiate discussion about the relationship and how each participant feels about it. Asking questions, reflecting feelings, providing constructive feedback, and immediacy may be useful helping skills here (see chapters 7 and 9).

Moving Through the Helping Process

Between the first session and the final session, the helping process consists of the four major activities described in Parts Four through Seven of this book: exploring client concerns, promoting client understanding, charting a new course, and working for positive change. If the process is working, the helper and client experience a sense of "movement" as the helping relationship evolves and the client makes changes (Nugent, 2000; Rogers, 1951). Some changes that may be seen include the client gaining new insights, learning new attitudes and behaviors, taking more risks in expressing himself or herself, and expressing feelings in a healthier manner (Moursund & Kenny, 2002; Nugent, 2000; Rogers, 1951). Clients may also experience better relationships with important people in their lives. For example, they may feel more connected to their families.

The latter part of the helping process is usually focused on working for positive change. Clients learn new attitudes and behaviors; goals and actions are put into effect and evaluated; and helpers facilitate the transfer of learning. That is, as discussed in chapter 12, helpers assist clients in applying what they have learned during the helping process to their "real-world" lives (see Ward, 1984). As clients make positive changes and move toward goal achievement, the issue of when to end the helping process becomes more prominent.

Ending the Helping Process

One thing that is certain about the helping process is that it will end at some point. The following are some common reasons for ending the process:

- Client goals have been achieved.
- Clients cannot have any more sessions (e.g., because of institutional or insurance limitations).
- Clients have gotten the most that they will get out of the helping process.
- Clients are ready to function on their own without further assistance from helpers.
- Clients are referred to other helpers.
- Clients decide to stop coming.
- The helping process is no longer productive.

Ending the helping process, commonly referred to as "termination," is typically viewed as a stage or phase of helping rather than as a one-time occurrence (see, e.g., Cavanagh & Levitov, 2002; Ward, 1984). This reflects that it is a process, one designed to help clients make a smooth transition out of helping by preparing them to function on their own, without helper assistance (Hackney & Cormier, 2001). When helpers prepare their clients for the end of helping, termination can be a positive, beneficial, and natural conclusion rather than a sudden—even traumatic— experience that leaves clients feeling abandoned.

When to Terminate

Sometimes it is known at the beginning of helping when the final session will occur. Factors such as institutional policies and limits on insurance coverage can result in helping relationships that last for a specified number of sessions. It is not unusual, for example, for sessions at a university counseling center to be limited to between 8 and 12. When the number of sessions is limited, clients should be told at the beginning of the helping process.

In other cases, the helping process is open-ended and terminates when helpers and clients choose to do so. In any event, whether helping is time-limited or open-ended, helpers and clients typically address termination at least a few sessions before the end of the helping process to give themselves time to prepare. The goal is to "come in for a soft landing," rather than to have the process come to an abrupt, startling halt.

The timing of termination is important. As Gladding (2000) noted, if the helping process ends too soon, clients may regress to earlier behaviors, and if the process goes on too long, clients may become dependent on helpers and fail to grow as people. The evaluation process described in chapter 13 can provide guidance on when to terminate. If evaluation reveals that client goals appear to have been achieved or clients seem ready to function on their own, it may be time to end the helping process. Maholick and Turner (1979, pp. 587–588) identified the following strategies that can be used to assess client readiness for termination:

1. Examining the initial symptoms, problems, and areas of conflict to see whether they have been reduced, eradicated, or resolved
2. Exploring the extent to which the stress that prompted clients to seek help has been managed and reduced
3. Searching for indications that clients have improved their coping abilities
4. Determining the degree to which clients demonstrate increased awareness, appreciation, and acceptance of self and others
5. Exploring the degree to which the capacity to love and be loved has been demonstrated
6. Reflecting on the ability of clients to plan differently and work more effectively
7. Evaluating the ability of clients to play rather than to merely obsess about the heaviness of life

Gladding (2000) noted that helper or client statements can indicate readiness to terminate (e.g., "I think we've made a lot of progress. Maybe we should talk about when we will end our meetings together."). He also listed various behaviors that may signal that the helping process is nearing an end, including "a decrease in the intensity of work; more humor; consistent reports of improved abilities to cope, verbal commitments to the future, and less denial, withdrawal, anger, mourning, or dependence (McGee, Schuman, & Racusen, 1972; Patterson & Welfel, 1994; Shulman, 1999)" (Gladding, 2000, p. 169). Boredom and lack of desire to participate in helping activities may also signal that termination is appropriate.

In addition, termination may be appropriate if clients do not appear to be making progress or benefiting from helping (American Counseling Association, 1995; American Psychological Association, 2002). Helpers need to make a judgment call about whether lack of progress or benefit warrants termination. Sometimes, lack of progress or benefit reflects client fears about change. These fears can be addressed and perhaps worked through. However, persistent lack of effort or lack of interest in the helping process may suggest that termination is appropriate. Helpers may provide referrals to other helping professionals if clients are interested.

The Termination Process

Termination of helping is typically characterized by several activities, as described in the following sections.

Initiate, Discuss, and Agree on Termination

Termination can be initiated by helpers or clients. Clients may want to terminate when they feel they have achieved their goals or reached a satisfactory level of relief from distress. Helpers may suggest termination when it appears that client goals have been achieved and positive changes have been made. For example, a helper might say: "Amy, it seems that you've come a long way since we started several weeks ago. You mentioned last time that you feel much better about your relationship with John. I wonder if we should start talking about how much longer we will be meeting. It seems to me that we might wrap up in the next few weeks. What do you think?"

Ideally, regardless of who raises the issue of termination first, when and how to terminate is decided by mutual agreement (Gladding, 2000). Both helpers and clients agree that it is time to end, and they decide when their last session will be. Sometimes, helpers or clients terminate the helping process prematurely, before it has had a chance to work as intended. Premature termination and various reasons for why it occurs are discussed later in this chapter.

Termination should be addressed before the final session. We mentioned earlier that it is typically addressed at least a few sessions before the end of helping. Many authors suggest that it should be raised and discussed early and from time to time throughout helping as a way to prepare clients for the inevitable end of the process (see, e.g., Kramer, 1986; Pipes & Davenport, 1999). How much time is devoted to termination varies from one relationship to another. The amount of time typically depends on the duration of the helping process, the strength of the helping relationship, the nature of the client's concerns and goals, and the client's feelings about termination. If clients feel apprehensive about termination but appear ready to function on their own, more time may be devoted to termination than with clients who are more comfortable with ending the helping process.

Some authors have asserted that, as a general rule, as much time should be spent concluding the relationship as was spent building it (see, e.g., Hackney & Cormier, 2001). Sometimes, helpers and clients decide to conclude their relationships gradually by increasing the time between sessions, such as going from weekly to biweekly sessions (Nelson-Jones, 1993). Doing so may help to slowly wean clients off the helping relationship.

Deal With Feelings About Termination

For clients, the end of helping can be a time of mixed emotions, such as sadness, fear, grief, confidence, satisfaction, and anticipation (see, e.g., Moursund & Kenny, 2002). They may feel a sense of loss and sadness that a good relationship is coming to an end. Sometimes, the end of the helping relationship reminds them of other difficult losses and "good-byes" that they have experienced (Maholick & Turner, 1979).

Some clients may feel angry about termination (Moursund & Kenny, 2002). In such cases, helpers might explore why clients feel angry and ascertain whether the anger is masking other feelings (e.g., anxiety, fear, sadness) about the end of helping (Moursund & Kenny, 2002). Spreading termination out over a few sessions gives helpers and clients a chance to discuss client feelings and make sure that clients are okay with the end of the helping process.

In addition to feelings of sadness, anxiety, and loss, clients may have positive feelings (Nugent, 2000). Termination may be a time when clients feel good about their successes and accomplishments. They may feel empowered, happy, and eager to put their new skills, attitudes, and behaviors to use as they make the transition out of helping. Indeed, it is important for helpers and clients to keep a positive focus as the relationship ends so clients can proceed with feelings of hope and confidence. While acknowledging the clients' feelings of sadness and loss, helpers should encourage clients to recognize what they have learned and gained in helping. Doing so may help clients feel better about ending the relationship.

Some clients react to the end of helping with strong emotions, whereas others are less emotional. In any case, helpers should support their clients and give them ample opportunity to discuss how they feel. The skills of listening, reflecting feelings, and immediacy are important here (see chapters 6, 7, and 9). Helpers and clients may, in some cases, decide to extend the helping process if client fears or concerns about ending are serious.

Of course, helpers also have reactions to and feelings about the end of the relationship (Goodyear, 1981). They may feel sad about seeing clients leave, especially if the relationship has been close or particularly productive. They may also feel competent and satisfied knowing that they were able to make a positive difference in their clients' lives. Sometimes, helpers feel that they were not as helpful as they could have been. In such cases, the end of the relationship may heighten anxiety, guilt, and self-doubt as helpers question their effectiveness and skill (Goodyear, 1981). Feelings of loss and sadness may also occur if helpers inappropriately use the helping relationship to satisfy their own personal needs for closeness and friendship. In addition, helpers often have to deal with the ambiguity and frustration of not knowing what happens to clients after they leave. Clients do not always communicate with helpers after termination.

Helpers may discuss some of their feelings with clients, including sadness about clients leaving and satisfaction and confidence about client gains. Expressing these feelings shows clients that helpers found the relationship to be positive and meaningful. However, it is inappropriate for helpers to expect clients to assist them in "working through" their feelings. Doing so shifts the focus of helping from clients to helpers. Supervision, consultation with colleagues, and various self-care activities, such as personal counseling, are ways in which helpers may cope with their feelings about terminating relationships.

In short, discussing feelings about termination permits helpers and clients to achieve "closure" (Ward, 1984). Both individuals may discuss how they feel so that they can be more comfortable with concluding the relationship.

Evaluate the Overall Helping Process

At the end of helping, evaluation of the overall helping process allows helpers and clients to assess the effectiveness and benefit of the process to clients. Helpers and clients review client progress, assess goal achievement, identify important client changes, and discuss client satisfaction with the helping process (Kramer, 1990; McClam & Woodside, 1994; Ward, 1984). Here are some questions that may be addressed when evaluating the overall helping process:

- How well have presenting problems and other problems been managed or resolved?
- How well have distress, anxiety, depression, and other uncomfortable feelings been mitigated?
- Were client goals achieved? To what extent?
- What new skills, attitudes, and behaviors have clients learned?
- How well have clients transferred what they have learned in helping to their real-world lives?
- What is the quality of clients' relationships with coworkers, friends, family, and significant others?
- How well are clients functioning in their daily lives (e.g., at work)?
- Were client expectations of the helping process met?
- How did clients feel about their helpers (e.g., the helpers' competence, skills, and understanding)?
- Would clients go through the helping process again if necessary? Why or why not?

As the helping process comes to an end, helpers and clients may verbally discuss these issues. The issues may also be addressed in some form on written surveys or questionnaires.

Helpers also usually evaluate their role in the helping process so they can improve their helping abilities. They may consider questions such as: Which techniques worked? Which ones did not work? What might be done differently with future clients? What are my strengths and weaknesses?

As part of the overall evaluation of helping, time is spent reviewing the helping process and summarizing client achievements. Reviewing and summarizing can effectively help clients see their strengths and what they have accomplished in helping. It also reinforces positive changes. Often, helpers summarize client achievements; however, sometimes they ask clients to summarize as a way to help the clients recognize for themselves what they have achieved. Clients may be encouraged to consider how they feel, think, behave, and interact now compared to how they did at the beginning of helping so they can see the progress and change over time (Kramer, 1990). Sometimes, videotapes or audiotapes of sessions are reviewed to assist in this process. Summaries are most effective when they are concrete and explicit, focusing on what clients have learned and what specific attitudes and behaviors have been changed. Specificity helps clients see clearly what they have achieved.

When reviewing and summarizing, helpers should also facilitate the transfer of learning (Ward, 1984). Because the helping process is almost over and helpers will soon be out of the picture, clients need to be able to take what they have learned in helping and make it work in real life.

Discuss Maintaining Gains, Dealing With Setbacks, and Handling Future Problems

Because clients will not always have helpers there to support them, they need to consider how they will handle problems and apply new learning after the helping process has ended. The following paragraphs describe three important issues for helpers to discuss with clients.

The first issue is how the clients will maintain the gains they made in helping. Several options exist to assist clients in maintaining gains, including scheduling future helping sessions, recommending support groups, making referrals to other helpers, and suggesting self-help resources, such as books and videos. Additional strategies that helpers can suggest to help clients maintain gains include self-monitoring, engaging in appropriate self-talk, visualizing, and using self-rewards (Nelson-Jones, 1993). Helpers may congratulate clients for their gains while reminding them to continue to monitor trouble spots.

The second issue helpers should discuss with clients is how the clients will deal with setbacks. Just because clients have finished the helping process does not mean their lives will be problem-free. They will likely face challenges as they work to maintain gains and live healthy lives. For example, a client who has succeeded in developing social skills and improving her romantic life may be rejected at some point by a romantic partner. Or, a client who has improved his study skills, and consequently his grades, may still get a bad grade on occasion.

Setbacks may also involve a return to ineffective attitudes and behaviors. Lapse and relapse are important concepts here (Brownell, Marlatt, Lichtenstein, & Wilson, 1986). "Lapse" refers to a brief, temporary indulgence in previous ineffective attitudes and behaviors. An example is a woman who recently quit smoking, then one day smokes a couple of cigarettes, but quickly thereafter gets back to her nonsmoking routine. "Relapse" involves a more substantial return to old habits, where clients essentially lose or give up newly learned skills, attitudes, and behaviors. An example is a man who stops drinking, only to start up again 2 months later. Relapse often continues until some intervention occurs, such as more helping. In short, a lapse is a momentary slip, whereas a relapse is more of a full-blown reversion to old ways (see Brownell et al., 1986). Lapse and relapse are very common occurrences, especially for hard-to-manage problems such as chemical dependency, obesity, and depression (Lambert & Bergin, 1994; Prochaska et al., 1992).

Often, it is beneficial for helpers and clients to discuss the possibility of setbacks and to recognize that challenges in maintaining gains may occur. Helpers and clients may role-play scenarios in which setbacks occur to see how clients would handle them. Helpers may also use many of the options discussed in the section on maintaining gains, including scheduling future helping sessions, recommending support groups, and making referrals. When clients understand the possibility of setbacks and have support systems to which they can turn, they have a better chance of minimizing the harm of setbacks and staying on track in maintaining gains.

A third issue that should be discussed is how the clients will handle future problems. As Peck (1978) observed in *The Road Less Traveled,* "Life is a series of problems" (p. 15). Helpers should assist clients in thinking about how they can apply their new skills, attitudes, and behaviors to future problems, even if those problems have little to do with the problems for which the clients sought help. In other words, helpers should assist clients in generalizing what they learned during the helping process to other problems and challenges in life (Hackney & Cormier, 2001). This is part of the transfer of learning. Role-playing and discussing hypothetical scenarios can be useful. Future sessions, support groups, and referrals to other helpers may also be options for addressing future problems.

Leave the Door Open

If allowed by the policies of the helping setting, helpers often leave the door open for future sessions or contacts should clients feel the need to return or keep in touch (Kramer, 1986, 1990). In addition, helpers may invite clients to call or write to say how things are going. Offering the chance for future contact minimizes the possibility that clients will feel abandoned and cast out to face the world alone. Clients may feel less anxious, more comfortable, and more confident knowing that helpers will be there if they need some support, have a desire to keep in touch, or are facing a relapse. Helpers need to guard against clients becoming too dependent on them, however. The offer of future sessions or contact can be abused, with clients contacting helpers so frequently that the helping process may never truly come to an end. In such cases, helping may have been terminated too early. In any event, the helper should make an effort to understand the reason for such client behavior and decide whether to continue the helping process.

Some authors have noted that in recent years and in many helping situations, the approach to termination has changed. The notion of a distinct, clearly defined end is being replaced in some cases by the idea of helping as an ongoing and intermittent process in which clients see helpers from time to time as needed to address problems, much as one sees the family doctor as needed (see, e.g., Budman & Gurman, 1988; Pipes & Davenport, 1999). Whether such an arrangement is possible or desirable depends on what helpers and clients decide as well as on the policies of the helping setting. When helping is viewed as ongoing, helpers need to be careful about clients becoming overly dependent. If clients see helpers every time challenges arise, they may struggle to develop personal responsibility for managing or resolving problems.

Skillfully Manage the Final Session

The final meeting is a time to reiterate and solidify client gains and discuss follow-up (described later in this chapter). This session is often less intense than previous sessions in terms of emotions and work. If it were as intense, the helping process may seem unfinished and end on an anxious, high-energy note that makes clients feel as if they still have a lot of work to do. Reviewing and summarizing accomplishments, engaging in some small talk, saying good-bye, and planning for follow-up are common activities in the final session.

After the final session ends, helpers often document client progress and current status in their case notes. They may address such questions as: What changes did clients make? To what extent were goals achieved? How well did the helping process work? If clients were referred to other helpers, this would be documented as well.

Resistance to Terminating the Helping Process

As noted previously, ending helping relationships can be difficult, especially when the relationships have been close, rewarding, and productive. Gladding (2000) stated that factors promoting resistance to termination include "the pain of earlier losses, loneliness, unresolved grief, need gratification, fear of rejection, and fear of having to be self-reliant" (p. 170).

Both helpers and clients may resist termination. Clients may have developed a dependency on helpers to assist them in working through problems. Thus, they may fear trying to maintain gains or trying to confront future problems without helper assistance. They also may not want to lose a comfortable, meaningful relationship with their helpers. Indeed, some clients become "addicted" to helping and helping relationships, especially if they have a history of loneliness and unstable relationships (Gladding, 2000). Resistant clients may respond to the end of helping with discomfort, anxiety, sadness, and anger. Some clients try to extend the helping process by regressing into old, ineffective behaviors or by identifying additional problems and goals. However, when the helping process has been productive and effective, clients tend not to react this way. In such cases, termination is generally viewed as a natural and logical conclusion to the helping process.

For most clients, discussing thoughts and feelings about termination and considering follow-up options relieve apprehension and help them become more comfortable with the end of helping. For clients who have strong reactions to termination, helpers may need to reevaluate the timing of termination—perhaps client problems and concerns have not been sufficiently addressed. Or, helpers may explore the resistance to termination and help clients become more comfortable with the end of helping.

Helpers may also resist termination. Helping relationships involve a strong human connection. In addition, successful helping relationships can reinforce helpers' sense of competence. For these reasons, some helpers find it difficult to end the helping relationship. Sometimes, helpers have difficulty letting go when helping does *not* seem to be progressing well. They may feel anxious about their abilities and determined to persist in their efforts to make the helping process work. Helper resistance to termination raises an ethical issue. Is the helper putting his or her needs ahead of the client's needs? Helpers may find it beneficial to consult with supervisors or colleagues to ensure that they end relationships at the appropriate time and in the appropriate way.

Premature Termination

Ideally, the helping process ends when client goals have been achieved (or clients are substantially on their way to achieving the goals), negative symptoms have been reduced, and client problems have, to some extent, been managed or resolved. In such cases, termination can be a positive, planned, and natural part of helping. This is how the helping process is designed to work. Often, however, helping ends before the process has had an opportunity to work as intended. In such cases, "premature termination" occurs.

Premature termination is very common in helping relationships. Garfield (1994) discussed research showing that most clients stay in helping for only a few sessions—if not just one—and that this pattern is the result of client dropout rather than deliberately planned brief helping processes. It appears that between 30% and 70% of all clients end helping prematurely (Garfield, 1994). As discussed earlier in this chapter, the drop-out rate for racial and ethnic minorities is higher than that for White clients. Sometimes, clients simply do not show up for more sessions, even if appointments have been scheduled, and do not notify helpers of their decision to terminate. In these cases, helpers may try to contact clients to ascertain their intentions and reasons for not returning. After discussing the matter, the client and helper might agree to continue working together. Or, they may talk about the client's feelings and perspectives, and the helper might identify alternative sources of help.

Premature termination is most commonly initiated by clients, but helpers can initiate it as well. In some cases, premature termination is caused by other factors, such as institutional or insurance policies that limit the number of sessions. When limitations are placed on the number of sessions, helpers should explain this in the first session and be prepared to offer referrals to other helping professionals once the sessions are completed so clients can continue to receive needed services.

Clients might terminate helping prematurely because they

- are not ready for helping (e.g., they feel unmotivated, uncomfortable, or uncooperative);
- do not like the theoretical orientation of their helpers;
- misperceive their helpers (e.g., they experience negative transference);
- want to test their helpers' commitment to them;
- do not relate well to their helpers (e.g., because of significant interpersonal or cultural differences);
- have disputes with their helpers about the course helping should take (e.g., the topics to address, the goals to set);
- become frustrated due to setbacks or slow progress;
- have concerns about their helpers' expertise, competence, or ability to be helpful;
- lack the time or money to continue;
- are uncomfortable with the development of healthy relationships;
- lose interest in helping;
- have greater priorities at the time;
- have experienced some relief from distress and unpleasant feelings;
- learn that the helping process is not what they expected;
- experience pressure to quit from other people, such as friends or relatives;
- feel that their helpers are unresponsive to their concerns and needs;

- feel that their helpers do not understand their problems and needs; or
- have personal issues that are unrelated to the helping process (e.g., health problems).

Helpers might terminate helping prematurely because they

- do not understand their clients' problems or needs;
- have values and beliefs that substantially differ from those of their clients (e.g., religious views, views on reproductive rights);
- experience countertransference, projecting their feelings and needs onto their clients (see chapter 15);
- lack objectivity (e.g., client problems may "hit too close to home");
- feel uneasy with particular problems or clients (e.g., very angry and confrontational clients); or
- have personal issues that are unrelated to the helping process (e.g., health problems, family matters, taking a different job).

When helping ends prematurely, both helpers and clients may experience negative emotions, such as frustration, anger, confusion, and disappointment. Clients may have less faith in the helping process as an effective way to resolve problems. Helpers may question their own abilities. It is beneficial for helpers to realize that they cannot always control whether clients terminate helping. Clients may end helping for reasons that have nothing to do with helper competence or the quality of service provided (Gladding, 2000). All helpers have clients who terminate prematurely, so helpers need to put the experience in perspective and not invariably see it as a negative comment on their abilities.

When helpers must end relationships prematurely, they should do so in a sensitive manner so that clients do not feel as if they are being rejected or abandoned. Typically, when helpers terminate prematurely, they provide referrals to other helping professionals (Gladding, 2000). They might emphasize that they are trying to make sure that the clients will see the proper professionals to get the best assistance possible. Because clients may feel reluctant about being referred, especially if the referral happens after many helping sessions have already occurred, helpers should address any client concerns about being referred and prepare clients for the transfer (Gladding, 2000).

If it looks as if premature termination may occur, helpers and clients can discuss the termination and try to avoid it, if possible and desirable. Asking questions, reflecting feelings, and immediacy can be useful helping skills here. If there is advance warning of premature termination, helpers and clients should discuss termination, work to achieve what they can in the time remaining, discuss referrals, and strive to accomplish a smooth transition from the helping relationship to the outside world or to the next helping relationship.

Although premature termination cannot always be avoided, helpers can reduce its chances by

- honoring their commitments to clients;
- respecting clients;

- recognizing and responding to cultural variables;
- responding to and discussing client needs, feelings, concerns, and complaints;
- showing interest in clients;
- demonstrating active involvement in the helping process;
- structuring the helping process;
- developing productive norms;
- maintaining their skills and competence (e.g., through continuing education);
- engaging in self-care activities; and
- consulting with supervisors and colleagues about client cases.

Giving Clients Their Wings

If helpers and clients have progressed well through the helping process, termination is usually not a difficult experience. Indeed, clients may be anxious to end the helping process and function on their own. Termination does not necessarily indicate that problems have been completely managed or resolved; rather, it indicates that the helping process has run its course and the client is now more prepared to function on his or her own, without regular helper involvement.

Follow-Up

Follow-up is essentially a post-helping evaluation process. After helping has ended, clients and helpers may check in to evaluate the quality of the helping services provided, to discuss client progress, to help clients maintain gains and minimize setbacks, and to evaluate the overall effectiveness of the helping process. Follow-up shows clients that they still have helper support after the conclusion of helping. During termination, talking about follow-up options can reduce client fears and anxiety about the end of helping.

Cormier and Nurius (2003) stated that follow-up may be conducted in a number of ways. The following are some of their observations as well as some of our own:

- Have one or more sessions after helping has ended. These sessions may occur weeks, months, or even years after termination.
- Have clients fill out written questionnaires, reports, inventories, or surveys about their experiences in helping and how they are currently doing.
- Arrange for clients to make brief visits to the helper's office.
- Arrange for telephone contact at some point. The telephone calls could be initiated by either helpers or clients.
- Send e-mails or mail letters to each other.
- Have clients engage in self-monitoring. This involves having clients record their attitudes and behaviors over a certain time period (e.g., 2 to 3 weeks). At some point thereafter, helpers and clients have a session to discuss the attitudes and behaviors and see how well clients are maintaining their gains.

Follow-up reinforces positive changes and reveals how well clients have been able to apply newly learned skills, attitudes, and behaviors in their real-world lives—

that is, how well they have transferred or generalized what they learned in helping to their actual environments outside of helping (Cormier & Nurius, 2003). Follow-up can aid helpers in improving their skills, interventions, and strategies. By learning how well and how long client gains have been maintained and what challenges clients have confronted, helpers may be able to ascertain which skills, interventions, and strategies worked and which did not. In some settings, follow-up is used for accountability and performance review purposes to evaluate helper competence and effectiveness.

Some clients want a lot of follow-up contact. Essentially, they are asking for a continuation of the helping process. Such behavior can be discussed to ascertain the reason for it. The timing of termination may also be reevaluated. Clients may not have been ready for termination.

Follow-up is often beneficial, but whether it occurs depends on the policies of the helping setting, helper style, and client needs and desires. Follow-up does not occur in many helping relationships. When clients feel good about the helping process and their achievements, they may not see any need for further contact with their helpers. When they see their helping experience as negative or unhelpful, they often do not want more contact with their helpers. So, in many cases, the final session is the last time that helpers see or hear from their clients.

Helping Outcomes

When helping works as intended, clients experience positive change, which is the overall goal of helping (Garfield, 1995). A significant growth and learning experience occurs. Positive changes that may be seen include

- reduction of painful feelings, such as depression and anxiety;
- reduced stress;
- more happiness and contentment;
- better interpersonal skills;
- richer, deeper, closer, more satisfying relationships;
- stronger, healthier connections to family;
- improved intimacy skills;
- more empathy;
- more positive, compassionate views of self and others;
- greater harmony between oneself and one's environment or the world;
- more assertiveness;
- greater self-awareness;
- more self-confidence;
- more independence and interdependence, less dependence;
- more responsibility and initiative;
- better relationship-building, problem-solving, and decision-making skills;
- more accurate perceptual skills, less distortion of people and experiences;
- healthier emotional expression;
- better academic and vocational performance;

■ healthier balance between work and leisure;
■ better physical health and grooming.

The following are three important comments about these positive changes. First, what constitutes a positive change depends on cultural variables. For example, in cultures that value family connections and have a more collectivist perspective than European American male culture (which tends to be individualistic), "more assertiveness," "more independence," and "less dependence" may not be desirable positive changes toward which clients strive. Instead, stronger family connections, for example, may constitute desirable positive change. Second, positive changes are not always permanent. Clients may relapse into old attitudes and behaviors. Maintaining gains often takes hard work. Third, determining how much or even whether positive change has occurred may be a matter of perspective and may depend on how one defines and measures change (Garfield, 1994, 1995; Hill & O'Brien, 1999; Lambert & Hill, 1994). For example, a helper may believe that her client made good progress and benefited from helping, but the client may feel less satisfied (Hill & O'Brien, 1999). These discrepancies are one reason why it is important for both helpers and clients to provide feedback and share their feelings and thoughts when evaluating the helping process. Concerns and differences in perception can be discussed as part of evaluation.

Summary and Concluding Remarks

This chapter focused on beginning, maintaining, and ending the helping process. There is much variability in this process across helping settings, but some general features, characteristics, and steps can be observed. The first session of helping is typically quite structured to set the stage for the rest of the process. The middle sessions are where most of the work in helping occurs. Ending the helping process is a stage or phase of helping—a gradual conclusion to the work that the helper and client do. The goal is to help the client make a smooth transition from helping to his or her real-world life. Follow-up may occur to check on how well the client has maintained the gains made in helping.

Successfully navigating the helping process truly is an art. When helping works as intended, clients typically see numerous positive changes, such as reduced stress, more satisfying relationships, and greater self-awareness. The process can be quite effective for those willing to make the effort to change.

Questions for Thought

1. What feelings, thoughts, and expectations might the helper and the client have during the first session? What difficulties might arise in the first session? How do the various first-session activities (e.g., structuring) promote the development of good helping relationships?

2. Imagine that you are a client who has already had an initial helping session. You are considering returning for another session. What factors would prompt you to continue with the helping process session after session? What might cause you to terminate helping early?

3. Think about a time in your life when a significant event or relationship came to an end—for example, you graduated from high school or one of your friends moved away. Think about how you handled the experience—what you did and how you felt. How was the end of this event or relationship similar to the end of a helping relationship?

4. In your view, from whose perspective should helping outcomes be measured? The perspective of helpers? Clients? Both? What are the advantages and disadvantages of measuring helping outcomes from helper perspectives? From client perspectives?

PART THREE

The Helping Relationship

4. The Context for Helping: The Special Relationship Between Helper and Client

CHAPTER 4

The Context for Helping: The Special Relationship Between Helper and Client

CHAPTER OVERVIEW

The relationship between the helper and the client is of fundamental importance in the helping process. This unique and special relationship lays the foundation for helping and establishes the context within which the activities of exploring client concerns, promoting client understanding, charting a new course, and working for positive change occur. In this chapter, we define the "helping relationship," discuss how attachment theory is relevant to helping relationships, and describe characteristics of good helping relationships. We also delineate helper and client factors that facilitate the development of good helping relationships, as well as those that do not. Finally, we discuss the cycle of caring, which describes how helpers build, maintain, and end helping relationships.

It is not upon the physical sciences that the future will depend. It is upon us who are trying to understand and deal with the interactions between human beings—who are trying to create helping relationships.

—Carl Rogers
(1962, p. 226)

What Is a "Helping Relationship"?

Often, the definition of "helping relationship" is assumed and is, therefore, not discussed. However, it is important to define this critical aspect of helping. The helping relationship basically refers to the way the helper and the client interact. Gelso and Carter (1985) described the relationship as "the feelings and attitudes that counseling [helping] participants have toward one another, and the manner in which these are expressed" (p. 159). Psychologist Carl Rogers, who developed client-centered counseling and emphasized the importance of a strong therapeutic relationship in the helping process, described a helping relationship as "a relationship in which at least one of the parties has the intent of promoting the growth, development, maturity, improved functioning, [and] improved coping with life of the other" (1962, p. 215). Both are useful definitions of the helping relationship.

Attachment Theory, Caregiving, and Helping Relationships

Attachment theory (Bowlby, 1988) provides a means to conceptualize relationships. It addresses the bonding and strong emotional reactions associated with connecting and disconnecting with others throughout the life span (Pistole, 1999). Attachment theory postulates that attachment and caregiving are interrelated, complementary systems.

Attachment refers to a person's need to maintain proximity, or closeness, to someone who provides a sense of security, such as a parent or romantic partner. When proximity is not maintained, the attachment system is activated. The individual who seeks proximity experiences separation anxiety and tries to reestablish proximity. When proximity has been reestablished, the attachment system is deactivated (Bowlby, 1988; Pistole, 1999).

The caregiving system involves providing emotional care and protection (Pistole, 1999). Caregiving gives the attached person a sense of security by providing soothing and closeness (a "safe haven") and a "secure base" from which to explore issues and concerns (Bowlby, 1988; Pistole, 1999). As Pistole (1999) noted: "Caregiving is aroused when the attached person signals a need for proximity, is in distress, or is perceived to be in some form of physical or psychological danger" (p. 438). Caregiving ends when the danger has passed or the attached person has established proximity (Pistole, 1999).

In recent years, attachment theory has been applied to helping relationships because of the significance of interpersonal relationships in the helping process. Attachment theory can explain how and why helping relationships develop. Helpers function as caregivers, and clients, who are in distress, seek attachment and security. Thus, helpers and clients work to form attachment-caregiving bonds (Pistole, 1999). Clients seek the assistance of helpers when in distress. This distress activates the attachment system in which clients seek proximity to helpers, who can provide care and a sense of security. The support, comfort, understanding, and accessibility of helpers allow clients to deactivate the attachment system as proximity and security are established. Moreover, by providing a "safe haven" for clients—by being comforting when clients feel distress—helpers support the secure base function, serving as an anchor to which clients can return (Bowlby, 1988; Pistole, 1999). The secure base serves as the starting point for providing guidance and exploring the troubling issues that prompted clients to seek help.

Characteristics of Good Helping Relationships

A helping relationship begins when a helper and a client meet for their first session. Both individuals come with experiences and perspectives that shape how they see the world and interact with people. One important task for them is to build rapport—to establish a bond of trust and respect that will encourage the client to share his or her problems in an honest, candid manner. It is the human bond or connection that develops—the feeling that the helper is paying attention, caring, empathizing, and understanding—that creates a comfortable environment for client change. In short, the helper and the client need to develop a high-quality relationship that will permit them to work together effectively.

Authorities on the helping process agree that a high-quality relationship is very important to effective helping (see, e.g., Bachelor & Horvath, 1999; Sexton & Whiston, 1994). They also note that a good relationship needs to be established early in the helping process, within the first few sessions. When helpers and clients get off on the right foot, clients are less likely to terminate the helping process prematurely and are more likely to see helping as beneficial.

In the following paragraphs, several characteristics that define good helping relationships and facilitate positive outcomes in the helping process are discussed. As you read, consider the ways in which helping relationships are similar to and different from other kinds of relationships, such as friendships, business relationships, and romantic relationships.

One-Way. Clients and their lives and problems are the focus of helping. Helpers participate in helping relationships to support and assist clients, not to address their own problems. In this respect, helping relationships differ from friendships and romantic relationships, which are two-way relationships. In friendships and romantic relationships, both people nurture each other and reciprocate support and assistance in difficult times. Referring to helping relationships as "one-way" does not mean that helpers never disclose information about themselves. Self-disclosure of feelings, thoughts, and life experiences, when done at appropriate times and in moderation, can be therapeutically valuable. A one-way relationship means that helping flows in one direction—from helpers to clients. Clients do not work with helpers to address helper problems.

Caring. Caring is an essential quality that must be maintained in helping relationships (Skovholt, 2001). Caring is associated with understanding, kindness, concern, attention, and nurturing. When clients feel cared for, they feel valued, which can instill motivation, confidence, and self-esteem. The nature of caring in helping relationships is described in more detail later in this chapter in the section on the cycle of caring.

Positive and Collaborative. People will typically discuss troubling concerns only with individuals whom they trust and respect. Thus, for good helping relationships to develop and ultimately for helping to be successful, helpers need to earn the trust and respect of their clients. Research has consistently shown that a positive, mutually interactive, collaborative relationship, as opposed to a more controlling, authoritarian one, is most likely to lead to positive change in clients (Albert, 1997; Bachelor & Horvath, 1999; Horvath & Symonds, 1991; Sexton & Whiston, 1991). In a positive, collaborative relationship, helpers and clients team up against problems, agreeing on the goals and tasks of helping. They develop a "working alliance" (Bordin, 1975; Gelso & Carter, 1985; Greenson, 1965; Horvath & Symonds, 1991). This cooperative endeavor helps to reinforce and empower clients by creating an environment in which they can feel comfortable, safe, respected, and free to express themselves. Authoritarian relationships, in contrast, may create a condescending, dominating atmosphere in which clients feel intimidated and controlled. Such relationships tend to stifle trust and open communication.

Centered on Communication. Communication is the essence of helping relationships. Helpers and clients constantly transmit and receive verbal and nonverbal messages during their meetings (Hackney & Cormier, 2001). Through discussion of these messages, clients become aware of how they interact with other people and can gain insight into the nature of their problems. The basis for professional helping is the "talking cure," a concept emphasized and refined by Sigmund Freud (Bankart, 1997). As clients talk about problems, they receive feedback from helpers and begin to see new ways of dealing with problems.

One aspect of helping relationships that may differ from other relationships in clients' lives is that helpers and clients communicate *about their relationship.* They talk about how they interact in the relationship, how they feel about the relationship, how well it is developing, and any problems that exist in the relationship. Helpers and clients can strengthen their rapport by discussing positive aspects of their relationship. They can also "clear the air" by discussing and working through any difficulties or misunderstandings they are having. This is important given that helpers and clients may perceive the helping relationship differently (Bachelor & Horvath, 1999). Talking about the relationship is a significant communication skill that clients may be able to transfer to other relationships in their lives. Because clients may not be accustomed to discussing relationships, helpers often have to take the lead in asking clients for their feedback about the helping relationship.

Confidential. Confidentiality was discussed in chapter 3. To reiterate briefly, confidentiality means that helpers do not reveal client information and statements to other people (although helpers are typically permitted to discuss client cases with colleagues and supervisors, who are also bound by confidentiality). Confidentiality is a significant aspect of helping. Without it, clients would probably choose not to discuss issues at all. Thus, confidentiality encourages candor, open expression, and the development of trusting relationships. Remember, though, that there are limits to confidentiality. For example, if a client reports child abuse, the helper is obligated to breach confidentiality and relay that information to law enforcement authorities or child protective services.

Governed by Ethical Guidelines. Each helping profession has its own ethical code, which states the principles and standards established by the profession to ensure the dignity, responsibility, and accountability of its members. The various codes tend to cover similar topics, such as confidentiality, client rights, respect for cultural and individual differences, assessment, and professional competence. Ethical issues are covered in more detail in chapter 14.

Guided by Clients' Needs, Desires, and Degree of Participation. Clients seek out helping services and participate in helping to the extent that they choose. Even though some clients are ordered by a court of law to seek professional help and face legal consequences if they fail to comply, helpers cannot compel clients to participate. Only clients can make the decision to modify their attitudes and behaviors. They determine what they want, and they are responsible for making decisions about how to live their lives. Helpers cannot force or impose changes.

Goal-Oriented and Purposeful. Helpers and clients do not meet merely to engage in conversation. They meet to help clients manage or resolve problems. Once client problems are defined and understood, helpers and clients work to establish goals that clients want to achieve. Helping is a deliberate process that involves planning, focus, and direction.

Structured. Helping usually is not a methodical, orderly process, but some degree of structure is established to define the nature of the helping relationship and the helping process. Helpers typically describe helping for clients, such as by discussing the roles and responsibilities of each person in the relationship. Helpers also discuss confidentiality, goals, expectations, and administrative matters (e.g., fees). Structuring helps clients see what they are "getting into" and assists them in developing realistic expectations about the nature of helping and what helping can accomplish.

Flexible and Adaptive. Each individual is unique, so each helping relationship is unique. The cultural and personality characteristics of the helper and client affect the development of their relationship. Because helpers bear primary responsibility for building relationships and because clients have unique attachment styles, helpers must be especially sensitive to client needs, responses, and characteristics and be prepared to adapt their helping skills, interventions, techniques, and strategies accordingly (see Pistole, 1999).

Flexibility is also required because helping relationships, like many other relationships, grow and evolve over time. Helpers initially focus on providing support and understanding as they listen to clients describe their problems. Helping, however, involves more than this. Indeed, too much support, such as excessive empathizing with client problems, can reinforce and ingrain the clients' current ineffective attitudes and behaviors and prevent the growth of helping relationships. Gradually, helping relationships move to a deeper level at which candid discussion, honest feedback, and action become important and valued along with support. Helpers challenge clients to develop a deeper understanding of their problems and to learn new ways of coping with them. In short, as helpers and clients get to know each other and client problems become more clear, helpers begin to balance support with challenge (Skovholt & Rønnestad, 1995). This balance allows helping relationships to continue to grow and move toward positive outcomes.

Focused on Feelings, Thoughts, Behaviors, and Interactions. In the process of living, everyone feels, thinks, behaves, and interacts with others. Clients demonstrate ineffective functioning in one or more of these areas. For example, a client may possess a good intellectual understanding of his or her problem (effective functioning in thinking) but experience great difficulty taking appropriate steps to solve or manage it (ineffective functioning in behavior). One of the goals of the helping process is to help clients function effectively in each area. Thus, depending on client problems and needs, helpers assist clients in expressing feelings in a healthy way, correcting negative thought patterns, learning more effective behaviors, and learning how to relate to others in a more satisfying way.

Although each of these areas—feelings, thoughts, behaviors, and interactions—is important, helping often contains a very strong affective component. That is, focusing on client feelings is usually a major part of the helping process. In general, feelings are important to healthy living and survival. They represent instinctual responses that have become deeply ingrained over the course of human evolution. Feelings are subjective, complex, and sometimes unpredictable; they are not rational, objective, and logical. They can change frequently and are very powerful motivators that often conflict with—and sometimes overwhelm—intellectual understanding. Indeed, clients may know intellectually how to manage or resolve their problems yet be stifled in their efforts by such feelings as fear, anxiety, and anger. For example, many people remain in abusive relationships not because they do not know how to leave, but because they fear change, loneliness, independence, and sometimes retribution. When they seek help for their problems, they do so not to hear helpers ask the logical and simplistic question, "If your situation is so unpleasant, why don't you leave?" (if it were that simple, they would have done so already), but rather to receive support, empathy, and an understanding of their feelings, which helps them feel that someone is on their side and cares about them. Once they know that their helpers are listening and caring, they may be ready to talk openly and explore their problems, which is the first step in determining how to manage or resolve them.

It is not unusual for clients to construct defenses and distort experiences to protect themselves from uncomfortable feelings. One of the most important roles of helpers is to identify these suppressed feelings, make them explicit, and help clients acknowledge, experience, and take responsibility for them (Cormier & Hackney, 1999). Often, little or no significant work can be accomplished in the helping process until clients recognize and own the feelings they suppress.

Helper Factors That Facilitate Good Helping Relationships

Although building good relationships depends on both helpers and clients, helpers bear primary responsibility for relationship development. This task can be challenging given that many clients have trouble developing healthy, satisfying relationships with people. This difficulty may be the reason they sought help in the first place. A major aspect of helping is interpersonal influence (see, e.g., Kottler, Sexton, & Whiston, 1994; Strong, 1968). Helpers do not merely apply learned *professional* skills to assist their clients in resolving or managing problems. The helper's "self," which includes *personal* characteristics, attitudes, and behaviors, is also a critical factor and constitutes a significant part of the helper's professional identity. Indeed, in a discussion of the effect of the helper on the outcome of the helping process, Wampold (2001) concluded: "The essence of therapy is embodied in the therapist. . . . Clearly, the person of the therapist is a critical factor in the success of therapy" (p. 202).

In the paragraphs that follow, we examine a number of personal characteristics, attitudes, and behaviors of helpers that facilitate the development of good helping relationships. By demonstrating these characteristics, attitudes, and behaviors, helpers model effective, functional behavior for clients and enhance their own credibility. Of course, no helper epitomizes every characteristic, attitude, or behavior discussed. Helpers demonstrate them to varying degrees. Effective helpers, however, tend to demonstrate them to a greater degree than ineffective helpers.

Empathy, Unconditional Positive Regard, and Genuineness. In the 1950s, psychologist Carl Rogers identified what he described as "the necessary and sufficient conditions of therapeutic personality change" (Rogers, 1957, p. 95). Though researchers and helpers now question whether the conditions he identified are *sufficient* for change, many of the conditions are seen as important in building good helping relationships. Specifically, empathy, unconditional positive regard, and genuineness are important. These conditions emanate from helpers and are widely viewed as essential elements in successful helping relationships regardless of helpers' theoretical orientations or work settings. We look at each of these conditions in more detail in the following list.

- *Empathy:* This is one of the defining features of helping. Helpers view the client's life through the client's eyes, a process often referred to as taking a phenomenological perspective. This perspective helps to facilitate a deep, nuanced understanding of clients and their concerns. Helpers express empathy by carefully listening to clients and then verbally demonstrating understanding of client feelings, thoughts, experiences, and perspectives. Empathy is not synonymous with sympathy. Empathy demonstrates understanding; sympathy demonstrates pity or compassion.
- *Unconditional Positive Regard:* Helpers accept and respect clients without judgment or criticism. Unconditional positive regard does not mean that helpers agree with clients and their viewpoints but rather that they accept and value clients as people worthy of respect.
- *Genuineness* (sometimes referred to as congruence): Helpers demonstrate that they are sincere, authentic, honest, "down-to-earth," and true to themselves. Helpers are comfortable with themselves, nondefensive, open-minded, and spontaneous. Helper statements are consistent with helper actions and expressions.

Since Carl Rogers identified these conditions in the 1950s, research has shown that they are related to positive client change, with empathy and unconditional positive regard being the most highly related (see, e.g., Sexton & Whiston, 1991). Genuineness has also been found to be related to positive change, but it seems to have the weakest relationship of the three conditions (Sexton & Whiston, 1991).

Why are these three conditions so important? Imagine being in a situation in which you were interacting with someone who criticized you, looked bored when you spoke, or made little or no effort to understand your experiences from your point of view. Would you want to build a relationship with that person? Would you want to share intimate details of your life with him or her? Empathy, unconditional positive regard, and genuineness reflect concern, interest, and trustworthiness. They establish a safe, warm, accepting, nonjudgmental environment that facilitates the development of positive, trusting relationships. In such an environment, clients tend to feel more comfortable expressing themselves, exploring troubling issues, and taking the necessary steps to work through those issues. Judgment, criticism, and inattention, in contrast, hurt open communication and reinforce the feeling that no one cares or understands.

The safe, supportive environment that helpers create has been referred to as a "holding environment" (Teyber, 2000). As described by Cormier and Hackney (1999) and Teyber (2000), the term holding environment refers to the fact that helpers stay with, or "hold," client feelings instead of distancing themselves from those feelings. Thus, helpers act as "containers." This holding environment is often quite different from the environments that many clients are used to, where significant people have responded by withdrawing or by dismissing or shaming client feelings, which clients then learn to repress. The role of helpers is to validate these feelings, to "hold" them. By doing so, helpers show that they can accept client feelings and that it is safe for clients to experience and express them. Sharing highly personal thoughts, experiences, and feelings and having helpers accept them without judgment, defensiveness, or dismissal is, for many clients, a new and fresh experience—one that can strengthen helping relationships.

Many clients appreciate the undivided attention and respect that helpers demonstrate; however, some clients do not believe that helpers' efforts to be understanding, accepting, and warm are genuine. Having had negative life experiences (e.g., abuse, discrimination, oppression) or having come from environments lacking in respect, they may see helpers' efforts as patronizing, insincere, and confusing. They are used to criticism, judgment, shame, disrespect, and disinterest, so that is what they expect from people. They may feel suspicious of helpers and see helpers' empathy, unconditional positive regard, and genuineness as smug, deceptive attempts to disarm them and get them to drop defenses that have had significant survival value. They feel that letting their guard down will leave them wide open to the kinds of attacks that they have experienced throughout their lives—abuse, racism, sexism, homophobia, and so forth. Indeed, empathy, unconditional positive regard, and genuineness, instead of promoting trust, may initially *increase* the suspicions of clients who are not accustomed to the respect and attention that helpers are trying to demonstrate or who are distrustful of helpers because they perceive them to represent the "system" or certain values (e.g., European American, male, heterosexual). Helpers need to recognize this wariness, be patient, and not give in to clients' efforts to re-create familiar disrespectful environments by evoking helper anger, hostility, or defensiveness. If helpers respond negatively to such client efforts, their credibility may be damaged in the eyes of their clients, who may see the helpers as being just like other people in their lives and, consequently, unable to provide assistance. Trust is earned over time. It is based on respect and consistent behavior. Helpers must be persistent and consistent in demonstrating empathy, unconditional positive regard, and genuineness and recognize that it may take time for clients to view their efforts as sincere.

Caring. Discussed earlier as a characteristic of helping relationships, caring deserves mention here as well. Recall that we described caring as an essential quality associated with understanding, kindness, concern, attention, and nurturing. Caring is the essence of helping. It is more important than any learned helping skill that helpers apply. Skills are important for accomplishing particular tasks and goals in helping, such as gathering information, promoting understanding, and facilitating action toward the resolution of problems. However, caring helps clients feel valued and important. It establishes the human connection that underlies the helping process. Multicultural research has also demonstrated the importance of caring. For example, in a study conducted by Pope-Davis et al. (2002) on helpers' multicultural competence from the perspective of clients who were racially diverse—White, Asian, Black, and in a few cases multi-racial (e.g., Black, White, and Native American)—all of the clients indicated that they "wanted the counselor to behave in ways that communicated caring" (p. 374). In D. Sue's (1997) study of counseling with Asian international students, the author reported that the students valued rapport, warmth, empathy, sincerity, friendliness, genuineness, and behaviors conveying "caring." Indeed, if helpers do not care about their clients, how effective will their helping skills and strategies really be?

Expertness. When helpers are perceived as experts, they tend to have more influence in the helping process and to be more successful in facilitating client change (Strong, 1968; Strong & Schmidt, 1970). When working with such helpers, clients may be more willing to continue in helping, develop good helping relationships, and change ineffective attitudes and behaviors. Clients may perceive expertness from the following: (1) professional titles (e.g., "Dr.," "Ph.D."); (2) diplomas and certificates on the wall; (3) shelves filled with professional books and journals; (4) helpers structuring the helping process and introducing clients to "therapeutic rituals"—for example, by telling clients how helping works, thus showing that the helpers know what they are doing; (5) helpers' confidence in their presentation and approach to helping; and (6) the helpers' reputation as an expert (Frank & Frank, 1991; Strong, 1968; Strong & Schmidt, 1970). For culturally different clients, helper expertness may be viewed as a function of cultural awareness, cultural knowledge, and skills, rather than as a function of degrees and titles (see D. W. Sue & Sue, 2003). Helpers need to be responsive to culture (e.g., recognizing and discussing differences) and show that they are capable of assisting their clients.

Trustworthiness. Trust facilitates open, honest communication. When helpers demonstrate consistent behavior over time, they establish themselves as reliable, and trust develops. Helpers also establish themselves as trustworthy by honoring their commitments to clients (e.g., abiding by ethical guidelines and keeping appointments) and by showing their clients that they will "be there" for them—they will not abandon their clients or shame them because of what they express. Strong (1968) stated that a helper's perceived trustworthiness is based on (1) the helper's social role as an extender of help and source of assistance, (2) the helper's demonstration of respect for and deep interest in clients' welfare, (3) the helper's close attention to client statements and behaviors, (4) the helper's lack of selfish or devious motives, and (5) the helper's maintenance of confidentiality. As discussed in chapter 3, for many clients, trustworthiness is also a function of how well helpers respond to client needs and cultural differences (Atkinson & Lowe, 1995).

Attractiveness. Strong (1968) described helper attractiveness in terms of likability, similarity, and compatibility. He asserted that a helper's unconditional positive regard may make the helper more likable to the client and that accurate empathy, which involves demonstrating understanding, can generate a sense of similarity and compatibility. Helpers can enhance perceived similarity by self-disclosing experiences, feelings, and problems similar to those revealed by clients (Strong, 1968). Attractiveness also has a physical component (see Harris & Busby, 1998). Some research has shown that clients may be more willing to self-disclose to physically attractive helpers than to less physically attractive ones (Harris & Busby, 1998). However, research has also shown that even when helpers are viewed as physically attractive, clients do not want to return for more helping sessions if the helpers possess poor helping skills (Vargas & Borkowski, 1982).

Self-Awareness. Because the helper's "self" is a significant factor in the helping process, helpers need to develop a deep, honest understanding of their own feelings, attitudes, motives, strengths, limitations, biases, and values. These aspects of the self can impact helping relationships and influence how helpers work with their clients. Helpers who possess a thorough understanding of themselves are better situated to understand and help others than are helpers with less self-knowledge. They are more likely to recognize and confront their biases and to understand that their own beliefs, views, and values are not held by everyone. Thus, they are less likely to impose their perspectives on their clients. This point is particularly important in light of research showing that individuals are much more apt to see the existence and operation of cognitive and motivational biases in others than in themselves (Pronin, Lin, & Ross, 2002).

Helpers who do not understand themselves well may also project their own feelings onto their clients and not realize it (Hackney & Cormier, 2001). For example, a helper who is angry about something while helping may perceive the client as being particularly difficult that day, when in fact, the negative feelings are emanating from the helper.

Active Involvement in the Helping Process. Helpers' high interest, vigor, and enthusiasm (shown, for example, through expressing emotions, giving feedback, and asking questions) tend to promote good relationships because they convey confidence, reflect competence, and show that the helpers are interested in their clients. Helpers who demonstrate high interest, vigor, and enthusiasm help their clients feel like they are the center of attention. A passive approach, in contrast (shown, for example, through offering little feedback and expressing little emotion), tends to convey disinterest and hinder open communication and the development of good relationships.

Cognitive Complexity. Effective helpers are able to view their clients' problems from multiple perspectives. They appreciate the ambiguity of the human condition and use complex and multiple criteria in judging helping outcomes (Jennings & Skovholt, 1999). Research on master therapists (exceptionally competent helpers) shows that these helpers not only tolerate complexity, they welcome it and even seek it out (Jennings & Skovholt, 1999). Helpers who view problems in rigid or simplistic terms (e.g., considering only one possible cause for client problems) are more likely to inaccurately describe client problems, impose inappropriate solutions, and apply ineffective interventions. In these cases, helping relationships may be damaged. Spengler and Strohmer (1994) found that counseling psychologists with lower cognitive complexity were more likely to form biased clinical judgments than were counseling psychologists who possessed higher cognitive complexity. Bieri (1955) observed: "Cognitive complexity relates especially to the tendency to predict accurately the differences between oneself and others. Similarly, the tendency to engage in inaccurate projections concerning the similarity between self and others relates significantly to cognitive simplicity" (p. 267).

Cultural Awareness and Responsiveness. Cultural characteristics (e.g., race, gender, age, and spirituality) introduce great variability into the helping process. When helpers recognize, respect, and respond to cultural variables, they stand a greater chance of building good relationships with their clients, being seen as credible, understanding client concerns, and selecting appropriate helping skills, interventions, and strategies (see Atkinson & Lowe, 1995). Conversely, inattention to culture, which can give the impression that helpers do not relate to, understand, or respect clients, can lead to premature termination of helping. Culturally aware helpers monitor their own attitudes, behaviors, and assumptions toward their clients. They understand their own cultural characteristics and how they may influence the helping process (see Arredondo et al., 1996; D. W. Sue et al., 1992).

A Strong Ethical Sense. Helpers who adhere to the ethical guidelines of their profession show their clients that they can be trusted. Ethical behavior demonstrates respect for clients and the profession. A strong ethical sense involves more than just avoiding wrongdoing and minimally complying with ethical guidelines. It means living up to the spirit of the guidelines and doing what is best for clients.

Patience. Many clients have poor relationship skills and have difficulty articulating their problems. Also, clients sometimes display strong emotions, such as anger, frustration, sadness, and hopelessness, which may be particularly intense when the clients enter helping. Patience is important when working with these clients. In addition, clients whose culture differs from that of the helper may need more time than culturally similar clients need to develop trust. They want to know, "Does the helper respect me and really understand my needs?" Helpers need to understand that it may take some time for clients to begin to trust them. It may also take a while for helpers to develop a clear understanding of client problems. Finally, making positive changes can be a long process, and helpers may experience frustration while working with clients who make very slow progress or resist change. Effective helpers try to understand the challenge of altering deeply ingrained attitudes and behaviors and try to keep in mind the courage that it often takes to change. Clients appreciate helpers who allow them to work at their own pace.

Sense of Humor. When used appropriately, humor can show that helpers are happy and well-adjusted. Expressing humor is not always appropriate in the helping process, but a complete lack of humor may create a somber, depressing atmosphere in the helping relationship, making it difficult for positive change to occur. A lack of humor may also make helpers seem distant and aloof. In addition to being valuable in relationship development, humor is valuable as an intervention. Helpers may teach their clients how to use humor appropriately to address problems and improve their quality of life.

Open-Mindedness. Effective helpers understand the client's world from the client's perspective. They are tolerant and understanding of values and beliefs that they may not share. They see beyond their own needs, perspectives, and values. Rigid adherence to particular perspectives, values, or belief systems can narrow and distort how helpers view their clients and cause them to perceive their clients' lives and problems inaccurately.

Objectivity. Hackney and Cormier (2001) defined objectivity as "the ability to be involved with a client and, at the same time, stand back and see accurately what is happening with the client and in the relationship" (p. 16). Objectivity means, in part, that helpers do not have a vested interest in the decisions that clients make in their lives. Helpers are able to look at client problems from a more neutral vantage point and offer fresh perspectives and new ways to address the problems.

Nonpossessive Warmth. Effective helpers demonstrate kindness and benevolence without attempting to use helping relationships to satisfy their own personal needs for attention, companionship, affection, and romance. They interact and empathize with their clients without becoming selfish, over involved, or focused on their own needs.

Positive View of Clients. Effective helpers have confidence in their clients. They view them as good, worthy of respect, and capable of change. They also try to focus on their clients' strengths and attributes rather than dwelling on their shortcomings. A positive view helps to instill hope and confidence in clients by showing that helpers believe in them. When helpers view their clients positively, the clients may see themselves more positively and feel more motivated to make changes.

Flexibility. As noted earlier, each client is unique, so each helping relationship is unique. Effective helpers recognize that there are few certainties, answers, or hard-and-fast rules in helping. They adapt their skills to accommodate the needs of each client and each relationship.

Sensitivity. Effective helpers demonstrate a keen awareness of their clients' needs, experiences, and feelings. They are tactful, perceptive, and respectful when addressing client problems.

Altruism. Effective helpers are concerned about the well-being of their clients. They have an unselfish desire to assist people in pain.

Self-Respect. Helpers treat themselves well—physically, emotionall[y] lectually. They regard themselves positively. By demonstrating self-respect, model self-respect for their clients.

Curiosity. Effective helpers are truly interested in their clients and have a ge[n]uine desire to learn about them. They possess "an enduring fascination with ideas and inquiries into the mysteries of being; a capacity to explore, pretend, and experiment" (Mahoney, 2000, p. 734). Their passion to explore, ask questions, and seek understanding in a positive and respectful way enables them to become intensely focused, interested, and involved in the helping process.

Good Grooming Habits. Helpers increase their attractiveness to clients by being well groomed. A clean, well-kept appearance shows clients that helpers take care of themselves. It also demonstrates respect for clients.

Commitment to Personal and Professional Growth. Effective helpers are committed to learning about themselves and others, increasing their knowledge, and improving their skills. Through personal reflection, continuing education, and talking with colleagues, among other activities, helpers improve their skills, enhance their self-awareness, and increase their competence. Helpers who possess self-awareness, broad knowledge, and essential therapeutic skills tend to be perceived by clients as more attractive, credible, expert, and respectable than helpers who are lacking in these areas (see, e.g., Strong, 1968).

Healthy Boundaries. This characteristic was described by G. Corey (2001). Effective helpers, when outside the helping process, try not to dwell on client problems. In addition, they know and respect the parameters of the helping relationship and are careful to avoid harmful dual relationships with clients (e.g., romantic relationships). Further, they know how to say yes and no appropriately and do not allow clients to manipulate them.

Self-Confidence. Effective helpers believe in themselves and their ability to accomplish what they set out to do. They tend to possess high levels of self-efficacy, which is the perception that they are able to influence their environment and obtain what they want in life (see Bandura, 1997).

Commitment to Self-Care. To serve as role models and effectively assist others (other-care), helpers themselves must stay healthy (self-care). Helping is a demanding activity. The stress involved can lead to burnout, evidenced by fatigue, boredom, exhaustion, and lack of interest in work. When helpers work under these conditions, they can make mistakes and appear uninvolved, thus hurting their clients more than helping them. The challenge for helpers is to avoid burnout. Helpers may do so by engaging in such activities as vacations, hobbies, exercise, spending time with friends and family, and maintaining a manageable workload. Self-care is addressed in more detail in chapter 15.

Skovholt and Jennings (2004) explored the world of "master therapists." In one chapter, Skovholt, Jennings, and Mullenbach (2004) described several characteristics of master therapists—those helpers recognized by their peers as being exceptionally competent. Ten master therapists were interviewed to identify these characteristics and develop a "portrait of the master therapist." In the following list, the characteristics are grouped into three domains: cognitive, emotional, and relational. Combined, these characteristics constitute the highly functioning self.

...ain, master therapists

- ...ambiguity
- cumulated wisdom
- ...rious
- a profound understanding of the human condition
- ...arners

...lomain, master therapists

- Have a deep acceptance of self
- Are genuinely humble
- Possess high self-awareness
- Have an intense will to grow
- Passionately enjoy life
- Are quietly strong
- Are vibrantly alive

In the relational domain, master therapists

- Are able to intensively engage others
- Possess acute interpersonal perception
- Have developed a nuanced ethical compass
- Are piloted by boundaried generosity
- Possess relational acumen
- Welcome openness to life feedback

Client Factors That Facilitate Good Helping Relationships

Helpers are not solely responsible for developing helping relationships. Clients also play an important role. The following paragraphs describe some of the numerous client characteristics, attitudes, and behaviors that facilitate the development of good helping relationships.

Readiness for Helping. One of the most important client factors in building good relationships is readiness for helping, which refers to the extent to which clients are aware of their problems and want to work on them. Clients who are ready for helping are typically more motivated to acknowledge and address problems than ones who are not ready. Readiness can be conceptualized in terms of stages of change. Several stages have been identified (Prochaska, 2000; Prochaska, DiClemente, & Norcross, 1992): (1) precontemplation (lack of awareness of problems), (2) contemplation (thinking about dealing with problems), (3) preparation (intention to take action soon), (4) action (modification of attitudes and behaviors), (5) maintenance (continuing gains and preventing relapse), and (6) termination (no return to unhealthy behaviors and coping styles). Most people do not reach Stage 6 but instead spend the rest of their lives at the maintenance stage.

Clients in the precontemplation stage may not be ready to benefit from helping. When such clients seek help, it is often under pressure from family members or friends or upon an order from a court of law (Prochaska et al., 1992). They may be unwilling to address problems with helpers. Clients in later stages of change may be more receptive to helping, are more willing to build good relationships, and may see greater benefits from the process. Such clients tend to possess more motivation to work on their problems.

Active Involvement in the Helping Process. It is difficult for a helping relationship to develop and thrive if the helper is doing all of the work to maintain the relationship. When clients demonstrate interest in the helping process by asking questions, being willing to address problems, being willing to trust, setting goals, and communicating openly, they can interact more productively with helpers and develop deeper, richer helping relationships (Bachelor & Horvath, 1999).

Patience and Persistence. The helping process may take some time and can be uncomfortable. Tough personal problems are rarely resolved quickly, and effective relationship skills are not learned overnight. Coming to trust helpers may take several sessions and may not be an easy process for clients who have had their trust betrayed by other people in the past. Learning relationship skills and new attitudes and behaviors can feel like swimming upstream. It requires the courage to try, an intense effort, and a strong commitment.

Positive Perceptions About the Helping Relationship and the Helper. If clients view the helping relationship positively early in the helping process (i.e., in the first several sessions), they tend to be more motivated to continue in helping and develop the relationship, and they are more likely to see positive results from helping (Bachelor & Horvath, 1999; Lambert & Bergin, 1994). Likewise, clients who view helpers as competent, knowledgeable, trustworthy, attractive, and interested are more likely to continue in helping than those who do not view helpers in this way (see, e.g., Garfield, 1994).

Positive, Realistic Expectations About Helping. Clients whose expectations about the nature of helping are most consistent with how helping actually works are more likely to continue in helping than those who expect something other than what they experience. Clients whose expectations are unrealistic may become frustrated and terminate helping.

Willingness to Express Emotions. Clients who learn to recognize, express, and take responsibility for their feelings often develop more emotional maturity, richer relationships, and greater motivation to address their problems honestly than clients who tend to stifle and disregard their feelings. Cultural characteristics help to determine how much emotional expression is desirable and healthy.

Willingness to Self-Disclose. When clients are willing to express their thoughts and feelings openly and talk about their problems, they give helpers the opportunity to respond with support and empathy. Such helper responses may encourage further client self-disclosure and promote deeper, more genuine communication. Sharing deeply personal material—letting someone else into your private world—and being accepted can be an intimate experience. It strengthens the bond between people and permits a rich relationship to develop.

At this point, you may be thinking: "Many of these client factors reflect what a lot of people would see as healthy behavior. Would people who possess these qualities really be in helping in the first place?" Your question would be on track. Many clients who enter helping are not feeling very positive about some aspects of life, and they may not be very good at self-disclosing or expressing emotions in a mature manner. Indeed, many of the factors that were identified may not be present in the initial sessions, forcing helpers to work hard to build relationships. However, clients who begin to develop in these areas (self-disclosing, active involvement, etc.) and persist in their efforts will likely establish better relationships with helpers.

Helper Factors That Hinder Good Helping Relationships

This book focuses primarily on processes and skills that promote positive change in clients. In other words, it focuses on what helpers *should do* within helping relationships. It is important, however, to also know what helpers *should not do*. Unhelpful attitudes, behaviors, statements, and responses can neutralize the best helping skills. In this section, we discuss helper attitudes, behaviors, statements, and responses that can hurt helping relationships.

Obviously, the opposite of many of the positive helper factors identified earlier can harm relationships (e.g., *im*patience, *lack* of self-awareness, and *closed*-mindedness). Here, we address some additional negative factors—attitudes, behaviors, statements, and responses that we refer to as "anti-skills." These anti-skills can derail helping relationships and prevent clients from receiving the assistance they need. Here is our list of anti-skills, which is based in part on Bolton (1979), Gordon (1977), and Okun (2002).

Becoming Defensive. Defensiveness is a natural response when one is challenged or attacked, even for helpers. However, helpers must work to avoid making defensive responses. Clients will sometimes express frustration and anger toward helpers. Some may try to put helpers on the defensive to divert attention from their own concerns. Some may try to evoke the same responses in helpers that they are used to receiving in their everyday relationships. Others may deliberately provoke helpers as a way to test them. In any case, helpers who respond with argument, debate, or combativeness will likely create a hostile, contentious environment and may damage their credibility. An example of a defensive remark is, "Don't get angry with me. That won't help you solve your problems."

Being Aggressive. A forceful approach to the helping process can damage relationships. Helpers who speak rapidly or in a loud tone, who press clients to self-disclose, or who are overly energetic can overwhelm clients. The clients may feel dominated, intimidated, and controlled. As a result, they may choose to withdraw and not express themselves. Alternatively, they may become equally aggressive.

Demanding, Ordering, or Insisting. Clients should be allowed to work at their own pace and disclose information when they feel comfortable. Helpers who press clients for information with persistent requests, warnings, orders, a barrage of questions, or an insistent tone of voice can cause the helping process to become tense and hostile. An example of this type of unhelpful comment is, "You have to tell me what you're feeling if you expect me to help you. What are you feeling?"

Being Sarcastic. Sarcasm represents indirectly expressed contempt, hostility, frustration, or anger. When helpers make sarcastic comments, clients will pick up on the underlying negativity and may wonder why the helpers are not expressing themselves in a more honest and direct manner. In relationships where openness, honest expression, and trust are important, sarcasm is inappropriate and may make clients suspicious of helpers.

Interrupting. Interrupting is a significant problem in interpersonal interactions. Some people start talking whenever a thought enters their mind, even if someone else is already speaking. In helping relationships, helpers interrupt when they fail to allow clients to finish their statements and expressions. They also interrupt when they do not give clients time to absorb, or "process," what transpires in the helping process. For example, if a client appears to be pondering a new insight, considering new information, or expressing an emotion, the helper usually should remain quiet until the client appears to be finished. In general, interrupting cuts off client expressions and is disrespectful. Sometimes, however, interrupting is acceptable and useful, such as when a client rambles a lot. If helpers must interrupt, they attempt to do so in a polite manner, showing that they are trying to sort through and understand a lot of information or make the most efficient use of session time, as opposed to simply communicating that they want their clients to be quiet.

Judging, Punishing, Criticizing, or Blaming. Helper statements that accuse, denounce, ridicule, or scold can cause clients to feel hurt, disrespected, and shamed. In response, the clients may withdraw or become angry. In addition, these statements may damage clients' self-esteem and create or exacerbate feelings of hopelessness. An example of this type of negative comment is, "This whole situation seems to be your fault. You wouldn't be in this mess right now if you had just stayed away from her like your friends told you to."

Moralizing. Helpers who convey condescension, arrogance, or dogmatism often hinder the development of helping relationships. These behaviors may scare, anger, or offend clients. Though there are individual differences, many people do not like being told what is best for them, what to think, how to feel, or how to behave. An example of a dogmatic comment is, "You shouldn't drink. It's not right."

Making Gratuitous Statements. The casual use of such phrases as "I understand," "I know exactly what you mean," or "I can relate" can sound phony and empty. These statements may seem presumptuous and patronizing, and clients may ask helpers to explain exactly how they "understand" or "can relate." When helpers respond with honest, insightful answers, clients may benefit. If, however, helpers have no meaningful answers to these questions, their credibility may be damaged.

Placating. Sometimes referred to as reassuring, sugarcoating, or band-aiding, this behavior involves making such statements as, "Everything's fine," or "Smile, it's no big deal." While appearing well-intentioned, these statements ignore the complexity or seriousness of clients' problems and effectively minimize concerns. They may reflect an attempt by helpers to prevent clients from experiencing unpleasant feelings, or they may reflect helper discomfort with clients or their problems.

Self-Indulging. Clients and their concerns are the focus of helping relationships. When helpers focus on issues of importance to themselves, clients may feel ignored. For example, a helper is being self-indulgent if he or she says, "I had a problem like that a few years ago and couldn't bear to tell my family about it. How would you tell your family?" Effective helpers sometimes share personal information (e.g., their past experiences and problems), but they do so to benefit their clients in some way, not to brag or satisfy their own needs. This skill is called "self-disclosing" and is discussed in chapter 9.

Providing Advice Inappropriately. Helpers must decide how much, when, and even whether advice should be given. Providing too much advice may prevent clients from taking responsibility for their problems. It may also cause clients to become dependent on their helpers to tell them what they should do. Providing advice too early in the helping process may prevent clients from developing an understanding of their problems.

Assuming. When helpers are not sure they understand client statements or expressions, they should seek clarification. Assuming that they understand their clients (or assuming that how they view experiences is also how their clients view them) can lead to misunderstandings that hurt relationship development. Helpers should also bear in mind that clients sometimes, deliberately or unconsciously, distort or omit experiences, facts, and feelings as they express themselves. Helpers may need to gather more information by asking questions or requesting details to ensure that they fully understand what is really going on. They may also rely on their intuitions and training. When helpers always assume that client expressions represent the "true" state of affairs, they risk incorrectly identifying client problems.

Thinking Simplistically. Client problems are complex and often do not lend themselves to easy explanations and solutions. Helpers who fail to consider many possibilities and perspectives when working with clients may have difficulty building productive relationships and facilitating positive change. Simplistic thinking can lead to inaccurate diagnoses or descriptions of client problems.

Stereotyping. Stereotypes are rigid generalizations that represent inaccurate or distorted ways of perceiving people. When helpers stereotype clients, they treat them unfairly, ignore their uniqueness, and often fail to conceptualize their concerns accurately.

Interrogating. Helpers need to ask questions to gather information; however, when they ask too many questions, the helping session can seem like an interrogation. Clients who are asked too many questions may feel highly scrutinized and uncomfortable. Sometimes, these clients assume a passive role in which they speak only in response to questions.

Imposing or Manipulating. Many clients seek the assistance of professional helpers because they see helpers as experts or, at least, as people who have the power to facilitate change and the resolution of problems. Thus, helpers often exert a great deal of influence in helping relationships. On the positive side, this influence can encourage clients to take the steps needed to work through their problems. On the negative side, helpers may, consciously or unconsciously, force their own values, views, or agendas onto their clients. Helping can be a controlling, imposing process when helpers fail to recognize their own values, biases, motives, and perspectives and how these factors can affect clients and the helping process.

Overanalyzing/Disregarding the Obvious. Some helpers feel inclined to search constantly for hidden meanings in client statements and behaviors. This inclination may cause them to ignore immediate issues, problems, and solutions. Their style may seem aggressive, threatening, and confusing, as they probe deeply into client concerns and make elaborate interpretations while overlooking explicit statements, feelings, and behaviors. Clients may become defensive or feel offended when helpers presume to explain why clients are expressing themselves in particular ways.

Ignoring Client Concerns. Sometimes, helpers who feel uncomfortable with clients' expressions or issues try to change the subject. Some helpers completely avoid exploring topics that are uncomfortable for them. Both behaviors are unhelpful, as they may cause clients to feel ignored.

Engaging in Discouraging or Distracting Nonverbal Behavior. Helpers and clients observe each other's nonverbal behavior. Slouching, yawning, stretching, fidgeting, and checking one's watch, to name a few behaviors, demonstrate boredom, inattention, and disinterest.

Avoiding Client Feelings. The helping process usually has a very strong affective component. When helpers ignore their clients' feelings, they may be missing the most significant aspect of the clients' expressions or problems. One way that helpers avoid feelings is by using logic. Bolton (1979) observed that logic creates emotional distance: "Logic focuses on facts and typically avoids feelings. But when another person has a problem or when there is a problem in the relationship, feelings are the main issue. When persons use logic to avoid emotional involvement, they are withdrawing from another at a most inopportune moment" (p. 24).

Ignoring Cultural Characteristics. Helpers who ignore their clients' cultural characteristics, such as race, gender, and spirituality, may demonstrate cultural encapsulation (Wrenn, 1962), as described in chapter 2. Culturally encapsulated helpers tend to narrowly define the helping process, its goals, and positive change. They tend to apply their skills in the same way with all of their clients regardless of the clients' culture. The result is an inflexible style that can be unhelpful or even harmful. Culturally encapsulated helpers may demonstrate bias, prejudice, discrimination, and oppression.

Many of these anti-skills represent attitudes, behaviors, statements, and responses that everyone expresses or feels like expressing at one time or another. Obviously, they can harm any kind of relationship. However, their use in helping can be particularly damaging due to the sensitivity, anxiety, and apprehension that most clients feel about sharing personal information and problems. These anti-skills are "high-risk responses": They do not inevitably harm communication in helping relationships, but they stand a good chance of doing so, and they may irreparably damage relationships if used repeatedly (Bolton, 1979). They tend to block discussion and honest expression, thwart clients' problem-solving abilities, increase emotional distance, and trigger such client responses as resentment, defensiveness, diminished self-esteem, resistance, and withdrawal (Bolton, 1979).

It is important to note that the greater the stress in helping relationships (resulting, for example, from the powerful expression of emotions or from client distrust), the greater the likelihood that anti-skills will have negative consequences. Unfortunately, it is precisely when stress is experienced that helpers are most likely to use these anti-skills (Bolton, 1979). In short, the times when these anti-skills are most likely to be used are also the times when they are most likely to have negative effects. Thus, as much as possible, helpers need to avoid expressing them.

Client Factors That Hinder Good Helping Relationships

Numerous client characteristics, attitudes, and behaviors can hinder the development of good helping relationships. Some of these are described in the following paragraphs.

Lack of Readiness for Helping. Clients who are not ready to recognize or address their problems often demonstrate low participation and interest in the helping process and an unwillingness to disclose much about themselves. These clients are often at the precontemplation stage of change, discussed earlier in this chapter (Prochaska, 2000; Prochaska et al., 1992). They may have been court-ordered to seek help, or they may have succumbed to pressure from friends or family members. They may also be individuals who, because of problems at work (e.g., significant conflicts with coworkers), must seek help as a condition of continued employment (Prochaska et al., 1992). In short, their reasons for seeking help are external or involuntary. They would not be in the helping relationship were it not for some outside influence. When clients do not want to address their problems, helpers find it very difficult to develop good helping relationships.

Excessive Defensiveness and Resistance. Defensiveness and resistance may be aspects of lack of readiness for helping. All people utilize defenses to some degree to protect themselves from perceived threats. Many clients overuse defenses (e.g., by completely avoiding feelings or lashing out at people) to protect themselves from feelings or experiences that they find too painful, anxiety-provoking, or frightening to confront directly. Helpers try to help clients face fears, explore repressed emotions, and challenge deeply ingrained, ineffective attitudes and behaviors, but some clients strongly resist doing so. Excessive defensiveness and resistance may prevent helpers and clients from connecting because clients will not let their guard down. Good relationships are hard to establish in such situations.

Negative or Inaccurate Perceptions About Helpers and the Helping Process. When clients perceive helpers as interpersonally unattractive or incompetent, good helping relationships usually do not develop. Further, when clients mistrust helpers (e.g., due to cultural differences) and that mistrust is not addressed, relationships may fail to develop. Clients may also have negative or inaccurate perceptions about the helping process and how it works. Those who see it as a process where helpers scrutinize and interpret every statement and behavior to expose negative underlying impulses and motivations may become defensive and suspicious, and may withdraw from their helpers. Clients who are in helping against their will (e.g., court-ordered clients) may see helping as irrelevant—"I'm not crazy! This process isn't for me!" Clients may also be skeptical about the ability of the helping process to do them any good. They may believe strongly that their problems are unsolvable. In all of these cases, good helping relationships may be difficult to build.

Negative Stereotypes About People Who Seek Help. Although attitudes have slowly been changing, many people still perceive a stigma attached to seeking help for personal problems. They view people who seek help as being weak or mentally ill. Clients who harbor this belief may possess a low self-opinion, which can make it difficult for them to see helping as a positive process. They may not self-disclose much or expend a lot of effort to build helping relationships.

Low Involvement in the Helping Process. Some clients may be motivated enough to seek help but not motivated enough to do the work needed to manage or resolve problems. Perhaps due to fear of change, they may demonstrate little interest in taking an active role in working on problems. When clients are very passive and let helpers take the lead on everything, relationships tend to be stagnant and unengaging.

Impatience. Some clients enter helping expecting quick answers and simple solutions to difficult, complex problems. This may reflect a fear of confronting problems. Clients who are unable to slow down and do the hard work that typically comes with problem resolution may become frustrated that the helping process is not fast and easy, and they may end helping prematurely.

Low Emotional Expression/Extreme Emotional Immaturity. Good relationships are typically characterized by a strong emotional connection. When clients are not emotionally involved or when they demonstrate an inability to control or moderate their emotions, deep, fulfilling, healthy relationships are difficult to build.

Low Self-Disclosure. It is very hard for helpers to assist clients who do not say much about their problems. Communication and the helping relationship itself may remain at a fairly superficial level if clients are not willing to share details about their lives and concerns.

Significant Psychological Impairment or Distress. Research has shown that clients who demonstrate greater psychological distress tend to be less capable of building positive helping relationships than are less distressed individuals (Bachelor & Horvath, 1999; Eaton, Abeles, & Gutfreund, 1988). Their distress may make it difficult for them to develop trust or to commit the energy necessary to build relationships with helpers. These clients may also demonstrate a significant lack of social skills.

Learned Helplessness. The theory of learned helplessness was developed by Abramson, Seligman, and Teasdale (1978), Maier and Seligman (1976), and M. E. P. Seligman (1975). Learned helplessness refers to an individual's expectation that there is little or nothing that he or she can do to create a desirable outcome or avoid a negative outcome in a particular situation—that is, the individual believes that he or she lacks control. Such expectations may develop as a result of prior repeated failures in situations requiring achievement, performance, or problem solving. Discrimination and oppression may also contribute to feelings of helplessness. Individuals who experience learned helplessness may feel hopeless, apathetic, and depressed. It can be difficult to develop good helping relationships with people who feel this way and believe that there is little or nothing they can do to change their situation.

Many of these client factors can be minimized or overcome in time and with effort on the part of clients and helpers. Negative stereotypes, negative perceptions about the helping process, and apprehension about self-disclosing or expressing emotions, for example, may gradually diminish or disappear as helping proceeds and trust develops. Helper patience and skill in handling difficult client behavior are important.

The Cycle of Caring: Building, Maintaining, and Ending Good Helping Relationships

Helping relationships are built, maintained, and ended. In particular, the course of helping relationships involves (1) empathic attachment, (2) active involvement, and (3) felt separation. Skovholt (2001) described this as "the cycle of caring," a process that helpers go through over and over throughout their careers. Note how the cycle of caring, as described in the following sections, reflects not only relationship development but also the way in which helpers begin, maintain, and end the helping process, as discussed in chapter 3.

Empathic Attachment

Empathic attachment involves developing caring relationships with clients. It starts in the first session as helpers begin to explore client concerns. Helper characteristics that facilitate good helping relationships (described earlier in this chapter), as well as many of the helper skills discussed in chapters 6 and 7 (e.g., attending, listening, reflecting feelings), promote empathic attachment. Attachment can be challenging because many clients have difficulty developing healthy, satisfying, committed relationships. Often, clients' primary relationships (e.g., relationships with parents and family members) are stressful and dysfunctional, and the ways the clients have learned to interact with individuals in these relationships tend not to work well with other people, such as friends, romantic partners, and coworkers. Clients bring these interactional patterns into helping relationships.

The primary goal of helpers may be to assist these clients in developing more effective behaviors, but the initial challenge is to attach—to build relationships with them—a task that can obviously be difficult with people who possess poor relationship skills. Nevertheless, that is the role of helpers. Helpers will probably find it easier to build good relationships with clients who possess some relationship-building skills and maturity, but they must be prepared to develop relationships with people who have difficulty doing so.

Contributing to the difficulty of building relationships with clients who possess poor relationship skills is the nature of attachment. To build successful relationships, helpers must attach with their caring side, which is soft and vulnerable. It is the opposite of the firm, protective side that shields people from harm. Consider an employer who has to tell several workers that they no longer have jobs. This person to some extent needs a "hard shell" to be able to tell people, "You're fired." Metaphorically, one could view this soft/firm dichotomy as the underside of the turtle versus the hard shell. With the hard shell, one cannot get hurt easily, but one also cannot attach very well. Helpers continually present their soft side so they can form an attachment—a positive human connection—with their clients. When clients are angry, frustrated, and have not learned how to relate well to other people, helpers, in trying to form an attachment-caregiving bond, take a lot from them and bear the brunt of many strong emotions.

The key is for helpers to attach to an appropriate degree. If they are too detached (the hard shell), good relationships will not likely develop. If they attach too much, they become engulfed in client problems, feeling client distress to a degree that compromises their ability to be helpful. Learning an optimal level of attachment, where helpers experience their clients' worlds but are not overwhelmed by them, takes years of practice and experience. It is also a paradoxical skill—learning how to be emotionally attached yet professionally distant, united but separate.

Active Involvement

Active involvement is the working part of helping and encompasses the major activities of helping: exploring client concerns, promoting client understanding, charting a new course, and working for positive change. It occurs in the context of attachment and takes up the majority of the helping process. Helper skills and content expertise (e.g., expertise in career issues, adolescent behavior, drug addiction) are important. Active involvement begins with the first session and continues until termination.

Felt Separation

Felt separation is the termination process. It represents a loss of the helping relationship. Effective separation permits helpers to attach again, as they must do throughout their careers with each new client. As described in Skovholt (2001), helpers separate effectively by "anticipating grief," which refers to the way helpers internally prepare for the end of relationships. They also "honor the loss" of relationships by committing time and energy to separating. Discussing feelings, reviewing progress, and saying good-bye all facilitate a conscious recognition of the significance of helping relationships. Understanding and respecting the importance of the relationship are what allow helpers to attach again, to develop new relationships with new clients. Sometimes, helpers engage in their own rituals to help them with separation, such as taking a walk before the last meeting or devoting some time to thinking about the helping process with their clients. Separation, or termination, is not just the end; it is an emotionally rich process of enjoying successes, solidifying gains, expressing feelings, letting go, and coping with loss.

Throughout this book, we describe several skills, activities, and procedures that helpers use to build, maintain, and end helping relationships. It is interesting to note that even some of the procedural and administrative aspects of helping, as discussed in chapter 3, facilitate good relationships. Some of these include creating a quiet, comfortable, private environment for sessions, structuring the helping process (e.g., describing it, discussing confidentiality, exploring client expectations), developing norms (e.g., determining when helpers and clients will meet), and skillfully managing time in sessions.

Summary and Concluding Remarks

In this chapter, we defined the helping relationship. We discussed attachment theory and its relevance and application to helping relationships. We also described the characteristics of good helping relationships, as well as helper and client factors that facilitate and hinder the development of good helping relationships. Finally, we discussed the cycle of caring as a way to conceptualize building, maintaining, and ending helping relationships.

The helping relationship establishes the context for the major activities of helping: exploring client concerns, promoting client understanding, charting a new course, and working for positive change. Helping relationships are not static; they grow and develop throughout the helping process. Establishing good relationships is critical to effective helping; it is perhaps even more important than therapeutic skills (Martin, 2000). Indeed, good helping relationships may themselves be therapeutic interventions because they allow clients to experience new, healthier ways of relating to people—something to which they might not be accustomed (Bachelor & Horvath, 1999).

It may take a few sessions for good relationships to develop. In some cases, they may never develop. How well, how quickly, and even whether helpers and clients build good relationships depend on a number of factors, including the extent to which a good "fit" exists between the individuals. Similarities and differences with respect to personalities, life experiences, expectations, and cultural characteristics can help determine the quality of the fit between helpers and clients (see Elkind, 1992; Young, 2001).

As discussed in this chapter, both helpers and clients can facilitate or hinder relationship development through their characteristics, attitudes, behaviors, statements, and responses. Sometimes, however, other factors can play a role. For example, limitations on the number of helping sessions that clients can have may hinder the development of relationships. This is not a negative characteristic or behavior on the part of helpers or clients, but rather a reality that must be accepted.

Next, we focus on the first of the major activities in the helping process: exploring client concerns. As helpers engage in this activity, they work to build, nurture, and strengthen helping relationships.

Questions for Thought

1. How are helping relationships similar to other kinds of relationships, such as business relationships, friendships, and romantic relationships? How are they different?

2. In addition to the helper and client factors described in this chapter, what factors can you think of that either facilitate or hinder the development of good helping relationships?

3. If you were a client in a helping relationship, what factors would be important to you in building a good relationship with your helper?

Exploring Client Concerns

CHAPTER 5

Exploring the Unique World of the Client

CHAPTER OVERVIEW

Exploring client concerns involves appreciating the uniqueness of each individual. Although people are similar in many ways, they are also different. Indeed, in many ways, people—and the ways in which they view the world—profoundly differ. In this chapter, we introduce the process of exploring client concerns by discussing what we call the "basic mistake," which has to do with the largely implicit, unconscious, and potentially problematic assumptions and beliefs that people may possess as they interact with one another. We then describe "worldview," or the way that people see, interpret, understand, and relate to the world. We also discuss "reality filters," the lenses through which each person sees the world. Next, we use the ocean as a metaphor for getting to know clients and exploring their concerns. Finally, we discuss processes, issues, and goals related to exploring client concerns.

*We shall not cease from exploration
And the end of all our exploring
Will be to arrive where we started
And know the place for the first time.*

—T. S. Eliot (1943)

Different Perspectives

A student walked into a classroom, sat down, and waited for his Introduction to Statistics class to begin. It was the first day of class. He looked around as unfamiliar students filed into the room and took seats around him. The professor entered, welcomed everyone to the course, and handed out the syllabus. As the student glanced down at the syllabus, he realized that he was in the wrong class. This was Counseling Procedures, not statistics. Embarrassed, he got up and walked toward the door as everyone in the class wondered what he was doing. "Excuse me, is there a problem?" the professor asked. The student responded, "I just realized I'm in the wrong class. Sorry to interrupt." "Well, what course are you looking for?" asked the professor, not prepared to let the student go just yet. "Intro to Statistics. Do you happen to know what room that's in?" inquired the student. Uncertain, the professor replied, "I'm not sure." The student said, "That's okay, I'll find it," as he quickly exited the room.

After this brief incident, the students in the class turned their attention back to the professor and the syllabus, expecting to address more details of the course. The professor, however, had other plans. He said, "Okay, on a sheet of paper, I'd like you to write down what just happened." The students looked a bit puzzled but began writing. After a few minutes, the professor asked the students to stop writing and to share their descriptions.

One student, Mary, said, "A man was mistaken about the classroom he was supposed to be in. He was pretty embarrassed about it and tried his best to hide it as he left the class."

Another student, Harold, said, "A student was lost and wanted the professor's help in locating his class."

George said: "Some freshman wasn't paying attention to what he was doing and walked into the wrong class. Doesn't this guy know how to read room numbers?"

Ann said: "This guy came in the wrong room. He got up and asked the teacher if he knew what room he was supposed to be in—which seemed kind of selfish. How would the teacher know and why would he care? I was annoyed that this guy disrupted the class."

The professor then asked each person in the class to describe the student who walked out.

Rosa observed that he was a White male about 6 feet tall, had brown hair and sharp features, and she remembered very clearly that he was wearing a white dress shirt with thin blue stripes.

Amy could not remember what he was wearing but observed that he had wavy, brownish-red hair, was about 5'10", had a thin build, some facial hair, and hard-soled shoes—she remembered hearing the sound of the heels as he left the room.

Reggie thought that the student was pretty average looking—not too tall, not too short. He observed that the student was wearing dark blue pants and a belt. He thought that the student's hair was fairly long and needed to be cut.

Finally, the professor asked how old the student looked. One person in the class said 24. Another said between 26 and 30. Still another said 27.

All of the students personally witnessed the same event at the same time, but each one gave a different response when asked to describe it.

This scenario draws attention to an important basic point: People often perceive the world around them in dramatically different ways. This point seems simple and obvious—and it is—but often what is simple and obvious goes unexamined and overlooked *precisely because it is so simple and obvious.* The students in the course know that people see the world differently, but actually hearing the various responses of their classmates and comparing them to their own observations encourages the students to explicitly recognize how profoundly people differ and to pay attention in a more intense way to these differences. In doing so, they gain a greater appreciation for differences and begin to recognize how differences can make human communication so complex. Communication, when effective, involves shared meaning—mutual understanding between at least two people. Accomplishing mutual understanding can be *much more* complicated than it seems because people often must communicate through significant differences to understand one another.

When exploring a client's concerns, the helper enters the client's world and strives to understand it from the client's perspective. Doing so is necessary to fully appreciate the client's life and problems. Recognizing that people view the world in very different ways is the first step in this process. One of the purposes of this chapter is to scrutinize human differences and their impact on communication—to explore at a deeper level what seems obvious. This can be likened to putting a leaf under a microscope. When you hold a leaf in your hand, you see a fleshy, green mass of a particular shape, but when you magnify it, examining it closer, you can see much more detail—an intricate network of veins and cellular structures. The leaf is not as simple as it appeared to be at first. The same is true with helping. Indeed, helping seems seductively simple and easy because it involves processes that people use every day, such as listening and talking; however, when helping is examined more closely—that is, when it is put under the microscope—it is not as simple as it appeared initially.

The Basic Mistake

People tend to focus on their own perspectives and may not immediately recognize or pay attention to other perspectives. They tend to believe that their perceptions are accurate; they may even believe that their perceptions represent the only valid way of viewing the world. This behavior is both self-preserving and limiting. We all create meaning for ourselves through our senses. For our own survival, we need to believe in our perceptions—what our senses, instincts, emotions, and intellect tell us about the world around us. They provide us with context to help us understand and explain our lives and experiences. Our perceptions give us predictability and a sense of security, and they motivate us to take action that we believe will promote our survival and well-being. In the "wrong class" scenario just described, when the students were asked to describe what happened, none of them said, "I can't do that." They readily provided their descriptions. *They trusted their perceptions.*

Although this need to believe in our own perceptions is important, it can lead to what we call "the basic mistake," which involves three assumptions:

1. *Everybody is just like me.* Look at the picture in Figure 5.1, which was drawn by cartoonist W. E. Hill in 1915. What do you see? An old woman? A young woman? Both? Neither? Something else? When we have shown this picture to students in our counseling skills course, some students have initially seen the young woman, whereas others have initially seen the old woman. Although all students have been able to see at least one of the images, a few students have struggled to see both of them. Some could do so only after prompting from other students. Why the differences in what students saw? If "everybody is just like me," then why did some students see one image before the other one? Why did some struggle to see both images? All of the students *looked* at the same picture, but they did not *see* the same thing.

People often function believing that other people are similar to them and see the world as they do (see Fiske & Taylor, 1991; Triandis, 1996). Indeed, research has demonstrated what is called the "false consensus effect," which refers to the tendency to view one's own behavior as typical and to overestimate the degree to which

FIGURE 5.1   Old Woman/Young Woman Drawn by W. E. Hill, 1915

other people share one's attitudes, beliefs, and behaviors (Fiske & Taylor, 1991; Ross, Greene, & House, 1977). People who agree with a particular position believe that a substantial percentage of human beings agree with that position; people who *disagree* with a position believe that only a small percentage of people agree with the position (see Mullen et al., 1985; Ross et al., 1977).

It is easy to generalize one's own experiences and perspectives to other people, to believe essentially that "If X is true for me, then it is true for you." This point can sometimes be seen when one person gives advice to another person, such as when Amy says to her friend, "I think you should tell him precisely how you feel." Amy's advice reflects her view of reality—what she would do in a similar situation. If all people were indeed alike, they would experience the world in the same way. Miscommunication would be practically nonexistent. In such a world, helping might be an easy process because people would share the same perspectives and readily understand one another.

2. *I understand things.* Humans often use their own lives to provide themselves with hints about other people's lives. We interpret other people's actions, behaviors, expressions, and experiences through our own filters—our own subjective ways of looking at the world. That is how we explain and make sense of what we see and hear. This behavior is natural and automatic, and like many things natural and automatic, it often goes unexamined. The belief "I understand things" becomes an underlying assumption, but it is a belief that can lead to misunderstandings. Think about cultural variations among people. What is considered normal in one culture may be viewed as deviant or abnormal in another. For example, a European American teacher may interpret an Asian American student's silence and lack of eye contact as disinterest when in fact they signal respect and deference to the teacher. The teacher's "understanding" is incorrect.

3. *Talking to people and understanding one another is not too hard. I do it successfully every day. It's easy!* If talking to people and understanding one another is easy, then why do misunderstandings exist? Why are there so many communication problems? The physical act of talking is easy for most people, but truly understanding another person's perspective requires intense, conscious effort and a suspension of one's own perspective. For many people, this process is not easy. It is not natural to suppress one's own needs, beliefs, and views (Kottler & Brown, 2000).

These three points, which make up "the basic mistake," reflect the largely implicit, unconscious, and potentially problematic assumptions and beliefs that people may possess as they interact with others. The need to believe in their own perceptions can blind them to the fact that other people may not see the world in the same way. The basic mistake reflects the reality that misunderstanding is often a norm of everyday life. Indeed, according to T. Benson (personal communication, October 21, 1984), "the basic fact about communication is misunderstanding."

Because of the natural inclination to interpret the world from one's own perspective, people may find it difficult to communicate effectively through their differences. In some cases, people may find it exceedingly difficult to talk to one another or communicate at all. We once had a male Palestinian student and a female

Israeli student in our counseling skills course. We asked if they would be willing to sit in front of the class and have a brief conversation. They agreed but found it virtually impossible to communicate. Religious and gender differences and the historical animosities between their peoples made it very hard for them to achieve shared meaning and feel comfortable communicating with each other.

It has been said that the most dangerous of all delusions is the belief that one's own view of reality is the only reality. Robinson, Keltner, Ward, and Ross (1995) described "naive realism," which refers to the tendency of people to fail to appreciate the subjective nature of their own construals (how people explain or interpret things). People do not make allowances for the subjectivity and uncertainties of construal when they are called upon to make behavioral attributions and predictions about others. They do not recognize the extent to which other people's judgments, decisions, and behaviors may be based on different beliefs, ontological assumptions, or interpretations of information (Robinson et al., 1995). Naive realism was encapsulated by Robinson et al. (1995) in this way:

> It speaks to the individual's unshakable conviction that he or she is somehow privy to an invariant, knowable, objective reality—a reality that others will also perceive faithfully, provided that they are reasonable and rational, a reality that others are apt to misperceive only to the extent that they (in contrast to oneself) view the world through a prism of self-interest, ideological bias, or personal perversity. (p. 405)

The important point here is that there are *realities*, not just one reality—*truths*, not the truth. The realities and truths that individuals take for granted may not be others' realities and truths. Effective helpers are good at recognizing many perspectives. The helpers' realities are multiple realities. They look at the world from the viewpoint of their clients—a phenomenological perspective. By appreciating the world as their clients see and experience it, helpers are able to understand and assist their clients. Helpers who encapsulate themselves in their own world shut themselves off from the realities of their clients and limit their ability to provide effective assistance.

Worldview

The unique way in which a client sees, interprets, understands, and relates to the world is often described as the client's worldview. The client's worldview reflects his or her beliefs and perceptions and impacts how he or she conceptualizes problems, understands experiences, interacts with other people, and makes decisions. Both helpers and clients have worldviews, and they may not be the same. Worldview is developed and influenced by numerous factors, including needs, cultural character-istics, and past experiences. In the next section of this chapter, we describe these fac-tors as "reality filters." As you will see, for individuals from many groups (e.g., racial/ethnic minorities, women), discrimination and oppression are significant fac-tors that define and shape worldview.

There are various ways to conceptualize and describe worldview. D. W. Sue and Sue (2003) defined a worldview as "how a person perceives his or her relationship to the world (nature, institutions, other people, etc.)" (p. 267). They discussed world-view in terms of locus of control (beliefs about the ability to affect one's fate through action) and locus of responsibility (beliefs about the degree of responsibility or blame that is placed on the individual or system). An individual has an internal or external locus on each dimension. For example, individuals who have an internal locus of control and an internal locus of responsibility believe that they are "masters of their own fate" (control) and that success is due to their own efforts (responsibil-ity). D. W. Sue and Sue (2003) observed that Western-oriented helping tends to reflect this perspective. Individuals who have encountered significant discrimination or oppression and feel that there is little they can do about it tend to possess an exter-nal locus of control and responsibility.

Kluckhohn and Strodtbeck (1961) are also frequently cited in discussions about worldview. They described several major value categories in which differences may be seen among cultures. For example, they noted that differences may be seen in time orientation, with cultures oriented toward the past, present, or future. European Americans tend to be future oriented (e.g., having long-range goals), whereas Native Americans and African Americans tend to be present oriented (Ho, 1987). Differences also exist in people's relationship to nature, with some cultures empha-sizing mastery over nature, others emphasizing subjugation to nature, and still oth-ers emphasizing harmony with nature. European Americans tend to emphasize mas-tery over nature (e.g., harnessing nuclear power, controlling resources), whereas other groups, such as Native Americans and Latinos/Latinas, tend to emphasize har-mony with nature (Ho, 1987).

Lonner and Ibrahim (2002) cited research asserting that client worldview is the most significant variable in cross-cultural assessment and helping. In fact, a paper-and-pencil instrument, entitled the Scale to Assess World View (SAWV), has been developed to examine client worldview (Ibrahim & Kahn, 1984, 1987; Ibrahim & Owen, 1994). It is used to assess client values, beliefs, and perspectives on five dimensions: human nature, social relationships, nature, time, and human activity. Within each dimension, helpers strive to understand the client's worldview, the worldview of the client's family, and the worldview of the client's cultural groups. The influences of gender, sexual orientation, sociopolitical history, and religion are considered particularly significant because these factors have historically been used as reasons to oppress people (Lonner & Ibrahim, 2002).

In short, helpers need to understand and appreciate the worldviews of their clients and recognize how their clients' worldviews may differ from their own. Helpers who fail to do so risk imposing their views and values on their clients, and they may be unable to develop good helping relationships with their clients.

Reality Filters: The Lenses Through Which Individuals See the World

If people look at the world in profoundly different ways and have unique world-views, then what creates these differences in perspectives? It is probably a combination of genetic and environmental factors. Indeed, people's life experiences, characteristics, and demographic variables essentially serve as "reality filters," affecting their behaviors, attitudes, choices, beliefs, values, and ways of relating to others. The concept of reality filters recognizes that life experiences, characteristics, and demographic variables create a unique set of lenses through which each individual views the world; thus, each person's perspective, or worldview, is different. Everyone sees, interprets, understands, and relates to the world in his or her own way. Several types of reality filters are described in the following sections.

Types of Reality Filters

Needs

People have various needs in life, such as food, shelter, friends, and vocational success (see, e.g., Maslow, 1954). Needs vary from person to person and depend on circumstances, thereby creating unique priorities and perspectives. For example, a person who struggles each day to find enough to eat has very different priorities and perspectives than a person who works to climb the corporate ladder.

Developmental Levels

Another reality filter is level of development. People differ in terms of intellectual, emotional, identity, and moral development. For example, some people are unsophisticated and immature, whereas others are highly intelligent and complex. Numerous authors and theorists have proposed stages of development through which individuals progress in life. Erikson (1950), for example, described psychosocial development throughout the life span; Levinson, Darrow, Klein, Levinson, and McKee (1978) discussed adult male development; Josselson (1987) and Levinson and Levinson (1997) discussed adult female development; and Kohlberg (1984) described stages of moral development. Individuals at different stages may possess different perspectives on the world around them. For example, under Kohlberg's theory of moral development, when determining whether a particular action is right or wrong, an individual at Stage 1 (punishment orientation) looks at the physical consequences (punishment) of that action, whereas a person at Stage 6 (universal ethics) looks more to abstract ethical principles of justice.

Self-Concept

How people view themselves can influence their perspectives. For example, people who see themselves positively (e.g., having high self-esteem or self-confidence) may perceive that they are attractive, worthy, and likeable. For many of these people, the world is a wonderful place, full of exciting challenges and opportunities. People who possess more negative self-images may believe that they are unlikeable and that other people find them unattractive. They may withdraw from the world, take fewer risks (e.g., avoid trying to make friends), and experience less zest for life than those with more positive self-images. For these individuals, the world may seem unpleasant, even hostile.

Self-Efficacy

This refers to people's judgments about their ability to handle situations that they encounter in life—for example, their beliefs about their ability to pass a test in school or to get a good job (Bandura, 1997). Self-efficacy judgments influence people's choices of activities and environments in which to function. People with high self-efficacy tend to exert great effort to master challenges, and they tend to perform at higher levels than low self-efficacy individuals, who have doubts about their abilities and may slacken their efforts, become resigned and apathetic, or give up (Bandura, 1982, 1997).

Occupational Personality

Occupational personality is another filter through which individuals view the world. Holland (1997) asserted that career choice is an extension of an individual's personality. He identified six personality types through which the individual and the work environment interact: Realistic, Investigative, Artistic, Social, Enterprising, and Conventional. For example, Realistic types are practical and tend to like to use tools or machines in their work. They may pursue such fields as plumbing or car repair. Social types like to help people, use verbal skills, and focus on ideas. They may pursue education and helping professions, such as teaching and counseling. The six different types vary in how similar they are to each other. Realistic and Social types tend not to be very similar. One of the challenges for social-oriented helpers is working with realistic-oriented clients, many of whom resist helping (if they seek it in the first place) because the social, verbal, affective, and sometimes abstract nature of the helping process is inconsistent with their practical, hands-on approach to the world. Helpers are not speaking their language.

Motives

Individuals' motives for engaging in particular behaviors or activities affect their perspectives. For example, consider the different motives college students may have for taking a course in a particular subject: to prepare for a career in the field, to satisfy a curiosity about the subject, to fulfill a degree requirement, to get those last few credits for graduation. Each student's motive may affect how he or she views the material in the course, how interesting the course seems, and what he or she gets out of it.

Family

The family systems in which individuals are raised can significantly affect their lives and perspectives (see, e.g., Bowen, 1978; Guerin & Chabot, 1992; McGoldrick, Giordano, & Pearce, 1996). The degree to which individuals define themselves in terms of family differs. For example, individuals with a collectivist orientation tend to define themselves more by family membership than do those with an individualist perspective (Triandis, 1996). Whether families are single-parent families, two-parent families, families in which children are raised by other relatives, such as aunts or uncles, or families in which extended family members (e.g., grandparents) live with parents and children, also affects family members' perspectives. Even birth order of the children has been identified as an important factor that affects development and ways of interacting (see, e.g., A. Adler, 1958). People learn norms, rules of behavior, and styles of interaction in their family systems. Many values are passed on through families. Some individuals have positive growth and development experiences in their families, where they feel supported and nurtured; others, however, are victimized by neglect or abuse. Obviously, these experiences can shape one's attitudes toward family and the world.

Physical Characteristics

Height, size, health, strength, senses, and disabilities, among other characteristics, all affect how people perceive the world. For example, think about how the life of a very tall person might differ from that of a very short person. An individual in a wheelchair might look at the world based on what is and is not accessible, whereas a person who does not need a wheelchair may not give accessibility a second thought.

Cultural Characteristics

Race, ethnicity, social class, national origin, gender, age, spirituality, political views/ideology, and sexual orientation, among other characteristics, influence perspectives. Different individuals and groups possess unique customs, values, characteristics, and experiences. Consider, for example, that many Western cultures tend to emphasize individualism and place less emphasis on family relationships than many other cultures. Also, some cultures value emotional control, whereas others value emotional expression. Discrimination and oppression, as noted earlier, are significant experiences for many groups and can influence the way members of the groups interact with others—for example, how much they trust people.

Majority/minority status can also affect perspectives. At a mostly White university, how might it feel to be an African American student? A White student? Sometimes, the challenge for majority groups is to recognize that different perspectives exist. With so many similar individuals around them, members of majority groups may find it easy to believe that all people view the world as they do. It can be difficult for them to see minority viewpoints.

The following sections describe in more detail some of these cultural characteristics and how they serve as reality filters.

Race and Ethnicity. Though there has been disagreement on how to define race, it can be viewed as a construct that combines physical features and historical and political characteristics (Fouad & Brown, 2000). In the United States, five major racial groups are usually identified: African American, Asian American, European

American, Latino/Latina, and Native American. There are differences be⌐
groups, but there are also significant differences *within* these groups. Thus
be careful to not stereotype individuals based on race. "Ethnicity" relates t⌐
graphic place of origin of a people. As noted by Fouad and Brown (2000), ⌐
"refers to the ways of thinking, feeling, and behaving shared among people ⌐ close
proximity who have had similar life circumstances over generations" (p. 381).

Several racial and ethnic identity development models have been created to
explain how individuals grow, see the world, develop and change attitudes, and relate
to other people and groups. These models recognize that unique cultural experiences, such as discrimination and oppression, are important factors in identity development. The models are typically described in terms of stages of development.
Models have been created for Blacks (Cross, 1971), Mexican Americans (Bernal,
Knight, Ocampo, Garza, & Côté, 1993), Asians (Sodowsky, Kwan, & Pannu, 1995),
and others.

An example of a racial identity development model is the Racial/Cultural
Identity Development model (D. W. Sue & Sue, 2003). The model identifies "five
stages of development that oppressed people experience as they struggle to understand themselves in terms of their own culture, the dominant culture, and the oppressive relationship between the two cultures" (D. W. Sue & Sue, 2003, p. 214). The
stages are as follows:

Stage 1. Conformity: Individuals of the nondominant culture who are in this stage
prefer the values of the dominant culture. They ignore or deny discrimination and
oppression. They devalue the values and belief systems of their own culture.

Stage 2. Dissonance: Gradually, denial of discrimination and oppression is shaken
and individuals experience conflict between self-depreciating and self-appreciating
attitudes and beliefs. Individuals increasingly recognize positive aspects of their own
culture. Sometimes, a major event (e.g., meeting a strong leader who is a member of
the individuals' culture) can more rapidly propel individuals into this stage.

Stage 3. Resistance and Immersion: Individuals become increasingly aware of personal and group discrimination. They feel guilty and angry that their denial of discrimination and oppression has contributed to the mistreatment of their own culture.
They begin to actively reject the values of the dominant culture and tend to rigidly
adhere to the values of their own culture.

Stage 4. Introspection: Individuals realize that they are spending their lives reacting
to discrimination and oppression and become disturbed by the rigidity and anger that
characterize the third stage. They want to better understand themselves and achieve
a greater sense of autonomy and freedom, which will allow them to think and do as
they please.

Stage 5. Integrative Awareness: Individuals develop a sense of inner security and are
able to accept aspects of many cultures.

How salient, or significant, race is for an individual depends on the individual.
Racial and ethnic identity development models typically assert that race and ethnicity

are more salient for individuals of racial and ethnic minority groups than for Whites (see Fouad & Brown, 2000). This difference is due largely to the majority status of Whites and the history of discrimination and oppression in the United States. However, Fouad and Brown (2000) have suggested that "the salience of race varies depending on how different one is (or is perceived to be), and with the importance of race to that difference" (p. 390).

Social Class. This often-overlooked factor can significantly affect perspectives. Social class includes such variables as income, wealth, education, occupation, power, control, prestige, and access to resources (see Argyle, 1994; Fouad & Brown, 2000; Liu, 2001). Fouad and Brown (2000) contended that social class and race do not directly influence development but, instead, influence how individuals view themselves as the same or different from other people in society. According to these authors, the perception of difference on salient dimensions affects development (Fouad & Brown, 2000; see also Liu, 2001).

Fouad and Brown (2000) discussed research showing that social class is a more powerful predictor of worldview than family structure, race, religion, or national origin. Lower social class can lead to feelings of alienation, demoralization, and frustration, and members of lower social classes often experience a keen awareness of social class when they are in higher social class environments. Fouad and Brown (2000) also cited research findings showing that lower social class has been connected to such problems as crime and poor health, whereas higher social class has been associated with internal locus of control, greater self-efficacy, higher educational aspirations, and less interracial group conflict.

D. W. Sue and Sue (2003) observed that many racial and ethnic minority groups are disproportionately represented in the lower social classes (see also Lewis, Lewis, Daniels, & D'Andrea, 1998) and that they are more likely to be diagnosed as mentally ill. These authors pointed out that helpers may unwittingly attribute client attitudes that result from adversity (e.g., poverty) to cultural or individual characteristics of the client.

Gender. Both biological factors (e.g., genetic traits) and social factors (e.g., gender-role expectations and peer group interactions) help to define and distinguish males and females and create differences in their perspectives. Consider, for example, how social factors may establish or influence gender differences. Through childhood and early adolescence, boys and girls tend to associate largely with others of their own gender—boys with boys, girls with girls. They socialize in their own separate cultures, learning how to communicate, interact, and behave in certain ways. Then, as they get older and begin to socialize more with the other gender (e.g., dating), they often experience surprise, confusion, and frustration when they realize that the other gender does not always see the world as they do or communicate in the same way.

Much research has been conducted on gender differences in behavior and perspectives. Gilligan (1982) asserted that identity and moral development differ between men and women, with men focusing more on rights and fairness (an ethic of justice) and women focusing more on caring and responsibility in relationships (an ethic of care). Tannen (1990) asserted that women and men talk in different ways, with women engaging more in "rapport" talk (talking to establish a connection between individuals) and men engaging more in "report" talk (talking to convey information, impart knowledge, and maintain status).

Discrimination, oppression, and gender-role stereotypes also influence the perspectives of men and women. Discrimination and oppression have been significant experiences for women and have had a range of consequences, including denied opportunities and depression. As for gender-role stereotypes, these attitudes and judgments can pressure both men and women to behave in certain ways (e.g., men are supposed to be strong and not cry; women are supposed to show emotion, except for anger). Such stereotypes are limiting for both genders. Even helpers are not immune from stereotyping. Women and men who deviate from traditional gender-role behaviors have been more likely than those who do not deviate in this regard to receive diagnoses of pathology (see, e.g., Robertson & Fitzgerald, 1990). For women, even engaging in traditional feminine gender-role behavior has led to diagnoses of pathology, a result of the fact that male norms have been used to define health and normality (Brown, 1992).

Age. A person's age can affect his or her perspectives in important ways. Age reveals the era in which one was born and raised. The technology, economy, societal values, political situation, and major events (e.g., war) of the time in which an individual was growing up can shape how that person views the world. For example, people who grew up during the Great Depression of the 1930s may have different attitudes toward money than people who grew up during the economic boom times of the late 1990s. Age also correlates with such factors as maturity, wisdom, experience, health, and attitudes about life and death. For example, a healthy person in her early 20s may not give much thought to her own mortality, whereas a person in his 80s may be more conscious of life nearing its end.

Spirituality. Most clients possess spiritual beliefs of some kind, and helpers are increasingly recognizing the importance of this aspect of life (see Fukuyama & Sevig, 2002). Spirituality is a broad concept that may be defined in many ways. It is not synonymous with organized religion, although that is one way in which spirituality is expressed. Spirituality is often associated with such concepts as hope, transcendence, higher powers, and meaning in life. Ingersoll (1994) discussed seven dimensions to spirituality:

- A sense of meaning
- A conception of divinity (theistic, atheistic, pantheistic, or panentheistic)
- A relationship to one's conception of divinity
- A recognition of and tolerance for mystery
- A willingness to give oneself to play—being playful
- An expression of spirituality through various activities, rituals, and experiences
- A way to integrate the aspects and dimensions of one's life

Historically, most helping professions have not emphasized spirituality, and in some cases, they have not been very accepting of it. Some possible reasons for this cool reception include (1) the fear that focusing on spirituality hinders a helping profession's quest for scientific status; (2) the assertion that spiritual beliefs, in some cases, cause psychological problems; (3) the belief that the ego-centered focus of psychology is incompatible with the spiritual search for the transcendent; and (4) the possibility that helpers would impose their spiritual beliefs and values on clients (Hansen, 1997; Mack, 1994; Worthington, 1989).

Today, however, spirituality is increasingly recognized in the helping process. Spirituality can be a powerful source of strength and hope in people's lives, and it can significantly shape their worldviews. For many people, including helpers, spirituality is a critical factor in understanding life, explaining and interpreting events, finding meaning in life, making decisions, providing comfort, coping with the unknown, and managing problems that do not have clear solutions.

Biases and Prejudices

Bias refers to a preference, tendency, or inclination toward particular ideas, values, people, or groups. An example is an employer who prefers to hire only male employees. Prejudice is a negative, overgeneralized belief or judgment about the nature and characteristics of a person or group of people (Allport, 1954; Ponterotto, 1991; Ponterotto & Pedersen, 1993). Prejudice is based on faulty, inflexible generalizations and unsubstantiated data, and it is held regardless of evidence or facts that contradict it (Allport, 1954; Ponterotto, 1991; Ponterotto & Pedersen, 1993). An example of prejudice is a White person's belief that all people who are not of his race are inferior. Biases and prejudices can lead to discrimination and oppression, which are harmful actions taken by a person or a group that has power. Bias and prejudice often stem from fear, intolerance, lack of empathy, and lack of respect for differences. They tend to affect a person's perspectives by narrowing them.

Roles

The roles that people assume—such as occupational roles and family roles—influence their perspectives and their perception of role-appropriate behaviors. Teachers, for example, impart knowledge, and students receive knowledge. Teachers may not care too much about grades, considering them indicators of performance and achievement that they are required to assign. Students, in contrast, tend to care a lot about grades, which may have a bearing on what schools they can get into or what jobs they can obtain. Consider also the role of a parent. Parents assume the role of caretaker, focusing on providing for their children, ensuring their safety, and nurturing their development as they grow. Adults who are not parents may not be as focused on or aware of child-rearing issues.

Education

The type and level of education a person has received can influence his or her perspectives. Individuals with training in business, for example, may look at the world from the perspective of a businessperson. Level of education can affect, among other things, the number and variety of career opportunities that one has.

Language

People use words (e.g., metaphors, descriptions, and stories) to communicate and describe their world to others. Words are linguistic representations of reality; that is, they symbolize or approximate reality. They are not reality themselves—just ways to capture it. The words a person uses to describe his or her reality depend in part on that person's language. Some languages have many words to describe something— for example, a particular emotion—whereas other languages may have only one or two words to describe the same thing. Also, the words that a person selects are filtered through that individual's reality. Based on intellectual development or culture, for example, a person may tend to use certain words and phrases more than others.

Past Experiences

People's past experiences can affect how they perceive the world. For example, a person who has survived a plane crash may perceive air travel as frightening and dangerous, whereas a person who has never been involved in a crash may feel quite comfortable flying, especially in light of often-cited statistics regarding the overall safety of air travel. The experience of discrimination and oppression, described in chapter 2, is another past (and perhaps continuing) experience that can affect perspectives and relationships to other people.

Expectations

People develop expectations about the various experiences that they have in their lives. At work, at school, and in relationships, for example, we have ideas about how things should work, what we want, and what we should get out of the experience. Our expectations can shape our perspectives on the experience. For example, when an employer announces a 5% pay raise, an employee who was expecting a 2% raise may feel quite pleased, whereas an employee who was expecting a 10% raise may be upset. At school, a student who expected more opportunities to participate in class and to ask the instructor questions may be disappointed by a professor who spends all of the class time lecturing, whereas another student may be pleased with this format.

This list of reality filters is not exhaustive, but it describes numerous factors that can affect people's perspectives. Note that many filters, such as needs, motives, and physical characteristics, can change over time. As people grow, develop, and encounter new challenges, their perspectives on the world may be modified to accommodate new information and changes in their lives.

One way to appreciate the impact of reality filters is to imagine yourself with different filters than the ones that you have. For example, think about what living as the opposite sex would be like. Or change one physical variable (e.g., close your eyes and imagine yourself blind) and experience the world that way for a few minutes. How does it feel to change your filters? What do you notice when you change them? Honestly examining your reality filters can be enlightening; however, it can also tap strong personal feelings and challenge your deeply ingrained perceptions about the world around you.

Selection, Organization, and Interpretation of Information

Reality filters affect how people process what they encounter in the world around them; that is, reality filters influence how individuals *select, organize,* and *interpret* information.

Selection of Information

Every day, people are bombarded with countless sights, sounds, and smells. They cannot process everything at one time, so consciously or unconsciously, they must select what they are going to attend to in their environment and omit other items. Of all the information available, what do people pick out? The intensity of something in the environment, such as a very loud noise, can influence what people select, as can repetition, such as a merchant's slogan or catch phrase that is consistently stated in every advertisement. Reality filters also influence what people select. For example, if an architect and a botanist (two different occupational personalities) were asked to look out a window and describe the view, the architect might focus on the skyscrapers on the horizon, and the botanist might point out the large number of trees. As another example, a female student in a classroom full of male students may be acutely aware of the gender disparity, whereas the men might not have noticed.

In short, people react to their environment differently, in part, because they attend to different things. The items that are most important to the individual are the ones that he or she will select. This is one explanation for variations in eyewitness accounts of events, such as the scenario described earlier involving the student who entered the wrong classroom. Reality filters such as needs, biases, prejudices, and past experiences may also distort what people observe, causing them to "see what they want to see."

Organization of Information

People organize the world around them—categorizing, arranging, and ordering it—based on their reality filters. For example, a male employee in a mostly female work environment may use gender as a way to organize what he sees—lots of female employees. Students who are asked to write term papers on a particular topic will arrange the discussions in their papers differently even though they are all writing on the same topic. How the students organize their papers may depend on such factors as what seems most important to them, their developmental levels, and their cognitive styles.

Interpretation of Information

Reality filters provide the context within which people explain, evaluate, and understand things in their environment. For example, those with strong religious convictions may see a natural disaster, such as a flood, as a sign from a higher power, whereas a meteorologist may provide a scientific explanation. A person with high self-efficacy may see a test as an exciting challenge to be successfully mastered, whereas a person with low self-efficacy may see the test as an insurmountable, anxiety-provoking obstacle. In each of these examples, the same event is viewed from a different perspective because of the reality filters of the individuals involved.

An important aspect of interpretation is "attributional style," or the way people interpret or explain what causes the behaviors, successes, and failures of themselves and others (Graham, 1991; Weber, 1994; B. Weiner, 1985). There are three dimensions to attributional style: (1) locus, which refers to whether the cause of the behavior, success, or failure is external (e.g., discrimination; the difficulty level of a task that one has to perform) or internal (e.g., effort; ability); (2) stability, which refers to whether the cause remains constant or varies over time; and (3) controllability, which refers to a person's perceived control over the cause (Arbona, 2000; Graham, 1991; B. Weiner, 1985). For example, ability is considered to be an internal, stable, uncontrollable cause, whereas effort is internal, unstable, and controllable (Arbona, 2000). The attributions that people make in each of the three dimensions have emotional, behavioral, and motivational consequences. For example, when people attribute failure to causes that they can control (e.g., effort), they tend to be more hopeful about the possibility of change; however, attributing failure to uncontrollable causes can create feelings of hopelessness (Graham & Brown, 1988; B. Weiner, 1985).

Cultural considerations come into play here. For example, as noted by Arbona (2000), research has suggested that people with worldviews other than "American mainstream" may not view ability and effort as the dominant causes of achievement, or they may vary in the extent to which they believe that certain causes of behavior, success, or failure (e.g., effort and ability) are controllable or uncontrollable (Maehr & Nicholls, 1980). Thus, caution is warranted—and additional research is needed—regarding attributional styles.

Getting to Know Clients

As helpers and clients build helping relationships, helpers begin the process of exploring client concerns. Exploring concerns involves learning about clients' lives, problems, and ways of viewing the world. Helpers strive to understand the reality of their clients. Gathering a lot of information helps to put client problems in context and permits helpers to get to know their clients as people.

As discussed earlier, reality filters help to explain how people can perceive the world in profoundly different ways. Communicating through these differences can be quite challenging and often requires hard work. Suspending one's own perspective in order to understand the perspective of another person is like swimming upstream, moving against the current of one's own views. But it is an important task. The client's reality is the most important reality in the helping process. The challenge for helpers is to comprehend this reality—to see, understand, and appreciate the world from the client's viewpoint. How do helpers do this? How do they communicate through differences and understand the client's reality? What we call "the ocean method" is a way for helpers to achieve understanding.

The Ocean Method

The phenomenological world of the client can be represented metaphorically as an ocean—a new, fascinating, and different place full of wonders and unique features. To fully appreciate, or "fathom," the client's world, helpers must enter and explore the ocean—sensing it, feeling it, experiencing it. The plant life, creatures, water depth, temperature, waves, currents, sand, and so forth, all serve as metaphors for the client's life and experiences. A problem may be represented by an iceberg. When clients seek help, helpers can often immediately see some manifestation of client problems, such as anxiety, depressed affect, anger, or defensiveness. These represent the tip of the iceberg, the part of the problem that rises above the surface for all to see. The bigger part of the problem, however, is submerged beneath the surface. Through the helping process, helpers gradually enter the ocean, going below the surface to see and understand the full extent and context of the problem and to help clients comprehend it as well.

Empathic Immersion

The key to exploring the client's world—the ocean—is empathic immersion. That is, helpers must be able to enter the world of the client and understand it from the client's perspective. Rogers (1961) described helper empathy as the ability of helpers to "sense the client's private world as if it were [their] own, but without ever losing the 'as if' quality" (p. 284). Helpers, of course, cannot completely know what it is like to be their clients, but through empathic immersion, they strive to adopt the internal frame of reference of their clients. Helpers become more skilled at this over time and after gaining exposure to a multitude of client issues and experiences.

Empathic immersion is dependent upon three elements. The first element is open-mindedness through the suspension of judgment (see Carkhuff, 2000). Helpers work to understand and accept the reality of their clients even if they do not agree with their clients or their perspectives. It is natural for people to make judgments. We all have values, beliefs, and perspectives. We have opinions related to the people we meet and the experiences we have. For helpers to understand their clients, they need to put their judgments on hold. This allows them to comprehend the world of their clients unfettered by the baggage of their own perspectives.

The second element of empathic immersion involves a concentrated focus on the client's world. Clients are the primary communicators in the helping process. Their lives, experiences, and problems are the focus of helping. Helpers have to take themselves out of the picture. They may have ideas, and in some cases answers, but first and foremost they need to understand their clients, demonstrate that understanding, earn trust, and not impose themselves. To understand the client's world, helpers must do more than surf the ocean, rapidly skimming across the surface. They must submerge themselves in the ocean—slowing down, focusing, and dwelling on all of its features. In this way helpers can amplify and magnify the client's experience (like examining a leaf under a microscope, to use an earlier metaphor), more fully understand it, and envision the world of the client. Imagine yourself in a new and unfamiliar place, perhaps under the sea while scuba diving or entering someone else's home for the first time. There is a strong need when in an unfamiliar place to remain focused, alert, and present. There is so much to attend to, so much to feel, see, smell, and hear. Taking all of it in requires concentration. To absorb and process as much information as possible, you must slow your internal dialogue—silence the internal "clatter and chatter"—and pay attention. This is how the unfamiliar becomes familiar. This is how understanding occurs.

The third element of empathic immersion is the intensity of effort required to understand the client's world. It is very hard work to go through one's own filters and constructions of reality. Suspending one's beliefs and judgments and focusing on the details of the client's world requires intense, conscious effort. Think of an actor who has to "stay in character" for the duration of a scene. This is a performance skill that requires constant focus and concentration. Helpers, likewise, must "stay in character" for the entire helping session and maintain their focus on their clients. This can be challenging and draining.

Empathic immersion is not as much a therapeutic skill as it is a mental stance that helpers take to allow themselves to receive and collect information about the client's world. Empathic immersion is reflected in the use of various skills and tools, such as attending, listening, asking questions, and intake interviewing. These skills and tools are the "scuba gear" and equipment that helpers use to explore the ocean, to chart it, and to learn as much as they can.

Processes, Issues, and Goals When Exploring Client Concerns

The process of exploring client concerns begins in the first helping session. The basic point of exploration is to understand the client's world and to identify, define, and understand the client's problems. In the next two chapters, various exploration skills that helpers use are described.

Whatever exploration skills and tools are used, exploring client concerns involves (1) *collecting* information: listening, asking good, relevant questions, making careful observations, and using appropriate tests, among other things; (2) *organizing* information: ordering and arranging large quantities of data gathered from helping sessions; and (3) *analyzing* information: identifying relevant themes in the data, drawing conclusions, and identifying potential goals and treatment strategies.

Collecting, organizing, and analyzing information may seem like a fairly simple, straightforward process—and many times it is—however, it can be challenging for a number of reasons. First, the exploration process often generates large amounts of data. Helpers must sort through all of it, decide what is relevant, and understand what it means. Expertise in this task largely comes with training and experience.

Second, helpers must decide which exploration skills and tools are most appropriate for a particular client and decide when to use them. Some tools, such as intake interviews, are used with virtually all clients. Others, such as tests, are used as needed and probably will not be used with all clients. Helpers need special training before using certain tools, such as tests.

Third, some clients are not very articulate. They present vague concerns and make rambling, confusing, scattered statements. Factors that may account for this include

- lack of knowledge or awareness regarding their problems (e.g., failing to recognize the ways in which their attitudes and behaviors contribute to their problems);
- reluctance to share information due to discomfort, shame, embarrassment, lack of trust, or fear of judgment;
- defensiveness;
- resistance;
- poor communication skills;
- difficulty with the language spoken in the helping session (i.e., the language may not be the client's native language);
- expression of intense emotions—frustration, confusion, anxiety, anger, sadness;
- omission or distortion of information (i.e., excluding or inaccurately describing feelings, facts, details, and experiences); and
- irresponsible behavior (e.g., blaming problems on other people).

Sifting through client defenses, behaviors, statements, and emotions to identify pertinent issues requires patience. In many cases, because of clients' apprehension, fear, or lack of trust, among other factors, the concerns that clients present when first seeking help are not the major problems the clients are experiencing. As trust develops and helpers gather information, clients may begin to reveal some of the deeper, more important issues. In short, it may take some time for helpers to develop a clear, thorough, accurate understanding of the problems with which their clients struggle.

Kottler, Brown, and Collins (2000, p. 187) noted that exploration (which they call assessment) accomplishes several important tasks or goals. It permits helpers to

- familiarize themselves with the world of their clients,
- learn about significant past events or developmental issues in the clients' lives,
- study the family history and current living situation of their clients,
- assess client strengths and weaknesses,
- identify problems,
- formulate diagnostic impressions, and
- develop treatment plans to accomplish mutually agreed-upon goals.

Helpers use a wide variety of skills and tools to gather comprehensive, meaningful, and complete information. Each skill or tool may help to provide another piece of the puzzle—one more piece of information—in understanding the client's life and problems. A personality test, for example, may provide information that was not obtained from an intake interview. Helpers must thoroughly explore the concerns of their clients. Doing so promotes an accurate understanding of client problems.

Summary and Concluding Remarks

In this chapter, we discussed how and why individuals experience the world in profoundly different ways and explained that, many times, people consciously or unconsciously make the mistake of believing that the way they see things is the way other people see them. We described worldview and how it is shaped by reality filters, which influence how people see and experience the world around them. Helpers need to be attuned, through empathic immersion, to their clients' unique perspectives in order to provide assistance. Helpers cannot assist people they do not understand. They collect, organize, and analyze information to understand the world and problems of their clients.

Questions for Thought

1. If people experience the world in profoundly different ways, how are they able to communicate with one another? How do they achieve shared meaning?

2. In this chapter, we discussed "the basic mistake," or potentially problematic assumptions that people may make in their interactions with others. What assumptions do you make when you interact with people? What are some possible explanations for the "false consensus effect"?

3. What reality filters can you identify in addition to the ones listed in this chapter? In what ways might they influence an individual's perspective on the world?

4. Take a moment to think about how the reality filters described in this chapter affect your own perspective on the world—your own worldview. How do your needs, physical characteristics, cultural characteristics, and past experiences, for example, impact your attitudes, behaviors, and values?

5. How might helpers' reality filters affect the process of collecting, organizing, and analyzing information about their clients?

6. We described some challenges that helpers confront when collecting, organizing, and analyzing information (e.g., managing large amounts of data). How might helpers deal with these challenges?

CHAPTER 6

Nonverbal Exploration Skills

CHAPTER OVERVIEW

In the helping process, helpers use various nonverbal skills to gather information, understand client concerns, and build good helping relationships. In this chapter, we focus on several of these skills: attending, listening, silence, and taking notice. As helpers dive into the ocean—the client's world—these skills serve as "scuba gear" and equipment that helpers use to see, experience, and understand this new and fascinating place. A hypothetical dialogue and several exercises are included at the end of this chapter to facilitate understanding of these skills.

What I remember most about the hour and a half I spent with him was the way he gave me all his attention.

—Norman Rockwell (1960, p. 87, cited in Bolton, 1979), speaking of the time he painted President Dwight Eisenhower's portrait.

Attending

At some point in your life, you were in a situation where you believed someone you were talking to was not paying attention to you. Perhaps the person was yawning, looking out the window, sighing, or fidgeting. How did you feel at that moment? Ignored? Offended? Irritated? Behaviors such as yawning and looking away demonstrate disinterest and boredom. They do not encourage the person who is speaking to continue. It is difficult for trust, respect, and comfort to develop in such situations. In the helping process, where trust and respect are the building blocks of good relationships, helpers need to demonstrate that they are interested in their clients and what they say. One primary way helpers demonstrate interest is through the skill of attending (Carkhuff, 2000; Ivey & Authier, 1978).

Attending is the physical and psychological stance that helpers take toward their clients to demonstrate interest and respect and to receive information communicated by their clients. Egan (2002) described attending (which he referred to as "visibly tuning in to clients") in terms of the helper's "presence" and noted that it represents the ways in which helpers can be with clients both physically and psychologically. He described what most people have found to be true: how comforting it can be to have another person there for us, especially during troubling times in our lives, even if very few words are spoken. Such attention demonstrates caring and concern—someone else is focusing on our thoughts, feelings, and needs. This is the essence of attending.

Attending is demonstrated through various behaviors that helpers use to show that they are interested in and focused on their clients. These behaviors include eye contact, facial expressions, body language, maintaining a comfortable physical distance, vocal qualities, and verbal tracking (Ivey & Authier, 1978; Ivey & Ivey, 1999).

Eye Contact

Making visual contact, usually eye to eye, is one of the most obvious and powerful ways that an individual demonstrates concern and interest in another person. It shows involvement and demonstrates that the individual is focused on the other person. For helpers, good eye contact is important in building relationships with clients. It helps clients feel like the center of attention. Good eye contact does not mean staring at clients. A long gaze may make clients uncomfortable. Rarely looking at clients is also problematic because it demonstrates disinterest and inattention. Bolton (1979) noted that "poor eye contact occurs when a listener repeatedly looks away from the speaker, stares at him constantly or blankly, or looks away as soon as the speaker looks at the listener" (p. 36). The helper's use of eye contact will vary from time to time and situation to situation, but helpers who use eye contact effectively typically look at the client's face for several seconds and then avert their gaze to something nearby or to another part of the client's body, such as a gesturing hand, before looking again at the client's face (Bolton, 1979).

There are significant cultural and individual differences regarding appropriate eye contact. For example, in some Native American cultures, sustained eye contact is considered offensive and disrespectful (Brammer & MacDonald, 2003; Sommers-Flanagan & Sommers-Flanagan, 1999). In European and North American cultures, direct eye contact tends to be most frequent when a person is listening but less so when one is talking; however, some African Americans do the opposite—more eye contact when talking, less when listening (Ivey & Ivey, 1999).

Facial Expressions

People express such emotions as anger, fear, happiness, surprise, and sadness through facial expressions. Cormier and Nurius (2003) observed that different areas of the face express different emotions. For example, fear is usually indicated by the eyes. Happiness and surprise may be conveyed through the lower face and the eyes. Anger is usually expressed through the lower face and brows.

Facial expressions communicate numerous messages. Cormier and Nurius (2003) noted that facial expressions "are used to initiate or terminate conversation, provide feedback on the comments of others, underline or support verbal communication, and convey emotions" (pp. 48–49). Research has shown that facial expressions that convey basic emotions (e.g., fear, anger, happiness, sadness) do not vary much from culture to culture and are largely demonstrated through the same expressions; however, cultural norms influence the intensity and frequency of emotional expression (Cormier & Nurius, 2003; Mesquita & Frijda, 1992).

Cormier and Hackney (1999) observed that helpers' facial expressions reinforce clients' verbal behavior and animate the helpers, showing that they are alert and responsive. These authors stated that it is important for helpers' facial expressions to reflect their clients' expressions. Thus, when clients express joy and happiness, helpers often smile. When clients express sadness or discomfort, helpers show concern. The helpers' expressions help clients feel understood and show that the helpers are following what their clients are expressing. Lack of expression by helpers may reflect apathy, boredom, disapproval, or lack of understanding. Such a stoic demeanor tends to stifle client expression.

Body Language

Helpers convey a lot of information with their bodies. Through their posture and gestures, helpers communicate involvement, attention, and interest. Bolton (1979) noted that "communication tends to be fostered when the listener demonstrates a relaxed alertness with the body leaning slightly forward, facing the other squarely, maintaining an 'open' position and situating [him- or herself] at an appropriate distance from the speaker" (p. 34).

Body language that communicates involvement, attention, and interest includes

- sitting with an open, comfortable, relaxed posture;
- sitting with the body facing the client;
- leaning forward slightly;
- nodding the head;
- smiling;

■ gesturing to punctuate statements; and

■ using moderate activity and variation in body movements (e.g., occasionally shifting posture).

Unhelpful body language may include

■ sitting with crossed arms and legs,

■ exhibiting nervous or repetitive behavior,

■ frowning,

■ making excessive or dramatic movements,

■ exhibiting a lack of animation—very little movement or gesturing, and

■ sitting with the body facing away from the client.

There are times, however, when some of these behaviors may be appropriate. Obviously, it would be unhelpful for a helper to sit completely still or frown throughout an entire session, as this body language will almost certainly convey the message that the helper is upset or uninterested in the client. Yet, if a client says something that confuses the helper, a brief frown can be a way for the helper to express that confusion. The client's message can then be clarified. As another example, crossed arms and legs may be unhelpful if such a posture appears tight and unnatural. However, some people look relaxed, comfortable, and "open" even with arms or legs crossed.

Maintaining a Comfortable Physical Distance

A comfortable distance between helpers and clients is necessary for good, productive communication. Too much space may make helpers seem aloof and prevent the development of an empathic connection. Too little space is invasive and can cause clients to feel anxious. Cultural and individual differences exist regarding the appropriate distance between individuals. A distance of 3 to 4 feet is typical and seems to be most comfortable for most European Americans (Brammer & MacDonald, 2003).

Compared to White Americans, however, many other cultural groups, such as African Americans and Latin Americans, tend to prefer less space between individuals when conversing (see D. W. Sue & Sue, 2003). Helpers who do not recognize cultural differences regarding distance may hinder communication in helping relationships. D. W. Sue and Sue (2003) noted that a client who prefers less space may be seen by the helper as expressing inappropriate intimacy. If the helper backs away, the client may interpret this as aloofness. Helpers and clients may benefit from discussing their needs regarding space, and helpers should look for cues (such as where clients choose to sit) indicating their clients' level of comfort with the space between individuals.

Gender, age, and other cultural variables may also affect what is considered a comfortable distance. For example, Cormier and Hackney (1999) discussed gender differences regarding space, noting that female clients may be more comfortable than male clients with a closer distance between themselves and helpers, particularly when the helpers are female. Female clients may feel intruded upon, however, with a closer distance if their helpers are male.

In addition, the amount of space that is appropriate may depend on the emotions that clients are expressing. Angry clients may need more space, whereas those feeling sad may be more comfortable with less space (Cormier & Hackney, 1999).

Vocal Qualities

The *manner* in which statements are made is an important aspect of communication. Pitch, rate of speech, volume, and articulation all relate to manner of presentation and provide cues for understanding expressions and verbal statements. For helpers, a soft tone of voice and a moderate rate of speech will generally help to create a warm, relaxed, supportive environment that facilitates client expression. A loud tone of voice may appear domineering, aggressive, and threatening, especially to clients from cultures in which people tend to speak more softly, such as Asian cultures (D. W. Sue & Sue, 2003). A rapid rate of speech can create a sense of urgency or anxiety, as can stuttering or fumbling over words. Helpers sometimes vary their rate of speech and volume depending on the topic being discussed and the client's speech patterns. For example, a volume level similar to the client's can show that the helper is following the client.

Verbal Tracking

Although we discuss attending under nonverbal skills, attending does have a verbal component (Ivey & Ivey, 1999). Helpers use various verbal statements and responses to show that they understand and are following what their clients are saying. Verbal encouragers such as "mm-hmm" and "I see" may accomplish this goal. Helpers may also paraphrase client statements or use words to reflect what clients appear to be feeling at the moment. These statements and responses assure clients that their helpers are listening to and following their statements. They also encourage clients to continue speaking about issues that are important to them (Brammer & MacDonald, 2003). Obviously, verbal responses themselves are not nonverbal skills. The important point here is that these verbal responses show that helpers are following and understanding client statements. In this sense, they reflect attending. Verbal responses are discussed in detail in chapter 7.

Ivey and Ivey (1999) noted that "selective attention" is a type of verbal tracking. Helpers cannot address every aspect of their clients' communications, so they must select the topics or statements to which they will respond. Effective helpers do not change the subject or add new meaning but rather select and respond to aspects of their clients' communications that seem important. Although clients largely determine the topics for discussion, helpers use selective attention as a way to focus and direct the discussion.

Final Comments About Attending

Attending is a powerful skill that shows clients that what they have to say is important and that they are the focus of the helping process. Such attention helps clients feel comfortable and encourages them to express themselves. It also facilitates the development of good, trusting helping relationships. Helpers who demonstrate appropriate attending behaviors tend to be seen by their clients as more skilled and attractive than those who do not.

Attending is the basis for other skills that helpers use. It is also one of the most continuously applied skills. Helpers use it throughout the helping process. In effect, helpers are like the driver of a car, maintaining concentration and vigilance at all times. Because clients want acceptance and often share problems that are difficult for them to discuss, they pay close attention to their helpers. Just as drivers who take their eyes off the road may scare their passengers and cause accidents, helpers who let up on their attending skills—looking out the window, yawning, slouching—may cause their clients to feel anxious and may jeopardize the development of trusting helping relationships.

At certain times, helpers may deliberately decide not to attend (Ivey & Ivey, 1999). For example, when clients ramble, helpers may interrupt or avert their eyes. In this way, helpers can communicate messages about ineffective client behavior. Many clients pick up on their helper's inattention.

Listening

The skills of attending and listening are often merged and discussed as one skill (e.g., "listening attentively"), but the skills are distinct. Attending involves physically and psychologically focusing on clients; listening involves understanding client statements and expressions. Attending prepares helpers to listen carefully to their clients.

Like attending, listening is a basic skill. It underlies the helping process and is critical to success in helping. It is *the* primary data-gathering method. Good helping is not possible without it. Careful, intensive listening requires effort, immersion, and concentration as helpers strive to comprehend the meaning contained in client statements and expressions. Listening, therefore, involves more than merely remaining silent or hearing clients speak.

Purposes of Listening

Listening serves several important purposes, as described in the following paragraphs.

Listening Permits Helpers to Understand the World and Problems of Their Clients. When helpers are listening, they are not talking. By listening, helpers gather the information they need to help clients address their problems.

Listening Conveys Respect and Facilitates the Development of Trust. Listening shows clients that they are the center of attention and that what they say and express is important. We know a client who said that one of his most poignant positive memories of counseling was that on the few occasions when he interrupted his helper to say something, the helper immediately stopped speaking to listen—no lectures about the rudeness of interrupting, no irritation expressed by the helper, no annoyed looks, no power struggling to see who would get to keep talking. For the client, this was a powerful gesture that he was not used to in everyday life. It made him feel important and showed him that he was the focus of helping.

Listening Gives Clients the Chance to Speak, Express Themselves, and Introduce All of the Aspects of Their Concerns. Through talking, clients have an opportunity to hear themselves—to sound out their problems. Talking about a problem can change it. Rather than the client experiencing the problem internally (e.g., through self-talk or brooding), the problem is now out in the open, in a different medium. Discussing the problem in the helping session and receiving feedback from the helper can encourage the client to begin to see the problem from a different perspective and perhaps identify more effective coping strategies. In addition, for many clients, talking about and sharing problems can be cathartic. The release of pent-up emotions and troubles can help clients feel better. Sharing problems and having helpers listen also helps clients feel that they are no longer alone in their understanding. They have an ally who will be there for them. It is indeed true that listening is a "gift," as one of our students put it.

Listening for Understanding: What Helpers Focus On

Effective listening involves more than concentrating on clients' verbal statements. Verbal statements are only one aspect of expression and may be insufficient for helpers to gain an accurate and complete understanding of clients and their problems. To listen accurately, helpers need to focus on clients' nonverbal behaviors as well. For example, helpers watch for such behaviors as crossed arms, furled eyebrows, and hand-wringing, which often "punctuate" verbal statements and permit helpers to read them more accurately (Egan, 2002). Helpers should also note discrepancies between verbal and nonverbal behaviors. A client who says, "I'm comfortable talking with you," while nervously tapping his foot and crossing his arms and legs sends a very different message than one who makes the same statement while smiling and sitting with an open, relaxed posture.

Egan (2002) pointed out that helpers must also consider contextual variables, such as client culture and personality, when listening to clients. Culture may influence, for example, the extent to which clients express feelings. A helper who does not take culture into account may mistake low emotional expression for depression when, in fact, low expression may be normal for the client's culture. Consideration of individual characteristics, such as personality factors, is also important. People express themselves differently, even in similar situations. At weddings, some people cry; others express joy. One person who has just achieved a major goal or won a contest may be moved to tears, whereas another may smile and shout in celebration. As helpers get to know their clients, they learn how their clients express themselves, verbally and nonverbally, and how contextual factors affect client expression. That is, helpers learn how to listen accurately.

Challenges in Listening

Listening seems like such a basic, easy skill—something that everyone does every day; however, truly understanding what clients are expressing can be challenging and requires intense effort and practice. The following paragraphs describe some reasons why the skill of listening can be challenging.

Clients Do Not Always Express Themselves Clearly. Due to such factors as mistrust of helpers, poor communication skills, expression of intense emotions, and language proficiency issues, client statements and expressions are not always concise and readily understandable. They may be confusing, disorganized, and convoluted. Clients may also omit important details (Egan, 2002). The challenge for helpers is to sort through, organize, and understand the content presented by clients. Helpers must derive meaning from what clients are expressing—and not expressing.

Reality Filters Affect Perceptions. Recall the discussion in chapter 5 about how reality filters influence what people "select," or pay attention to, in their environment. People, including helpers, listen in the context of their experiences, culture, and characteristics. Hutchins and Cole Vaught (1997) observed: "As helpers we respond to people in terms of our personal history, especially if we have little or no knowledge of them. Thus, we enter into each interpersonal relationship with a predisposition to see, hear, and react to people and events in certain ways" (p. 69).

Hutchins and Cole Vaught (1997) also noted that "we tend to look for what we 'see' and hear" (p. 69), which can lead to inaccurate listening and faulty understanding. This phenomenon is known as "confirmatory bias." In the context of helping, it refers to helpers seeking out, selecting, and remembering information that confirms their hypotheses, assumptions, and beliefs about their clients' lives and problems, even in the presence of disconfirming information—information that is *inconsistent* with their hypotheses, assumptions, and beliefs (M. Snyder, 1981; M. Snyder & Campbell, 1980; Strohmer & Shivy, 1994; Strohmer, Shivy, & Chiodo, 1990). Consider an example: Many cultures tend to stress family relationships and connections (collectivism) more than Western culture does; Western culture tends to place more emphasis on individuating from the family (individualism). A Western-trained helper who does not realize this difference while assisting a culturally different client may see the client's focus on her family as a sign of unhealthy dependence. As the client speaks, the helper may *listen* for clues that support this belief and then later share the belief with the client. The helper may even smile or nod when the client says something that supports the helper's belief, thereby subtly encouraging the client to accept the belief as accurate.

Helpers cannot remember everything their clients say, but they need to listen as carefully and objectively as possible, identifying and responding to the important details and issues in their clients' expressions. To minimize confirmatory bias, helpers may find it beneficial to continuously examine their clinical thought and assessment processes and practice seeking out disconfirming information in order to come to a more complex understanding of client lives and problems (Strohmer & Shivy, 1994).

Human Beings Can Mentally Process Meaning Faster Than They Can Speak. This point was made by R. B. Adler, Rosenfeld, and Towne (1980) and Bolton (1979). Because of this faster mental processing, it is easy to anticipate what another person is going to say, stop listening, and let one's mind wander while the other person is still talking. If helpers stop listening while their clients are expressing themselves, they risk appearing uninterested and missing important issues.

It Is Easy to Dwell on Things That Clients Say or Express. Sometimes, something in clients' statements or expressions may prompt helpers to dwell on those statements or expressions. Perhaps the client raised what the helper views as a very important issue or said something that reminds the helper of his or her own problems. In such cases, helpers may dwell on the statement or expression and, in doing so, stop listening and miss other important ideas or issues. In a sense, listening is like viewing a movie at a theater. You must constantly keep pace with the action in front of you. You cannot stop the movie and go back to review something you missed. Of course, in the helping process, helpers can interrupt their clients and seek clarification, but if they do this too often, they disrupt the flow of client expressions and convey the impression that they are not listening. The point is that listening requires continuous effort and concentration.

Effective Listening Is an Intense Skill That Many People Have Never Learned. The intensity and effort required to suspend one's own perspectives and focus on and understand what other people are saying make effective listening a challenging skill. This point is reflected in R. B. Adler et al.'s (1980) assertion that one of the myths of listening is that it is a natural process. People engage in listening all the time, but they often do it poorly. Indeed, mediocre listening is easy; effective listening is hard. Many people have never learned how to listen effectively. There are times when helpers may deliberately not listen, such as when interrupting clients who are rambling, but, in general, helpers need to avoid ineffective, or mediocre, listening. R. B. Adler et al. (1980) identified several "poor listening habits," including

- pseudolistening—giving the appearance of listening (e.g., through eye contact, nodding) while actually focusing on other things;
- stage-hogging—allowing people to speak only long enough for the stage-hogger to catch his or her breath;
- insulated listening—avoiding uncomfortable topics;
- defensive listening—taking innocent comments, questions, or expressions as attacks (e.g., a parent who interprets her child's question as a challenge to her authority); and
- ambushing—listening only to gather information to use against someone.

Egan (2002, pp. 75–76, 90–91) also described forms of "inadequate" and "distorted" listening, including

- partial listening—picking up on only parts of the speaker's message, and not necessarily the essential points;
- rehearsing—mentally preparing and practicing a response while the speaker is speaking;
- evaluative listening—judging what the speaker is saying as good or bad, right or wrong, acceptable or unacceptable;
- fact-centered listening—focusing primarily or solely on the facts of the speaker's situation while ignoring the person; and
- sympathetic listening—commiserating or becoming an "accomplice," thus losing objectivity and possibly failing to help the speaker/client take action to address ineffective attitudes and behaviors.

It is easy to engage in these types of ineffective listening, and most people have probably done so at some point. Among the numerous reasons why people may not listen effectively are preoccupation with other issues, boredom, too much to listen to (message overload), noise and other distractions, hearing problems, the greater appeal of talking, and lack of training (R. B. Adler et al., 1980). Helpers need to be conscious of when and why they might not be listening effectively and strive to minimize ineffective listening.

Effective Listening (and Attending) Must Often Be Balanced With Note-Taking. Note-taking is important for documentation, remembering numerous details, and planning treatment strategies, but helpers need to be careful not to focus or rely too much on note-taking. Clients want to see that their helpers are focusing on them, not just recording the content of their statements. As helpers improve their listening skills, they become better able to commit client statements and expressions to memory. This allows helpers to focus more on their clients than on their notepads. Further, clients tend to be impressed and feel important when helpers demonstrate how much they remember about them without the prompting of written notes. Not all helpers take written notes during sessions. In many cases, helpers record important information after the session is over.

Active Listening: How Helpers Demonstrate Understanding

As has been discussed, it is important for helpers to listen to client statements and expressions so that they can understand their clients' problems. Rogers (1951) noted that it is also important for helpers to *demonstrate* their understanding to their clients. Doing so builds rapport and shows that helpers are paying attention and accurately following along. Feeling understood can be powerful, especially for people who have had trouble getting others to pay attention, much less understand.

Helpers demonstrate their understanding through the use of various verbal skills, such as verbal encouragers, paraphrases of client statements, and reflections of client feelings. Using such skills to show that one is listening is often referred to as "active listening." Several of these verbal skills are described in detail in the next chapter.

A Final Comment on Listening

Good listening is an important skill—and perhaps a lost art. Americans, in general, tend to value talking and expressing themselves more than listening. For example, we have free *speech*, assertiveness training, and communication classes. In school, students learn about speaking, reading, and writing but usually not about listening (R. B. Adler et al., 1980). Yet, being listened to and understood is so important to everyone and is critical to healthy relationships. In the helping process, listening is a fundamental skill. Helpers learn to be good listeners through training, practice, and experience.

Silence

Many helpers, particularly novices, struggle with the skill of silence. It seems so simple not to say anything, but perhaps because silence often feels awkward in social situations, not saying anything can be quite uncomfortable. Silence can make inexperienced helpers feel that they are not helping and can compel them to speak to fill the void. Fear of silence can prompt them to rehearse what they plan to say next rather than to focus on client expressions (Hutchins & Cole Vaught, 1997). Of course, silence may occur because helpers or clients feel uncomfortable or do not know what to say, but here we focus on silence as a skill intentionally used by helpers to facilitate the helping process.

Purposes of Silence

The following paragraphs describe several reasons why helper silence is important.

Helper Silence Gives Clients the Chance to Fully Present Their Concerns. In light of the inclination of many people to speak constantly, interrupt, and not listen, a helper's silence can be a profound and refreshing change for clients. It can show clients that their statements and expressions are important, thereby conveying respect and allowing clients to feel heard.

Helper Silence Gives Clients Time to Process and Experience What Transpires in the Helping Session. During the helping process, clients may discuss troubling concerns, express powerful emotions, and develop new understandings related to their problems. Helper silence, which may last for a few seconds or a couple of minutes, allows clients to "percolate"—to consider what they have said, experience feelings, and reflect on new information and understandings. Hutchins and Cole Vaught (1997) explained the importance of silence in critical moments, such as when clients gain insight, as follows: "Let clients think about the situation without interruption. At such times, you can virtually see the 'wheels turning' in their brains. Let it happen! More important things are probably occurring during this silence than any words could express, so use the silence and allow this unique process to be completed" (p. 105).

Helper Silence Allows Clients to Collect Their Thoughts. While expressing themselves, clients may pause for a few seconds as they consider what to say next. This silence is not a cue for helpers to begin speaking. If helpers do begin to speak, important client expression may be interrupted.

Helper Silence Shows That Helping Is a Dialogue. Both helpers and clients contribute to the helping process. Helpers do not do all of the talking. If helpers talk too much, clients may rely on them to initiate and carry the conversation. Silence allows clients to take the lead and express themselves freely.

Helper Silence Can Moderate the Pace of Helping (Cormier & Hackney, 1999). When there has been a lot of talking or strong expression, both helpers and clients sometimes need a moment to pause and regroup.

Helper Silence Allows Helpers to Use Other Important Skills, Such as Attending and Listening. When remaining silent, helpers can more intensely focus on their clients. They can, for example, show interest, observe their clients' body language, listen to the clients' verbal statements, and develop ideas about the clients' problems.

Points to Consider When Using Silence

The following paragraphs describe some points for helpers to keep in mind concerning the use of silence.

Be Aware of Cultural Differences Related to Silence. D. W. Sue and Sue (2003) noted that the use of silence varies from culture to culture. For example, according to these authors, in Japanese and Chinese cultures, silence by a speaker may indicate a desire to continue speaking after making a point. It often signals respect rather than a desire not to speak further. European Americans tend to be less comfortable with silence and talk to fill the gaps in conversation. Observing and understanding how clients use silence can give helpers clues about when to speak and when to be silent.

Use Silence in Moderation—Not Too Much or Too Little. Not allowing for silence is a form of interrupting. When helpers talk too much, too quickly interject statements, or ask too many questions, clients' expressions and internal processing may be disrupted. As a result, open communication, growth, and awareness tend to be stifled. Too much talking by helpers and not enough silence can also make it seem as if helpers, not clients, are the focus of the helping process. Too much silence can be a problem because it conveys disinterest and can cause helpers to appear disengaged from the helping process. When helpers use too much silence, clients may feel unsupported or alone, especially at times when they need feedback and guidance from their helpers (e.g., when they need assistance in managing anxiety).

Taking Notice

As helpers work with their clients, they mentally note various client behaviors, statements, expressions, and characteristics. Combined with other skills, the skill of taking notice aids helpers in exploring client concerns. This skill is similar to what many would describe as "observing" (see, e.g., Carkhuff, 2000). However, taking notice involves more than helpers noting what they "see" as they look at their clients. It also describes what helpers mentally perceive, discern, and detect as they interact and converse with their clients. For example, a helper may "take note" of a particular word or phrase that a client uses frequently and consider that in his or her assessment of the client.

What Helpers Notice

The following are many of the client behaviors, statements, expressions, and characteristics that helpers mentally note:

- Level of distress (e.g., level of anger, agitation, or anxiety)
- Level of affect or animation
- Amount of eye contact
- Facial expressions

- Body language
- Social skills
- Physical appearance, description, and condition/health
- Physiological behaviors (e.g., sweating)
- Vocal/speech patterns (e.g., volume and rate of speech)
- Articulation; clarity of expression
- Words and phrases used and how frequently they are used
- The way words and phrases are emphasized or accented
- Manner of speaking (e.g., past or present tense)
- Use of metaphors, idioms, and analogies
- Manner of responding to helper statements and questions
- Apparent inconsistencies in aspects of the client's presentation
- Level of self-awareness
- Cultural characteristics (e.g., race, gender, age, social class)

Noting these behaviors, statements, expressions, and characteristics permits helpers to more accurately understand their clients and client problems. Helpers use the information they notice to (1) identify patterns and themes; (2) give context to client statements and expressions; (3) develop hypotheses about the nature of client problems; (4) make diagnostic and treatment decisions; (5) select appropriate helping skills, interventions, and strategies; and (6) ascertain client progress in helping. Through written notes, audiotape, or videotape, helpers may record what they notice.

For the most part, taking notice involves focusing on four major aspects of clients: physical aspects, nonverbal behavior, verbal behavior, and culture.

Physical Aspects. Physical aspects include physical appearance, description, and condition/health. Helpers note, for example, whether clients have any diseases, illnesses, or disabilities that could factor into their problems. Helpers also notice grooming. Does the client look disheveled, or does the client appear neat with clean clothes and combed hair? Observations about grooming can indicate to helpers how well clients take care of themselves.

Nonverbal Behavior. A significant aspect of communication is nonverbal behavior, such as facial expressions and body language (see Mehrabian, 1972; Scherer & Ekman, 1982). When two people interact face-to-face, each sends numerous nonverbal messages. Even when no words are spoken, communication still occurs. Helpers, therefore, must be aware not only of their own nonverbal behaviors and what they communicate but also of their clients' nonverbal behaviors and the messages that these behaviors send.

Observing clients' nonverbal behavior provides context for understanding their verbal statements and enables helpers to see and understand what the clients might not verbalize. Clients' nonverbal behavior also provides clues about the emotions the clients are experiencing. Clients may cross their arms when feeling angry or defensive. Their breathing may become more rapid and pronounced when they feel anxious. Their eye contact with helpers may be sporadic when discussing particularly difficult issues. Indeed, much is communicated through nonverbal behavior.

Nonverbal behavior "leaks" messages that clients may not intend to send; thus, it helps to show what clients really mean when they speak (Egan, 2002; Passons, 1975). Although verbal statements can be edited and controlled fairly easily, non-verbal behavior is more spontaneous and difficult to control (Passons, 1975). For this reason, when there is an apparent contradiction between verbal and nonverbal behaviors (e.g., a person saying, "I'm not nervous," while repeatedly tapping her fingers and fidgeting in her chair), people tend to believe the nonverbal behavior.

Effective helpers pay attention to apparent contradictions in client words and nonverbal behaviors. When contradictions seem to exist, both the words and the nonverbal behaviors are important, as together they convey an important message (Bolton, 1979). For example, Bolton (1979) observed that when a person laughs while talking of a personal tragedy, this behavior may indicate that the person desires to share the experience but does not want to burden the listener with the issue or that she is ambivalent about discovering and sharing the depth of her feelings on the matter. In short, helpers consider client nonverbal behavior in conjunction with verbal statements to help them understand the messages their clients send.

Verbal Behavior. The statements that clients make indicate the topics that are important to them, how they communicate, and how they see the world. By focusing on verbal behavior, helpers may note, among other things, metaphors, words, and phrases that clients use.

Ivey and Ivey (1999) noted that people have individual ways of receiving information from the world and that the way in which people perceive events, experiences, and other people is reflected in their language. Some people describe things primarily in terms of what they see; others in terms of what they hear or feel. Paying attention to how clients describe things allows helpers to understand how clients conceptualize their world. Ivey and Ivey (1999) stated that when helpers respond by "matching" the language of their clients, the development of rapport and understanding is facilitated. Thus, if a client speaks in visual terms (e.g., "As I *see* it . . ."), the helper may find it beneficial to use visual terms, such as "see" and "view," to paraphrase the client's statements, reflect the client's feelings, and ask questions.

Culture. When taking note of client behaviors, statements, expressions, and characteristics, helpers need to consider the cultural characteristics of their clients. Verbal and nonverbal behaviors vary from culture to culture. For example, little eye contact by a client can be a sign of embarrassment, self-consciousness, or disinterest; however, in many Native American and Asian cultures, it is a sign of respect. Culture provides context for understanding clients' verbal and nonverbal behaviors. Failure to take culture into account can cause helpers to draw inaccurate conclusions about their clients.

Accurately Taking Notice

Accurately taking notice can be a challenging task. For example, for one client, silence may signal respect and deference to the helper, whereas the same behavior in another client may signal boredom, disinterest, or a passive expression of anger. Another complicating factor is that behavior in a client may have different meanings depending on the situation. Shifting in a chair may signal discomfort with the topic of discussion, or it may mean that the client has become tired of sitting in one position. Tears may signal happiness or sadness. A smile may reflect happiness or embarrassment. Further, helpers need to be careful not to draw hasty conclusions or give undue weight to any single, particular behavior, such as one puzzled look or one angry statement. To accurately take notice of client behaviors, statements, expressions, and characteristics, helpers need to consider the topics being discussed, how much they currently know about their clients, and the clients' personality traits, cultural characteristics, and overall behavioral patterns.

Sharing What Has Been Noticed

Sometimes, helpers share with their clients what they have noticed. They may do so through immediacy, a skill discussed in chapter 9, or through reflection of feelings, a skill discussed in chapter 7. With the latter, helpers share their observations about the apparent emotional state of their clients. Helpers may also share what they have noticed by pointing out patterns they have observed in client body movements. A helper might say, for example, "I notice that when you talk about your boss, you begin fidgeting in your chair. Did you know that?" When helpers share what they have noticed, clients are encouraged to elaborate on their behaviors, statements, and expressions and to develop a deeper understanding of what they mean.

A Hypothetical Dialogue

The following is a brief hypothetical dialogue between a helper and a client. The client is a female college student discussing academic and social concerns. As with any dialogue that would occur during a helping session, this dialogue contains both verbal and nonverbal components. Although you cannot "see" the helper's nonverbal skills in this printed dialogue, try to visualize the helping session and focus on the helper's use of nonverbal skills, as indicated by the written prompts.

Client (low emotional expression; flat manner of speaking): I said last time that I was thinking about dropping out of school. I'm just getting so tired of it.

Helper (makes eye contact with the client; look of concern on helper's face; open posture focused on the client; soft tone of voice): Yes, I remember. What don't you like about it?

[The helper uses attending skills—eye contact, appropriate facial expression, good posture, and a soft tone of voice—to demonstrate that she is focused on the client. The helper has taken notice of the client's somber mood by observing the client's low affect. The helper matches this mood with a look of concern.]

Client: I just don't feel like I belong there. The people in my classes have their own little cliques. They talk about things that don't interest me that much; most of them like doing things that I don't—like going to bars. And my major, biology, is okay, but kind of boring. It's not something I feel passionately about. All the other biology majors I know get so excited about it, and I just can't relate to that.

Helper (following what the client is saying): It sounds like you believe you don't fit in very well.

[This verbal response is a paraphrase of the client's statement. Paraphrasing is discussed in more detail in chapter 7. The helper's response here is a form of attending in the sense that the helper is showing that she is verbally tracking the client. The response also reflects active listening—understanding the client's statements and then demonstrating that understanding to the client with a verbal response.]

Client: Right, and I've thought about changing my major so I could find something interesting and meet some new people who I *can* relate to (helper nods head, says "mm-hmm"), but I've already done that twice, and it hasn't helped. (Client's face contorts a bit.) It just seems like nothing will make things better.

[The helper demonstrates attending with a nod of the head. The helper also shows that she is verbally tracking the client (a form of attending) by using a verbal encourager ("mm-hmm"). These behaviors encourage the client to continue speaking, and they show the client that the helper is paying attention.]

Helper (observing what the client appears to be feeling): You seem pretty frustrated that nothing you've tried has worked.

[The helper takes notice of the client's apparent emotional state (frustration) based on cues in the client's previous statement and the client's nonverbal behavior (face contorting). The helper reflects the emotion back to the client. The verbal response here is called reflecting feelings and is discussed in chapter 7. With this response, the helper demonstrates that she is actively listening and following what the client is expressing.]

Client (looks somber): Yeah.

Helper (observes the client's somber look; does not say anything, but focuses on the client)

Client (looks at the floor): Actually, I feel like I'm beyond frustration—more like hopeless. Not many things interest me that much anymore. I've had trouble making friends and finding interesting things to do for a few years now. I don't go out much, and things just keep getting worse. I don't connect with people like I used to back in high school.

[The helper's silence gave the client a moment to ponder and clarify her feelings without interruption. As the client considers what the helper said previously ("You seem pretty frustrated . . ."), she realizes that she feels more than frustrated; she feels hopeless. If the helper had too quickly interjected a statement, this moment of clarity for the client may have been cut off. In that case, both the helper and the client would have missed out on an important understanding of what the client is feeling.]

Helper: So, before, you were sociable and active, and now you're much more isolated.

[This is another paraphrase. It also demonstrates verbal tracking and active listening.]

Client (looks down toward the floor): Yeah. It's like something happened that's turned me off and put a dark cloud over my head. I keep to myself a lot now.

Helper (observes what the client appears to be feeling; soft tone of voice): You feel pretty lonely.

[The helper reflects feelings. The helper takes notice of the client's emotional state based on her previous verbal statement and nonverbal behavior (looking down). The helper's tone of voice matches the client's affect.]

Client: Yeah, things aren't going too well right now.

This dialogue shows how a helper might explore concerns and build rapport with a client by using a combination of nonverbal and verbal skills. Note how the helper used various nonverbal skills to focus her energy and effort on the client, immersing herself in the client's world, striving to understand it. This intense focus not only aids the helper in exploring client concerns, it also demonstrates that the helper cares about the client and will be an ally in addressing the client's concerns.

Summary and Concluding Remarks

In this chapter, four nonverbal skills that helpers use to explore client concerns were discussed: attending, listening, silence, and taking notice. These skills allow helpers to gather information, understand client concerns, and build good helping relationships with their clients. One important theme throughout this chapter was the importance of cultural awareness in exploring client concerns. To effectively use the skills discussed, helpers need to adapt each one as appropriate—for example, adapting attending by reducing or increasing the physical distance between themselves and clients based on client cues. Helpers also need to appreciate how culture may affect clients' verbal and nonverbal behaviors.

Nonverbal skills are, of course, not sufficient for a complete exploration of client concerns. Helpers also use various verbal skills, such as asking questions, paraphrasing, and reflecting feelings. These skills complement nonverbal skills and enable helpers to more thoroughly explore and understand the lives and problems of their clients. Verbal skills are addressed in the next chapter.

Questions for Thought

1. If you were a client, what helper attending behaviors would make you feel most comfortable with the helper? What helper behaviors would you find distracting or discouraging?

2. How well do you listen to other people? How intensively do you listen? To what extent do you consider nonverbal behavior and culture when listening to others?

3. How do you deal with silence in your conversations with people? What statements or behaviors do you make or engage in to break up silence? If silence is uncomfortable for you, what can you do to increase your comfort level?

4. In your interactions with other people, which of their behaviors and characteristics do you tend to notice and focus on the most? How do your experiences and characteristics (your "reality filters") influence what you notice?

Exercises

The following exercises cover the skills discussed in this chapter. Many of these exercises require more than one person and thus may be useful as classroom exercises. If you do not have exercise partners available, we encourage you to read through the exercises that require more than one person and visualize how you might perform if you were doing the exercises with other people.

ATTENDING EXERCISES

EXERCISE 1: This exercise requires two people: a speaker and a listener. It has two parts.

Part A: The speaker should choose a topic, such as career interests, a favorite hobby, or activities during a recent vacation, and begin talking about the topic. The listener's role is to give the speaker very little attention—for example, little or no eye contact or lack of facial expression. The participants should stop the exercise after a few minutes and discuss what happened, with each person sharing his or her observations and feelings. For example, how did the speaker feel about the listener's lack of attention?

Part B: Now, the speaker again selects a topic and begins talking, but this time the listener should attend carefully to what the speaker is saying, using the attending behaviors described in this chapter. After a few minutes, the participants should stop the exercise and discuss it. If you were the listener, what did you change when you did the second part of the exercise and attended carefully? What behaviors did you engage in when you attended carefully? If you were the speaker, how was the second part of the exercise different from the first? How did the listener's behaviors in each part affect your presentation? If you wish, switch roles and repeat the exercise.

EXERCISE 2: This exercise requires three people: a helper, a client, and an observer. The client selects a topic to discuss, such as a relationship problem or difficulty finding a job. The helper and the client address this topic in a role play for about 5 minutes, with the helper using good attending behaviors, as described in this chapter. The observer's role is to watch the role play and note the attending behaviors displayed. The observer may find it useful to keep written notes. Following this exercise is a template that the observer can use as a guide. When the role play is completed, each person should share his or her comments about it. If you were the client, what impact did the helper's attending behaviors have on you? What did the helper do well? Not so well? If you were the helper, which attending behaviors do you believe you demonstrated well? With which ones did you struggle? The observer should also share his or her observations on what attending behaviors were demonstrated, how well they were demonstrated, and what effect they appeared to have on the client. The observer should balance positive and corrective feedback. The exercise should be repeated often enough for each individual to play each role.

OBSERVER TEMPLATE FOR ATTENDING EXERCISE 2

Behavior	**Comments (e.g., note to what extent and how well the behavior was demonstrated)**
Eye Contact	_____
	_____
	_____
Facial Expressions	_____
	_____
	_____
Body Language	_____
	_____
	_____
Comfortable Physical Distance	_____
	_____
	_____
Vocal Qualities	_____
	_____
	_____
Verbal Tracking	_____
	_____
	_____

LISTENING EXERCISES

EXERCISE 1: This exercise requires two people: a speaker and a listener. The speaker selects a topic, such as a favorite activity or the most unusual experience he or she has had. The speaker should spend up to a minute talking about this topic while the listener listens. When the speaker is finished, the listener should say back to the speaker the major points, topics, or themes contained in the speaker's statements. The speaker should then indicate whether the listener correctly identified and understood what was important in the speaker's statements. Did the listener understand what the speaker said? What nonverbal behaviors (if any) by the speaker helped to promote understanding? Following this discussion, the participants should switch roles and repeat the exercise.

EXERCISE 2: Over the next few days, pay attention to how well you listen as you go about your daily activities and interact with people. What do you notice about the way you listen to other people? When conversing with someone, how well do you truly understand what the person is communicating to you? Do you engage in any of the types of ineffective listening described in this chapter? If so, which ones? What prompts you to listen carefully to people? What prompts you to tune people out? Make a deliberate effort to listen more and speak less. What do you notice when you do so?

SILENCE EXERCISES

EXERCISE 1: This exercise requires two people: a speaker and a listener. The speaker and listener should sit facing each other and discuss a topic of the speaker's choice (e.g., career goals, a relationship concern). The listener should focus on using the skill of silence. Before verbally responding to anything the speaker says, the listener should consider whether silence would be more appropriate than making a statement or asking a question. In other words, the listener should not too quickly begin speaking. Also, he or she should pay attention to cues the speaker gives that signal whether the speaker has finished speaking. At times, the listener may deliberately choose not to say anything after the speaker finishes speaking in order to see whether the speaker will continue. After about 5 minutes, the participants should stop the exercise and discuss how the silence affected their interaction. If you were the listener, did the silence allow you to better understand what the speaker expressed? What did you notice during silences? How well were you able to pick up on cues from the speaker that the speaker was done and that it was your turn to say something? As you were listening, what cues told you that the speaker was not finished speaking? If you were the speaker, what impact did the silence have on you? Following this discussion, the participants should switch roles and repeat the exercise.

EXERCISE 2: Pay attention to silence as you go about your daily activities. How well do people use silence as they converse with others, including yourself? How well do you use silence in conversation? What impact does the silence or lack of silence have on the conversation? What cues tell you when silence is appropriate?

TAKING NOTICE EXERCISES

EXERCISE 1: To help you appreciate the importance of nonverbal behavior, watch a televised or videotaped interview or interaction between two people, such as that of a counseling session. Turn the volume all the way down so that you cannot hear the people speaking. After several minutes, describe the interview or interaction. What was the mood of the discussion—happy, sad, angry, serious? What emotions were present? What nonverbal behaviors did you see that support your conclusions? Could you tell what the individuals were talking about?

EXERCISE 2: This exercise requires three people: a helper, a client, and an observer. The client should select a topic for the helper and the client to role-play for about 5 minutes. For example, the client could be a student who wants to discuss academic difficulties or a person who wants to address a relationship problem. While engaging in dialogue with the client, the helper should note the client's behaviors, statements, expressions, and characteristics. (The list at the beginning of the section on taking notice identifies several behaviors, statements, etc., to look for.) For example, what patterns or themes are present in the client's statements? What emotions are present? What body language does the client engage in? Does the body language seem congruent with the client's words? How do cultural characteristics factor in? The observer should also note the client's behaviors, statements, expressions, and characteristics. The observer may wish to write his or her observations on paper. After the role play, the three participants should discuss the observations made. For example, if you were the helper, what did your observations (e.g., of client nonverbal behavior) tell you about the client and his or her concerns? How did your observations help you understand the client's concerns? If you were the observer, is there anything about the client's verbal or nonverbal behavior that the helper seems to have missed? The exercise should be repeated often enough for each person to play each role.

CHAPTER 7

Verbal Exploration Skills

CHAPTER OVERVIEW

In addition to the nonverbal skills discussed in chapter 6, helpers use various verbal skills to explore client concerns. These verbal skills, which are described in this chapter, include invitations, verbal encouragers, asking questions, paraphrasing, reflecting feelings, focusing, and summarizing. As with nonverbal skills, verbal exploration skills aid helpers in gathering information, understanding client problems, and building helping relationships. A hypothetical dialogue and several exercises are included at the end of this chapter to facilitate understanding of these skills.

I got down to business and asked my standard opening question: "What ails?"

—Irvin Yalom (1989, p. 89)

Invitations

Invitations are brief statements or questions designed to encourage clients to begin speaking, to continue speaking, or to elaborate. They are sometimes referred to as openers or leads. Here are some examples:

"What would you like to discuss today?"
"Maybe you'd like to say what's on your mind."
"Would you like to tell me what's going on?"
"What would you like to do?"
"How are things going?"
"Please start wherever you wish."
"Please continue."
"What else do you want to talk about today?"
"Can you tell me more about that?"

When helpers use invitations, they show that they are interested, focused, and ready to listen to what their clients have to say. Invitations are often used at the beginning of the helping session (e.g., "What would you like to discuss today?"), but they may be used whenever clients seem to need encouragement to speak (Bolton, 1979). For example, if a client seems agitated or irritated, the helper might say, "You seem irritated. What's going on right now?" The helper's comment invites the client to address the feeling.

Invitations are usually nondirective and do not pressure clients. They allow clients to decide what to talk about and to determine the direction of the conversation. They also encourage clients to actively participate in the helping process. Helpers are not going to do all of the talking. Indeed, it is important for helpers to use attending and silence while waiting for responses to their invitations (Bolton, 1979). These skills communicate that helpers are focused on clients and are ready to receive information. In fact, sometimes, attending and silence serve as "nonverbal invitations."

Because many clients feel apprehension, reluctance, or fear about sharing their concerns, invitations do not always immediately open the lines of communication. A helper might ask a client what he would like to talk about only to hear a response like, "I don't know." Also, even with invitations from helpers, clients with particularly distressing concerns may find it difficult to talk about their concerns. In such cases, helpers may find it useful to use other skills, such as silence or reflecting feelings. Sometimes, helpers may choose to speak for a while to help clients feel more comfortable and to reduce client feelings of being in the spotlight.

Helpers need to consider client cultural characteristics when using invitations. With Western-oriented helping processes, clients typically are expected to play a fairly active role in beginning, directing, and sustaining dialogue with helpers, and helpers play a less direct or active role as they attend, listen, remain silent, and strive to understand the lives and concerns of their clients (D. W. Sue & Sue, 2003). In many cultures, however (e.g., Asian American, Latin American, Native American), respect for elders and deference to authority are very important values. When working with clients from these cultures, helpers may have to be more direct and active (D. W. Sue & Sue, 2003). As noted by D. W. Sue and Sue (2003), "A racial/ethnic minority client who is asked to initiate conversation may become uncomfortable and respond with only short phrases or statements. The therapist may be prone to interpret the behavior negatively, when in actuality it may be a sign of respect" (p. 114). Thus, with members of some cultures, broad invitations (e.g., "What would you like to discuss today?") may not facilitate conversation. More directive statements (see, e.g., the skill of focusing, described later in this chapter) may be more helpful.

Finally, when presented with the opportunity to use invitations, helpers need to avoid making comments that effectively function as "door closers." Rather than opening conversation, these comments, which may include judgment, reassurance, or advice, shut it down (Bolton, 1979; Young, 2001). Some examples include:

"You seem angry right now. Don't worry, you'll feel better later."
"Your bad mood sure is putting a damper on things."
"If you feel so bad, why don't you do something that makes you feel good?"

Statements like these may provoke an angry response. In any case, these statements do not invite clients to elaborate on what is going on—what they are thinking or feeling. The helper has just demonstrated little or no interest in hearing about it.

Verbal Encouragers

Verbal encouragers are short statements that show that helpers are listening to, following, and understanding what clients are saying. These statements are typically just one to three words in length. Here are some examples:

"Mm-hmm."
"I see."
"Okay."
"Ah."
"Of course."
"I hear you."
"Really."
"Sure."
"Yes."
"Right."

Verbal encouragers are often used in conjunction with eye contact and head nods to show attention, involvement, and comprehension. With these statements, helpers are implicitly saying, "I'm following you." Verbal encouragers do not necessarily indicate agreement or disagreement with client statements; they simply indicate that the statements have been heard and understood (Bolton, 1979).

Verbal encouragers promote continued talking and expression by clients, who know that their helpers are following along. Verbal encouragers are nondirective. With minimal disruption, they allow clients to continue talking and expressing

themselves on the topics of their choice and to determine the direction of the helping session (Ivey & Authier, 1978). Helpers, however, need to use verbal encouragers in moderation. When overused, verbal encouragers sound artificial, mechanical, and unconvincing. When they are underused, clients may wonder whether their
helpers are listening and may feel anxiety or concern.

Asking Questions

Asking questions is one of the primary ways that helpers learn about their clients'
lives, problems, needs, and desires. Sometimes, clients do not provide information
unless they are asked. Good questions emanate from good listening and can elicit a
wealth of information—like finding treasure in the ocean. Poor questions, however,
tend to elicit responses that are unhelpful or irrelevant. It is important for helpers to
ask good, appropriate questions so they can develop a complete and accurate understanding of their clients' lives and problems.

Purposes of Questions

Helpers ask questions to

- open conversation;
- show interest and concern;
- gather information;
- obtain details;
- gain insight into client problems and perspectives;
- clarify client statements, behaviors, and feelings;
- encourage clients to elaborate on statements and expressions;
- introduce new topics;
- formulate and test diagnostic impressions and hypotheses;
- inquire about unverbalized issues in the session (e.g., tension between the helper
  and the client);
- understand what clients want and need;
- acquire information needed to prepare treatment strategies; and
- focus and direct the helping process.

Types of Questions

There are two major types of questions: open and closed. Open questions are
exploratory and call for a response of more than just a word or two. They are "open"
in the sense that they give the responder considerable flexibility in how to answer,
thus allowing for rich, personal, and varied responses. Here are some examples:

"What was your previous job like?"
"How do you respond when he treats you that way?"
"What are your concerns about going back to school?"
"How would you like for things to be different?"

Open questions are the most valuable type of question in helping. They ask clients to respond as they choose with as much detail as they want. They typically elicit a lot of information. Also, because of the freedom that clients have in responding, open questions often illuminate numerous topics for helpers and clients to explore.

One kind of question that is typically asked as an open question is the "clarifying" question, which is designed to ensure that helpers understand what their clients express. Clients sometimes use words and phrases that are not readily understandable. At times, they also make vague, ambiguous statements that could be understood in many different ways. Consider, for example, a client who says, "Mark is going to pay if he takes my car." Does this statement mean that the client expects monetary compensation from Mark? Does it mean that the client is going to contact the police and have Mark arrested? Is this a threat of violence? Does "takes my car" mean purchase, borrow, or steal? Helpers should not assume too readily that they know what their clients mean. They should check out anything that is unclear to them. Here is an example of a clarifying question that could be asked in the situation just described: "What do you mean when you say that 'Mark is going to pay'?" Another example is: "I'm not sure I'm following you. Can you explain that statement, please?"

Closed questions are designed to elicit a specific piece of information. They tend to generate rather brief responses, such as "yes" or "no." Here are some examples:

"Is your father still alive?"
"Do you like your job?"
"Where do you work?"
"How old are you?"
"What is your brother's name?"

Closed questions tend to be more directive and focused than open questions. They restrict client choice in how to respond and request only a brief answer on a specific topic. Responses to closed questions tend not to be as deep and rich as responses to open questions.

The overuse of closed questions typically results in minimal information being offered and often creates a heavy reliance on helpers to do the talking. Novice helpers commonly ask too many closed questions (Ivey & Authier, 1978). The minimal responses they receive give these helpers very little information about the lives and concerns of their clients. With the supply of questions soon exhausted and minimal information obtained, helpers may not know what to say or do next. At this point, the session reaches an impasse because the clients have been relying on the helpers to take the lead by asking questions.

In general, closed questions are less valuable than open questions and should be used less frequently because they do little to illuminate client concerns, experiences, and feelings. Sometimes, however, clients—especially very verbal ones—will volunteer additional information when asked a closed question.

Sommers-Flanagan and Sommers-Flanagan (1999) discussed two other types of questions that helpers sometimes ask: (1) swing questions, which can technically be answered with "yes" or "no" but are intended to elicit longer responses (e.g., "Can you tell me more about that?"); and (2) indirect or implied questions, which are essentially questions phrased in the form of a statement (e.g., "I wonder how you're feeling about the job interview tomorrow."). These types of questions can also be useful for eliciting information.

Considerations and Cautions When Asking Questions

The following are several points for helpers to keep in mind to ensure that they ask questions appropriately.

Make Sure That Questions Have a Legitimate Purpose. This point was discussed by Cormier and Nurius (2003). Helpers should not ask questions merely to keep the conversation going, to appear expert and knowledgeable, or to indulge their own curiosity. Their questions need to serve a beneficial purpose that is relevant to the helping process, such as gathering information, encouraging clients to talk, or requesting that clients elaborate on something they said. Once questions have been asked and responded to, helpers need to determine whether they received the information they needed. For example, if a helper asked a clarifying question, did she obtain the clarification that she needed?

Ask Questions on Important Issues and Relevant Topics. Questions are great tools for drawing out information, but if they do not address important issues, the responses probably will not contain helpful information. For example, if a client is going through a divorce and is worried about the effect of the split on her children, good questions may focus on the children and how they are coping (e.g., "How did they respond when you said that you and their father were divorcing?"). A poor question when addressing the children's well-being might focus on how the two spouses plan to divide their property.

Determine Which Type of Question Would Be Most Appropriate Under the Circumstances. When seeking very specific information, a closed question may be most appropriate. When helpers want clients to describe experiences, issues, or feelings, an open question would be best (Cormier & Nurius, 2003).

Be Aware of the Leading Effect That Questions Can Have. Helpers' questions can be directive, requesting responses on topics selected by the helpers. Questions allow helpers to take the session in the direction that they choose. For this reason, helpers should ask questions in moderation and consider using less directive skills, such as silence and reflecting feelings. The moderate use of questions in conjunction with the use of less directive skills allows clients to describe their concerns in their own way and to direct the course of the discussion. Remember, though, that clients from many racial and ethnic groups prefer a more directive helping style (e.g., structuring, providing information, making suggestions); thus, in some cases, helpers may opt to ask questions and use more directive skills (e.g., making suggestions) rather than remain silent or reflect feelings.

Be Prepared to Receive Very Different Reactions and Responses to Questions. Cormier and Hackney (1999) made this point, observing that some clients see questions as intrusive, whereas others see them as a sign that helpers are interested.

Sometimes, merely asking questions can be provocative and annoying to clients, as if helpers are supposed to already know the answers. One client even asked: "Are you going to ask me questions or are you going to help me?" In cases in which clients are reluctant to speak, perhaps because they do not want to be in helping or because they are apprehensive about disclosing details of their lives and problems, questions may not elicit much of a response. With these clients, helpers might remain silent and let the clients speak when ready, or they may choose to speak for a while and try to encourage the clients to participate. In any case, peppering clients with questions when they do not want to speak can cause clients to become even more entrenched in their silence and resistance.

Be Careful About Too Quickly Probing Deeply Into Client Concerns. Many clients are hesitant about sharing their concerns and freely volunteering information. Indeed, the concerns they discuss first may not be the concerns that are bothering them the most. They may not fully understand these deeper concerns or be prepared to address them. In any case, clients may disclose information on a surface level only. Helpers can use questions to go beneath the surface and begin to understand client concerns; however, clients may feel threatened or offended if helpers proceed too quickly. Probing too deeply too quickly usually feels intrusive and may harm helping relationships. It is often prudent for helpers to proceed in a delicate manner and gradually pursue client concerns in depth over time as the helping relationship grows stronger. If clients have strong negative reactions to helper questions, helpers may drop the subject or ask their questions at a later time.

Avoid Asking Questions Beginning With "Why." An example of a "why" question is, "Why do you feel so anxious?" Questions beginning with why, more so than questions beginning with who, what, where, when, and how, tend to elicit "I don't know" responses. "Why" questions also can sound judgmental or provocative. The questions imply that clients have to justify their statements, expressions, and feelings rather than explain or clarify them. In some cases, "why" questions may suggest that helpers do not understand, agree with, or approve of client statements and expressions. Imagine, for example, a client having just expressed anger and the helper responding, "Why are you so angry?" To the client, this question may imply, "I don't see any reason for you to be this angry." The client may feel misunderstood and become even angrier. Helpers can usually get the information they need by phrasing their questions in a way that does not use the word "why."

Consider Cultural Characteristics. Ivey and Ivey (1999) observed that the "rapid-fire" North American questioning style may be perceived as rude and offensive by people in other cultures. In addition, questions that ask for personal information may be perceived as intrusive. Helpers may need to proceed slowly and cautiously when trying to gather information.

Avoid Asking Too Many Questions. Novice helpers, in particular, tend to ask too many questions and, compared to more experienced helpers, ask a higher proportion of questions on unimportant topics. Asking too many questions can hinder the development of trust and rapport, especially with resistant or less talkative clients. A barrage of questions can cause clients to feel highly scrutinized, defensive, and uncomfortable. The helping session may feel like an interrogation. Asking a lot of questions may even create the expectation that when all of the questions are asked and answered, helpers will have solutions for clients. Helpers may be asking too many questions if they (1) interrupt their clients to gather more information; (2) ask a series of questions in a row before giving clients an opportunity to answer; (3) do not allow for silence; or (4) observe that clients consistently assume a passive role, waiting for the helper to speak.

Avoid Asking Too Few Questions. Helpers may not ask enough questions for a number of reasons. For example, they may believe that asking questions shows that they are not listening; they may fear that asking about clients' personal concerns is intrusive; they may fear that asking questions reflects ignorance or naïveté—that they should already know the answers; or they may assume that they fully understand their clients' statements and expressions. If helpers do not ask enough questions, however, they risk gathering insufficient information, which can lead to an inaccurate understanding of client problems. Helpers develop a feel for how many questions to ask through practice, experience, and careful observation of their clients.

Paraphrasing

Helpers must not only strive to understand clients through careful listening, they must also *verbally demonstrate* that understanding to their clients (Rogers, 1951). Doing so shows that helpers are following client statements, feelings, and expressions. You can probably relate to the positive, reinforcing, validating feelings created by knowing that someone else understands you. For clients, these feelings facilitate trust and a sense of connection and encourage them to continue expressing themselves.

Client communication can be divided into cognitive/objective content and affective/subjective content. Facts, details, descriptions, thoughts, and experiences represent the cognitive or objective portion of client communication, whereas feelings, expressed in words and nonverbal behaviors, represent the affective or subjective portion (Hackney & Cormier, 2001; Ivey & Authier, 1978). Some clients provide cognitive content much more than affective content; for others, the opposite is true. In any case, helpers demonstrate understanding of cognitive content by paraphrasing, and they demonstrate understanding of affective content by reflecting feelings. Sometimes, helpers paraphrase and reflect feelings in the same statement, but we discuss the two skills separately in this chapter to promote understanding of each one. In this section, we consider cognitive content and paraphrasing.

Getting the Gist of Client Statements

Paraphrasing is basically a two-part process. The first part involves identifying the cognitive content of client statements—the facts, details, descriptions, thoughts, and experiences. The second part involves demonstrating understanding of the cognitive content by feeding back the content in new words. We will explain these two parts in more detail by way of an example. Consider the following client statement: "When people say I'm not good enough to do something, that just makes me want to demonstrate my talents and prove them wrong."

To paraphrase this statement, the helper first needs to identify the cognitive content of the statement, which is the client's desire to demonstrate his talents and prove wrong people who doubt his abilities. Second, the helper needs to demonstrate understanding of the cognitive content by feeding back the content in different (or mostly different) and fewer words than the client used. The helper accomplishes this with a paraphrase. He or she might say, for example, "So you want to show people how capable you are when they doubt your abilities."

A paraphrase responds to the overt, explicit content in the client's statement without altering it, introducing new topics, making judgments or evaluations, or searching for hidden meanings. In other words, a paraphrase basically says the same thing as the client's statement, just in a new way. In this sense, a paraphrase is largely a nondirective response. It allows clients to set the course of the helping session and decide what issues to discuss. Hackney and Cormier (2001) noted that sometimes client statements contain only affective content (e.g., "I'm angry"); in such instances, the cognitive content must be inferred from the context of the statement or determined by asking clients to elaborate.

When paraphrasing, helpers try to relay the "gist" or essence of what clients are saying (Ivey & Authier, 1978). They do not methodically replace client words with synonyms. Paraphrases may be worded in many ways, but some common examples of how helpers might introduce paraphrases include, "So you're saying . . . ," "It sounds like . . . ," "It seems as though . . . ," and "Let me see if I understand . . . ."

Paraphrases show the client that the helper understands what the client has expressed. They also allow the helper to make sure that his or her understanding is correct. Sometimes, helpers may not be sure that they have heard clients correctly, so they paraphrase to double check. There are many clues that helpers look for to determine the accuracy of their paraphrases. For example, they look at client body language. Head nods and hand gesturing can indicate that the paraphrases were accurate. A puzzled look or a shaking of the head can indicate that they were off base.

In addition, helpers listen to their clients' verbal responses. Sometimes, after paraphrasing, helpers will ask clients whether their paraphrases were accurate (e.g., "Is that right?"). Accurate paraphrases tend to elicit responses such as, "Right," "Yeah," or "Exactly." Such paraphrases encourage clients to continue speaking and to elaborate on their previous statements. If paraphrases are inaccurate, clients may say something like, "No, what I'm saying is . . ." and then proceed to correct the helper. Repeatedly making inaccurate paraphrases can shut down dialogue and damage trust. Clients may feel that they are not being heard or understood.

Helpers also determine the accuracy of their paraphrases by noting how quickly clients respond to the paraphrases. The more accurate paraphrases are, the more quickly clients tend to respond with head nods or verbal statements such as, "Exactly." The sense of connection and mutual understanding is a good feeling and is quickly acknowledged. When paraphrases are inaccurate, they derail the client's train of thought and are often met with brief silence. The client has to "jump the tracks" to process and understand the helper's response. Once clients realize that their helpers did not understand, they may respond with puzzled looks, perhaps some irritation, and corrective statements.

Paraphrasing shows clients that they are being listened to and understood and thus encourages them to continue exploring their problems. By demonstrating understanding of their clients' overt expressions through paraphrasing, helpers may earn the privilege of probing deeper into their clients' concerns. Trust develops gradually in relationships. When clients know they have been understood, they may be more willing to let helpers into their lives.

Paraphrasing also encourages specificity, clarity, and concreteness. By distilling the essence of client statements, which may be vague, complex, or lengthy, paraphrasing can aid clients and helpers in sorting through all of the words to pull out the important elements of client communication.

Characteristics of Good Paraphrases

Helper paraphrases that possess the following characteristics stand the greatest chance of being effective:

Well-Timed. Helpers do not paraphrase every client statement. Typically, helpers allow their clients to speak for a while (from several seconds to a few minutes) and then paraphrase important topics or ideas. Thus, paraphrases are used when helpers have gathered sufficient information and believe that responding to the cognitive content will demonstrate understanding. Helpers tend to use paraphrases more frequently when clients present a lot of cognitive material. When the content of client expressions is largely feeling-oriented, however, helpers tend to focus more on reflecting feelings.

Focused on Important Topics. Paraphrases should address what appear to be the most significant facts, details, thoughts, and experiences in client expressions. They should not address apparently trivial material.

Accurate. Through paraphrasing, helpers strive to accurately feed back the cognitive content of client expressions. In their paraphrases, helpers should not add content (e.g., topics that clients did not express in any way) or distort or change the meaning of client expressions. Inaccurate paraphrases convey the impression that helpers do not understand or are not listening.

Tentatively Expressed. Helpers may begin paraphrases with such introductory words as, "It seems as though . . ." or "Let me see if I understand . . . ," which suggest that the helpers are asking the clients to verify the accuracy of their paraphrases. When such words are used, paraphrases may seem less threatening, presumptuous, or imposing than more blunt responses, which may convey that helpers are telling clients, "This is what you're saying." A soft, even inquisitive, tone of voice can also suggest tentativeness. Tentatively expressed paraphrases show respect, encourage clarification, and facilitate open communication. When paraphrases are delivered tentatively, clients also are more likely to correct their helpers if the paraphrases are off base. Helpers, however, need to be careful about sounding apologetic or uncertain. If they sound this way, clients may believe that their helpers do not understand them, and their perception of helper competence and credibility may be negatively altered.

Brief. Paraphrases are concise, to-the-point responses, not long, rambling statements. Talking too much tends to take the focus off clients and put it on helpers. It also disrupts the flow of client expression. When helpers use lengthy paraphrases, clients may think the helpers are not listening well and are fumbling for responses.

Natural. Helpers should use simple, clearly understandable, age-appropriate language and avoid the excessive use of sophisticated, esoteric words and phrases. They should try to speak in concrete terms, being specific about facts, details, thoughts, and experiences. Paraphrases should simplify and clarify, not confuse.

Balanced With Other Skills. Paraphrases should be used in conjunction with other skills. When helpers use paraphrasing too frequently, clients may feel that important parts of their concerns, such as their feelings, are being ignored and are not worthy of attention. Excessive paraphrasing may also encourage clients to ignore important feelings when recognizing and experiencing those feelings may be a critical part of successfully addressing their problems. In addition, excessive paraphrasing may convey the impression that helpers are not contributing much to the helping session beyond serving as a mirror for client expressions. Conversely, infrequent paraphrasing can cause some clients to wonder whether their helpers understand them. As discussed in the next section, how much—or even whether—helpers use this skill depends in part on cultural variables.

Cultural Considerations

Not all clients are receptive to paraphrasing, and cultural differences exist in reception to this skill. For example, a White woman in our counseling skills class who had worked in an inner-city school that had a high percentage of African American and Native American students related that students accused her of "trying to act smart by putting things into White folks' talk" when she paraphrased their comments. She did not find paraphrasing to be very useful with the population that she served because the skill did not promote exploration and good relationship development.

Some research has also questioned the effectiveness of paraphrasing with Asian clients. Exum and Lau (1988) suggested that paraphrasing may be viewed by Asian clients as hesitancy on the part of helpers. In one counseling study involving Asian international students, the students viewed periodic paraphrases during the helping session as unnecessary (D. Sue, 1997). Some of the students thought that the paraphrases represented helpers questioning the students' truthfulness. The female students were more positive about paraphrases than the male students were.

In short, although paraphrasing can be a valuable skill, helpers need to gauge client responses to paraphrases to determine whether to continue using this skill and, if so, how much to use it.

The Restatement

Sometimes, helpers respond to client statements with a restatement, a response similar to the paraphrase. Both respond to explicit cognitive content; however, unlike the paraphrase, which involves helpers using their own words, the restatement merely repeats or parrots, word for word, part or all of what clients have just said. Here is an example:

Client: We had some unpleasant news yesterday. John has decided that he's leaving the company. I guess we won't be doing the project after all.

Helper: You won't be doing the project after all.

The restatement is useful in some circumstances. For example, it may be beneficial when helpers are not certain that they heard clients correctly—perhaps their clients spoke very softly or a noise interfered with careful listening. In addition, the restatement can be useful, on occasion, as a way to get clients to elaborate on statements that helpers think are important. The restatement also may be useful when clients

- are not native speakers of the language spoken in the helping session,
- have speech impediments or mental disabilities,
- are elderly or very young, or
- are somewhat immature or unsophisticated.

In these cases, helpers' judicious use of the restatement ensures that they are following what clients are saying and reinforces that clients were heard correctly.

Beyond these reasons, the restatement is of limited value in the helping process because it can sound like helpers are mocking their clients. Furthermore, the restatement does not demonstrate that helpers understand, only that they heard client statements and can repeat them. When helpers paraphrase, they select their own words, which requires that they process the meaning in client statements and then feed that meaning back to the clients.

Reflecting Implied Cognitive Content

Related to paraphrasing is the process of reflecting implied cognitive content. Clients do not always directly and explicitly state what is going on in their lives. Helpers may sense implied messages in client statements and expressions. Sometimes, clients are not consciously aware of the implied content because it is content that they are afraid to confront. Other times, clients simply do not explicitly state what they mean. They may not think to do so, or they may not articulate their messages very well. Effective helpers listen for this implied content as they explore client concerns. Both helpers and clients can come to a better understanding of client problems when such content is made explicit and explored. Consider the following example of reflecting implied cognitive content:

Client (teacher talking about her students; somber expression; little emotion): My students all seem uninterested and bored. Only a handful of them have gone on to college. Each year, student evaluations of my course are mixed, but most of them don't like the course.

Helper: I'm wondering whether you believe that you've failed as a teacher.

Based on the information gathered at this point and considering the client's nonverbal and verbal behavior, the helper has made explicit what she believes is implied in the client's statement. Note how the helper's response is similar to a paraphrase in that it focuses on cognitive content, but it differs from a paraphrase in that it reflects implicit, not explicit, cognitive content. A paraphrase of the client's statement might be, "It sounds like you have a lot of unmotivated and dissatisfied students." This paraphrase feeds back, in different words, what the client explicitly expressed. The reflection of implied content, however, goes beyond explicit words and reflects what the client seems to be suggesting.

When helpers reflect implied cognitive content, they do so cautiously, offering their reflections in a tentative, nonimposing manner. They do not present them too forcefully, as they realize their reflections may be incorrect or prompt negative responses from clients, such as confusion or denial, especially if the implied content is uncomfortable or threatening. Indeed, both a good relationship and a good understanding of explicit client statements are important when using this skill. Early in helping relationships, helpers generally use this skill infrequently because of its potential for exposing content that clients are not yet ready to confront. Because implied content is uncovered, this skill is useful for exploring client concerns and promoting client understanding. That is, helpers use this skill to learn more about their clients, and clients can learn more about themselves when helpers draw out and clarify their implied messages.

Reflecting Feelings

Recognizing and responding to client feelings are significant aspects of the helping process. Carkhuff (2000) asserted that "responding to feelings is the most critical single skill in helping because it reflects the helpees' affective experience of themselves in relation to their worlds" (p. 104). Most client problems and issues have emotional components that need to be addressed. The client who has trouble making friends, for example, may be struggling with low self-confidence and feelings of inadequacy, not merely difficulties in identifying ways to meet people. Often, little or no significant work can be accomplished in the helping process until clients recognize and own the feelings that they avoid. Through the skill of reflecting feelings, among other techniques, helpers aid clients in bringing their feelings into awareness and expressing them in healthy ways.

It should be noted that although feelings are typically important to address in helping, clients vary in their level of emotional expression. Culture, upbringing, and environment all affect how people express feelings. Helpers do not try to get all of their clients to express feelings to the same degree. They assist their clients in expressing themselves in a healthy way that is consistent with client culture and personality characteristics. Cultural considerations are addressed in more detail later in this discussion.

Identifying and Responding to Client Feelings

Reflecting feelings is a two-part process. The first part involves identifying what clients are feeling—that is, identifying the affective content, not the cognitive content, of client expressions. To do this, helpers must be able to "read" their clients and recognize their nonverbal emotional cues, such as facial expressions and body language (Carkhuff, 2000). Helpers also listen to the words clients use and consider what they already know about their clients' lives. Finally, helpers use their own perceptions and intuitions, which can give them clues about what their clients are feeling.

Often, clients experience more than one feeling, and sometimes those feelings are ambivalent, confusing, and contradictory (Rogers, 1942). For example, a woman may experience love and affection for her husband while at the same time feel hurt and angry that he does not spend more time with her. Helpers need to watch for all of the feelings.

When identifying their clients' feelings, helpers consider not only the type of feeling (e.g., anger, fear, happiness), but also the intensity of the feeling (Carkhuff, 2000; Cormier & Nurius, 2003; Young, 2001). There are many levels of anger, for example, from irritated to mad to enraged. Likewise, happiness can range from okay to happy to ecstatic. Intensity might also be indicated through the use of such words as "very" and "somewhat" (e.g., "mad" versus "very mad"). See Figure 7.1 for a list of feeling words.

The second part of reflecting feelings involves responding to the feelings that clients express (Carkhuff, 2000; Rogers, 1942). Helpers do this by "reflecting" the feelings; that is, they state what their clients appear to be feeling. When reflecting feelings, helpers may simply state the feeling (e.g., "You feel frustrated."), but they often state the feeling and add some content afterward to put the feeling in context (e.g., "You feel frustrated by your husband ignoring your needs.") (Carkhuff, 2000; Ivey & Ivey, 1999). The reflections focus on mirroring client feelings (Rogers, 1942); they do not judge or evaluate feelings or add content that was not expressed by clients.

Many clients, especially those who have difficulty expressing emotions, may not overtly state how they feel. Their statements may contain no words indicating their feelings. In these cases, helpers must infer feelings from contextual factors, such as verbal statements and nonverbal behaviors. They may also ask the clients how they feel (Ivey & Ivey, 1999). Other clients have little problem expressing how they feel. When clients use specific feeling words to describe how they feel (e.g., "I'm very anxious right now."), helpers usually do not merely repeat the feeling ("You feel very anxious."). Such a response would probably prompt clients to say something like, "Yes, that's what I said." Instead, helpers might ask clients to elaborate on their expressed feelings (e.g., the anxiety).

It is common to begin reflections with, "You feel. . . ." Helpers, however, need to be careful not to overuse this way of introducing reflections. Overusing these words can cause reflections to seem insincere and mechanical. It should also be noted that simply using the word "feel" does not make a response a reflection of feelings (Young, 2001). Consider, for example, a client saying, "I just don't think our relationship will work any longer. George and I need to go our separate ways," and the helper responding, "You feel that it would be best to end the relationship." The helper's response is a paraphrase, not a reflection of feelings. The helper did not identify and respond to the client's feelings but rather addressed cognitive content and selected the word "feel" in place of words such as "think" or "believe."

This list illustrates the wide variety and intensity levels of feelings.

TYPE OF FEELING

Intensity	Happiness	Sadness	Confusion	Anger	Fear	Shame
Low	comfortable confident content glad justified okay pleased relaxed satisfied	blue bored disappointed discontent numb resigned	caught distracted stuck uncertain undecided unsure	aggravated agitated annoyed displeased dissatisfied irked irritated vexed	apprehensive concerned hesitant insecure jumpy reluctant uncomfortable uneasy vulnerable	apologetic humbled sorry
Medium	cheerful delighted eager encouraged happy joyful	discouraged dispirited distressed down gloomy glum hurt lost melancholy morose mournful sad somber sorrowful troubled unhappy upset	confused flustered foiled rattled skeptical surprised torn	betrayed bitter cheated contemptuous disgusted frustrated huffy imposed-upon indignant jealous mad offended persecuted perturbed pressured provoked rebellious resentful sullen thwarted wronged	afraid alarmed anxious disturbed fearful frightened intimidated nervous threatened trapped worried	abashed ashamed blameworthy embarrassed foolish guilty regretful remorseful repentant stupid
Strong	blissful ecstatic elated energized excited fantastic fulfilled gleeful thrilled tickled wonderful	crushed defeated dejected depressed despondent devastated distraught forlorn hopeless miserable neglected rejected	bewildered overwhelmed perplexed shocked stunned	angry enraged exasperated fuming furious infuriated irate outraged pissed off seething vengeful	petrified scared terrified	degraded disgraced humiliated mortified

FIGURE 7.1　Feeling Words

The following example shows how a helper might reflect a client's feelings. The client's demeanor is somber and flat as she says, "My friend Becky just moved to another state. I thought I was prepared for her leaving and not being around any longer, but I guess I'm really not. I keep thinking about her and how I don't have a close friend around here anymore." The helper would first identify what the client is feeling. Because the client did not explicitly use any feeling words in her statement, the feeling must be inferred. The client's words combined with information about her demeanor (nonverbal behavior) seem to indicate feelings of sadness and loneliness. The intensity appears to be moderate. Next, the helper would respond to the feeling with a reflection. One possible reflection is, "You feel lonely now that Becky has moved away."

After offering a reflection of feelings, helpers note their clients' verbal and nonverbal behaviors to determine the accuracy of their reflections. They may also directly ask clients whether their reflections were accurate. When accurate, reflections may elicit responses similar to those elicited by paraphrases (e.g., head nods, statements like "Right" or "Yes"), though clients who have difficulty recognizing and expressing emotions may respond defensively or with denial, stoicism, or confusion.

Reflections, like paraphrases, confirm that helpers understood what was expressed. They also help clients feel heard and respected. Rogers (1942) noted that when helpers respond to client feelings, "it gives the client the satisfaction of feeling deeply understood, it enables him to express further feeling, and it leads most efficiently and most directly to the emotional roots of his adjustment problem" (p. 141).

Helper reflections encourage clients to continue expressing themselves—to stay with their feelings and to elaborate on them, thus leading to deeper self-disclosure and expression. Because reflections signal to clients that it is okay to express themselves, using this skill can sometimes open the floodgates, prompting a significant release of emotion. At times, as a way to help clients accept their feelings and see that it is okay to express them, helpers may use a more directive response. Sommers-Flanagan and Sommers-Flanagan (1999) called this type of response a "feeling validation." Such a response might be phrased, "It's okay to feel sad about your friend moving away."

Helpers' acceptance of client feelings can be refreshing and profound to the clients and can empower clients to accept the feelings. Clients may experience a sense of relief and recognize that having feelings is normal. The feelings can now be discussed, experienced, and explored instead of repressed. In short, reflecting feelings and validating feelings both convey emotional acceptance, which can strengthen the rapport between helpers and clients.

Surface Versus Underlying Feelings

Expressed feelings sometimes mask underlying feelings that may be too threatening or uncomfortable for clients to face. Anger, for example, may mask fear or pain. It is important for helpers to identify feelings that might be below the surface, hidden beneath more obvious feelings or behind defenses, such as a stoic façade. Helpers do so by carefully listening to clients' verbal statements, which may indicate underlying feelings, by observing clients' nonverbal behaviors, by considering what they know about their clients, and by using their intuitions and professional judgment.

Early in helping relationships, helpers tend to focus on obvious feelings. Demonstrating awareness of these feelings not only helps to build rapport and trust as helping relationships develop, it also allows helpers to earn the privilege to probe deeper later on.

Trying to draw out underlying feelings too early in the helping process can threaten the helping relationship. Such attempts can be provocative, offensive, and presumptuous. Helpers may not yet know enough about their clients to justify deep reflections, and they may not have earned the trust of their clients. Furthermore, clients may not be ready to address the underlying feelings. If, for example, a client appears to express anger when talking about recently breaking up with his girlfriend, the helper probably would not start by suggesting that the anger masks the client's underlying pain and sadness because of the loss of the relationship. Instead, the helper probably would start by reflecting the client's anger. Suggesting that the client feels sad could cause the client to become defensive and even angrier because he may not be ready to acknowledge his pain. He may also be offended by the helper's presumptuousness. Early in the helping process, before trust has developed, increasing a client's anger may cause the client not to return for another session. Eventually, the client needs to address his pain, but early on, it is more important for the helper to focus on and understand explicit expressions, learn about the client's life and concerns, and build the helping relationship.

Helpers may choose to reflect feelings at a deeper level once good relationships have been established and clients are ready to explore such feelings. Such reflection may come later in the process of exploring client concerns and may also serve as an attempt to promote client understanding—to help clients honestly examine, understand, and express their feelings.

Characteristics of Good Reflections of Feelings

Helper reflections that possess the following characteristics stand the greatest chance of being effective.

Well-Timed. Some degree of rapport must be established before most clients will express their feelings openly and honestly. For this reason, helpers consider the strength of the helping relationship in determining when and how much to reflect feelings. Early in the helping relationship, helpers need to use this skill judiciously.

Focused on Important Feelings. Helpers do not reflect every client feeling. They reflect feelings when the feelings appear to be the most important and prominent aspect of what clients are expressing.

Accurate. As discussed earlier, it is important for helpers to correctly identify both the type of feeling and its intensity (see Figure 7.1). In addition, helpers must identify and reflect the specific feeling or feelings the client is experiencing. Inaccurate reflections communicate to clients that helpers do not understand or are not paying attention.

Tentatively Expressed. When reflecting client feelings, helpers may use a soft, sometimes inquisitive, tone of voice to convey that they are testing their reflections with their clients. Helpers may also introduce reflections with such words as, "It sounds like you feel . . ." or "Maybe you're feeling. . . ." Finally, they may ask clients whether their reflections seem accurate. Tentatively expressed reflections show respect; they show that the helpers are not imposing their observations. They also encourage clients to continue expressing themselves and to correct their helpers if the reflections were off base. As with paraphrasing, helpers should avoid reflecting feelings in an apologetic or uncertain manner. Reflections that sound apologetic or uncertain may cause clients to question helper credibility or competence.

Brief. Reflections should be concise responses. When helpers say too much, the feelings may become lost in the jumble of words. A short reflection of what clients appear to be feeling helps to keep the focus on the clients and the feelings.

Natural. Helpers should use simple, clearly understandable, age-appropriate language. Their reflections of client feelings should be specific and concrete.

Balanced With Other Skills. Reflections should be balanced with other skills, such as silence, asking questions, and paraphrasing. Overemphasizing feelings may cause discomfort and may make clients feel that other aspects of their concerns, such as the facts and details, are being ignored. Conversely, underemphasizing feelings may encourage clients to ignore their feelings.

Consistent With Clients' Cultural Characteristics. Emotional expression varies from client to client based on personality characteristics and cultural background. Effective reflections consider cultural variables, as discussed in the next section.

Cultural Considerations

The extent to which helpers focus on feelings—and how they do so—is dependent on the client's cultural characteristics. Some cultures (e.g., Asians) tend to value privacy and emotional control and may be less receptive to extensive focusing on feelings. When helpers focus extensively on feelings and encourage the expression of feelings, clients from these cultures may feel that they are losing face. One way to address feelings with clients from these cultures is to discuss feelings along with content and situational variables rather than focusing on feelings alone (D. Sue, 1997). For example, consider the following helper responses listed in D. Sue (1997, p. 188):

1. "I can see that you are distressed." (individual and emotion focus)
2. "Trying to decide what to do in this situation is difficult for you." (situation and emotion focus)
3. "You are trying to decide how to deal with this situation." (situation focus)

These helper responses are from D. Sue's (1997) counseling study involving Asian international students. The students valued empathy (helpers demonstrating understanding of client feelings and perspectives) but found the discussion of emotions most valuable when combined with content. The students were more likely to feel that the helper was empathetic with responses 2 and 3 than with the first response, which they felt was too direct and personal. For these students, focusing only on emotions detracted from the helping relationship. As D. Sue (1997) stated, "Acknowledging emotions enhanced empathy but only when it was more indirect, involved the situation, was not too frequent, or was followed by some directive statement by the counselor" (p. 188). The study also found that the Asian female participants were more open to emotional content alone than were the males and that the Caucasian comparison group was comfortable with all three responses listed above.

Focusing

In certain situations, helpers may find it beneficial to focus the conversation on particular issues, statements, feelings, or expressions (see Brammer & MacDonald, 2003). Such situations include

- when helpers want to discuss particular issues, statements, feelings, or expressions that they believe are relevant and significant;
- when clients say or express something that helpers consider particularly important and worthy of further attention and exploration;
- when clients raise many issues or concerns;
- when clients are not expressing themselves clearly; and
- when helpers are not sure that they heard or understood what their clients said or expressed.

In these cases, helpers may use the skill of focusing. The following are some examples of focusing:

"Tell me more about your job."
"Can you describe that experience in more detail?"
"Tell me what it feels like when you get angry."
"Let's talk about the incident at school."
"You said earlier that you had an argument with your husband yesterday. Can you say more about that?"

Helpers may also focus discussion by repeating particular client words or phrases in an effort to encourage clients to say more (Brammer & MacDonald, 2003). For example, if a client says, "I tried to tell him what I thought, but I froze up," the helper might respond with, "Froze up?" This response will likely prompt the client to elaborate on and clarify what she meant by "froze up."

Focusing is a directive skill in which helpers identify specific issues, statements, feelings, or expressions that seem confusing or particularly important and try to get clients to address them further (see Brammer & MacDonald, 2003). The helper's focusing statements and questions encourage clients to explore and consider the issues, statements, feelings, or expressions—to ponder or elaborate on them and perhaps develop greater awareness. This further exploration can reduce confusion and facilitate greater understanding for both helpers and clients (Brammer & MacDonald, 2003).

The skill of focusing should be used in moderation. It puts helpers in the driver's seat—they decide which topics to address. If focusing is used too often, clients may feel that helpers are dominating the session and not allowing them sufficient opportunity to discuss issues that are important to them. As a result, clients may become frustrated or withdrawn, and helping relationships may deteriorate. However, clients from some cultural groups may want helpers to take a more direct, active role in the helping process. Indeed, studies have found that many racial and ethnic minority clients tend to prefer more directive helping techniques and strategies (see, e.g., Atkinson & Lowe, 1995; D. Sue, 1997), such as structuring, providing information, making suggestions, and giving advice. For such clients, focusing may be used more frequently.

Summarizing

In the helping process, summarizing involves synthesizing information provided by a client and highlighting major themes or points in the client's feelings, thoughts, behaviors, and experiences (Brammer & MacDonald, 2003; Okun, 2002). Summarizing helps to identify major issues, focus discussion, clarify statements and expressions, and assess client progress.

Summarizing is similar to paraphrasing and reflecting feelings in that it involves helpers using their own words to feed back what clients have expressed without altering the meaning, changing the subject, or adding new topics. However, summaries are different from paraphrases and reflections in that they tend to be longer responses and may cover dialogue over a greater span of time. They may address topics discussed over several minutes, an entire session, or several sessions (Ivey & Ivey, 1999; Sommers-Flanagan & Sommers-Flanagan, 1999).

When Helpers Summarize

Summarizing is beneficial throughout the helping process. For example, it can be used at the beginning of a session as a way for helpers and clients to review what was discussed in previous meetings. This type of summarizing helps to provide continuity from one session to the next. It also assists helpers and clients in picking up where they left off in the previous meeting and focusing quickly on important topics as they begin the current session. Here is an example:

> "Well, in our last meeting, we were talking about some of the academic problems you've been having in your classes. You said that you've been pretty stressed out about your grades and that you're worried that you won't get into a good graduate school program. You said you were going to try to think of some ways you could improve your grades. Would you like to start with that today?"

Summarizing can also be used at various points in the session to focus on important topics or feelings, demonstrate and ensure understanding, identify themes in client statements and expressions, provide clarity when helpers are confused, assist helpers and clients in digesting large amounts of information, assist clients in organizing and clarifying their issues, and assist clients in seeing the "big picture." Summarizing can be especially useful if clients have presented a lot of information or are discussing complex topics. Here is an example:

> "Let me see if I'm following you here. You and your wife have tried marital counseling, but that didn't work. Now, your wife says that she wants to get a divorce. You've tried to talk her out of it and salvage the marriage. That, too, doesn't seem to be working. Now, you're feeling resigned about a divorce and think that it probably can't be avoided. Is that right?"

Finally, summarizing can be used at the end of a session or the end of the helping relationship to review what has been discussed or accomplished. In D. Sue's (1997) counseling study involving Asian international students, the students found summarizing at the end of helping sessions to be helpful. Here is an example of this type of summarizing:

> "Well, why don't we look at what we've covered today. We talked about how you've struggled to make friends since moving here, and you told me how upsetting that's been. You said that you might think about some ways you could meet people, and we agreed to talk about that some more next time. We also began to address some possible goals as we move forward. How does that sound to you?"

As shown in these examples, summaries

- can address feelings as well as facts, thoughts, details, and experiences;
- are concise, specific, and concrete, not long, vague, or rambling; and
- often end with a question (e.g., "How does that sound to you?") that invites clients to verify accuracy, correct inaccuracies, or add their own ideas.

Demonstrating Continuous Attention Through Summarizing

One of the benefits of summarizing is that it reflects a sustained effort to follow and understand what clients have expressed over time. Helpers do not merely respond to one statement or one expressed feeling, but respond to several, thus demonstrating continuous attention. Clients are often impressed when helpers demonstrate how much they remember and that they have been listening the entire time. Thus, summarizing can enhance helper credibility and expertness. At the same time, it can increase client investment in the helping process by showing clients that what they have to say is important and is being understood. Further, summarizing can empower clients, reinforcing that they are the focus of the helping process.

Encouraging Clients to Participate in Summarizing

Sommers-Flanagan and Sommers-Flanagan (1999) recommended that summarizing be an interactive, collaborative effort between the helper and the client in which both individuals recall and discuss important topics, thoughts, and feelings. Having clients participate, and having them offer their summaries at times, places some responsibility for recalling important topics on them and helps to reveal what they believe is important (Brammer & MacDonald, 2003; Sommers-Flanagan & Sommers-Flanagan, 1999). Having clients summarize may also help clients see their issues more clearly and recognize and take credit for their progress.

Learning and Practicing Helping Skills: An Important Note

The skills discussed in this chapter are typically the first verbal skills that students learn in helper training programs. We have found that students often raise a few issues as they learn and practice the skills. We discuss these issues here.

First, students often ask how a helper knows when to use a particular skill (see Young, 2001). In the discussion of the skills in this chapter, we provided some guidelines for when to use them. For example, when clients discuss a lot of facts, a paraphrase might be appropriate. When feelings are expressed, a reflection of feelings would probably be a good choice. When helpers want details or clarification, a question might accomplish that goal. Invitations can be used when clients need encouragement to speak.

The order in which the skills were presented in this chapter is one possible way in which these skills might be applied in helping; however, there is no precise formula for when to use particular skills. Through training and practice, helpers gain a feel for when to use them. Although reading a book about helping skills can provide information and guidance, more is needed. Just as one must get behind the wheel of a car and practice driving to learn to drive, doing exercises and role plays and actually helping people in "real-life" helping settings are the best ways to learn and practice helping skills and develop a feel for when to use particular skills.

A second issue students often raise is that learning and practicing these skills seems mechanical and artificial. It is true that learning about helping skills one at a time through written text, dialogues, and exercises can introduce an element of artificiality. However, learning helping skills is no different from learning any other skill for the first time. One does not learn a new batting stance or dance move in the midst of a game or a performance. Nor does one learn a multitude of new skills all at once. New skills are often learned one at a time in a practice setting, and they may feel awkward at first (Bolton, 1979). In this chapter, we discussed the skills one at a time, and in the exercises at the end of the chapter, we ask you to practice them that way to promote understanding of each skill.

People tend to have fairly ingrained patterns of communication, so trying to modify the way they communicate, such as when they are learning the skills discussed in this chapter, can be uncomfortable for them and evoke resistance. Bolton (1979) observed:

> There is no such thing as unstructured communication. Some of the
> rules that foster clear communication have been transmitted fairly

effectively in our society while other important structures of communication, like reflective listening skills, are rarely transmitted. As a result,
when we learn these new skills, they seem strange and artificial at first.
But they are no more artificial than the rules of sentence structure,
spelling, and so on. (p. 64)

The skills discussed in this chapter are used throughout life, not just in helping.
People just tend not to focus on them, and often they do not use the skills very well.
Feelings may be ignored. Questions may be overused. Responses may be laced with
advice, defensiveness, or judgment—all of which can be unhelpful and damaging in
relationships. Helpers need to learn the skills that foster productive relationships and
the exploration of concerns, and they need to avoid the unhelpful responses that
people are sometimes inclined to use in everyday life. Initially, many students and
helpers do not use skills such as paraphrasing, reflecting feelings, and summarizing
very effectively. They may use them in a way that sounds mechanical and artificial;
however, with practice, they learn to use these skills more naturally and to integrate
them into their own personalities, thereby creating a unique helping style (Bolton,
1979).

A Hypothetical Dialogue

The following hypothetical dialogue between a helper and a client demonstrates how
several of the skills discussed in this chapter might be used in a helping session. The
client is a woman who is dealing with the demands of graduate school and marriage.

Helper: Well, near the end of our meeting last time you mentioned something that has
been troubling you recently. You started talking about how you've been trying to balance marriage and being a student. It sounded like that's been quite a struggle lately.

*[The helper briefly summarizes what was discussed in the previous meeting. This sum-
mary establishes continuity between sessions and helps to immediately focus the discussion on an important topic. The summary helps to "get the ball rolling," so to speak.]*

Client: Yeah, I'd say so.

Helper (remains silent for a moment to see whether the client will continue): Would
you like to say more about that?

*[The helper invites the client to share more about her struggle with school and marriage.
Combined with the summary earlier, the invitation helps to get the session started. With
the client's brief response ("Yeah, I'd say so."), the client may have needed some encouragement to begin.]*

Client: Well, my life just seems so burdened right now. I got married last year, and I
started graduate school several months ago. It just takes so much time and energy to
make both work—to do homework and spend time with Chris. It feels like they both
require more time and energy than I have available.

Helper: You feel overwhelmed by the demands that both are making on you.

[The helper reflects the client's feelings. The client's words indicate feeling overburdened and overwhelmed and the helper demonstrates understanding of those feelings. Note that the helper adds some content ("by the demands that both are making on you") to provide context for the feeling.]

Client: Definitely. And I worry that both of them are going to fail because I'm not giving enough time to each one. (Helper nods and says, "Mm-hmm.") In fact, I've noticed that when I'm doing schoolwork, I'm constantly thinking that I should be spending time with Chris, and when I'm with Chris, I keep thinking that I should be studying.

[The helper's reflection encouraged the client to recognize and elaborate on her feelings—to provide more information. In addition to feeling overwhelmed, the client indicates that she is worried. Note that the helper also demonstrated attending (head nods) and used a verbal encourager ("Mm-hmm"), which showed that the helper was following the client's statements.]

Helper: It seems kind of like you're being pulled in two different directions and can't seem to fully commit to both school and the marriage. When you're doing one activity, you're focused on the other.

[The helper paraphrases the client's statement. The paraphrase shows that the helper understands the client. It also helps the client identify in a concrete, succinct, and specific manner the struggle she has been having—difficulty fully committing to school and her marriage.]

Client: Exactly. "Commit" is the word. It does feel hard to fully commit myself to both. (Helper nods and says, "Mm-hmm.")

[The client indicates that the paraphrase was accurate. The helper uses attending and a verbal encourager.]

Helper: How much time would you say you spend doing schoolwork each day?

Client: Probably about 4 hours, outside of class.

Helper: How much time do you spend with Chris each day?

Client: Maybe 1 hour.

[The helper has asked two closed questions here. The helper's goal was to elicit two specific pieces of information—how much time the client spends on schoolwork and how much time she spends with her husband. The client's responses are informative and important, but not content-rich. With this information, the helper can begin to see how the client manages her time. Note the pattern of interaction between the helper and client over the last few lines of dialogue. The helper asks a question; the client responds. If this ping-pong pattern continued for too long, their meeting might resemble a police interrogation more than a helping session. Such a pattern could also establish a style of *interaction in which the client speaks only in response to the helper's questions. For these reasons, as well as others, helpers balance asking questions with other skills, such as listening, silence, paraphrasing, and reflecting feelings.]*

Helper: What do the two of you do during the time you're together?

[The helper asks an open question.]

Client: Usually we just talk about the day. Sometimes, we have dinner together. That happens once or twice a week. Occasionally, we run an errand together, like grocery shopping. It's all pretty superficial and shallow.

[Note how the open question allows the client to respond as she chooses and gives the helper a lot of information—more than a closed question would.]

Helper: So you spend some time together and do some activities, but it's not quality time. It's not very meaningful.

[The helper paraphrases the client's previous statement to demonstrate that the helper understands it.]

Client: Yeah. There's no substance to it. Chris has even said a couple of times recently that it seems like the time we spend together is dull and boring. (Client pauses; her face contorts a little.) Those comments have made it really hit home that our marriage is starting to falter. It's not just my own perception. Chris doesn't seem to be very happy. That creates stress and makes it difficult for me to focus on school. So that's why everything seems on the verge of failing. It's a downward spiral that seems unstoppable. (Helper nods and says, "Mm-hmm.")

[Note how the paraphrase encouraged the client to continue speaking, thus providing more information to the helper. The paraphrase did not change the subject or alter the meaning. It stayed on the topic and prompted further disclosure by the client. Note again the use of attending and the verbal encourager.]

Helper: It sounds like you feel not only overwhelmed but maybe helpless as well, like there's nothing you can do.

[The helper reflects the client's feeling (helplessness). This feeling is a little deeper than "overwhelmed," which the helper reflected earlier. The helper has learned so far that the client not only feels the stress of being overwhelmed, she also feels powerless to do anything about her situation.]

Client (sighs): Yeah. It feels like things are out of control. I don't know what to do, but I know that something has to give.

Helper: What do you mean by "something has to give"?

[The helper asks a clarifying question. The purpose of this question is to understand more clearly what the client means by "something has to give." By itself, this statement is

vague and could have many meanings. The helper needs to ask the client to explain what she means.]

Client: I can't keep going on like this. I need things to change. And it seems like what's going to happen is I'm going to fail in school or get a divorce—or both. It just seems like that's the direction this is all headed.

In this dialogue, the verbal skills used by the helper permitted the helper to explore the client's concerns. Their use gave the helper a lot of information about the client's life and problems. By the end of the dialogue, the helper possessed a greater understanding of the client's struggle to balance graduate school and marriage.

Summary and Concluding Remarks

In this chapter, we discussed several verbal skills that helpers use to explore their clients' concerns: invitations, verbal encouragers, asking questions, paraphrasing, reflecting feelings, focusing, and summarizing. These skills build rapport, provide helpers with information, and facilitate an understanding of client problems. We also addressed some of the challenges in learning and practicing these skills. We believe that patience and openness to learning are key qualities for students and helpers to possess as they develop and hone their skills.

Questions for Thought

1. In your daily interactions with people, do you tend to ask a lot of questions? Which type of question, open or closed, do you ask more frequently? Do you tend to assume that you know what people are saying, or do you ask them to clarify their meaning when you are unsure?

2. How would you respond to someone who asserts that paraphrasing and reflecting feelings are unnecessary in helping because they merely reiterate what clients have just expressed?

3. In what situations might helpers summarize client statements and expressions? When do you find it useful to summarize in your interactions with people?

Exercises

The following exercises cover the skills discussed in this chapter. Many of these exercises require more than one person and thus may be useful as classroom exercises. If you do not have exercise partners available, we encourage you to read through the exercises that require more than one person and visualize how you might perform if you were doing the exercises with other people.

INVITATIONS EXERCISE

This role-play exercise requires two people: a helper and a client. The client should select a topic to discuss for a few minutes (e.g., academic goals, a relationship concern). The helper should focus on using invitations to begin the role play. The helper should also use invitations in places throughout the role play where the client seems to need encouragement to speak or where the helper would like the client to elaborate on something. After a few minutes of role-playing, the helper and client should stop and discuss how well invitations facilitated discussion in the role play. The exercise partners should then switch roles and repeat the exercise.

VERBAL ENCOURAGERS EXERCISE

EXERCISE 1: This exercise consists of two parts and requires two people: a helper and a client.

Part 1: The client should select a topic to role-play for 3 to 5 minutes (e.g., vocational goals, a relationship concern). The helper and client should then begin the role play. The helper can respond to the client and use skills described so far in this book, but he or she should *not* use any verbal encouragers. At the end of the allotted time period, the partners should discuss the role play. To what extent did *not* using verbal encouragers hurt communication? What impact did the nonuse of verbal encouragers have on the client? How easy or difficult was it *not* to use verbal encouragers?

Part 2: Now, the partners should repeat the exercise for another 3 to 5 minutes, but this time, the helper *should* use verbal encouragers. Either the same topic or a different topic may be used for the role play. At the end of the allotted time period, the partners should discuss the role play. To what extent did the verbal encouragers facilitate communication? What impact did their use have on the client? What differences did the partners notice between the two role plays? The partners should now switch roles and repeat both parts of the exercise.

ASKING QUESTIONS EXERCISES

EXERCISE 1: Three brief descriptions of client problems follow. For each one, write an open question, a clarifying question, and a closed question that a helper might ask to explore the client's problem. Examples of questions that a helper might ask for each description are provided at the end of this chapter.

Description 1:

A student is called in to see her guidance counselor about some academic concerns. Her grades have been slipping recently. She says, "I'm tired and don't have much interest in school."

Open question: _____

_____

_____

Clarifying question: _____

_____

_____

Closed question: _____

_____

_____

Description 2:

A man seeks help because his marriage appears to be headed for divorce. He does not want a divorce, but he thinks that divorce is inevitable and nothing he can do will stop it.

Open question: _____

_____

_____

Clarifying question: _____

_____

_____

Closed question: _____

_____

_____

Description 3:

A woman seeks counseling to address an eating problem. She is trying to lose weight but is having great difficulty succeeding. She says, "I feel like food calls out to me—begs me to 'come and get it.' I then go to the store and buy everything in sight."

Open question: _____

_____

_____

Clarifying question:_____

_____

_____

Closed question: _____

_____

_____

EXERCISE 2: This exercise requires three people: a helper, a client, and an observer. The client should select a topic to discuss (e.g., a relationship concern, academic goals). The helper and the client should conduct a role play on this topic for about 5 minutes. The helper may use any of the skills discussed up to this point in this book but should focus on asking good questions. The helper should also focus on asking questions appropriately (e.g., asking open questions as opposed to closed questions when encouraging the client to explore a topic). The observer's role is to note the questions asked and the responses they elicited. The observer should also note places where the helper could have asked a question but did not, as well as places where other skills or responses (e.g., silence) might have been more appropriate than questions. It may be helpful for the observer to write his or her observations on paper. When the role play is finished, each person should share his or her comments. What information did the helper gain from the questions he or she asked? What type of question did the helper ask most frequently—open or closed? What impact did the helper's questions have on the client? The exercise participants should switch roles and repeat the exercise often enough for each person to play each role.

PARAPHRASING EXERCISES

EXERCISE 1: Four client statements are presented in this exercise. In the space following each statement, write a response that paraphrases the client's statement. An example of a helper paraphrase of each client statement is provided at the end of this chapter.

Statement 1:

Client (talking to an academic advisor at her college): I'm starting to have second thoughts. I'm not sure that biology is for me.

Helper paraphrase: _____

_____

_____

Statement 2:

Client (talking about problems in a romantic relationship): Mark is always focused on his work. He seems to have very little time for me and what I need. I'm always second in line.

Helper paraphrase: _____

_____

_____

Statement 3:

Client (talking about a recent work session): We got a lot done at the meeting yesterday. It was very successful.

Helper paraphrase: _____

_____

_____

Statement 4:

Client (speaking about how he responds to other people): When people jerk me around, I call them every name I can think of. Nobody disrespects me and gets away with it.

Helper paraphrase: _____

_____

_____

EXERCISE 2: This exercise requires three people: a helper, a client, and an observer. The client should select a topic to discuss (e.g., academic goals, a relationship concern). The helper and the client should conduct a role play on this topic for about 5 minutes. The helper may use any of the skills discussed up to this point in this book, but the helper should focus on paraphrasing when responding to the client's statements. The observer should note the paraphrases used, what effect they had on the client, how well they promoted exploration of the client's concerns, and places where the helper might have used paraphrases but did not. It may be helpful for the observer to write his or her observations on paper. After 5 minutes, the three participants should stop and discuss the role play. What effect did the paraphrases have on the client? How well did they promote exploration of the client's concerns? Did they lead to greater understanding of the client's concerns? Did the paraphrases possess the characteristics of good paraphrases discussed in this chapter (e.g., focused on important topics, accurate, brief)? After each person has shared his or her observations, the participants should switch roles and repeat the exercise until each person has played each role.

REFLECTING FEELINGS EXERCISES

EXERCISE 1: Four client statements are presented in this exercise. In the space following each statement, write a response that reflects the feelings expressed in the statement. An example of a helper reflection for each client statement is provided at the end of this chapter.

Statement 1:
Client (face contorted; forceful, loud tone of voice): I don't understand why I didn't get that job! I deserved it more than any of those other incompetent applicants!

Helper reflection of feelings: _____

_____

_____

Statement 2:
Client (smiling; relaxed posture): I think the session went well yesterday. We got a lot done.

Helper reflection of feelings: _____

_____

_____

Statement 3:

Client (low emotional expression): Other people just don't seem to want to be around me that much. I keep to myself a lot now.

Helper reflection of feelings: _____

_____

_____

Statement 4:

Client (appears somewhat tense; taps his finger while speaking): I just know I'm going to mess up on the test tomorrow.

Helper reflection of feelings: _____

_____

_____

EXERCISE 2: This exercise requires at least two people. It may be done in small groups or in a classroom setting with the entire class. One person (the speaker) should describe an event or experience in life that had an emotional impact on him or her; however, the speaker should *not* directly state how he or she felt about the event or experience. The description should be brief—no longer than 1 minute. After the speaker describes the event or experience, the other people (the listeners) in the group or the class should try, one at a time, to identify and reflect the speaker's feelings about the event or experience. After a listener identifies and reflects a feeling, the speaker should say whether the listener is accurate. However, if the listener does not get the feeling right, the speaker should *not* say what the correct feeling is. Listeners should continue to try to identify and reflect the speaker's feelings until a listener does so accurately. If no one has correctly identified the feelings after all the listeners have had a turn, the speaker should say what he or she was feeling about the event or experience. Then, a new speaker should be selected and the exercise repeated. When everyone has had a chance to be the speaker, the group or the class should discuss the exercise. What did you learn about identifying and reflecting feelings? What did you learn about the different types and intensity levels of feelings? How easy or difficult was it for you to identify and reflect feelings?

EXERCISE 3: This exercise requires three people: a helper, a client, and an observer. The client should select a topic to discuss (e.g., academic concerns, a relationship issue). The helper and the client should conduct a role play on this topic for about 5 minutes. The helper may use any of the skills discussed up to this point in this book, but the helper should focus on reflecting feelings when responding to the client. The observer should note the reflections used, what effect they had on the client, and places where the helper could have used reflections but did not. It may be helpful for the observer to write his or her observations on paper. After 5 minutes, the participants should stop and discuss the role play. What effect did the reflections have on the client? How well did they promote exploration and understanding of the client's concerns? Were the reflections accurate? After each person has shared his or her observations, the participants should switch roles and repeat the exercise until each person has played each role.

FOCUSING EXERCISE

This exercise requires two people: a helper and a client. The client should select a topic to discuss (e.g., a relationship concern, vocational goals). The helper and the client should conduct a role play on this topic for 3 to 5 minutes. During the role play, the helper should, as needed, use the skill of focusing. As the client speaks, the helper can identify issues, statements, feelings, or expressions that he or she believes are confusing or particularly important. He or she should then use the skill of focusing to gather more information about these issues, statements, feelings, or expressions. After the role play, the partners should consider these questions: What additional information did the helper learn through focusing? How did using this skill aid the helper in understanding the client's concerns? Did the use of focusing aid the client in developing greater awareness? After completing the role play and addressing these questions, the partners should switch roles and repeat the exercise.

SUMMARIZING EXERCISES

EXERCISE 1: In this exercise, two client statements are presented. In the space following each statement, summarize what the client expressed. An example of a helper summary of each statement is provided at the end of this chapter.

Statement 1:
Client (gesturing nervously, speaking fairly quickly): Things are getting increasingly difficult at work. New policies and procedures have been put into place that have made my job more difficult. I've got tons more paperwork to fill out, and I feel like my boss is breathing down my neck to do it precisely according to procedures. I feel like if I make one little mistake, I'll be fired on the spot. I'm beginning to think that maybe I should start looking for another job. I just can't take it anymore. I don't need this. The job is okay, but it's not that great. I want to feel relaxed in my work.

Helper summary: _____

_____

_____

_____

_____

Statement 2:

Client (somewhat agitated): My wife Ann told me last week that she wants to get a divorce. After 20 years of marriage, she drops this bombshell. I didn't see it coming at all. And I had no reason to. She hasn't complained to me about anything. She hasn't said anything about wanting to go to marriage counseling or anything like that. We both have good jobs. The kids are happy. So why is she doing this? I don't know what to think or where to go from here. What's the next step? Is this what it all comes to after 20 years?

Helper summary: _____

_____

_____

_____

_____

EXERCISE 2: This exercise requires two people: a speaker and a listener. The speaker should select a topic (e.g., a recent vacation, vocational goals) and should talk about this topic for about 1 minute while the listener listens. The listener should be sure to pay attention to feelings, facts, thoughts, details, and experiences. When the speaker is finished, the listener should summarize what the speaker has said. After the listener finishes summarizing, the partners should discuss whether the listener's summary captured the important elements of the speaker's statements and expressions and whether the summary was accurate and complete. If it was not accurate or complete, what was inaccurate or left out? The partners should then switch roles and repeat the exercise.

Exercise Responses

Note that these responses are examples of good responses. They are not the only correct responses.

ASKING QUESTIONS EXERCISE

Description 1:
Open question: What do you believe is causing your lack of interest in school?
Clarifying question: What do you mean when you say that you are tired?
Closed question: Have you ever had academic problems in the past?

Description 2:
Open question: What would you do if a divorce occurred?
Clarifying question: Could you explain your reason for thinking that a divorce is inevitable?
Closed question: How long have you been married?

Description 3:
Open question: How have you tried to lose weight?
Clarifying question: What do you mean when you say that food calls out to you?
Closed question: What is your ideal weight?

PARAPHRASING EXERCISE

Statement 1 helper paraphrase: You're beginning to have doubts about pursuing biology.

Statement 2 helper paraphrase: I hear you saying that Mark's not paying enough attention to you.

Statement 3 helper paraphrase: It sounds like your meeting was very productive.

Statement 4 helper paraphrase: So you insult people who cross you.

REFLECTING FEELINGS EXERCISE

Statement 1 helper reflection of feelings: You're pretty angry about not getting hired.

Statement 2 helper reflection of feelings: You feel satisfied with how the session went.

Statement 3 helper reflection of feelings: It sounds like you feel lonely.

Statement 4 helper reflection of feelings: You're anxious about the test and how you'll do.

SUMMARIZING EXERCISE

Statement 1 helper summary: It sounds like you're feeling pretty stressed about your job and you feel anxious with all of the pressure put on you to do things right. It seems that all of this stress and anxiety are not worth it to you in the long run, so you're considering finding a job that would be more comfortable for you. Is that right?

Statement 2 helper summary: Let me make sure I'm following you. You thought things were going quite well. Then, Ann says she no longer wants to be married. It sounds like you're pretty shocked and confused because this came out of the blue and is so much at odds with how you thought your relationship was going. Now, you're searching for answers: Why is this happening? What do I do now? Is that right?

Promoting Client Understanding

CHAPTER 8

Striving Toward Honest Understanding

CHAPTER OVERVIEW

This chapter focuses on the process of promoting client understanding; that is, it describes how clients are helped to develop a thorough, honest awareness and understanding of themselves and their problems. In many cases, promoting understanding involves helping clients learn more about problems that they already recognize and know. Often, it involves helping clients recognize and understand issues that are outside of their awareness. Developing understanding can help clients take new perspectives, which is often an important aspect of problem management or resolution. Numerous topics are discussed in this chapter, including why helpers promote understanding, problems and behaviors that may be outside of client awareness, the process of promoting understanding, and points to consider about promoting understanding.

Everything can be taken from a man but one thing: the last of the human freedoms—to choose one's attitude in any given set of circumstances, to choose one's own way.

—Viktor Frankl (1963, p. 104)

Why Promote Understanding?

When clients fully and honestly understand their problems, they are in a better position to make positive changes. Indeed, Hanna and Ritchie (1995) found that developing insight or new understandings, confronting problems, and perceiving problems in new ways were potent and active ingredients in psychotherapeutic change.

The exploration process allows *helpers* to understand their clients' lives and problems. The next step is to help *clients* develop a good understanding. This understanding helps them take responsibility for their problems—what Carkhuff (2000) called "personalizing." As Carkhuff stated, "We facilitate personalized understanding when we assist the helpees in internalizing, or owning, the meaning of their experiences, their problems or deficits, and their goals or the assets they want and need" (p. 135).

The extent to which it is necessary or desirable to promote client understanding depends in large part on the client—his or her reasons for seeking help, cultural characteristics and values, motivation to take action, psychological sophistication, desire to understand, and ability to accurately identify and assess his or her problems. Most clients need help seeing aspects of their problems that are outside of their awareness, and they need help learning to see their problems and themselves in more productive ways. Promoting understanding, therefore, is often an important feature of helping. Rogers (1951) stated: "One of the most characteristic and perhaps one of the most important changes in therapy is the bringing into awareness of experiences of which heretofore the client has not been conscious" (p. 147).

What Clients Might Not See

Clients might not demonstrate a complete, honest understanding of themselves and their problems, which can make it difficult for them to set realistic goals and work for positive change. If understandings are inaccurate, related goals will probably be inappropriate. The following paragraphs describe some of the things that clients sometimes do not see and may need help seeing for accurate understanding.

Sources of Problems. Clients may not understand what is causing their problems. Identifying the source may be an important way to help clients understand their attitudes, feelings, behaviors, and experiences, put problems in proper perspective, and determine how to manage or resolve the problems. For example, a client who is overly critical of her children may feel more empowered to change her ways if she recognizes that her parents were overly critical of her, that she is responding in the way she was treated, and that she can change her response. As another example, a racial minority client might be better able to cope with feelings of low self-esteem and low self-confidence if he recognizes and understands the extent to which external factors, such as discrimination, contribute to his feelings. He can then focus on how to cope with the discrimination and challenge the belief that there is something wrong with him.

Relationships Between Feelings, Thoughts, Behaviors, and Experiences. Clients may need help seeing relationships between feelings, thoughts, behaviors, and experiences—that is, they may need help understanding what their feelings, thoughts, behaviors, and experiences mean and identifying how they affect one another. For example, a client may fail to recognize the relationship between being the sole survivor of a multi-car accident and currently engaging in excessive risk-taking behavior and having feelings of guilt. The helper may assist the client in understanding that these are common reactions to such an experience. As another example, a client struggling with alcoholism may need help seeing and accepting the relationship between his drinking and the negative turn of events in his life, such as losing his job.

Inconsistencies in Attitudes and Behaviors. Clients may express attitudes and demonstrate behaviors that appear inconsistent, such as smiling or laughing while describing very painful experiences. Lauver and Harvey (1997) observed that one way clients maintain inconsistencies is by keeping the different parts separate in their awareness. Compartmentalizing inconsistent attitudes and behaviors in this way prevents clients from confronting the inconsistent pieces. Helpers work with clients to connect and relate the pieces—to understand, for example, what smiling means when it occurs while discussing very difficult experiences.

Distorted or Inaccurate Perceptions. People have a need to understand things in their lives, and they often trust that their perceptions are accurate. Being able to understand and explain feelings, thoughts, behaviors, and experiences helps people feel a sense of control (Hill & O'Brien, 1999). Perceptions, however, may be distorted or inaccurate. For example, a client may feel that he is stupid because he received a low grade on a test or because a caregiver in his life referred to him in this way. In reality, these experiences do not indicate that he lacks intelligence. Clients may also selectively attend to details in their lives, screening out (or in some cases dwelling on) unpleasant material. In many cases, distortions and inaccuracies are due to fear and anxiety. That is, viewing problems honestly may create too much discomfort, so clients create less threatening explanations. For example, a student who has just moved 500 miles away from home to go to college may say to her parents that she made a big mistake and wants to come home—college is too expensive, her classes are too difficult, and she is having a hard time making friends. The student is uncomfortable and attributes her discomfort to factors that are less threatening and easier for her to accept than a more personally threatening reason: her fear and anxiety about being on her own, away from her parents for the first time in her life.

Transference. This topic could be discussed under "distorted or inaccurate perceptions," but we discuss it separately because of its importance in helping relationships. Helpers and clients have emotional reactions to each other as they interact. For example, a client may feel good about a positive comment made by his helper. Sometimes, the emotional reactions reflect inaccurate perceptions about the other person. Such reactions are known as transference when they come from clients and countertransference when they come from helpers. These phenomena were first described in psychoanalytic theory, and they are now widely recognized as significant aspects of helping relationships. In this chapter, we focus on transference. Countertransference is described in chapter 15.

Transference occurs when clients project onto helpers feelings or attitudes they have possessed toward important people in their lives, such as parents and relatives (Brammer & MacDonald, 2003; G. Corey et al., 2003). That is, clients displace emotional reactions from past relationships onto their helpers, and they erroneously see their helpers as exhibiting the attitudes, behaviors, and feelings that the significant people in earlier relationships exhibited (Gelso & Fretz, 2001). For example, a client who sees the helper as similar to his mother in terms of physical appearance and authority may respond to the helper in a manner similar to how he has responded to his mother. The client may also inaccurately see in the helper the same attitudes, behaviors, and feelings expressed by his mother (see Gelso & Fretz, 2001).

Transference likely occurs in most relationships, helping or otherwise (Gelso & Carter, 1985). However, it may be particularly significant and powerful in helping relationships. As noted by Gelso and Carter (1985), "The therapeutic situation . . . with its emphasis on a kind of controlled help-giving, magnifies and intensifies this natural reaction" (p. 169).

Whether the projected feelings are positive or negative, they represent distorted, erroneous ways of viewing helpers. Watkins (1983) identified five transference patterns (ways that clients distort helpers) in helping: (1) helper as ideal (perfect); (2) helper as seer (expert); (3) helper as nurturer (client plays the role of being dependent and helpless, needs care and soothing from the helper); (4) helper as frustrator (client is defensive and cautious, expects that the helper may frustrate what the client wants); and (5) helper as nonentity (helper has no needs, wishes, or problems).

Helpers react in various ways to transference (Watkins, 1983). They may feel competent and important when the transferred feelings are positive (e.g., affection, idealization). They may feel defensive and hostile when the feelings are negative (e.g., anger, hatred) (Watkins, 1983). It is important for helpers to identify transference when it occurs so that they can handle and address it appropriately with clients. However, identifying transference can be difficult, especially when the transferred feelings are positive. Helpers may be more inclined to accept such feelings as genuine, rather than see them as distortions (G. Corey et al., 2003). Helpers must be skilled at recognizing client emotions and distinguishing transference from legitimate responses to helper statements, expressions, and behaviors. They need to understand their own needs, motivations, and personal reactions and be prepared to assist their clients in developing awareness of transference (G. Corey et al., 2003).

Transference is not always addressed in the helping process. If it is fairly mild (e.g., the client idealizing the helper a little bit), it may not warrant attention. Helpers tend to focus on transference when it is very strong, interferes with or blocks the helping process, or is a key element of client problems (see Young, 2001). For example, if a client is transferring a great deal of anger onto the helper, causing difficulty in building a good helping relationship, the helper would likely address the transference. In addressing transference, the task is to help clients recognize transference, understand where the emotions are coming from, and take steps to develop more accurate and appropriate responses. This may be done with such skills as interpreting (see chapter 9), asking questions, reflecting feelings, and focusing. As long as significant transference occurs and is not worked through, clients may be stifled in their ability to grow.

Ineffective Attitudes and Behaviors. This general category may include most of the other categories discussed thus far. In many cases, problems continue to go unmanaged or unresolved because of ineffective attitudes and behaviors that prevent clients from addressing the problems in healthy, productive ways. For example, clients may insist on blaming other people for their problems or they may avoid confronting troubling issues. Some clients have never developed mature social skills. They communicate in the ineffective ways they learned and may not realize the effect of their behavior on other people. Clients often remain mired in these ineffective attitudes and behaviors until the attitudes and behaviors are brought into conscious awareness and corrected. Examples of ineffective attitudes and behaviors include

- avoiding problems with such behaviors as drinking or working excessively;
- reactive behavior, such as anger and aggression;
- blaming other people for problems;
- misinterpreting attitudes, feelings, behaviors, and experiences;
- projecting perspectives, attitudes, feelings, and behaviors onto other people;
- denying feelings or troubling experiences; and
- engaging in self-defeating attitudes and behaviors, such as negative self-talk.

Promoting Client Understanding

Broadly stated, promoting understanding involves helping clients

- increase self-awareness;
- accept responsibility for their attitudes, feelings, behaviors, and experiences;
- experience feelings;
- realistically and accurately appraise their strengths, assets, skills, and weaknesses;
- see aspects of problems that are outside of their awareness;
- view problems from a fresh perspective—that is, develop "a new way of perceiving" (Rogers, 1942, pp. 206–207); and
- develop a useful, accurate, honest, and thorough understanding of their problems.

With the attainment of understanding, clients may find that their problems lose the power to control and negatively affect their lives. Further, clients learn to accept themselves and feel free to choose more satisfying directions and goals in life (Rogers, 1942). Thus, understanding puts clients in a better position to set realistic goals and make positive changes.

The Challenge of Promoting Client Understanding

Promoting client understanding can be a challenging part of the helping process. Clients are often highly invested in their unique perspectives, attitudes, feelings, and behaviors. Although how they express themselves and live their lives may be ineffective in many ways, clients are used to these familiar patterns. It can be difficult to imagine life any other way with such deeply ingrained perspectives, attitudes, feelings, and behaviors.

When helpers promote client understanding, they are asking their clients to change. Effective helpers do not impose their own views or values on their clients or tell their clients what their problems are. They assist clients by challenging them to confront feelings, fears, attitudes, and behaviors that they have avoided, to increase their self-awareness, to develop a more honest understanding of their problems, and to consider their problems from new perspectives. This is not an adversarial process. Helpers encourage their clients to change while also supporting them within the safe environment of the helping relationship. Indeed, this "challenge/support" balance is what promotes change (see, e.g., Skovholt & Rønnestad, 1995). Nevertheless, change involves the often scary process of exploring the unknown, so it can increase discomfort and anxiety.

Efforts to promote understanding represent a challenge to the client's world as he or she knows it. What clients have known to be true about their lives and problems is now being questioned. Clients may respond defensively or angrily to the helper's efforts. They may not easily abandon the perspectives, attitudes, and behaviors that have become so familiar to them.

The Process of Promoting Client Understanding

Promoting client understanding starts with the development of good helping relationships, which are characterized by empathy, unconditional positive regard, genuineness, and trust (see, e.g., Hill & O'Brien, 1999; Rogers, 1942). Think about your own interactions with people. You probably find it easier to accept someone commenting on things that appear to be outside of your awareness when that person is a good friend as opposed to a stranger. Your friend has earned the privilege of entering your life and sharing observations with you. Because of the established relationship, you know that your friend's comments emanate from support and a desire to help rather than from criticism. The same is true in helping. When good helping relationships have been established, clients are more likely to increase their self-awareness, entertain new perspectives, and see the helpers' efforts to promote understanding as supportive rather than presumptuous and disrespectful. When promoting understanding, helpers may be shaking up the client's world, so they need to approach this process delicately, within good relationships.

Before attempting to promote understanding, helpers need to make sure that they have thoroughly explored the client's concerns and that they understand those concerns (Hill & O'Brien, 1999). After all, it is difficult for helpers to promote understanding of something that they do not fully understand. Much information-gathering typically occurs before helpers try to promote understanding. This information-gathering maximizes the ability of helpers to accurately identify client concerns, observe patterns in client behaviors, see aspects of problems that clients do not appear to recognize, and draw conclusions. By demonstrating their understanding of the problems that clients describe (e.g., through paraphrasing and reflecting feelings), helpers may earn the privilege of exploring further and assisting clients in seeing aspects of problems that are outside of their awareness.

At this point in the helping process, helpers—if we use our ocean metaphor— begin deep-sea diving, probing at greater depths than before. In doing so, they may open up new topics for discussion and encourage clients to share thoughts, feelings, and experiences that they were reluctant to share earlier. As clients begin to look beyond their familiar, ineffective attitudes and behaviors, they may experience new feelings. For example, a client who expresses anger and resentment toward his ex-fiancée for breaking off their marriage may begin to cry if the helper suggests that the client feels hurt by the loss of an important relationship. The client may respond defensively and dismiss the suggestion, or he may be open to bringing new feelings into awareness and exploring them. As the client develops a more honest understanding of his situation, he becomes better positioned to manage it in a healthy manner.

Helpers strive to promote both intellectual and emotional understanding (Gelso & Fretz, 2001; Hill & O'Brien, 1999). Intellectual understanding provides an objective explanation for problems. By itself, intellectual understanding may be merely a logical, cognitive, abstract awareness that is insufficient to motivate change. In contrast, emotional understanding connects affect to intellect and creates a sense of personal involvement and personal responsibility for problems (Gelso & Fretz, 2001; Hill & O'Brien, 1999). Indeed, Rogers (1942, 1951) contended that "insight" substantially arises out of being able to accept and express emotions. In the helping process, emotional understanding involves experiencing feelings. The feelings reflect the client's own subjective experiences, not an objective, academic explanation. It is one thing to *know* that one is happy, angry, or sad; it is another thing to *feel* happy, angry, or sad. Greenberg and Safran (1987) wrote: "If a client accesses a thought in a vivid fashion and the response is affectively laden, we know the client is truly experiencing what is being said rather than abstractly hypothesizing something. It is this type of experiential processing that is important in therapy in general" (p. 192).

Young (2001) described the following steps that helpers may take to increase emotional awareness in clients. First, helpers observe client attempts to move away from or avoid emotions. They note avoidance behaviors, such as changing the subject or fidgeting, and they point out nonverbal behaviors that might indicate emotions, such as eye movement or bodily tension. Second, helpers stop the movement away from the emotions and encourage clients to focus on the emotions. They may ask clients what they are feeling right now. Third, helpers invite clients to become aware of the emotions—to explore their meaning and express them. Finally, helpers challenge clients to follow through and act on what they have learned from expressing the emotions.

Emotional understanding gives clients the sense that significant, core issues are being addressed and that the helping process is working (Greenberg & Safran, 1987; Young, 2001). Emotional understanding is important for another reason as well. When clients allow themselves to experience emotions, their defenses tend to go down to some degree. Clients become less resistant to change, so new attitudes and behaviors often can be instilled.

To promote client understanding, helpers use various skills, such as providing constructive feedback, confronting, and interpreting. These skills are described in the next chapter.

Developing honest understandings can be difficult and uncomfortable for clients. They are charting new territory. They need time to digest new information and awarenesses. They also need helper support as they experience new emotions. But when clients begin to develop new understandings of themselves and their problems, they often experience a feeling of hope that their lives can change. They become aware of a sense of "movement" and feel they are getting out of a rut that they have been in (Rogers, 1951). This can be revitalizing and motivating for clients. Their unsolvable problems begin to look solvable. As clients develop some degree of understanding, they and their helpers can begin to identify goals and actions and take steps to make positive changes.

We conclude this section with an important point, which is that the development of understanding is a continuous process. Understanding comes with hard work and honest exploration of one's attitudes, feelings, and behaviors, and it often requires time and patience. Understanding usually comes in layers or plateaus and does not always proceed in an orderly fashion or at a constant pace (J. Dagley, personal communication, May 23, 2002). Furthermore, understanding is not a final state that one achieves in life. People are always learning and growing. Clients may reach a point at which they possess sufficient understanding to set realistic goals and take action for positive change, but that does not mean they no longer work to understand themselves. Understanding may continue for a lifetime. As noted by J. Dagley (personal communication, May 23, 2002), "Promoting client understanding is by nature a process, not a destination. One doesn't understand one's self once and for all."

An Example of Promoting Client Understanding

The following example shows how a helper might promote client understanding.

Marcus is having trouble making friends. He feels angry and says that people ignore him and demonstrate no interest in being around him. While exploring Marcus's problem, the helper learns that Marcus spends much of his time watching television and playing video games at home. When he does go out, he rarely speaks to anyone and tends to engage in fairly solitary activities, such as going to movies by himself. He rarely makes an effort to approach anyone. On occasions when someone invites Marcus to socialize, Marcus makes excuses for why he is unavailable. The helper notes to herself that it does not appear to be other people who are ignoring Marcus but rather Marcus is ignoring other people by isolating himself. He appears to be projecting his own attitudes and behaviors onto other people, blaming them for his lack of a social life.

When the helper has sufficient information and a good relationship has been established, she shares her observations and uses various skills, such as providing constructive feedback and confronting (discussed in chapter 9), to help Marcus see that he appears to be the one who is ignoring people, not the other way around, and that he has established a pattern of isolating himself from others. The helper suggests that Marcus's anger could be a way of expressing underlying sadness about being isolated and not knowing how to meet people.

Marcus may deny the helper's statement. If he does, the helper would explore the reasons for Marcus's denial, consider other possible explanations for Marcus's situation (because the helper may have been wrong), or decide to address the issue at a later time.

Alternatively, Marcus may accept the helper's ideas as accurate. He may come to see the ineffectiveness of his own behaviors, such as isolating himself, and realize that he is ignoring others, not the other way around. Yet Marcus's new intellectual understanding of the helper's point, by itself, may not be sufficient motivation for Marcus to make positive changes. Marcus feels angry, which suggests that there is a significant emotional component that he needs to recognize. As noted earlier, the helper may suggest that Marcus is ignoring other people and that he may be feeling hurt and sad. If Marcus appears to be holding in emotions (e.g., based on his non-verbal behavior), the helper may point that out and ask what he is feeling. Although Marcus may continue to deny feeling hurt or sad, with the helper's support, patience, and empathy, he may begin to experience sadness and express his underlying pain about being lonely and isolated. This emotional understanding would emanate from within him, not from the helper, thus making it a powerful experience.

With these intellectual and emotional understandings, Marcus would possess a more useful and accurate understanding of himself and his problems. He would then be able to focus his attention on setting realistic, positive goals for change.

Two Important Points to Consider About Promoting Client Understanding

Helpers should keep the following points in mind.

Consider the Motivation of Clients to Develop Understanding of Themselves and Their Problems. The extent to which helpers focus on and promote client understanding in the helping process depends largely on the clients. Hill and O'Brien (1999) noted that some clients do not need or want insight into their problems. They want support or immediate behavior change and are not interested in understanding why they feel, think, or behave the way they do. With these clients, helpers may try to determine the reasons why the clients do not want to develop understanding. If clients are protecting themselves from issues that they are afraid to acknowledge, helpers may, at some point, confront the clients. If clients ultimately choose not to develop understanding, helpers can try to provide what the clients do want, such as referrals or assistance in making behavior changes, with minimal focus on promoting understanding (Hill & O'Brien, 1999).

It is possible for people to make changes in behavior with little understanding. Many proponents of behavioral theory assert that understanding is not necessary for behavior change and that, in fact, behavior change may lead to understanding (D. W. Sue & Sue, 2003). According to Rogers's (1942) model of helping, insight leads to action, and action leads to further insight.

Take Cultural Variables Into Account. Helpers need to be knowledgeable about client cultures. They also need to understand how their own cultural perspectives may differ from those of their clients. Failure to consider culture can lead to inappropriate and unhelpful attempts to promote understanding. For example, a Western-oriented helper assisting an Asian American client who is concerned about receiving his parents' approval may see the client as being overly enmeshed in his family. However, the helper's understanding would probably be inaccurate in light of the client's culture, in which collectivist values and family connections tend to be emphasized more so than in Western society. If the helper were to encourage the client to see her viewpoint, the client may feel uncomfortable and insulted and perceive the helping process as irrelevant.

D. W. Sue and Sue (2003) observed that although developing understanding, or insight, is often a significant part of Western-oriented helping processes, it is not highly valued in all cultures. They noted, for example, that people in some Asian cultures deal with unpleasant emotions, such as anger, anxiety, and frustration, by not thinking about them and by occupying their time with other activities. The belief is that thinking about these feelings too much may actually cause problems.

Another important cultural variable to consider is social class. Clients of lower social class may be less interested than those of higher social class in developing understanding. Because clients of lower social class are often concerned with trying to satisfy basic survival needs, they may see efforts to promote understanding as inappropriate or undesirable (D. W. Sue & Sue, 2003). When one is struggling to survive, the promotion of understanding may seem too abstract, impractical, and unimportant. Clients of lower social class may be more interested in learning how to access resources, such as child support, emergency housing, medical assistance, or unemployment benefits. They often want information, suggestions, and advice (see D. W. Sue & Sue, 2003).

Summary and Concluding Remarks

Martin (2000) observed that "the natural aftermath of exploration is understanding, as the client clears away the fog by facing it and grappling with it. New ideas start coming; new solutions to old problems become apparent; the person feels a new strength and knows him- or herself better" (p. 75). Promoting client understanding is the process of helping clients see themselves and their problems from new, healthier perspectives. In most cases, clients need to recognize the ineffectiveness of their current ways of functioning and develop a thorough, honest, meaningful understanding of themselves and their problems before they can set realistic goals for change.

Understanding can occur fairly quickly. In a moment of insight or clarity, clients may suddenly seem to "get it." In many cases, however, understanding is a more gradual process that occurs over time. Rogers (1942) contended that "insight comes gradually, bit by bit, as the individual develops sufficient psychological strength to endure new perceptions" (p. 177). Helpers use several skills to promote client understanding, including asking questions, reflecting implied cognitive content, and reflecting feelings. Six additional skills for promoting understanding are described in chapter 9: providing constructive feedback, confronting, providing information, interpreting, self-disclosing, and immediacy.

Questions for Thought

1. Why do many clients resist change and cling to ineffective attitudes and behaviors?

2. How do helpers and clients know when some degree of understanding (intellectual and emotional) has been achieved?

3. What challenges and risks might helpers encounter as they try to promote client understanding? How might helpers deal with these challenges and risks?

CHAPTER 9

Skills for Promoting Client Understanding

CHAPTER OVERVIEW

Helpers use a number of skills to promote client understanding, including some of the skills discussed in previous chapters. We will briefly revisit three of the more significant ones here: asking questions, reflecting implied cognitive content, and reflecting feelings. In addition, helpers use six skills that we have not described yet: providing constructive feedback, confronting, providing information, interpreting, self-disclosing, and immediacy. These skills, which are discussed in this chapter, help clients develop awareness and new perspectives, see options and possibilities, identify their strengths and assets, take responsibility for their feelings, thoughts, and behaviors, and develop a more thorough understanding of their problems. A hypothetical dialogue and several exercises to facilitate understanding of these skills are included at the end of this chapter.

I can see clearly now; the rain is gone.

—Johnny Nash (1972)

Previously Described Skills

Asking Questions

Helpers can use questions to help clients develop understanding. For example, if clients are reluctant to express themselves, especially when discussing difficult topics, questions can be used to give them "permission" to address those topics (e.g., "What's going on inside you when you hear your parents arguing?"). By talking about the issues—sounding them out—the clients may arrive at their own understandings. Questions can also be helpful as a way to encourage clients to think about their problems from new perspectives (e.g., "What are some other possible reasons why you didn't get the job?"). Further, questions can be used to inquire about client feelings and to encourage clients to explore those feelings (e.g., "What are you feeling right now as we're talking about your divorce?").

Reflecting Implied Cognitive Content

As discussed in chapter 7, clients do not always directly and explicitly state what is going on in their lives. There may be implied messages in their statements and expressions that helpers may sense. Sometimes, the implied content is kept out of the clients' conscious awareness because the clients are afraid to confront it directly. Both helpers and clients can come to a more useful understanding of client problems when such content is made explicit and explored. Here is an example:

Client: My job is so tiresome. I do the same thing day after day with no change in routine and no chance for advancement. It's a dead-end position.

Helper: It sounds like you'd rather have a different job.

The helper makes explicit what she believes is implied in the client's statement. Note that the response does not just feed back what the client said in different words, as in paraphrasing. The helper goes beyond the words the client stated and reflects what the client seems to be suggesting. Hearing the helper explicitly say what he is suggesting may encourage and empower the client to explore and seriously consider what he wants. He may start thinking more explicitly about leaving his current, undesirable position and finding a new job.

Reflecting Feelings

This skill can promote client understanding by encouraging clients to recognize, express, and focus on their feelings. Reflecting feelings gives a name to the clients' affective experiences. When clients recognize and explore their feelings, they may develop a greater understanding of those feelings. An example of reflecting feelings is, "It seems that you're very hurt by Amy's comments. Is that what you're feeling?"

Six New Skills

The following six skills—providing constructive feedback, confronting, providing information, interpreting, self-disclosing, and immediacy—can have a powerful effect in promoting client understanding. They are very useful skills; however, some of them are controversial because while they can lead to understanding, they can also be provocative. They can even be harmful if used inappropriately. Although these six skills may be used as needed at any point in helping, helpers usually use them after good helping relationships have been established and after they have developed and demonstrated an understanding of their clients' concerns (see, e.g., Hill & O'Brien, 1999). Under these circumstances, clients are more likely to be receptive to these skills.

The six new skills should also be used in moderation. Whereas the skills that you have encountered so far in this book, such as attending, listening, silence, asking questions, and reflecting feelings, are the "bread-and-butter" skills of helpers, the six new skills discussed in this chapter can be described as "salt-and-pepper" skills. They are most effective when used in moderate amounts. They "season" the helping process, enhancing its quality.

Providing Constructive Feedback

Providing feedback involves helpers offering their observations, opinions, impressions, and reactions to their clients. It also involves helpers discussing with clients their performance on activities such as tests and role plays. Through feedback, clients learn how they affect and appear to other people as well as how well they have performed particular tasks. In these ways, among others, this skill promotes understanding. Feedback may be provided at the request of clients or on the helpers' own initiative.

Much of helping involves providing feedback in some form. For example, reflecting feelings involves helpers feeding back the feelings that clients appear to be expressing. Even helpers' nonverbal behaviors can be forms of feedback. A smile or a grimace, for example, may reflect how something the client has said or done affects the helper.

Effective helpers do not merely provide feedback; they provide *constructive* feedback. Constructive feedback addresses specific client attitudes and behaviors, is offered in response to both effective and ineffective client attitudes and behaviors, and is provided when clients are ready and willing to receive it. These points and other criteria for constructive feedback are discussed in more detail later in this chapter. In their daily lives and relationships, clients may receive very little constructive feedback for either effective or ineffective behavior. People in the clients' lives may feel it is not their place to provide feedback. When feedback is provided on ineffective behavior, it is commonly of poor quality. Poor feedback is nonspecific and is presented in an unsupportive way. Examples include "You're too self-absorbed" and "You're not a very good listener." Such feedback comes across as an insult and can evoke defensiveness or withdrawal. It does not seem to emanate from a sense of concern or a desire to be helpful.

With regard to feedback on effective behavior—or positive feedback—people often do not provide it because it seems unnecessary. The underlying assumption is that if other people are doing things well, they are doing what is expected, probably already know it, and do not need to be told about the quality of their behavior. In reality, however, people have a need for positive reinforcement. It makes them feel good, and it encourages the continued expression of effective attitudes and behaviors. In short, people need to know when they are doing things well, and they need to know, in a supportive and respectful manner, when their attitudes and behaviors are ineffective and may need to change.

The Nature of Constructive Feedback

As noted, constructive feedback addresses effective as well as ineffective attitudes and behaviors. "Positive" constructive feedback focuses on client strengths and effective attitudes and behaviors. It not only helps to reinforce those strengths, attitudes, and behaviors, but it also helps clients recognize that they are capable people, not merely a collection of problems and ineffective attitudes and behaviors. An example of positive constructive feedback is: "You have a strong voice. You articulate well and clearly ask for what you want."

When helpers provide constructive feedback on ineffective attitudes and behaviors and other areas for improvement, their feedback is not intended as an attack, a negative judgment, an insult, or a criticism. It is provided to help clients become aware of attitudes and behaviors that may make it difficult for them to obtain things they want in life. Often, helpers not only address the ineffectiveness of the attitude or behavior, but they also provide guidance and options for ways to change and improve. In these cases, the feedback is referred to as "corrective." An example of corrective feedback is: "When you get nervous, you tend to talk a lot and speak very rapidly. The people around you may want to tune you out. How about if you try to speak slower and focus more on what the other person is saying?"

The Value of Providing Constructive Feedback

The value of constructive feedback in the helping process is that it helps clients

- develop awareness of how they are seen by people and how their attitudes and behaviors affect others;
- recognize and continue to express effective attitudes and behaviors;
- become aware of ineffective attitudes and behaviors and areas for improvement;
- grow and develop as people by encouraging modification of ineffective attitudes and behaviors;
- learn how to engage in "self-feedback," in which clients monitor their own attitudes and behaviors, recognize how other people respond, and make adjustments (Hutchins & Cole Vaught, 1997); and
- learn an effective communication skill (clients themselves learn how to give and receive constructive feedback).

Points and Guidelines for Providing Constructive Feedback

Select an Appropriate Way to Provide Feedback. Most often, feedback is provided verbally by helpers. Sometimes, however, feedback is provided by having clients listen to audiotapes or watch videotapes of all or part of a helping session (Hutchins & Cole Vaught, 1997). Because most people are not accustomed to hearing or seeing themselves on tape, simply listening and watching can be a fresh and interesting experience and can help clients realize how other people see them. The content of the tapes can also be discussed. For example, the tapes may be stopped as needed to address particular statements, behaviors, or situations.

Recognize Cultural Variables. Feedback needs to be culturally appropriate. For example, if a client is from a culture that values emotional control, the helper probably would not say, "You seem to be holding back a lot. It would help if you were more expressive and assertive." Also, with all clients, but especially with culturally different clients, it is important for helpers to ascertain how their feedback was received. What did the client hear? How did he or she interpret the feedback? This point is addressed later in this chapter in more detail.

Time Feedback Appropriately. Feedback is most effective when it is provided soon after the event that prompts the feedback, while the event is still fresh in the client's mind. Feedback loses its impact and relevance the longer helpers wait.

Ask Clients Whether They Are Willing to Receive Feedback. For feedback to be effective, clients must be ready and willing to receive it. Helpers may introduce feedback with a question such as, "Can I give you some feedback?" Clients may say yes or no. If clients say no, helpers should respect their wishes. Feedback that is provided when clients do not want it will probably not be heard.

Provide Feedback (Especially Corrective Feedback) in a Supportive Manner. Helpers provide feedback to promote awareness and understanding, not to hurt or criticize. A respectful, steady tone of voice, carefully chosen words, and good eye contact increase the likelihood that clients will accept the feedback and reduce the likelihood of a defensive response. A loud, commanding tone and strong language can sound harsh and critical. Helpers do not want to come off sounding as if they are saying, "You know what your problem is?"

Focus on Behavior and Other Things That Can Be Changed. Brammer and MacDonald (2003), as well as many other authors, have stressed that constructive feedback focuses on behavior, not on people. Thus, a helper might say, for example, "When you yell at people and get in their faces, it may cause them to become defensive. It feels intimidating and disrespectful." This statement has a better chance of being accepted and promoting client understanding than, "You're mean," which is a judgmental comment that focuses on the client rather than on his or her behavior. Constructive feedback should also focus on changeable behaviors rather than on aspects of clients that may be very hard to change, if they can be changed at all (e.g., physical characteristics) (Brammer & MacDonald, 2003).

Be Clear, Concise, and Specific. Clients need to know exactly what attitudes and behaviors are being addressed. A poor feedback statement might be, "You seem unprepared today." This statement is a general conclusion that does not give the client enough information about what the ineffective behavior is or what to do about it. As a result, the client might feel anxious and confused and dwell on trying to figure out what the helper meant. The client also might ask the helper for clarification. A better statement might be, "You didn't seem ready for our session today because you hadn't done any of the exercises that we talked about last time. Maybe a different strategy would be a good idea." Feedback statements should also be fairly short so clients can digest what is said. Providing too much feedback at once can overwhelm clients and make it difficult for them to remember and process everything that is said.

Make the Feedback Meaningful. Constructive feedback typically involves more than just saying something like, "You're twiddling your thumbs right now" or "You're speaking very fast." One can imagine a client responding with, "Okay, I'm speaking very fast. So what?" Merely pointing out a behavior does not explain why the comment is being made. If clients are not aware of their behaviors, statements that identify the behaviors may be the starting point for feedback, but good, constructive feedback often adds an observation or insight. An example is, "You're speaking very fast. It's hard to follow what you're saying when you talk at that rate. People might get frustrated and stop listening. Try slowing down a little and see what that's like."

Provide Feedback in a Balanced Way. Clients benefit from feedback that addresses effective attitudes and behaviors as well as from feedback that addresses ineffective attitudes and behaviors. Providing only positive feedback ignores areas in which clients may need to change or improve. Too much feedback on ineffective attitudes and behaviors can seem overly critical and cause clients to feel that there is nothing positive about them. Often, it is a good idea to provide positive feedback first.

Discuss the Feedback With Clients. One of the most important aspects of providing feedback is ascertaining client responses and reactions to the feedback. This is particularly important when working with culturally different clients, who may have very different understandings than their helpers about why specific feedback has been provided. Often, helpers ask a question such as, "What do you think about that?" as a way to begin a discussion about the feedback and the attitudes and behaviors that are the subject of the feedback.

The following is an actual event that demonstrates how important it is to discuss feedback. A supervisor scheduled individual meetings with his employees for their annual performance reviews. One of the employees was a Somali woman whose work performance was exemplary. During the meeting, the supervisor gave the woman positive feedback about her work and then provided some corrective feedback, which is common in American workplaces. The woman listened politely and carefully. The supervisor never asked for her reactions to the feedback. After the review, the woman left and did not return to work. A few days later, the supervisor, somewhat puzzled, called the woman and asked why she had not been coming to work. The woman responded, "Because you fired me." The woman thought the corrective feedback meant that she was not doing her job well and that she was being terminated. She thought the supervisor's initial positive feedback was provided merely to soften the blow. The miscommunication was resolved and the woman came back to work.

However, discussing the feedback and ascertaining how it was heard and interpreted during the performance review might have avoided this significant misunderstanding.

Confronting

Confronting involves helpers pointing out inconsistencies, distortions, and contradictions in client expressions, behaviors, perspectives, and circumstances (see Ivey & Authier, 1978). Often, clients do not seem to recognize these incongruities. They may lack awareness or they may be trying to avoid the incongruities because they are too distressing, painful, or anxiety provoking. Confronting helps to make the incongruities explicit so clients can recognize and understand them. As noted in Sommers-Flanagan and Sommers-Flanagan (1999), "The goal of confrontation is to help clients perceive themselves and reality more clearly" (p. 107).

To many people, the word "confronting" suggests contention, antagonism, or hostility. In the helping process, confronting is not at all intended to be adversarial or contentious. Effective helpers always remain allies with their clients. When they use this skill, they do so to promote awareness, growth, and change, not to punish, criticize, blame, or hurt their clients.

The Nature of Incongruities

Incongruities can be manifested in numerous ways. Clients express themselves through feelings, statements, attitudes, beliefs, verbal behaviors, and nonverbal behaviors—any one of which may conflict with another. For example, a statement might conflict with nonverbal behavior (e.g., saying one is angry while smiling), or two statements might be in conflict (e.g., a client saying that she is pleased with a job interview she just had but shortly thereafter saying that she is disappointed with how it went).

Incongruities may also exist between

- client perceptions and reality (e.g., a client believing that nobody likes her when, in reality, she has many friends);
- client perspectives and other people's perspectives;
- client goals and behavior;
- what clients are and what they wish to be (see Egan, 2002).

Phrasing Confrontations

Confrontations are often phrased in a "you say . . . but . . ." format. Carkhuff (1983) suggested a "milder" format: "On the one hand, you say/feel/do _____, while on the other hand, you say/feel/do _____." This format is a little less "hard-hitting" than the "you say . . . but . . ." format because it does not contain the word "but," which bluntly indicates that a contradiction exists. Clients may respond less defensively when helpers "ease into" addressing incongruities. Confrontations can also be phrased as questions, such as, "How do you believe your grades will improve if you don't go to class and make an effort to study more?"

The following are some examples of confronting. For each one, note the incongruity that is being observed (e.g., conflict between a statement and a behavior).

"You said earlier that you were pleased with how the interview went, but now you're saying you're disappointed with it."

"You say that you're angry, but you're smiling as you speak."

"On the one hand, you want your son to be independent, while on the other hand, you wish that he would stay at home and live with you."

"You blame yourself for not getting a job at Acme, but the company was not hiring."

The Value of Confronting

The value of confronting in the helping process is that it helps clients

- develop awareness of incongruities that may be interfering with honest understanding;
- examine their current perspectives and prepare to consider new ones;
- develop increased self-awareness;
- more deeply explore feelings, thoughts, behaviors, and experiences;
- integrate the various parts of themselves and their experiences; and
- learn how to monitor their feelings, thoughts, and behaviors and explore incongruities on their own.

Points and Guidelines for Confronting

Be Careful About Imposing Perspectives on Clients. In the helping process, confronting involves helpers pointing out things that appear inconsistent or discrepant. Some authors believe that this gives too much weight to helpers' notions of what is inconsistent or discrepant. Lauver and Harvey (1997), for example, asserted that "what needs to be confronted in those instances when we perceive discrepant counselee behavior is our own ignorance" (p. 87). They maintained that all client behavior is logical in the moment and that confronting, which they call "collegial confrontation," should focus on helper confusion about something helpers perceive as discrepant. It should not focus on persuading clients to come around to helper viewpoints. Collegial confrontation may involve saying, for example, "I'm confused right now. I'm wondering what it must be like to express such anger toward your parents while laughing about the situation at the same time." Here, the helper is confronting his or her own confusion about a perceived discrepancy. The helper and the client can then collaboratively examine and explore the client's expressions and come to understand them together. According to Lauver and Harvey (1997), the more conventional form of confrontation ("you say . . . but . . .") assumes the validity and superiority of helper viewpoints and could come across as arrogant and presumptuous.

Helpers need to decide for themselves how to confront their clients. In all cases, they need to carefully examine their own perceptions about what constitutes an inconsistency or a discrepancy and ensure that they do not impose their perspectives on their clients.

Recognize Cultural and Individual Variables. People from relatively outspoken cultural groups, such as European Americans and African Americans, may respond more favorably than people from other cultural groups to confrontations presented in a direct, candid manner (Ivey & Ivey, 1999). People from cultures that place more emphasis on subtlety, such as Asian Americans, Latinos/Latinas, and Native Americans, may find direct confrontations to be offensive and disrespectful (Ivey & Ivey, 1999). With these clients, a gentler approach may be needed. Phrasing confrontations in the ways described earlier by Carkhuff (1983) and Lauver and Harvey (1997) may be helpful with clients from these cultural groups.

Lauver and Harvey's (1997) perspective on confrontation also has another important cultural implication. When confrontation is viewed by helpers as a way to confront their own ignorance, and phrased accordingly, the helpers may be more inclined to seize the opportunity to learn more about their clients and cultural differences. Understanding—by both helpers and clients—may be facilitated. The more forceful "you say . . . but . . ." format may discourage clients from trying to explain their behavior, and it may cause them to feel that they are doing something wrong.

Individual differences must also be recognized. For example, passive, sensitive clients may prefer fewer or gentler confrontations, whereas clients with stronger personalities may respond better to more direct confrontations (Ivey & Ivey, 1999). Substance abusers and males who act out may need or respond better to assertive, direct confrontations as opposed to softer ones (Ivey & Ivey, 1999; Sommers-Flanagan & Sommers-Flanagan, 1999).

Confront Clients on Positive Aspects, Too. Confronting should not be used only to dwell on the negative. It should also be used to help clients recognize their strengths, resources, and assets (Evans, Hearn, Uhlemann, & Ivey, 1998). Thus, confronting can reinforce clients, reminding them of their abilities (e.g., "You say you're not going to do well at the swim meet, but you've taken first place at all three meets so far this year.").

Confront in a Sensitive and Prudent Manner. Some helpers shy away from confronting because they worry that it may be too threatening, hurtful, or offensive to their clients. They may also worry about arousing client anger. Indeed, confronting is one of the most potentially provocative skills that helpers use because it can put clients on the spot. It is difficult to dismiss inconsistencies and discrepancies once they are pointed out. To maximize the chances that clients will be receptive to confronting, helpers need to consider a few points. First, they should avoid hostility. Effective confrontations are often presented in a tentative manner, which may be expressed through a soft tone of voice or through phrases such as, "I'm wondering about some things you've said . . . ." Presenting confrontations in this way is more likely to have the desired effect of encouraging client awareness and exploration of the incongruities. Even confrontations that are more blunt and direct should be offered in the spirit of support and understanding, not contention. Second, helpers should confront in moderation. When used too often, even if offered tentatively, confronting may create a frustrating, hostile environment in which clients feel highly scrutinized. Third, helpers should confront at the right time. If clients seem receptive to exploring their concerns and if they seek understanding, confrontation may be appropriate. However, helpers often refrain from confronting when clients demonstrate high levels of stress, agitation, or anger because confronting at such times may amplify these feelings and harm helping relationships.

Be Clear, Concise, and Specific. Confrontations should clearly, concisely, and specifically describe the incongruities observed. For example, a helper should not merely say, "You're sending mixed signals here." This statement is unspecific and does not promote awareness and understanding. The client may be unclear about what the mixed signals are. Instead, the helper might say, "You say you want to graduate, but you're not studying or going to class." Specific statements allow clients to clearly see incongruities.

Present the Incongruities and Nothing More. Confrontations should not contain speculation, criticism, judgments, labels, or solutions. Helpers should simply present the incongruities for clients to consider. Clients then have the opportunity to recognize, ponder, and respond to the incongruities in their own way. Helpers and clients can explore together the meaning of the incongruities.

Discuss the Confrontations With Clients. It is important to ascertain client responses and reactions to confrontations. The skills of listening, taking notice, and asking questions are important here. Client reactions can range from defensiveness and denial to acceptance, depending on the accuracy and timing of the confrontations and client readiness to hear them (see, e.g., Hill & O'Brien, 1999; Ivey & Ivey, 1999). Helpers might follow up confrontations with a question such as, "What are your thoughts on that?" as a way to initiate discussion.

Providing Information

Providing information occurs when helpers identify resources or give answers, facts, options, or descriptions of research to clients. This skill is used throughout helping. For example, helpers may describe research that is relevant to the problems that motivated clients to seek help. They may also discuss resources, such as support groups, that clients can take advantage of to help them maintain the gains they have made in helping.

The Nature of Information

Information in helping comes in many forms. It may involve providing or describing research findings, diagnoses, helping procedures, psychological concepts and terms, and vocational and educational information. Helpers may also suggest books, videotapes, computer programs, and Internet sites. Further, helpers may offer referrals to community or government resources or to other professionals who specialize in areas relevant to client needs.

Providing information is not synonymous with advising, suggesting, or directing. Information is more factual in nature (see Doyle, 1998). Once helpers provide information, clients do with it as they choose. Advice, suggestions, and directives, in contrast, are more prescriptive. Helpers in these cases propose steps to take or tell clients what they think should be done. The skills of advising, suggesting, and directing are discussed in chapter 11.

The Value of Providing Information

Providing information promotes client understanding by educating and enlightening clients. For example, a client with insufficient information about job possibilities may believe that his occupational choices are limited. The helper may be able to identify resources or describe numerous options that the client has not considered. Armed with this information, the client can approach his job search from a new, more informed, more confident perspective. The resources and wider range of options open up new possibilities and may increase the client's chances of finding a job that suits his interests.

Specifically, as part of the process of promoting client understanding, providing information helps clients

- increase knowledge;
- correct misconceptions and misinformation;
- identify and consider options, opportunities, and possibilities;
- take new perspectives on problems and situations; and
- make good, well-informed decisions.

Helpers do not impart information to show off their knowledge, but providing information can communicate to clients that helpers are knowledgeable and competent. This, in turn, may strengthen helping relationships and increase helper credibility.

Points and Guidelines for Providing Information

Ascertain Why Clients Need Information. Whether helpers provide information at their own discretion or at the request of clients, they need to first ascertain why clients require the information (see Hill & O'Brien, 1999). For example, clients may need information to allow them to make important decisions or to understand the helping process. In such cases, providing information is beneficial. Sometimes, however, clients want information for less beneficial reasons. For example, they may believe that the role of helpers is to tell them what to do through information and advice. Or, they may seek information as a way to avoid self-exploration or painful feelings (Gelso & Fretz, 2001). Effective helpers avoid providing information as a "quick fix" solution to client problems. If this skill is overused, clients may come to rely on helpers to provide answers and solutions.

Determine What Clients Already Know. This point was made by Hill and O'Brien (1999). Learning what clients already know can assist helpers in determining how much more information clients need and whether clients possess any misinformation. It also prevents helpers from wasting time explaining things that are already within client knowledge. Helpers can ask questions to ascertain what clients currently know.

Recognize Cultural Variables. Much information is culture-bound (e.g., educational techniques and parenting practices). If helpers lack cultural awareness or are careless, they may force their own beliefs, values, and perspectives on clients by virtue of the information they choose to provide (see Cormier & Nurius, 2003). For example, a helper who opposes divorce on religious grounds may provide a client with articles on ways to save a marriage when the client would prefer information about ending a marriage. As another example, a helper may discuss research findings from studies conducted on members of his or her own cultural group without realizing that the findings might not be relevant for clients of different groups. Helpers need to recognize cultural variables and strive to provide information that is suited to their clients' needs and cultural characteristics.

Provide Information at the Right Time. When clients lack important information, possess misinformation, or seem aimless or confused, providing information may be appropriate. It is less likely to be appropriate when clients are immersed in talking about their concerns or when they are expressing powerful emotions.

Ensure That the Information Provided Is Accurate, Relevant, and Complete. To be helpful, information must be accurate and relevant (see Cormier & Nurius, 2003). Helpers need to be educated, trained, qualified, and knowledgeable to provide information that relates to clients' concerns. Information also needs to be complete. For clients to make appropriate use of information, they need to be fully informed, which sometimes means the helper must impart information that may be difficult for them to hear. Clients need to know the "good" and the "bad"—risks and benefits, advantages and disadvantages, positive news and negative news (Cormier & Nurius, 2003). Helpers, however, are not expected to be knowledgeable about everything. Sometimes, providing information means making referrals to resources that can give clients the information they need.

Provide Information in Formats That Are Appropriate and Useful to Clients. To provide information in a manner that will be most useful to a client, the helper must be familiar with the client's needs and characteristics as well as with various sources of information. For example, a computer-oriented client may want computer-related or Internet resources. A client who has trouble reading may benefit more from videotapes or audiotapes than from written materials. Some clients, such as those with memory difficulties, may benefit most from written information, as opposed to verbally provided information. When providing written or taped information, helpers may assist clients by discussing where the clients might store the information (e.g., in a special place at home) so it does not get lost (M. Kiselica, personal communication, May 12, 2002).

Provide Difficult Information With Sensitivity. Some information is fairly innocuous, such as telling a client where she can pick up an application for financial aid. Other information may be emotionally difficult and tough to hear, such as providing details about a disorder with which the client has just been diagnosed. Helpers need to be prepared to address concerns, questions, feelings, and reactions that clients may have when difficult information is provided (see Cormier & Nurius, 2003).

Be Articulate, Succinct, and Specific. When providing information, helpers should speak clearly and slowly and use terminology that clients understand. Such client factors as age, sophistication, and language skills influence how helpers provide information. Helpers should also provide information in moderate amounts so clients can remember it and so that they avoid inundating clients with information (Cormier & Nurius, 2003; Hill & O'Brien, 1999). Being specific increases the usability of the information. Information that is vague or overly general may be of limited value.

Discuss the Information, as Well as Client Reactions and Understanding. Helpers need to observe client reactions to the information provided and explore those reactions with the clients (Hill & O'Brien, 1999). Helpers also need to make sure that clients understand the information provided. Various problems can occur as information is communicated from helpers to clients. For example, information may be provided too quickly, or clients may confuse or distort the information and thus not accurately hear it (Evans et al., 1998). To minimize misunderstanding, helpers may, after providing information, ask clients if they have any questions or want anything clarified or repeated. For example, they may ask, "Did you follow that?" or "Do you need me to clarify or repeat anything?" To ensure understanding, helpers might also ask clients to repeat the information (Evans et al., 1998).

Interpreting

Helpers differ in how they define interpreting, due in part to different theoretical perspectives on interpretation. We have chosen to define interpreting broadly, describing it as helper statements that offer new ways of viewing and describing feelings, thoughts, behaviors, and experiences. The goal of interpreting is to assist clients in developing more thorough, effective, and useful understandings of their lives and problems. Helpers do not use interpreting to criticize, judge, or condescend to clients.

Interpreting is different from paraphrasing, reflecting feelings, reflecting implied cognitive content, and reflecting underlying feelings, all of which were described in chapter 7. Paraphrasing and reflecting feelings mirror the overt, explicit message expressed; that is, they maintain the client's frame of reference. Interpreting, however, involves helpers adding their own understanding of what is going on. Thus, helpers provide a new perspective or new frame of reference (Brammer & MacDonald, 2003). Likewise, reflecting implied cognitive content and reflecting underlying feelings both maintain the client's frame of reference, even if that frame of reference is implicit or ambiguous (hidden in client words, behaviors, and expressions). Interpreting, once again, provides a new frame of reference, one that clients apparently have not experienced or considered.

Forms of Interpretation

Hill (1985, 1989) and Hill and O'Brien (1999) described several forms of interpretation. These are discussed in the following paragraphs.

Interpretations That Identify and Describe Patterns and Themes in Client Statements and Expressions. As clients communicate, helpers may observe patterns and themes in their statements and expressions. Helpers may use interpretation as a way to help clients see these patterns and themes. Consider the following example:

Client (describing a romantic relationship that she ended after 3 months): Once again, another relationship that's ended in failure. Each time, I keep thinking this will be the one that lasts. It always seems, though, that I end up thinking that there's someone else out there who is better for me.

Helper: I've noticed that most of the relationships you've had have lasted about 3 months. It seems that when it looks like the relationship is starting to get serious, you break it off.

In this example, the helper identified a pattern or theme that she noticed over time and shared it with the client. The interpretation may help the client better understand her behaviors.

Interpretations That Make Connections Between Feelings, Thoughts, Behaviors, and Experiences. When a helper realizes that different aspects of problems and experiences are separated in a client's awareness or are kept out of the client's awareness, the helper may strive to connect them through interpretation. Consider the following example:

Client: I'm wary of my supervisor. I question whether he's really capable of doing his job. I just don't think he has the interests of the company or his employees at heart.

Helper: Could it be that your attitude toward your supervisor is not so much about his behavior as it is about your overall distrust of authority?

This example assumes that the helper has thoroughly explored the client's concerns and has noted statements and expressions in the past that would suggest that the client distrusts authority. In this example, the helper connects the client's distrust of authority to the client's attitude toward his supervisor, thereby suggesting a new way of looking at how the client relates to his boss. The client may come to understand that his attitude stems not from his supervisor's actual behavior but rather from his own perspective on authority. If the client accepts this interpretation, he will have a greater understanding of his attitudes and how they affect his relationship with his boss. The client may then be able to approach this relationship from a fresh perspective.

Consider another example:

Client: I quit my job recently because I wanted to make a stronger commitment to my family. I feel like I've been neglecting them lately. I was really disappointed to leave that job. I had been there for 5 years, I loved the work, and the people were great. What's odd is that I'm finding that I don't want to spend a whole lot of time with my family, even though I have plenty of time. I feel kind of bored when I'm around them. I mean, I left that job so I could be with my family, and now I don't want to be with them that much. What's going on?

Helper: Could it be that the disappointment you feel over giving up a job that you loved so much has made it difficult for you to want to spend time with your family?

In this example, the helper makes a connection between the client's disappointment about giving up her job and her lack of desire to spend time with her family. Seeing this connection may help the client understand her problem.

Interpretations That Point Out Transference, Resistance, and Defenses. Clients may need help seeing these behaviors. Consider this example, in which interpretation is used to identify transference:

Client: Everybody told me not to go out with this guy because he was no good. I remember when I described him to you, you said I should be careful. I should have listened. You must be thinking how stupid I am. I know you want to say, "I told you so." Go ahead, let me have it.

Helper: It sounds like you're expecting me to respond like your mother always has.

By pointing out how the client ascribed to the helper characteristics and behaviors that the helper does not possess (transference), the helper may aid the client in seeing where her expectations originate and that she is not perceiving the helper accurately. With the helper's assistance, the client could explore the effect of her mother's hurtful comments and criticisms. Doing so could increase the client's understanding and improve her ability to develop effective relationships with other people.

In addition to being used to identify transference, interpretation can be used to point out resistance and defenses, such as intellectualizing or lashing out in anger (Hill & O'Brien, 1999). Interpretations can help clients understand resistance and defenses and learn why they engage in these behaviors. For example, a helper might say to a client, "I wonder if you talk intellectually about your situation because the feelings related to it are so painful for you."

Interpretations That Encourage Clients to Reframe Their Perceptions. When client perceptions are distorted, self-defeating, or incorrect, helpers can use interpretation to assist the clients in developing different, healthier, or more accurate perceptions. Through the interpretations, clients are encouraged to redefine or reframe their current perceptions, and thus assign new meanings to problems, behaviors, and situations (Cormier & Nurius, 2003). Helpers are effectively saying to their clients, "You see things this way, but how about considering another perspective?" When the meaning assigned to problems, behaviors, or situations is changed, client responses can change and new options and possibilities can be explored (Cormier & Nurius, 2003).

Often, helpers reframe clients' problematic and negative perceptions by encouraging clients to look at their problems and situations in a more positive and productive way (e.g., "You're not a troublemaker; you're assertive."); however, helpers can also offer reframes that may be more difficult for clients to hear and accept, such as reframing a client's statements about being tired during helping sessions as a manifestation of lack of interest in the helping process.

In a sense, all of the types of interpretation that have been discussed so far involve helping clients reframe perceptions. Here, however, we are focusing on encouraging clients to take new perspectives on particular feelings, thoughts, behaviors, experiences, and situations in their lives. We are not talking about identifying patterns and themes, making connections, or pointing out transference, resistance, or defenses.

Here is an example of an interpretation that encourages a client to reframe her perception:

Client: My colleagues are a little frustrated with me. I wanted to do the project a particular way, and they wanted to do it a different way. They wanted to cut corners, but I insisted that we not do that. This caused a delay in finishing. I feel like a troublemaker.

Helper: I hear that you feel bad about causing a delay and about causing some negative feelings with your colleagues, but could it be that what you call being a "troublemaker" is your own healthy sense of assertiveness? You stood up for what you thought was right.

In this example, the helper encouraged the client to see her behavior from a new perspective. If she sees herself as assertive, the client may cope more effectively with challenging situations and develop a more positive self-image than she would if she sees herself as a troublemaker. The helper might even ask the client to try to reframe her behavior and the situation for herself—to consider other possible ways of looking at her behavior and the situation, besides troublemaking.

Consider another example:

Client: People just ignore me. They don't invite me to parties or ask me to socialize.

Helper: Is it possible that you're ignoring other people rather than the other way around? As you said earlier, you rarely go out or invite people to socialize.

Note that in this example, the new perspective that the helper offered was very different from the client's perspective. In fact, it was the opposite of the client's perspective. When such a reframe is offered, the likelihood increases that the client will dismiss the reframe. The helper in this case would probably make such a statement only after having established a good relationship and having developed a solid understanding of the client's life and problems. By this point, the helper would probably have earned the privilege of challenging the client. Under such conditions, even if the client did not initially agree with the reframe, he would be more likely to consider and discuss the helper's statement. Without a good relationship or understanding, the client would likely be more inclined to dismiss the statement as ridiculous and not give it a second thought.

D. W. Sue and Sue (1990) summarized a case presented by Nishio and Bilmes (1987) that shows how reframing, when used in a manner that considers cultural variables, can be a valuable skill in multicultural helping. In this case, a Western therapist who was seeing a Laotian couple encouraged the wife, who was subjected to abuse by her alcoholic husband, to leave her husband and lead an independent life. The couple did not return for another session with the helper. They went to another helper who also recognized the unhealthy situation but was more understanding of cultural norms and expectations (e.g., family orientation, interdependence). After building a trusting helping relationship, the helper pointed out the merit of a more independent wife (e.g., if the wife assumed more responsibility, she would be less of a burden on her husband, who would have more time for himself) (Nishio & Bilmes, 1987, p. 344). Thus, the helper redefined, or reframed, independence in a more culturally sensitive and acceptable way. This new perspective combined with attention to the drinking problem and the abuse permitted a successful resolution in which the drinking and the abuse stopped.

In addition to using reframing themselves, helpers can encourage clients to use this skill on their own. As challenging situations and problems arise in life, clients can focus on how they view the situations or problems and then consider other possible perspectives.

The Value of Interpreting

Though some helpers are reluctant to use it, interpreting can be an important skill in helping. The value of interpreting is that it can

- promote greater client understanding of feelings, thoughts, behaviors, and experiences;
- encourage clients to reevaluate current perspectives and begin to view problems or situations in new ways;
- strengthen helping relationships by showing clients that helpers understand them on a deep level;
- show clients that it is okay to discuss issues that they may be reluctant to address specifically;
- promote deeper exploration of problems;
- create a sense of movement in managing or resolving problems; and
- create feelings of hope, relief, and motivation as clients begin to see their problems in new ways.

Points and Guidelines for Interpreting

Get to Know Clients and Their Problems Before Making Interpretations. Interpretations are well-considered statements that are based on helpers' intuitions and the information they have gathered. Interpretations are not uninformed speculations or wild guesses in which helpers take a "stab in the dark" at understanding their clients. Thus, interpretations tend to be used after helpers have developed a fairly good understanding of their clients' lives and problems. Early in the helping process, when helpers do not yet know their clients well, interpretations are more likely to be incorrect or threatening.

Be Careful About Imposing Perspectives on Clients. When interpreting, there is a risk that helpers may impose their own values and beliefs on clients. Also, like clients, helpers can distort reality or latch onto perspectives and explanations that may be inaccurate. If helpers are not familiar with their own reality filters—if they possess poor self-awareness—they may suggest new perspectives that are inappropriate for clients. For example, if a client with religious convictions expresses guilt over not faithfully adhering to one of the tenets of his religion, a helper who is not too keen on organized religion might try to reframe the client's feelings and behavior as a healthy rejection of an oppressive religious belief. This response, however, would reflect the helper's values and viewpoint and might be offensive, inaccurate, and unhelpful to the client.

The risk of imposing perspectives on clients explains why some helpers rarely use the skill of interpreting, if they use it at all. The argument against using this skill is that interpreting gives too much weight to helpers' own views, perceptions, beliefs, and intuitions, thus taking the focus away from what clients believe (see Belkin, 1988). Because clients may see their helpers as experts, they may accept their helpers' interpretations as accurate even if they feel inclined to disagree. The argument for using interpretation is that it helps clients face important issues, problems, and feelings that they might otherwise avoid. In addition, interpretation encourages clients to view situations and problems in new, more meaningful ways.

Recognize Cultural and Individual Variables. When making interpretations, helpers strive to ensure that their interpretations take cultural variables into account, as in the reframing example described earlier. This point ties in with the idea just discussed: making sure that helpers do not impose their perspectives on clients. For example, clients who come from cultures in which family connections are very important may not respond well to interpretations suggesting that they are overly dependent on their families. Such interpretations could be incorrect and harmful to the helping relationship. Also, as noted in chapter 8, some clients may not value developing understanding. Helpers might choose not to use interpretation with those clients.

Make Interpretations at the Right Time. Clients who seem to be searching for understanding may be most prepared to receive interpretations. Clients who blame others for their own problems, want to talk a lot, or want advice may not be ready (Hill & O'Brien, 1999).

Be Mindful of the Depth of Interpretations. Interpretations that are slightly discrepant from clients' current views tend to be more effective and facilitative of change than interpretations that are highly discrepant, or "very deep" (Claiborn, Ward, & Strong, 1981). Slightly discrepant interpretations, which are closer to clients' current beliefs than highly discrepant interpretations are, may be more immediately understandable than the deeper interpretations (Claiborn et al., 1981). As helping progresses and relationships strengthen, helpers may gradually increase the depth of their interpretations. For example, a helper might initially suggest that an employee's problems with his boss could be due, not to the actual behavior of the boss, but to the employee's distrust of authority. As helping progresses, the helper might go deeper and suggest, for example, that the problems may stem from conflicts the employee has had with his father.

Some novice helpers interpret too often and feel inclined to share what they believe are important insights or interpretations whenever they come to mind, regardless of how deep they are or how much the helping relationship has developed. This common mistake can harm relationships and put off clients. Before they make interpretations, helpers need to consider such questions as, "Am I making this interpretation to benefit the client or to show off and feel like an expert?" and "How might the client respond to this interpretation at this point in the relationship?"

Offer Interpretations Tentatively. It is a good idea for helpers to offer their interpretations tentatively (Evans et al., 1998). Tentativeness may be expressed with such language as, "Could it be that . . . ?" "I'm wondering if . . ." or "What about this . . . ?" Tentative statements suggest that helpers are checking out their beliefs rather than imposing them. Such statements encourage clients to respond to or correct the interpretations.

Be Clear, Concise, and Specific. Because interpretations offer new perspectives, they need to be specific and understandable. Vague statements, such as, "It seems like there's something more to this than just anger," do not promote understanding. Instead, they may confuse and frustrate clients or cause anxiety.

Discuss the Interpretations and Client Reactions. Effective helpers pay close attention to how their clients react and respond to their interpretations (Hill & O'Brien, 1999) and may ask clients for their comments (e.g., "What do you think about that?"). They also watch for nonverbal cues, such as pauses and facial expressions. Clients may accept interpretations and be willing to explore the new perspectives. Alternatively, they may deny interpretations or become puzzled by them. In the latter cases, the interpretations may be incorrect or they may be on target but address issues that clients are not ready to face. When clients do not accept interpretations, helpers may choose to explore the clients' reactions (if the clients are willing) or may decide to back off and offer interpretations further down the road when the clients seem more prepared to develop their own understandings (see Hill & O'Brien, 1999).

Self-Disclosing

Helpers often divulge much about themselves in the helping process. At the beginning of the process, they may share information about their education, training, credentials, professional experiences, and work style as part of informed consent. By doing so, they let clients know what they are getting into and with whom they will be working. Helpers also share information about themselves through their responses, nonverbal behavior, and personal characteristics. As Strong and Claiborn (1982) put it: "The [helper] communicates his or her characteristics to the client in every look, movement, emotional response, and sound, as well as with every word. Clients actively construe the personal characteristics, meanings, and causes behind [the helper's] behaviors in order to evaluate the personal significance of the [helper's] remarks" (p. 173). Here, we discuss a specific form of self-disclosure: helpers deliberately deciding to share information about themselves, including feelings, experiences, and problems.

Sharing Personal Information

When helpers share information about themselves, including feelings, thoughts, attitudes, experiences, opinions, and problems, they are self-disclosing (see Jourard, 1971). Helpers do not self-disclose as a way to shift the focus onto themselves and work on their own problems. They do so to strengthen the helping relationship and to benefit their clients. By providing personal information that relates in some way to client issues, helper self-disclosure encourages clients to self-disclose and to explore in greater depth their feelings, thoughts, behaviors, and experiences. It may also prompt clients to reexamine and reevaluate their perspectives on their lives and problems. They are encouraged to see new solutions and options. Effective self-disclosure tends to enhance rapport and create the feeling of a human connection between helpers and clients. Consider the following examples of self-disclosing:

Client (college student): It just seems impossible to make friends. I'm not very outgoing, and I always think that nobody will like me.

Helper: You know, I, too, had trouble making friends when I was in college. I was pretty shy and it felt really scary to meet people. It took courage and some practice, but I found that once I took some chances and opened up, I made some good friends.

In this example, the self-disclosure helps to establish a connection with the client by describing a relevant experience from the helper's own life. Also, the helper's disclosure of a problem similar to that of the client and the "happy ending" to the problem may help the client begin to see that his situation is not hopeless. The client may feel empowered to see his problem as solvable and persist in trying to make friends.

Here is another example:

Client: When I received the divorce papers, I was stunned. I started thinking, "Where am I going to live now?" "How am I going to survive on just one income?" I thought we would be together for the rest of our lives, and now I just see a solitary existence.

Helper: I got a divorce myself several years ago. I remember thinking, "What do I do now?" "What's next?" I also remember feeling very lonely, like there was no one to support or help me now. Is that like what you're experiencing?

As in the first example, the self-disclosure in this example helps to establish a connection between the helper and the client. The client may feel better knowing that with regard to divorce, the helper has "been there," too, and can assist her in dealing emotionally with the situation. The helper's credibility in the eyes of the client may be enhanced. The self-disclosure also encourages the client to elaborate and further explore her situation. By showing that the helper knows what the client is going through, the self-disclosure may help the client feel more comfortable talking about the impending divorce and her feelings about it.

Self-disclosing is a controversial skill. Research on its effectiveness is mixed, with some studies showing that it has a positive impact on clients and other studies showing that it does not favorably impact the helping process or its outcome (see, e.g., Donley, Horan, & DeShong, 1989; Hill, 1989; Watkins, 1990). Authorities also disagree on its appropriateness in helping. DeJong and Berg (1998) stated bluntly: "We do not recommend that you [helpers] tell clients about your own experiences" (p. 29). In their view, describing personal experiences is unnecessary and impairs the ability of clients to arrive at their own solutions. Concerns have also been raised that self-disclosing takes the focus off clients and that acknowledging personal problems may reflect negatively on helper credibility. In support of self-disclosing, many helpers believe that moderate self-disclosing strengthens rapport and helping relationships. It shows that helpers are "human" and that they cope with the challenges of life like all people.

Helpers ultimately need to draw their own conclusions about self-disclosing and decide for themselves how much or even whether to use this skill. We believe that it can be an effective skill when helpers carefully weigh its benefits and risks and consider the points and guidelines described later in this discussion.

The Value of Self-Disclosing

Self-disclosing can be a valuable skill. Specifically, it can

- increase helper attractiveness, as well as trust, rapport, and confidence in helping relationships, by showing that helpers are "real" human beings, not distant professionals who have no problems;
- elicit feelings of relief by showing clients that they are not alone, that all people face challenges and struggle with problems;
- encourage clients to learn from helper experiences;
- put client problems in perspective, making them seem less threatening or overwhelming;
- encourage self-exploration by clients;
- model the discussion of feelings, thoughts, and experiences, thus encouraging clients to self-disclose;
- help clients consider new perspectives and see options or solutions to problems; and
- instill hope that problems are solvable, that they can be successfully managed or resolved.

Risks of Self-Disclosing

Self-disclosing can be risky because it may

- shift the focus of helping from clients to helpers;
- overwhelm and confuse clients (helper self-disclosure of feelings, thoughts, and experiences may cause clients to feel that they are supposed to assist their helpers, thus blurring the roles and boundaries of helping relationships);
- offend or unsettle clients (helper self-disclosure involves sharing personal details, and clients may feel that helpers are getting uncomfortably close);
- convey the impression that helpers are trying to "one-up" their clients: "You think *your* problems are tough! Listen to this . . . !";
- damage helper credibility and respectability (helper self-disclosure of problems may cause clients to wonder whether their helpers are mentally healthy and able to help);
- encourage clients to "follow the leader" and solicit advice on how to deal with their problems (clients may believe that the way in which helpers addressed particular problems is how they should as well—the assumption being that what worked for helpers will work for them, too); and
- spread personal information beyond the helping relationship (helpers are bound by confidentiality, but clients are not; helpers may want to keep to themselves anything they would not want everyone else to know).

Points and Guidelines for Self-Disclosing

Consider Motives and Reasons for Self-Disclosing. Simone, McCarthy, and Skay (1998) suggested several questions that helpers might ask themselves in deciding whether to self-disclose. Some of these questions include:

"Have I thought through why I am disclosing?"

"Do I know enough about the client to disclose appropriately?"

"Is my timing right?"

"Am I disclosing for my needs or the client's?"

"Will my disclosure pull the focus from the client?"

"Will this disclosure improve or diminish our rapport?"

"Will it help the client look at different viewpoints, or will it confuse the client?"

"Does this client need me to model disclosure behavior?" (pp. 181–182)

One of the most important points to remember about self-disclosing is that this skill should be used with clients' best interests in mind. When self-disclosing, helpers are talking about themselves, but they do not self-disclose to be liked, to brag, to impress, to gain sympathy, or to seek assistance with their own problems.

Recognize Cultural Variables. D. W. Sue and Sue (2003) observed that culturally different clients may approach their helpers with some hesitation and mistrust and may not self-disclose until their helpers do. For example, when seeking assistance from helpers who are of the majority racial group, clients of minority racial groups may not want to talk about their problems until they get answers to such questions as, "Do you really understand what it means to be a minority person in this society?" and "What makes you any different from the racist majority group members I have encountered in my life?" (Ivey & Ivey, 1999, p. 290; D. W. Sue & Sue, 2003). The basic point of these questions ("How can you relate to me?" "How can I trust you?") can be extended to other groups that have encountered discrimination and oppression, such as women and gays and lesbians. When clients of these groups see helpers of different groups, they may want to know how the helpers can understand and relate to them before they reveal their concerns. In short, helpers who self-disclose some feelings, thoughts, and experiences may be more effective at getting culturally different clients to self-disclose. They may also be seen as more credible.

Use Self-Disclosures in Appropriate Circumstances. Self-disclosing may be appropriate and beneficial at times when helpers want to motivate clients, promote client self-disclosure, help clients develop understanding, or enhance the helping relationship. For example, if a client seems hopelessly stuck and feels that his problems are unsolvable, a helper might consider disclosing a relevant personal experience. Self-disclosing is often avoided when clients are expressing very powerful emotions or when they are not having any difficulty talking about their problems. Other skills, such as paraphrasing and reflecting feelings, are more appropriate in these situations. Long (1996) asserted that if there is any doubt, helpers should not self-disclose.

Self-Disclose Relevant Material. What a helper discloses should be "similar in content and mood to the client's messages" (Hackney & Cormier, 2001, p. 60). The helper self-disclosures in the two examples provided earlier (the college student and the divorcing spouse) meet this criterion. In the divorce situation, for example, the helper reveals a personal experience with divorce (similarity of content) and describes feelings of loneliness and concern about what to do now, with the intensity of the experience being about the same as that of the client's experience (similarity of mood).

In all cases, helpers need to exercise discretion in what they reveal. Not all experiences, even ones that are similar to the client's, are appropriate to share, and deeply personal disclosures may be uncomfortable and too intimate for clients. Helper sexual practices and fantasies, for example, may fall into this category.

Make Self-Disclosures Brief and to the Point. Self-disclosures should be brief, succinct statements, not long stories. Self-disclosing momentarily shifts the center of attention from clients to helpers. However, clients are the focus of helping, so helpers should not dwell too much on themselves. Helpers need to remember that even though self-disclosures focus on them, the point of offering the self-disclosures is to benefit their clients. Hill and O'Brien (1999) and Long (1996) suggested that after self-disclosing, helpers should return the focus to clients (e.g., "I wonder if that's like what you're experiencing." "Would that fit for you?").

Self-Disclose in Moderation. Self-disclosing seems to be most beneficial and effective when it is done in moderate amounts (see, e.g., Edwards & Murdock, 1994). Too little or no self-disclosure may make helpers seem distant and aloof. Too much self-disclosure can cause clients to believe that they are no longer the focus of helping.

The extent to which helper self-disclosure is used depends on each unique helping relationship. Hendrick (1988) noted in her study of self-disclosure that clients like and want helpers to self-disclose, and that helpers need to match their disclosures to client needs.

Immediacy

Immediacy is often described as a form of self-disclosing because it involves helpers sharing their feelings, thoughts, reactions, and observations. However, unlike self-disclosing, where helpers focus largely on the past, immediacy involves making "here-and-now" statements in which helpers share feelings, thoughts, reactions, and observations as they are occurring, while they are fresh and present. Basically, something about the helper/client interaction impacts helpers, who decide to immediately comment on it and share their feedback and responses. In other words, helpers address "what is going on" between themselves and their clients within the relationship (Turock, 1980, p. 168). Immediacy calls attention to aspects of helper/client interactions that have not been explicitly addressed. Carkhuff (1984) stated that "immediacy is probably one of the most critical variables in terms of communicating a depth of understanding of the complex interaction between the parties to a relationship" (p. 192).

Types of Immediacy Statements

Helpers make immediacy statements about themselves, their clients, something that is occurring in the helping session, or the overall helping relationship (Cormier & Nurius, 2003; Egan, 2002).

Helpers' Immediacy Statements About Themselves. Helpers may share their immediate responses to their clients (e.g., how they are feeling at the moment). Examples include the following:

"I feel annoyed when you interrupt me like that."

"I'm feeling confused and overwhelmed right now. You're talking about a lot of
   things at once."
"I'm very pleased to hear you say that."
"I'm so happy that your new job is working out for you."

Helpers' Immediacy Statements About Their Clients. Helpers may observe
something about their clients that they believe warrants attention, such as the clients'
facial expressions, demeanor, or body movements. Examples follow:

"You seem bored right now. You haven't said much in the last 10 minutes."
"I've noticed that you've been shifting around in your chair a lot. Are you nervous
   about something?"
"You're beaming. I take it you're happy with how the meeting went."

*Helpers' Immediacy Statements About Something That Is Occurring in the
Helping Session.* Helpers may comment on a specific aspect of the helping relationship at that moment. Examples include the following:

"It feels to me like there's some tension between us right now. Does it seem that way
   to you?"
"It feels like we're making a lot of progress."

Helpers' Immediacy Statements About the Overall Helping Relationship.
Helpers may comment on the status of the helping relationship. Examples follow:

"I'm very pleased with how our relationship has grown over the past several weeks.
   You've really opened up a lot in that time."
"I think we've come a long way, but there's still more work to be done."

Immediacy statements can be positive or negative (see Egan, 2002). Positive
immediacy statements (e.g., "I'm very pleased to hear you say that.") help clients
feel good about the helping relationship and more invested in it. Positive statements
also reinforce effective client behavior. Negative immediacy statements (e.g., "You
seem bored right now. You haven't said much in the last 10 minutes.") are used to
call attention to unhelpful behaviors or nonfacilitative conditions that, if unchecked
and unaddressed, could undermine the helping relationship. Positive immediacy
statements are beneficial throughout helping. Negative immediacy statements may
be more effective after good helping relationships develop than at an earlier time
because they may evoke defensive responses and because they address factors that
clients may be uncomfortable discussing.

The Value of Immediacy

Immediacy is a powerful and beneficial skill in many kinds of relationships because
it involves talking about interactions in the relationships (Carkhuff, 1984).
Immediacy strengthens helping relationships by increasing rapport and closeness
and by improving communication. Without it, relationships may become distant,

stagnant, dull, and tense. When immediacy is not used, miscommunication often occurs and misconceptions may develop, potentially causing the relationships to end out of frustration, anger, or boredom.

Many clients have a history of being in relationships in which they have not talked about the relationships—and what was going on in them—with the other people involved. When they have been involved in relationships in which talking about the relationship has occurred, ineffective statements and behaviors, such as criticizing, insulting, blaming, yelling, and making sarcastic remarks, have been quite common. Especially in dysfunctional family environments, people do not learn healthy, effective communication skills.

Clients typically bring these ways of interacting into helping relationships, behaving toward helpers in the same way they behave toward other people. For example, a client who generally acts in a confrontational manner with people will likely relate to the helper in the same way. Immediacy is a way for helpers to point out and comment on client behaviors and relationship dynamics and bring them into clients' awareness. Through immediacy statements, clients are encouraged to ponder and explore their feelings, thoughts, behaviors, and ways of interacting. They may begin to see how they relate to and affect other people, and they may come to understand why people respond to them in the way they do. With this knowledge, clients are in a better position to make positive changes.

Immediacy provides clients with a fresher, different, and better communication experience than they have had in other relationships. When helpers make immediacy statements, they demonstrate an effective communication skill that many clients have rarely experienced: mature, honest discussion about what is going on in the relationship, how the participants see the relationship, and how they feel about it. Immediacy also gives clients permission to express themselves and to address any concerns or problems in the helping relationship.

The point of immediacy is not for helpers to share their feelings, thoughts, reactions, or observations and then move on to other topics. The immediacy statement should be the beginning of a dialogue about what is going on in the relationship, a dialogue in which helpers and clients share their perspectives and feelings about their relationship (see Cormier & Nurius, 2003). For example, immediacy can give helpers and clients an opportunity to "clear the air" when negative, relationship-damaging factors are present, including aimlessness, resentment, client reluctance to self-disclose, stress, misunderstandings, or apparent client mistrust (Egan, 2002). An immediacy statement (e.g., "It seems like there's some tension between us right now.") can serve as the starting point for a discussion about these factors. The helper may then invite the client to respond to the immediacy statement (e.g., "What do you think about that?"). Relationships and rapport are usually strengthened when the participants are able to release frustration and tension.

Because many clients are not used to talking about their relationships, immediacy can be uncomfortable for them. They may become defensive and not want to discuss the issues that helpers have raised. However, other clients may appreciate the opportunity to express themselves. In some cases, immediacy opens the floodgates and prompts a significant release of emotion and energy. As helpers and clients talk about what is going on in their relationship, clients may feel a sense of relief and even greater confidence in the relationship now that they have had the opportunity to express themselves. Using immediacy in the helping process can lead to important discussions about having effective, healthy relationships with other people.

Points and Guidelines for Immediacy

Strive for Accuracy and Be Aware of the Influence of Helper Biases, Personal Problems, and Needs. Biases, personal problems, and needs can distort helpers' perceptions of what is going on in the relationship (see Cormier & Nurius, 2003; Hill & O'Brien, 1999). For example, if a client begins to talk about a sexual problem and the helper feels uncomfortable with sexual topics, the helper might try to avoid discussion of the issue by making an immediacy statement such as, "It seems like we're straying off the topic here. I'm confused about where this is going. We were talking earlier about your new job. Can you say more about that?" In this case, the immediacy statement is unhelpful. It is based on the helper's discomfort, and it stifles discussion of an important issue for the client. Helpers need to be self-aware and try to minimize the likelihood of these types of distortions (Turock, 1980).

Recognize the Benefit of Immediacy in Cross-Cultural Situations. An important use of immediacy is to address cultural differences and clear up cultural misunderstandings. Differences between helpers and clients in age, gender, race, religion, sexual orientation, and social class can affect trust and compatibility in helping relationships (Evans et al., 1998). When these differences are not addressed, underlying mistrust can damage the relationship. When helpers acknowledge differences, limitations in their understanding, and client concerns, these factors can be discussed. Helpers and clients can determine whether they will be able to successfully manage their differences or whether referrals would be appropriate. Simply recognizing differences and airing concerns about them can increase trust and rapport in relationships.

Take Care to "Own" Feelings, Thoughts, Reactions, and Observations. This point was made by Cormier and Nurius (2003) and Hill and O'Brien (1999). Immediacy statements typically contain such words as "I" or "me" to show that helpers are owning their feelings, thoughts, reactions, and observations (e.g., "I'm really glad you decided to share that." "I feel hurt and offended when you insult me like that."). With this type of wording, helpers model responsibility for and acceptance of one's own expressions. They also show clients how client statements, expressions, and behaviors impact other people. "You" statements, such as, "You seem a little uncomfortable right now," can be helpful if carefully worded, but they sometimes sound accusatory and can evoke defensive responses from clients.

Make Immediacy Statements in Moderation. If immediacy statements are used too frequently, clients may feel uncomfortable and highly scrutinized. If immediacy statements are underused, helping relationships may feel like other poor relationships in clients' lives, characterized by lack of effective communication. In such cases, clients may feel reluctant to express concerns about the helping relationship, and they may not learn how they are seen by others or how their attitudes and behaviors affect their relationships.

A Hypothetical Dialogue

The following hypothetical dialogue between a helper and a client demonstrates how a helper might promote client understanding using many of the skills described in this chapter. The client is a man who is having marital difficulties. A good helping relationship has developed between the helper and the client. This dialogue is from the fifth session of the helping process.

Client: I tried talking to my wife a couple of days ago. I picked a time when I knew she wasn't doing anything, and I tried to start a conversation about some of the things we needed to talk about, like money and picking a good school for the kids. I was trying hard to be calm and levelheaded. Within 1 minute, things had deteriorated. Same old story. It happens every time we try to talk about these things.

Helper: When you started the conversation, what did you say?

[The helper asks an open question to gather more information.]

Client: I said, "Honey, we need to talk." She seemed kind of defensive and said, "What about?" I said, "About money, the kids, and stuff." She sat down, and I told her that we need to decide these things. I gave her a list that I wrote up that stated how we would do things—how we would split expenses, who would be responsible for which bills, and so on. She looked at it and got this look on her face like my list was ridiculous. I said, "You got any better suggestions? At least I'm thinking about these things and willing to work them out." She said, "No, you're not." Then she shoved the list back at me.

Helper: Is that how your conversation ended?

[The helper asks a closed question.]

Client: Yeah. Then she left the room. You see, she's not willing to work anything out. I'm willing, but she isn't.

Helper: Well, I'm wondering about some things you just said. You said that you're willing to work things out, but you gave her a list that basically told her how everything would be done.

[The helper uses a confrontation to point out an apparent incongruity between the client's words (willing to work things out) and his actions (giving his wife a list telling her how they would do things). The helper simply presents the incongruity for the client to consider—without passing judgment, interpreting, adding commentary, or criticizing.]

Client: Well, I wanted to go into the conversation having a clear idea of how things would work. I thought that getting her agreement on what I came up with would be simple and quick and would avoid hassle.

[The client responds to the confrontation by explaining his intentions when giving his wife the list. The client does not indicate in his response that he clearly sees an incongruity.]

Helper: But then she doesn't feel like part of the process of working things out. You're not working together, you're giving her orders.

[The helper follows up the earlier confrontation by further explaining the perceived incongruity.]

Client: I've always worked this way. It's assertive and efficient to take charge and be prepared and know what you want.

[The client responds by stating that he has always worked this way, thus giving the helper information that this is a pattern. It may reflect how the client addresses issues in his marriage.]

Helper: Let me check something out with you, if I may. I'm wondering if you might be afraid to give up some control in working out marital issues with your wife. Working together is harder and riskier than taking charge. You might not get everything you want. There's give-and-take on both sides. Taking charge is assertive and efficient, as you say, but in a personal relationship, it can seem dominating rather than collaborative.

[The helper uses interpretation to offer a possible explanation for the client's "take-charge" approach to his marriage: The client may be afraid of giving up some control. The helper offers the interpretation tentatively ("I'm wondering if . . ."). The interpretation is designed to encourage the client to look at his situation from a new perspective, namely, that he tries to control because he fears that he will not otherwise get what he wants, and that he may not be as willing as he says he is to work things out with his wife. The interpretation also encourages the client to consider reframing his "assertive and efficient" take-charge behavior as dominating. Finally, the helper is providing constructive feedback with this statement by explaining how the client may be "coming across" (i.e., as dominating).]

Client (pauses and speaks more softly than before): I don't know. It just seems like I have to be tough when I deal with her or I won't get what I want. She can be pretty inflexible and demanding herself.

[The client appears to consider the interpretation. He offers an explanation for his take-charge approach, but he does not immediately accept the interpretation.]

Helper: It sounds like there's a lot of power struggling in your relationship.

[The helper paraphrases to show understanding of the client's response to the interpretation.]

Client (soft tone of voice): Yeah, you could say that.

Helper (remains silent)

[The helper uses the skill of silence to see whether the client will elaborate.]

Client (also remains silent; looks at the helper and around the room)

Helper: I'm noticing that you've been quieter since I mentioned that you might be afraid of giving up some control. What are you thinking?

[The helper uses immediacy to address changes that she sees in the client, namely, that he has become quieter recently. The immediacy statement focuses on what is going on at the moment. The helper shares her observation at the time she makes it. The helper then asks an open question to invite the client to comment on what is going on.]

Client: Well, you know, as a supervisor at the plant, I'm used to giving orders. I tell people what to do and they do it—that's my job. But the rules seem so much different in marriage, and I've struggled to figure out how to make things work smoothly. I feel like an idiot and sometimes like a failure.

[The client has been thinking about the helper's earlier interpretation. If the helper had not made an immediacy statement to raise the issue of the client's quieter demeanor and silence, the client may have remained fairly subdued for the rest of the session. He may not have shared his thoughts about the rules of marriage seeming so much different from the way things work at his place of employment. He may not have shared that he feels like a failure sometimes. The helper's immediacy statement and the open question inviting a response allow these issues to come out into the open and be discussed.]

Helper: I hear that you feel frustrated about trying to make things work smoothly in your marriage, but consider this way of looking at your relationship: Marriage is rarely mastered. It's often an ongoing process of trying to improve and enrich the relationship and make it work. Some of the tactics you're using may need to be modified, but you're working hard to make your relationship work when many other people in your shoes would just give up. You know, about half of all marriages end in divorce. Your efforts don't sound idiotic or like the actions of a failure; they show a commitment to making things work. How does that sound to you?

[The helper begins with a reflection of feelings to show understanding of the client's struggle to make things work smoothly in his marriage. She continues by offering an interpretation that reframes the client's situation. She encourages the client to change his perspective about seeing himself as an idiot and a failure and to recognize that he is persisting and working hard to make his marriage work. The helper follows the interpretation with a perception check ("How does that sound to you?") to get the client's feedback. Note that the helper also provides information by telling the client about divorce statistics. This information may help the client appreciate that a significant number of couples end their marriage when difficulties arise, but that the client and his wife have not done so. This information may help the client change his perspective about sometimes feeling like a failure.]

Client: Makes sense, I suppose. We are still married after 10 years, and neither one of us has ever threatened divorce. We seem to make things work one way or another, though not always smoothly.

[The client demonstrates some acceptance of the helper's interpretation and information. If the client changes his perspective on marriage and roles in the relationship, he may be in a better position to take action to improve his relationship with his wife.]

Helper: It sounds like both of you are committed to your relationship even though there are some rough spots.

[The helper paraphrases the client's statement.]

The skills the helper used in this dialogue assisted the client in developing an understanding of his marital problems. The client was encouraged to take a new perspective. With this new understanding and a fresh perspective, the client, with the helper's assistance, could set goals related to improving communication with his wife and working out marital issues in a more collaborative manner.

Summary and Concluding Remarks

This chapter described several skills that helpers use to promote client understanding. A few skills that were discussed earlier in this book were revisited, and six new skills were described: providing constructive feedback, confronting, providing information, interpreting, self-disclosing, and immediacy. These six skills help clients develop awareness and new perspectives, see options and possibilities, identify their strengths and assets, take responsibility for their feelings, thoughts, and behaviors, and develop a more thorough understanding of their problems. These six skills are typically used after good helping relationships have developed and helpers have learned a lot about their clients' lives and problems.

Although these skills can help clients develop important understandings, they can also evoke strong reactions. For example, constructive corrective feedback and negative information ("bad news") can be tough to hear. Confronting and interpreting challenge clients to carefully examine their feelings, thoughts, and behaviors and to consider issues and aspects of themselves that they might prefer to avoid. Clients might respond to the use of these skills by withdrawing, discrediting their helpers, changing the subject, arguing, pretending to agree in order to get helpers to move on to other issues, telling helpers that they are wrong, or minimizing the importance of the topic (see Egan, 2002; Evans et al., 1998). Whether clients react favorably or unfavorably to the skills described in this chapter, helpers tend to follow up with skills such as listening, asking questions, paraphrasing, and reflecting feelings to demonstrate understanding of client reactions and to assist clients in exploring the new areas for discussion that these skills may open up (Hill & O'Brien, 1999).

With some degree of honest understanding achieved, clients are prepared to clarify "possible decisions, possible courses of action" (Rogers, 1942, p. 41). They are ready to chart a new course toward effective functioning by setting goals and identifying actions to achieve those goals. They are ready to begin to put their new understandings to work. This process is the focus of the next part of this book.

Questions for Thought

1. Think about a time in your life when someone gave you feedback. Was the feedback constructive or poorly provided? What aspects of the experience (e.g., how the feedback was provided, how well you knew the person, the person's expertise) made the feedback helpful or unhelpful?

2. What can helpers do to maximize the chances that confrontations will be well received?

3. What do you see as the benefits and risks of providing information to clients?

4. Do you believe that interpreting is a valuable skill in the helping process? What are the benefits and risks of interpreting? Which clients might benefit the most from this skill? The least?

5. What is your position on self-disclosing in helping? Should helpers use this skill or not? Why or why not?

6. What makes the skill of immediacy powerful? Why is this skill important in helping relationships? What are the potential consequences if it is not used?

7. How do cultural variables affect how helpers use the skills described in this chapter?

Exercises

The following exercises cover the skills discussed in this chapter.

PROVIDING CONSTRUCTIVE FEEDBACK EXERCISE

Three client statements follow. After each statement, write a helper response that provides constructive feedback. An example of a helper response to each client statement is provided at the end of this chapter.

Statement 1:
Client (client is very friendly and always has a smile, but she is quiet and somewhat passive; she is having difficulty establishing a satisfying social life): I try to socialize and make friends, but it just seems like no one likes me.

Helper feedback: _____

_____

_____

Statement 2:
Client (other people tend to distance themselves from the client; client speaks in a loud tone of voice): I always talk loud. It gets attention and it's assertive. There's no mistaking what I'm saying.

Helper feedback: _____

_____

_____

Statement 3:
Client (client is a student who is seeing a helper about improving his grades and passing his math class; he has been spending his time after school with friends instead of studying; he does not seem to care much about the class): I've just got other things I would rather do after school. I mean, I need time away from all this schoolwork.

Helper feedback: _____

_____

_____

CONFRONTING EXERCISE

Three client statements follow. After each statement, write a helper response that confronts the client. An example of a helper response to each client statement is provided at the end of this chapter.

Statement 1:
Client: My fiancé and I had a big fight last night about our finances. I think we should be saving more, and he thinks we should focus solely on paying off debt. Whenever we try to talk about money, it seems like we end up in a big argument. We are making good money, at least, so I feel like we have some security. Overall, I guess we don't have too much of a problem around money.

Helper confrontation: _____

_____

_____

Statement 2:
Client (client is trying to improve performance at work): I just don't want to spend that much time in training. It's boring, and I've got other things I could be doing. I just don't have time for it.

Helper confrontation: _____

_____

_____

Statement 3:
Client: I went to a friend's party last weekend. I met some nice people there and had some good conversations. I even made plans to have lunch tomorrow with one person I met. But I left the party feeling worse than I did when I walked in. It just felt like the people there were humoring me—talking with me simply because I was there, not because they really liked me. It always seems that way—like no one ever truly likes me.

Helper confrontation: _____

_____

_____

PROVIDING INFORMATION EXERCISE

Three client statements follow. After each statement, write a helper response that provides information. An example of a helper response to each client statement is provided at the end of this chapter.

Statement 1:
Client: I'm trying to find out what the requirements are for the psychologist position opening up at the clinic. Can you tell me what they are?

Helper information response: _____

_____

_____

Statement 2:
Client (a victim of domestic violence who has decided to end her abusive relationship): I'm not sure what to do or where to go now. Where can I get help?

Helper information response: _____

_____

_____

Statement 3:
Client (after considering applying to an academic degree program at Metro University; the program has a 20% acceptance rate): I thought about applying to the degree program in educational policy at Metro University. I'd like to go to school there because they have a good program and it's close to home, but I heard that the program has only a 3% acceptance rate. I don't think I have a chance, so I'm considering other schools.

Helper information response: _____

_____

_____

INTERPRETING EXERCISE

Three client statements follow. After each statement, write a helper response that interprets the client's statement. An example of a helper response to each client statement is provided at the end of this chapter.

Statement 1:
Client: My wife seems to think that I'm a little child who can't take care of himself. When I tell her I'm going out for a while, she wants to know where I'm going. That's what my mother used to ask!

Helper interpretation: _____

_____

_____

Statement 2:

Client (client's father abandoned the family when the client was young): I just don't trust my husband. I bet he's looking around for some younger woman he can run off with, and then he'll be gone. I'm thinking about filing for divorce.

Helper interpretation: _____

_____

_____

Statement 3:

Client: I'm an A student, but that doesn't seem to be good enough. The teacher keeps pushing me so hard because she doesn't like me. She always suggests ways that I could improve.

Helper interpretation: _____

_____

_____

SELF-DISCLOSING EXERCISE

Three client statements follow. After each statement, write a helper response that demonstrates self-disclosing. An example of a helper response to each client statement is provided at the end of this chapter.

Statement 1:

Client: I was going to ask Amy out on a date last week, but I lost my nerve. It seems like this always happens. I meet someone I like and want to ask out, and then at the last minute, I bail out. It's so frustrating to see everyone else going on dates while I'm having so much difficulty getting one.

Helper self-disclosure: _____

_____

_____

Statement 2:

Client: I just started college last week. I'm so far away from home, and I feel so alone. The work is so much more demanding than it was in high school. I don't see how I will ever get it all done and do well.

Helper self-disclosure: _____

_____

_____

Statement 3:

Client: My job search isn't going too well. There's just nothing out there that appeals to me. It seems like I'm never going to find a job that I really enjoy. I feel like I'm going to spend my life going from one miserable little job to another, like some vocational transient.

Helper self-disclosure: _____

_____

_____

IMMEDIACY EXERCISE

Three client statements follow. After each statement, write a helper response that demonstrates immediacy. An example of a helper response to each client statement is provided at the end of this chapter.

Statement 1:

Client (fairly silent for the first 10 minutes of the session; makes little eye contact with the helper; shrugs his shoulders): I don't know what I want to talk about.

Helper immediacy statement: _____

_____

_____

Statement 2:

Client (yelling): I don't know how many times I have to tell him to ask me before he takes my car! We've talked about this so many times, but he just doesn't listen! I mean, is it so much to ask? I bet you don't take other people's things without asking! Do you? What am I supposed to do?

Helper immediacy statement: _____

_____

_____

Statement 3:

Client (has been motivated and actively involved in the helping process over the past several sessions and seems increasingly comfortable with the helper): I feel like I'm getting a huge burden off my chest by talking with you. And most important, I feel like I've learned a lot over the past several weeks.

Helper immediacy statement: _____

_____

_____

Exercise Responses

Note that these responses are examples of good responses. They are not the only correct responses.

PROVIDING CONSTRUCTIVE FEEDBACK EXERCISE

Statement 1 helper feedback: I can give you some feedback if you wish. You're very friendly and pleasant to be around, and your smile is very warm. I think these are important and attractive qualities. But I notice that you seem shy, and that may be why it's hard to socialize.

Statement 2 helper feedback: Can I give you some feedback? Speaking loudly is assertive, and you are very clear on what you want. At the same time, I think you tend to overwhelm and intimidate people with your voice. That may be why they tend to keep their distance from you.

Statement 3 helper feedback: Can I give you some feedback? It seems like you're not very interested in passing the class. You haven't been studying, and you're spending most of your time with your friends. What are your thoughts on that?

CONFRONTING EXERCISE

Statement 1 helper confrontation: You said that when you try to talk about money, you end up in a big argument, but then you said you don't have too much of a problem around money.

Statement 2 helper confrontation: You want to improve your work performance, but it sounds like you're unwilling to do the training that's necessary to accomplish that goal.

Statement 3 helper confrontation: You say that it seems no one truly likes you, but you said you had some good conversations and made lunch plans with one person.

PROVIDING INFORMATION EXERCISE

Statement 1 helper information response: You have to be a licensed psychologist in this state and have at least 5 years of experience working as a psychologist. For additional requirements and more details, I'll give you a copy of the job posting.

Statement 2 helper information response: There are several resources you can consider. There's a women's shelter a few miles from here where you can stay for a while, and I can give you the phone numbers for other community agencies and support groups that help women in your position. You may also want to contact the police or the court clerk and look into getting an order for protection.

Statement 3 helper information response: Actually, the acceptance rate for that program is about 20%.

INTERPRETING EXERCISE

Statement 1 helper interpretation: Is it possible that she doesn't see you as a child, but she just cares about you and wants to know where you are so she won't worry?

Statement 2 helper interpretation: I'm wondering if you fear that your husband will leave you because that's what your father did a long time ago. Perhaps you're thinking of leaving your husband by divorcing him so he can't abandon you like your father did.

Statement 3 helper interpretation: Could it be that she pushes you so hard because she sees you as a very good student and is trying to help you reach your full potential? Her suggestions for improvement could be her way of showing that she believes in your ability and wants you to succeed.

SELF-DISCLOSING EXERCISE

Statement 1 helper self-disclosure: I had some trouble getting dates, too, when I was your age. I remember how frustrating and lonely it was to watch other people on their dates while I didn't have one. I could hardly ever get up the courage to ask for a date because I feared rejection and embarrassing myself. Is that how it is for you?

Statement 2 helper self-disclosure: You know, when I started college, I remember feeling the same way. It was my first time living away from home. I didn't know anyone at the university, and the work was overwhelming. It seemed like the professors thought I had nothing else to do but study for their classes. For most students, it gets better, though, and it did for me. It takes a little time to adjust to such a major change in life. Making some friends and joining a study group helped me a lot.

Statement 3 helper self-disclosure: When I finished college, I didn't see any attractive job prospects, either. I remember thinking that there wasn't a good job out there for me. For a couple of years, no matter how hard I looked, I just couldn't find anything I was happy with. It was a little scary. Is that how it is for you?

IMMEDIACY EXERCISE

Statement 1 helper immediacy statement: It seems to me that you're bored. What are you feeling?

Statement 2 helper immediacy statement: When you yell like that, I feel annoyed. I feel like I want to tune you out because it's very hard to talk with someone who's yelling. I'm wondering how you believe that yelling helps.

Statement 3 helper immediacy statement: That's great! I want to tell you how pleased I am with the progress you've made over the past several sessions. I feel good about the positive steps you're taking. Would you like to say more about what you've learned?

Charting a New Course

CHAPTER 10

Setting Goals

CHAPTER OVERVIEW

This chapter focuses on the first aspect of charting a new course: setting goals. At this point, helpers assist their clients in deciding and articulating what they want to accomplish. That is, what goals do the clients want to achieve? In this chapter, we define goals and describe their purposes and benefits. We also discuss characteristics of effective goals, the process of setting goals, whether to set goals verbally or in writing, difficulties related to setting goals, and skills used in setting goals. A hypothetical dialogue and exercises are included at the end of this chapter to facilitate understanding of setting goals.

The mind that has no fixed goal loses itself.

—Michel de Montaigne
(1580/1925, p. 39)

Setting Goals: Reducing Complexity and Increasing Precision

When exploring client concerns, helpers immerse themselves in the "ocean"—the world of their clients—and strive to appreciate the uniqueness, intricacies, and complexity of their clients' lives and problems. When promoting client understanding, helpers assist clients in fully and honestly appreciating the nature, intricacies, and complexity of their problems. When helping clients set goals—the first aspect of charting a new course—the task is to *reduce* complexity. Helpers assist clients in translating difficult problems, complicated issues, and general desires into clear, precise goals for change. Helpers begin to move from the somewhat passive process of exploration and understanding to the more active process of helping their clients articulate the changes they want to make. Adopting a more concrete, active, structured, and behavior-focused approach than they may have used earlier allows helpers to function effectively and assist their clients in setting goals. Such an approach may be particularly useful for clients of many racial and ethnic minority groups (e.g., African Americans and Latinos/Latinas) and clients of lower social class, who tend to prefer more directive, structured, active helping approaches (D. W. Sue & Sue, 2003).

What Are Goals?

In the helping process, goals are verbal or written expressions of what clients want to accomplish. They reflect what clients hope to achieve with helper assistance. Here are some general points about goals in helping.

Goals Focus on Results, Ends, or Outcomes, Not Actions. Goals address what clients want to achieve, not what clients are going to do to get there (see Egan, 2002). For example, if a client wants to receive straight As this semester, that is the result, end, or outcome toward which the client will strive. It is the client's goal. Studying 3 hours per night and joining a study group are actions that the client could take to help her reach the goal. Actions are discussed in chapter 11.

Goals Reflect the Changes That Clients Want to Make in How They Feel, Think, Behave, or Interact With Others. For example, goals could be set to

- reduce anger and increase positive feelings (a feelings-related goal),
- improve decision-making skills (a thought-related goal),
- improve physical health (a behavior-related goal), or
- make more friends (an interaction-related goal).

Goals may also address a combination of feelings, thoughts, behaviors, and interactions.

Goals Focus on Prevention, Remediation, or Growth. Goals can be set for the purpose of avoiding or minimizing the chances of undesirable events or consequences, managing or resolving current problems, or enhancing client skills, knowledge, potential, and quality of life.

Goals Can Be Immediate, Short-Range, Middle-Range, or Long-Range. Some goals address immediate needs, such as getting access to urgently needed services (e.g., those offered by a women's shelter). Other goals are short- or middle-range in nature. Such goals are intended to be accomplished at some point in the near future, in many cases while clients are still in helping. For example, a client who wants to improve his grades may create a short-range goal of achieving an A on a midterm exam coming up in 2 weeks. Still other goals are long-range. These goals may take many months—even years—to achieve (e.g., a first-year college student's goal to graduate in 4 years). Of course, multiple goals may be set in helping, depending on the amount of time available and the nature of the client's problems. The goals may include an assortment of immediate, short-range, middle-range, and long-range goals.

Purposes and Benefits of Goals

Setting well-prepared, carefully considered goals increases the chances of success-fully managing or resolving problems (Dixon & Glover, 1984). In helping, goals—and the process of setting them—are important for the following reasons.

Goals Provide Structure, Focus, and Direction for the Helping Process. Helping would be aimless without goals. Without goals, helpers and clients would have dif-ficulty knowing the purpose of their meetings and what clients want to accomplish.

Setting Goals Strengthens Helping Relationships. The process of setting goals supports, continues, and reinforces the collaborative nature of helping (McClam & Woodside, 1994). Clients ultimately decide what they want to accomplish, but helpers offer guidance and feedback. Working together in this way creates a feeling of teamwork and strengthens rapport.

Goals Ensure That Helpers and Clients Are Pursuing the Same Objectives in the Helping Process. Without clearly stated goals, helpers and clients may have entirely different ideas about why they are meeting and what they want to accomplish.

Setting Goals Assists Clients in Articulating Their Needs and Desires. Setting goals requires clients to specify what they want to accomplish and assists them in clearly understanding what outcomes they will pursue. Those clients who have a clear sense of their goals are more likely to benefit from helping (Tallman & Bohart, 1999).

Goals Motivate Clients. As noted by Egan (2002) and Locke and Latham (1984), clients' identification of what they would like to accomplish can encourage positive thinking and empower the clients, helping them focus their attention and energy, mobilize resources, reduce anxiety and confusion, search for ways to accom-plish their goals, and achieve a sense of movement in the management or resolution of their problems.

Setting Goals May Elicit Feelings of Hope, Liberation, and Relief. Setting goals may allow clients to feel, possibly for the first time, that they are getting out of the rut they have been in and are finally moving forward with managing or resolving their problems. Their "unsolvable" problems begin to look solvable.

Goals Aid Helpers in Developing Ideas and Plans for Working With Clients. Once goals have been set, helpers can identify relevant skills, interventions, and strategies to facilitate achievement of the goals. For example, if a client sets a goal related to making more friends, the helper may decide that role-playing could be an effective technique to assist the client in achieving this goal.

Goals Permit Evaluation of Progress and Measurement of Success in Helping. When specific goals are established, helpers and clients can use them to chart client progress and determine how well the helping process is working. Are the goals being achieved? What challenges are clients facing as they work toward their goals? Do the goals need to be modified? Without goals, helpers and clients would have difficulty evaluating helping. How would they know when they have finished and whether they accomplished anything?

Setting Goals Teaches Clients a Useful Skill. Setting effective goals is a skill that many clients do not possess. Learning how to set effective goals can help clients become adept at specifically identifying and articulating the things they want in life. This skill can benefit clients long after helping has ended.

Characteristics of Effective Goals

Effective goals tend to possess the characteristics described in the following paragraphs.

Effective Goals Are Based on Careful Exploration and Sufficient Understanding of Client Problems and Needs. A reasonably good understanding of client problems and needs is typically required before meaningful, relevant goals can be set. Even goals set in the first session must be based on a sufficient understanding of client problems and needs. The basic point here is that one must know what the problem is in order to take steps to manage or resolve it. Goals that are set before understanding is achieved may focus on unimportant or irrelevant concerns and fail to address the real issues for which clients need help.

Effective Goals Are Established by Mutual Agreement. Helpers and clients decide together what goals to pursue. Clients know themselves, their problems, their needs, their desires, and what they are willing to do. They are also the ones who ultimately must do the work to manage or resolve their problems. Helpers contribute to the goal-setting process by sharing their knowledge, insights, and skills. They also offer new perspectives on client lives and problems. Through guidance and feedback, they help clients set realistic, specific, and beneficial goals. In short, helpers work with clients to articulate, prioritize, and revise goals and to facilitate the process of achieving them.

Although goals are mutually agreed upon, clients ultimately bear most of the burden of setting them. Only clients know what they want, and they are responsible for the changes that they want to make in their lives. Moreover, when clients set goals that reflect what they want (as opposed to helpers setting the goals they think are best), the goals tend to be more personally meaningful. It should be noted that for some clients with a collectivist perspective, consulting with family members may be part of the process of setting goals, making decisions, and making changes (see D. W. Sue & Sue, 2003). Such consultation is not a sign of unhealthy dependence or enmeshment. Instead, it reflects the fact that choices and decisions made by one individual in the collective may have an impact on the other members of the collective.

Effective Goals Are Focused on Significant Problems. Many problems may be discussed in the helping process. Due to time constraints, financial limitations, and helper and client choices, among other factors, goals are not always set for every problem. Helpers and clients may need to prioritize problems and then address the most important ones.

Effective Goals Are Focused on Positive Change. Sometimes, clients want to set goals that would probably not be beneficial. For example, a client may want to set the goal of taking revenge on a coworker who has angered her. A goal that satisfies many of the characteristics of effective goals could probably be set, but would this goal really help the client solve problems and improve her quality of life? Exacting revenge on a coworker would not likely lead to positive change and improved well-being for the client. By using such skills as asking questions and confronting, helpers can assist clients in carefully considering whether goals will lead to positive change.

Effective Goals Are Desirable and Practical When Assessed With a Cost/Benefit Analysis. To determine whether particular goals are worth setting and pursuing, helpers assist clients in assessing the costs and benefits of the goals (Dixon & Glover, 1984; Egan, 2002). For example, pursuing the goal of raising one's grade point average (GPA) from 3.0 to 3.5 during the current school year would probably require more study time. Social activities and free time might need to be sacrificed to some extent. These would be the costs of the goal. The benefit would be a higher GPA, which might increase the client's chances of getting into graduate school or getting a good job.

The discussion of both costs and benefits is important. It helps clients decide whether to proceed with particular goals and also helps clients recognize that making positive changes involves some costs, not just benefits. When clients understand that there will probably be some costs, they are less likely to give up on their goals when they experience those costs. Identifying benefits may increase client motivation to pursue goals.

Effective Goals Are Realistic. In the broadest sense, realistic goals are ones that are possible to achieve. For example, losing 8 pounds in 10 weeks is probably realistic for most people, but losing 150 pounds in the same time period is not. Egan (2002) described realistic goals in terms of resources and control. He stated that goals are realistic if (1) clients have access to the resources needed to accomplish them; and (2) the goals are within the clients' control, not hampered by external circumstances. For example, a client who wants to make her father stop drinking may be setting an unrealistic goal because her father's drinking is not within her control. A more realistic goal may relate to addressing how the client responds to her father's drinking (e.g., learning to more effectively manage her anger). During the goal-setting process, helpers assist clients in focusing on what the clients can do, rather than focusing on trying to control or change other people. Clients may not be able to control their environment or other people, but they can control how they respond to them.

Effective Goals Are Challenging. Goals should not be so lofty that failure is almost certain. Nor should they be so easy that clients would hardly have to expend any effort or take any risks to accomplish them. Effective goals are challenging—not too easy, not too difficult. Clients expend more effort and feel more motivated when their goals challenge them (Egan, 2002; Locke & Latham, 1984).

Effective Goals Are Expressed in Positive, Active Language. Goals that are expressed in positive, active language (i.e., goals that suggest what clients want to affirmatively accomplish, as opposed to what clients want to prevent or avoid) tend to be more appealing and motivating than goals stated in negative language (see DeJong & Berg, 1998). Goals that are described negatively or only in terms of the absence of problems (e.g., "to not be upset all the time") can reinforce discouragement, negative thinking, and feelings of being stuck (DeJong & Berg, 1998). They can also make it difficult for clients to know what they are supposed *to do*. If a client does not want to be upset all the time, then what does she want in place of being upset? The answer to that question is what the goal would focus on.

Effective Goals Are Specific and Focused on Behavioral Changes. In general, effective goals clearly, concretely, and specifically describe observable, desirable behavioral changes. Although clients may present vague concerns, making it difficult initially to identify specific goals, they work with helpers to gradually define goals with more precision. Specific, behavior-focused goals often address in some way (1) the behavior to be performed or changed; (2) the level, degree, or amount of the behavior; and (3) the conditions under which the behavior will occur—for example, where and when the behavior is to take place (Cormier & Hackney, 1999). As an example, consider the goal "to increase the number of family meals at home from once per week to three times per week by the end of the month."

    Behavior: increasing the number of family meals
      Amount: from once to three times per week
  Conditions: at home, by the end of the month

Specific, behavior-focused goals are important for a couple of reasons. First, when goals are stated in specific terms and focus on explicit behaviors, clients know exactly what is to be achieved and are, therefore, more likely to identify the steps they need to take to make changes. Vague goals (e.g., "to be emotionally stronger") may create uncertainty as to what the goals mean and what clients are supposed to do to achieve them. Second, it is easier to measure progress and achievement in attaining specific, behavior-focused goals than it is to measure progress and achievement in attaining less specific ones (see Cavanagh & Levitov, 2002). For example, achievement of the goal "to maintain a 3.5 grade point average in all course work this school year" is easier to measure and confirm than is achievement of the goal "to do well in school" or "to be happy with my academic performance." How would one measure "doing well" or "happiness"? What do these terms mean to a particular client? Happiness is the general state toward which the client strives. Specific goal statements help the client reach happiness (McClam & Woodside, 1994).

Goals vary in their level of specificity. They do not have to be as specifically stated as possible, but they need to be specific enough for progress to be assessed and achievement to be determined. In addition, some insurance carriers, as a condition for payment, require that helpers identify specific, behaviorally measurable outcomes for their clients (i.e., specific behavioral changes to be made in helping). Thus, helpers and clients need to set goals that can be measured.

Effective Goals Are Attainable Within a Certain Period of Time. A time frame within which goals will be accomplished motivates clients and encourages disciplined action (see Egan, 2002; Locke & Latham, 1984). The absence of a time period can cause clients to put off goals or turn their attention to other activities. They may never get around to working toward the goals they set. The period of time that is established varies based on client needs and the nature of the goals. Of course, helpers and clients can extend or shorten the time period if necessary.

Effective Goals Are Consistent With Client Characteristics, Skills, Resources, and Circumstances. Effective goals take into account such client factors as age, intelligence, maturity, cultural characteristics, worldview, life experiences, resources, living arrangements, commitments, and problem-solving styles. All of these factors impact what clients want and need, and also what they are able or willing to do. Client characteristics, skills, resources, and circumstances often help to determine what goals are realistic. For example, the goal of attending a prestigious university may not be realistic for a client with poor grades or limited financial resources.

Also, such variables as race/ethnicity and social class may influence goals and goal-setting. For example, as noted in the discussion of worldview in chapter 5, European Americans tend to be future-oriented. Such an orientation may make European Americans more agreeable to long-range goals. Many other cultures, however, have a different time orientation. For example, Native Americans and African Americans tend to be present-oriented (Ho, 1987). Immediate and short-range goals may be most desirable for clients of these groups (D. W. Sue & Sue, 2003). Clients of lower social class who have immediate survival needs, such as accessing public resources or emergency services, may also prefer immediate and short-range goals. Of course, these are generalizations. In addition to cultural group characteristics, helpers must consider the unique needs and desires of their individual clients as they help their clients set realistic goals (e.g., not all European Americans value long-range goals).

Effective Goals Are Consistent With Helper Abilities and Obligations. Several points are important here. First, helpers must possess skills and training relevant to helping clients achieve their goals. A school guidance counselor, for example, who sees a teenage student who has academic difficulties and a substance abuse problem will likely focus on addressing the academic difficulties and refer the student to a more qualified professional to address the substance abuse issues. Second, helpers need to consider the policies and functions of the settings in which they work. The kinds of clients served in the setting, the types of problems the setting addresses, and the resources available to helpers can affect what helpers can do and what types of goals can be set. For example, in a setting that focuses on crisis counseling, goals tend to be immediate and short-range. Third, helpers must abide by ethical guidelines and laws when helping clients set and pursue goals (Brammer & MacDonald,

2003; Hutchins & Cole Vaught, 1997). Although clients, on their own, can set and pursue whatever goals they choose, helpers cannot always ethically or legally assist them in achieving their goals. For example, Brammer and MacDonald (2003) noted that it would be inappropriate for a helper to assist a client in cheating on an examination or taking advantage of a weaker person. Finally, helper values may conflict with client values and needs to such an extent that it would be difficult for helpers to accommodate client goals (Hutchins & Cole Vaught, 1997). For example, a helper and a client may have different views on reproductive rights and may not be able to find much common ground. In such cases, a referral to another helper may be needed.

Effective Goals Are Changeable. As helpers and clients work together, they may discover that it would be a good idea to modify goals (see Locke & Latham, 1984). Goals that initially seemed achievable may turn out to be too difficult to accomplish, new information may have come to light about client problems, or clients may choose to reveal issues that they did not feel comfortable discussing earlier. In each of these cases, helpers and clients may decide to modify the goals.

The Process of Setting Goals

Helpers and clients set goals as they choose to, based on their preferences, the clients' needs, the helpers' theoretical orientation, and the policies and procedures of the helping setting. There are, however, some basic steps that typically characterize the process of setting goals, as described in the following paragraphs.

Consider the Status of the Helping Relationship. Goals sometimes are set early in the helping process before strong helping relationships have developed. This is often the case when clients have urgent or immediate needs (e.g., a goal to reduce anxiety). In general, however, goals are set after good helping relationships have developed, when clients are usually more willing to talk about what they want to accomplish. At this point, they are more likely to trust helpers as people who can facilitate change.

Ensure Understanding of Client Problems. Setting goals can occur at various points in the helping process, but whenever goal-setting happens, helpers need to possess sufficient knowledge and understanding of client problems and needs to ensure that the goals address relevant issues.

Discuss Goal-Setting With Clients. It is helpful to explain to clients how setting goals can increase the chances of success in helping by clearly and specifically identifying the objectives to be pursued. Clients also need to understand that setting and working toward goals often require hard work and a strong commitment (see Nelson-Jones, 1993) and involve both costs and benefits. Although clients may find that setting goals helps them become more focused and motivated, they often have to give up attitudes and behaviors that are familiar and comfortable, such as blaming other people and avoiding responsibility (Nelson-Jones, 1993). Helpers can discuss these issues with their clients. They need to know that their clients are ready and willing to set goals.

Instill Hope About Change. Clients may want more than a description or a reason for setting goals. They may also want to know whether setting goals will really help them make positive changes. Thus, helpers often instill hope in clients that change is possible, despite past failures or inaction. Some clients use their history as a reason for not changing and for believing that their situation will not improve (J. Dagley, personal communication, May 23, 2002). As a way to instill hope, helpers can tell their clients that they will be there for support. They may also describe some of the purposes and benefits of goals, as described earlier. However, helpers need to be realistic. Although helpers can encourage and facilitate change, they cannot guarantee it.

Help Clients Translate Their Problems and Desires Into Specific Goals. Clients usually do not enter helping prepared to state highly specific goals. Typically, they describe their problems and express a desire for change, often in vague or general terms. These problems and desires need to be translated into specific goals (see Brammer & MacDonald, 2003). For example, "I am overweight" (the problem) leads to "I want to lose some weight" (the desire), which then becomes "I want to lose 20 pounds in the next 6 months following the 'New You' weight loss plan" (the specific goal). To help clients translate problems and desires into specific goals, helpers consider the characteristics of effective goals, described earlier, and use such skills as listening, asking questions, focusing, and confronting.

Prioritize Goals. This point was made by Locke and Latham (1984). Some problems are more important than others and require more immediate attention. Goals related to these problems are typically addressed first. Further, if helpers and clients identify more goals than they can reasonably work toward in the time they have together, they need to select from among the many possible goals, deciding which ones will be pursued and in what order. Some goals may ultimately be discarded, either because there is not enough time to pursue them or because they address less important issues.

Develop Subgoals, If Needed. You have probably noticed that it is a lot easier to eat an apple if you cut it up into little pieces than if you try to stuff the whole thing in your mouth at once. Subgoals are smaller goals that are set to facilitate the achievement of larger goals. For example, if a client sets a middle-range goal of getting an A in her English class this semester, she may set one or more subgoals (e.g., short-range goals) to be achieved along the way, such as getting an A on the quiz the next week. Subgoals promote disciplined, focused action and may make larger goals seem less overwhelming. When subgoals are achieved, clients see results and feel a sense of accomplishment. This progress encourages clients to persist in their efforts as they work toward achieving their larger goals. In short, achieving subgoals increases the chances that the larger goals will be achieved. The characteristics of effective goals also apply to subgoals, and helpers use the same skills when assisting clients in setting subgoals as they use when helping clients set larger goals.

Note and Discuss Client Reactions to the Process of Setting Goals. Setting goals can be challenging for clients as they consider the specific changes that they want to make. Helpers may find it beneficial to ask clients how they are responding to the process of setting goals. Do they have any concerns or questions? How comfortable are they with the process? How do they feel about the goals that they want to pursue? In many cases, clients do not verbalize their concerns or feelings unless helpers ask. Clients may feel more comfortable, motivated, and invested in the goal-setting process if they have the opportunity to express themselves.

Modify, Add, or Discard Goals as Needed. The process of setting and pursuing goals should be flexible, with helpers and clients making adjustments when necessary (Locke & Latham, 1984). Here are some reasons why goals might need to be modified, added, or discarded:

- Clients might not reveal everything about their problems early in the helping process due to such factors as mistrust and fear of judgment; it may take a few sessions for them to disclose important or sensitive information.
- Problems may be complex and take a while to be fully described and understood.
- New developments in clients' lives and problems may occur during the helping process.
- Difficulties may be encountered as clients attempt to achieve goals—for example, a goal that initially seemed realistic and desirable may turn out not to be.
- Clients may simply change their mind and want new goals.

For all of these reasons, goals that have already been set may need to be modified as new information becomes available. New goals may be added, and existing goals may be cast aside. Consider, for example, this situation. A client presents her concern as having a problem finding a job. It appears initially that the client lacks vocational information, but as the client becomes more comfortable and open with the helper over the course of a few sessions, the helper begins to see that the client lacks self-confidence. Indeed, the client believes that she will never find a good job. An initial goal related to gathering information about possible careers may be modified, put on hold, or even dropped in order to set goals related to increasing self-confidence.

Setting Goals: Verbally or in Writing?

Whether to verbally discuss goals or put them in writing depends on many variables, including the helping setting, the helper's style and theoretical orientation, and the client's needs and desires. Verbal and written goal processes both possess advantages and disadvantages. Verbally discussed goals are flexible and easy to modify, but they may be forgotten. Written goal statements, which are common in helping settings that emphasize systematic procedures and careful measurement of treatment outcomes, require clients to articulate specific goals and actions on paper and thus encourage careful thinking about what is to be accomplished. Written goal statements also serve as concrete reminders of the commitments that clients have made. A disadvantage of written goal statements is that they may discourage the modification of goals by making goals seem "set in stone." Helpers and clients usually decide together whether they want to verbally discuss goals or write them down.

Difficulties Related to Setting Goals

The following paragraphs describe difficulties that are sometimes associated with the process of setting goals.

Premature Goal-Setting. Goals that are set too early, before helpers understand client problems, may be irrelevant and inappropriate. Helpers, especially novices, sometimes find it tempting to jump to setting goals and providing solutions before problems have been thoroughly explored. A quick answer is simpler than delving into complex emotions and complicated problems. Therefore, helpers may proceed too fast to setting goals and taking action to achieve them. M. S. Corey and Corey (2003) stated that this impatience and need to solve client problems can block helpers from hearing what clients are communicating about their problems. The exploration process is cut off and clients may feel that important parts of their problems are being ignored. As M. S. Corey and Corey (2003) noted, "This problem-solving focus aborts the struggle of clients in expressing and dealing with feelings and thoughts and eventually coming up with alternatives that are best for them" (p. 128). Helpers who provide early solutions may be uncomfortable with client problems or they may be too focused on their own need to feel competent and see results (M. S. Corey & Corey, 2003). Helpers need to allow clients to express their feelings and fully describe their concerns so meaningful goals can be set.

Inaccurate Identification of Client Problems. Even with thorough exploration, helpers may incorrectly identify client problems, which are often intricate and complex. Sometimes, helpers have difficulty understanding the problems and identifying what their clients need. Sometimes, they latch onto unimportant topics or focus on issues that are important to themselves. In any case, inaccurate identification can lead to irrelevant and unhelpful goals. To avoid this problem, helpers should verify their understanding of client problems by using such skills as asking questions, paraphrasing, and reflecting feelings. They may also consult with supervisors or colleagues.

Client Resistance. Setting goals requires clients to think specifically about how they want things to be different in their lives. It asks them to commit to change. Although the majority of clients want to manage or resolve their problems, the prospect of making changes and abandoning ineffective—but familiar—attitudes and behaviors can evoke conflicting feelings and resistance to setting goals. Clients may manifest resistance by

- continuing to blame other people for problems;
- expressing fear of change;
- expressing fear of failure;
- expressing confusion or frustration;
- demonstrating a lack of readiness, motivation, desire, or commitment to change;
- letting helpers take the lead (e.g., allowing helpers to set goals; going along with whatever helpers want to do);
- clinging to negative beliefs that problems will never be managed or resolved;
- maintaining that they do not know how to be different;
- putting off change;

■ expressing beliefs that goal-setting in helping is an artificial and overly methodical process that is too different from their usual ways of making decisions; and
■ refusing to participate in goal-setting.

Hackney and Cormier (2001) asserted that resistance to setting goals can stem from (1) clients' confusion about their priorities, desires, and needs; (2) helpers pushing clients in certain directions; or (3) clients not wanting to give up the benefits that current behaviors offer. For example, a client who wants to lose weight may resist doing so because he or she does not want to reduce fat and sugar consumption. Eating rich food gives pleasure and satisfaction even though it causes problems.

Helpers often work to understand resistance by "joining," or going along with, the resistance rather than fighting it. For example, a helper might say, "I see that you're hesitant to work on setting goals, and there's probably a good reason for that. Would you like to talk about some of your concerns?" (S. Neufeldt, personal communication, May 6, 2002). Helpers may even learn that something they are doing is causing the resistance (e.g., pushing for goals that the client does not want to set). In such cases, resistance is understandable and requires changes on the helper's part. Helpers may explore resistance using such skills as listening, asking questions, confronting, interpreting, and immediacy. They may also acknowledge that planning for and making changes often require a lot of courage and personal strength. Often, helpers need to be patient, and they may need to delay goal-setting until clients are ready.

Struggling to Define or Decide on Goals. Some clients enter helping with fairly clear ideas about what they want to accomplish and have little difficulty setting specific goals. For many clients, however, identifying specific goals is challenging. The clients know they want things to be different, but they are not entirely sure how. Even after exploring and understanding their problems, they may still struggle to articulate what they want. For these clients, asking questions and focusing may be useful helper skills. Other clients may identify a vast array of potential goals but then struggle to select good ones to pursue. Helpers may assist these clients by doing a cost/benefit analysis for each goal.

Setting Goals That Do Not Possess Characteristics of Effective Goals. As discussed earlier, effective goals tend to possess certain characteristics. For example, they are mutually agreed upon, realistic, and specific. If goal-setting is not taken seriously, done carefully, or given sufficient attention, the goals that are set may not possess these characteristics. Such goals may be nonspecific, unrealistic, too easy or too difficult, focused on the negative, or focused on unimportant issues. Setting goals with these characteristics can result in a multitude of problems, including uncertainty as to what is to be achieved, difficulties in measuring progress, and the inability of clients to accomplish the goals. Thus, helpers and clients need to take goal-setting seriously and strive to set high-quality goals.

Helpers Imposing Their Own Perspectives, Needs, and Biases. Clients are the focus of helping, and the goals that are set need to be consistent with clients' needs and desires. Sometimes, helpers' perspectives, needs, and biases can interfere with setting goals. Helpers may deliberately or unconsciously pressure clients into setting goals that they believe would be best. Or they may suggest goals that reflect their own cultural beliefs rather than those of their clients. For example, a helper who has an individualist perspective (see chapter 2) might push a client toward setting highly individual goals that focus solely on the client. This may be a problem if the client has a collectivist perspective. Clients who view the world from a collectivist perspective may want to consider the impact of family and sociocultural variables when setting goals (see, e.g., D. Sue, 1997). Helpers may find it beneficial to consult with supervisors or colleagues to address situations where conflicts have arisen between their own needs and perspectives and those of their clients. If helpers experience significant conflicts in this regard, referrals to other helping professionals may be in order.

Goal-Setting Processes That Are Either Too Formal or Too Casual. If goal-setting is too formal (e.g., producing highly detailed, lengthy written goal statements), it can seem overly methodical, orderly, and complicated. Highly formal goal-setting processes may promote precision and specificity, but they may also detract from the personal nature of helping and make the process seem like a school or work project. Goals then become dry, impersonal objectives that may have little meaning to clients. Very casual goal-setting processes (e.g., generally talking about what clients want) can also be problematic in that they may convey the impression that setting goals is unimportant. When the process is too casual, clients may not take goal-setting seriously or feel motivated to work toward the goals they set. Helpers can alleviate some of these problems by deciding with their clients how they want to go about setting goals.

Skills Used in Setting Goals

Many of the skills discussed in previous chapters are useful in the process of setting goals. In the following sections, we briefly revisit several skills that are particularly useful in this regard.

Listening

Listening involves hearing and comprehending client statements and expressions. As helpers listen to clients, they pick up clues about the clients' problems and what the clients want and need. Lauver and Harvey (1997) stated that helpers "must listen closely and recognize and mentally list counselee utterances and nonverbal messages that are potential goal indicators" (p. 113). These authors encouraged helpers to listen for expressions of pain, frustration, dissatisfaction, and unhappiness as well as expressions related to wishes, hopes, aspirations, ambitions, and needs—all of which may be developed into specific goals. For example, a client statement such as, "If I had more computer skills, I could probably get a better job," could be developed into a specific goal such as, "to complete and pass a course in basic computer training at the local college by the end of the year."

Asking Questions

Helpers can ask open and closed questions to identify and understand what clients want and need. They can ask questions to learn how clients would like to feel, think, behave, and interact differently. Further, they can ask questions to help clients state their goals with specificity. Examples of questions that may be asked in the process of setting goals include the following:

"How would you like for things to be different?"
"What would you like to change in your life?"
"What would you like to accomplish?"
"If your problems were resolved and you were living the life you wanted, what would you be doing?"

Focusing

Helpers use focusing to identify and address in detail specific topics, statements, and expressions that seem particularly important. Focusing is particularly helpful during goal-setting, which is a process of going from vague to clear, from general to specific, from abstract to concrete. Focusing promotes clarity and precision in goal statements. Examples of focusing in the process of setting goals follow:

"Please tell me what spending more time with your husband would involve. What would you be doing?"
"Describe more specifically how much improvement you would like to see in your job performance."
"How would you define a good social life?"

Sometimes, there is an overlap between focusing and asking questions. To the extent that questions request specifics and details, they are a form of focusing.

Confronting

Through confronting, helpers point out inconsistencies, distortions, and contradictions in client expressions, behaviors, perspectives, and circumstances. Confronting can be used in goal-setting to point out apparent incongruities in client desires and goals (e.g., a client wanting to make more friends without venturing out of the house very often). Confronting can also be used to address client resistance to setting goals. In addition, it may be helpful as a way to encourage clients to assess how realistic their desires and goals are. Examples of confronting in the process of setting goals include the following:

"You say that you want to make changes, but when we start talking about what you'd like to change, you always want to discuss something else."
"I hear that you want to force Mark to seek help, but he is the only one who can make that decision."

A Hypothetical Dialogue

The following hypothetical dialogue between a helper and a client demonstrates how a goal may be set. The client is a male college student who is struggling to meet people and make friends. This dialogue is from the fourth helping session.

Helper: Well, last time near the end of the hour, we began talking about your goals. Have you given any more thought to that?

[The helper opens the session by reintroducing the issue of the client's goals. This is a way to begin focusing on goal-setting. The helper asks a closed question to invite the client to respond.]

Client: A little. Not a lot. I just know I want things to be different. I'm tired of being alone all the time.

Helper: How do you want things to be different?

[The helper asks an open question to get the client to be more specific.]

Client: I want a satisfying social life.

Helper: Tell me what a satisfying social life involves.

[The helper uses the skill of focusing to encourage the client to elaborate. Note how the helper and the client are moving from the problem ("I'm tired of being alone all the time") to the client's desire ("I want a satisfying social life"). This desire is very general and probably would not be sufficient as a goal statement. It represents what the client ultimately wants to achieve, but the helper and the client need to get more specific to facilitate taking action, charting progress, and confirming achievement.]

Client: More friends, mainly. I want a few friends that I could do things with during the week.

Helper: What kinds of things would you like to do with your friends?

[The helper asks an open question to elicit more details.]

Client: Football games, movies, shopping. I'd like to go to the coffee shop sometimes—things like that. Maybe get a few dates now and then, too.

Helper: Okay, so you do have a fairly clear idea of what you want—what a good social life is for you. I remember last time we talked about some of your ways of approaching people in the past, and how they seemed a little forward. You also only approached people in your classes and, even then, on only a few occasions.

[The helper indicates understanding of the client's desires. The helper also summarizes material from the previous session to reiterate the client's efforts to satisfy those desires. The client's efforts have been limited and largely ineffective. Thus, identifying new ways to satisfy the client's desires may be the next step and may provide material from which a goal could be developed.]

Client: Yeah, I remember. I've thought about that a little bit since last time. I guess I never really paid much attention to how I've tried to get to know people. I just did what seemed natural, and obviously it hasn't worked.

Helper: Are there other places besides your classes where you're around people you might like to meet?

[The helper asks a closed question.]

Client (pause): Not really. I don't get out a whole lot.

Helper: I remember you saying a couple of weeks ago that you like soccer quite a bit.

Client (nods): Yeah.

Helper: Did you know that there's a soccer club on campus? They accept new members all the time.

[The helper provides information about a potential option for getting out and meeting people.]

Client (seems a little surprised): Really? No, I didn't know that.

Helper: What do you think about joining the soccer club as a possibility for meeting people?

[Note how the helper connects meeting people with the client's enjoyment of soccer, thus giving the client an opportunity to meet people in an environment in which he is doing something he likes. The client may be more relaxed in such an environment.]

Client (ponders his response a moment; seems to perk up a little): That could work. I could try it.

Helper: Okay. Well, how about if we think of becoming a member of the university soccer club as a goal? It's obviously not your ultimate goal here, but it may be something to shoot for as a first step. How does that sound?

[Based on the client's agreeable response to joining the soccer club, the helper suggests a goal: becoming a member of the university soccer club. This goal statement allows both the helper and the client to be clear on what the client will pursue. The helper then checks to see what the client thinks ("How does that sound?").]

Client: That sounds fine. I've got a couple of exams in a few days, so I'm not going to do anything right now. I'll do it next week.

[Note that a time frame has been established for joining the soccer club: next week. This goal could be described as a short-range goal.

A specific goal has now been set: to become a member of the university soccer club next week. The helper and the client have gradually moved from the problem ("I'm tired of being alone all the time") to the client's desire ("I want a satisfying social life") to a specific goal ("to become a member of the university soccer club next week").]

Note that the goal possesses characteristics of effective goals. For example, the goal is specific and focused on behavioral changes: The client will become a member of the soccer club. Because of the goal's specificity, the helper and the client will be able to determine whether the goal is achieved. The goal is also challenging. The client is required to engage in new behavior, namely, taking the initiative to join the club, which involves entering a new social environment. The goal is attainable within a certain period of time: next week. Finally, the goal is consistent with the client's resources and circumstances. The client likes soccer, and as a student, he has access to the university soccer club.]

Helper: Okay, great. Next week it is. (pauses) How do you feel about what we've just talked about and the goal we've discussed?

[The helper asks an open question to solicit the client's feedback about the goal-setting process. This can help to determine whether there are any concerns or difficulties that should be addressed at this point.]

Client: Fine. More hopeful. I really didn't know there was a soccer club on campus. I feel like I've got something to pursue now.

Helper: Good. You seem a little more upbeat. (pauses a moment while the client nods) Let's talk for a minute about how you can get hooked up with the soccer club.

[The helper takes notice of the client's apparent change in demeanor (more upbeat) and shares this observation. By raising the issue of how to get hooked up with the soccer club, the helper is assisting the client in preparing to take action. That is, the helper is beginning to address the matter of what the client is going to do to achieve his goal.]

In this dialogue, the helper assisted the client in setting a goal. The helper and the client chose to verbally set the goal and not make a written goal statement.

The goal that they established may be one of many goals that they set. They may set additional goals that expand the client's social horizons. They may also set goals related to increasing the client's self-confidence. Because the client has had some past failures in meeting people, he may be apprehensive in social situations and may possess some self-defeating attitudes (e.g., "I'm unattractive to people." "I just don't know how to meet people."). If so, a goal that encourages more positive self-statements, for example, could be set. Any of the goals that the helper and the client set may be modified, if necessary, as new information becomes available. Once specific goals have been set, helping focuses on assisting the client in achieving the goals and confronting any challenges encountered in the process.

Summary and Concluding Remarks

This chapter addressed several aspects of goal-setting—specifically, the nature of goals, purposes and benefits of goals, characteristics of effective goals, the process of setting goals, whether to set goals verbally or in writing, difficulties related to setting goals, and skills used in setting goals.

Goal-setting reveals what changes clients would like to make in their lives. Change involves clients feeling, thinking, behaving, and interacting better, but change also means altering familiar attitudes and behaviors and accepting new responsibilities. Thus, setting goals and committing to them can be exciting and difficult at the same time. Some clients embrace goal-setting, whereas others are less comfortable with it. In any event, helpers need to take this process seriously and assist clients in developing high-quality goals. Once goals have been set, it is time to identify the actions that will be taken to achieve the goals. This is the focus of chapter 11.

Questions for Thought

1. Consider how your own personal method of setting goals in life compares to the way goals are set in helping. Think of a time in your life when you set a goal. How did you set your goal? How many of the characteristics of effective goals described in this chapter did your goal possess? What difficulties did you encounter? How did you measure progress? How successful were you in achieving your goal?

2. Do you believe the helping process can be successful without goals being set? Explain your response.

3. How do client characteristics, such as culture, education, and sophistication, factor into the goal-setting process? How do these characteristics affect the way goals are set?

4. This chapter identified several difficulties related to setting goals. Can you think of any other difficulties? If so, what are they? How might helpers deal with them?

5. If you were a helper, what factors would you consider in determining how formal or casual the goal-setting process should be with a particular client?

Exercises

The following exercises cover the process of setting goals. Exercise 2 may be most beneficial as a classroom exercise.

EXERCISE 1: Three brief descriptions of clients and their problems follow. For each client, identify one possible goal that you believe might be appropriate and write it down. As you identify goals, consider the characteristics of effective goals described in this chapter. You may do this exercise on your own or in a group of three or four people. A possible goal for each client is provided at the end of this chapter.

Client 1:

The client is a graduate student who is trying to finish her master's degree in social work. She feels that she has not been very disciplined as a student and explains that this is why she still has not finished her degree after 3 years. She estimates that she is about 60% done with the degree. Her priority in helping at the moment is to find a way to finish her degree in a reasonable amount of time and with a good grade point average.

Possible goal: _____

_____

_____

Client 2:

The client is a man who is trying to stop drinking. He has not sought treatment until now. He is inquiring about the 4-week alcohol treatment program at the hospital and is interested in pursuing it.

Possible goal: _____

_____

_____

Client 3:

The client is a man who is working in a job that he does not enjoy. He wants to find a new job. He likes writing and editing and has some editing experience. He wants to find a job in the editing field in the metropolitan area where he lives.

Possible goal: _____

_____

_____

EXERCISE 2: This exercise involves a 5–7 minute role play and requires three people: a helper, a client, and an observer. In the role play, the helper assists the client in setting a goal. The client should select a topic for the role play (e.g., an academic or vocational concern). The helper should spend a few minutes exploring the client's concern and developing understanding. After doing so, the helper and client should discuss what the client wants and identify a specific goal to be achieved. The helper should keep in mind the characteristics of effective goals while working with the client to set the goal. The observer should take notes about the goal-setting process: the level of formality of the process, the skills the helper uses, the extent to which the goal that is set possesses characteristics of effective goals, and any difficulties that arise in the process. After the role play is completed, each individual should share his or her observations about the role play. The following questions should be considered and discussed: How did the helper assist the client in setting the goal? How formal or casual was the goal-setting process? What skills did the helper use? Does the goal that was set possess characteristics of effective goals as described in this chapter? Did any difficulties arise when setting the goal? If so, how well were they handled? The exercise should be repeated often enough for each person to play each role.

Exercise Responses

The following are possible goals for the clients in Exercise 1. Note that these goals are not the only possible goals that could be set.

Possible goal for Client 1:
To finish my master's degree within the next year and a half with a 3.5 grade point average.

Possible goal for Client 2:
To stay sober and successfully complete the 4-week alcohol treatment program at the hospital.

Possible goal for Client 3:
To obtain a position as an assistant editor at a newspaper or with a magazine publisher in the metropolitan area within the next year.

CHAPTER 11

Identifying Actions

CHAPTER OVERVIEW

This chapter focuses on the second aspect of charting a new course: identifying actions. At this point, helpers assist clients in determining what actions the clients will take to achieve their goals. In this chapter, we define actions and describe their purposes and benefits. We also discuss characteristics of effective actions, the process of identifying actions, whether to identify actions verbally or in writing, difficulties related to identifying actions, and skills used in identifying actions. A hypothetical dialogue and several exercises are included at the end of this chapter to facilitate understanding of identifying actions.

Life is a series of problems. Do we want to moan about them or solve them?

—M. Scott Peck (1978, p. 15)

From Setting Goals to Identifying Actions

Once goals have been set, it is time to help clients identify the actions they will take to achieve their goals. Numerous authors have discussed the importance of actions, typically in the context of "action plans," "action steps," or "action strategies" that clients develop to work toward their goals (see, e.g., Carkhuff, 2000; Cormier & Nurius, 2003; Egan, 2002; Locke & Latham, 1984). Whatever they are called, and however they are conceptualized, actions grow out of client goals.

What Are Actions?

Actions are the steps, activities, and behaviors that clients undertake to achieve their goals. Helpers and clients identify actions for each goal that is set. Here is an example. Suppose a client has set the following goal: to achieve a 3.5 grade point average in all course work this school year. The helper and the client identify the specific actions that the client will take to achieve this goal. In this example, the client will

1. study at least 2 hours per night, Monday through Thursday, at home;
2. purchase and review study aids, including books on effective test-taking skills;
3. attend a study group at school each Wednesday afternoon through the end of the school year.

As another example, consider a client who wants to achieve the goal of losing 25 pounds in 6 months by following the "New You" weight loss plan. She may identify the following actions:

1. Follow the diet plan specified in the "New You" booklet.
2. After work, walk 1 mile per day, 5 days per week, on the university campus.
3. Purchase exercise equipment at a sporting goods store.
4. Begin the exercise regimen described in the "New You" booklet.

Purposes and Benefits of Actions

In the helping process, actions and the process of identifying actions

- instill hope in clients that problems can be managed or resolved—actions "chart a course";
- motivate clients to work toward their goals by focusing their energy and effort;
- promote progress toward goal achievement by clearly spelling out what clients will do;
- provide structure and focus for the helping process;
- help clients see what skills and resources are required to achieve their goals;
- aid helpers in preparing specific treatment plans;
- help to identify problems that might interfere with goal achievement;
- facilitate evaluation of progress toward goal achievement; and
- teach clients a beneficial skill—namely, how to identify steps, activities, and behaviors that will help them reach the goals they set, now and in the future.

Characteristics of Effective Actions

Most of the characteristics of effective goals apply to effective actions as well. Actions are most likely to result in goal achievement when they are

- established by mutual agreement;
- relevant to client goals (actions must facilitate the achievement of client goals);
- focused on positive change (actions must promote improvement in well-being and quality of life);
- desirable and practical when assessed with a cost/benefit analysis;
- realistic (clients must be able to perform the actions; the actions must be not only possible, but also likely to be successfully undertaken);
- challenging—not too difficult or too easy (it is best if actions require at least moderate effort and risk so clients can experience a sense of progress and accomplishment);
- expressed in positive, active language that focuses on what clients will do, not on what they want to prevent or avoid (e.g., "I will eat five servings of fruits and vegetables each day" is more likely to promote goal achievement than "I will not eat foods that are bad for me");
- specific and focused on behavioral changes (such actions allow clients to know exactly what to do and they facilitate the measurement of progress);
- capable of being performed within a certain period of time;
- consistent with client characteristics, skills, resources, and circumstances (actions must take into account what clients are able and willing to do);
- consistent with helper abilities and obligations; and
- changeable (actions may need to be modified, added, or discarded).

The Process of Identifying Actions

The following paragraphs describe basic steps that characterize the process of identifying actions.

Discuss Identifying Actions With Clients. When clients understand that identifying and taking specific actions can increase their chances of achieving goals, they may be more willing to participate in the process of identifying actions. Identifying actions requires clients to articulate what they will do to make changes in their lives, so helpers need to be prepared to address any concerns or fears the clients may have.

Instill Hope About Change. As with goal-setting, clients may want more than a description or a reason for identifying actions. They may want to know whether identifying actions will really help them make positive changes. Thus, helpers often instill hope in clients that change is possible, despite past failures or inaction. They may do so, for example, by offering their support and encouragement to clients throughout the process of identifying actions.

Consider Clients' Past Efforts to Manage or Resolve Their Problems. When considering possible actions, the helper and client need to take into account the client's past efforts to manage or resolve his or her problems. Past ineffective efforts may not be worth repeating. Doing so may be a waste of time. In many cases, however, past efforts can serve as the starting point for identifying actions. It may be the case that the client's past efforts were ineffective because the client was going about them in the wrong way. For example, a client who is trying to improve his social life may do a good job of putting himself in social situations, but instead of actively trying to meet people, he passively waits for others to introduce themselves. In this case, the client's actions may need to be modified so that he takes a more active role in meeting people.

Identify Actions. Asking questions and brainstorming (discussed later in this chapter) often are useful skills for generating ideas for action. Other skills described later in this chapter are helpful as well. As potential actions are identified, helpers and clients should consider the characteristics of effective actions to help them decide which of the actions they identify are worth pursuing.

Prioritize Actions and Prepare a Timeline. Often, actions are sequenced, ordered, or ranked in some way (Carkhuff, 2000; Cormier & Nurius, 2003). For example, if a client's goal is to take and pass an introductory computer course by the end of the year, he might identify and order actions as follows: (1) Work 5 extra hours per week at my job for the next 6 weeks to earn money for course tuition, (2) identify local colleges that offer introductory computer courses and order their catalogs, (3) review the catalogs and select a college and a course that fit my needs, (4) register for the college's computer course, and (5) attend class regularly and complete all homework assignments. To identify when the actions will be undertaken and completed, the client may create a timeline or timetable that is consistent with the time frame for his goal. This may give the action sequence further structure and motivate the client to take action. He not only knows what actions he will take, but in what order and when. Not all clients require or desire this much structure. Helpers talk with their clients to decide how much structure is necessary.

Discuss Rewards and Reinforcements. Clients need to feel motivated to pursue the actions that they identify. Thus, helpers may assist clients in identifying rewards for completing each action. For example, suppose a client is trying to find a better job. One of the actions that he will take is to contact two of his former professors to inquire about career options in his field. The client may decide that upon successful completion of this action, he will have a nice dinner and attend a movie (see Bandura, 1997; Carkhuff, 2000; Egan, 2002; Watson & Tharp, 2002).

Discuss How to Determine Whether the Actions Are Working. Helpers and clients need to be able to determine the effectiveness of the actions the clients take. Thus, when identifying actions, they need to also identify what they will see if the actions are working—that is, they identify the attitude and behavior changes that will indicate progress toward goal achievement. For example, suppose a client sets a goal related to losing weight and identifies several actions that she will take to accomplish that goal. She will know that the actions are facilitating goal achievement if she sees the following: (1) more active lifestyle, (2) trimmer appearance, (3) more positive feelings and overall feeling of good health, and (4) more self-confidence and socializing. To aid in determining how well clients' actions are facilitating goal achievement, helpers may teach clients how to self-monitor (note and record) their attitudes, feelings, and behaviors.

Discuss How to Handle Problems or Setbacks That May Arise When Taking Action. Identifying actions is often easier than taking action. Thus, in the process of identifying actions, helpers must both convey confidence in their clients' abilities to take action and address what the clients will do if the actions are not working as well as hoped. It may be beneficial for helpers to assist clients in identifying the personal sabotage strategies that the clients have used in the past to keep themselves stuck in problems (J. Dagley, personal communication, May 23, 2002). For example, if a client who is trying to improve his social skills tends to make excuses about why he never approaches other people (e.g., "They probably won't like me."), the helper can work with the client to become aware of this negative self-talk and counter it with more positive statements. Helpers may also address potential problems and setbacks by helping clients identify alternate actions, or "contingency plans" (Egan, 2002). Anticipating possible problems and having backup plans may help to prevent clients from becoming too demoralized about setbacks or slow progress.

Note and Discuss Client Reactions to the Process of Identifying Actions. Determining what actions to take can be challenging for clients because they are being asked to identify new, more effective behaviors. Helpers need to pay attention to how their clients respond to this process. Are clients resisting it? Do they have any concerns? What do they need?

Modify, Add, or Discard Actions as Needed. As the helping process progresses, helpers and clients may decide to modify, add, or discard actions. For example, if a client finds that a particular action is not working, she and the helper may decide to brainstorm other possible actions that could be taken. If the client set a goal to locate a new job as a social worker within 3 months but has not been successful in doing so by conducting Internet searches and networking with friends who work in the helping professions (the actions she took to try to achieve the goal), she may discard these actions and identify new actions to be taken, such as contacting her former graduate school professors to inquire about job prospects in her field.

Keep the Goals in Mind. Clients may focus so much on actions that they lose sight of their goals. Or, they may think that by successfully completing a sequence of actions they will have reached their goals. It is important for clients to understand that successful completion of actions does not *equal* goal achievement; it *leads* to goal achievement. Clients can successfully complete all of the actions that they identified and still not achieve their goals. Thus, clients need to keep their goals in mind and attend to how well the actions they take are facilitating achievement of the goals. Evaluation of progress toward goal achievement is discussed in chapter 13.

Identifying Actions: Verbally or in Writing?

Actions can be identified verbally or in writing. The option that is selected depends on how goals are set, helper and client preferences, and the requirements of the helping setting. Verbally discussing actions, rather than writing them down, may be a realistic option if the actions are not too numerous, complex, or detailed.

If helpers and clients identify actions in writing, they usually list the problems to be addressed, the goals and subgoals to be pursued, the actions to be taken for each one, when the actions are to be taken, and what attitude and behavior changes are anticipated. Clearly spelling out on paper what is to be done can help clients feel more committed to taking action.

Difficulties Related to Identifying Actions

The following paragraphs describe difficulties that are sometimes associated with the process of identifying actions.

Premature Identification of Actions. Sometimes, helpers suggest actions and try to offer solutions before goals have been set or even before problems have been thoroughly explored (see M. S. Corey & Corey, 2003). For example, a client might express her desire to lose weight or to make more friends, and the helper might immediately suggest actions that the client could take, such as starting a diet or joining a singles club. Such haste by the helper may preclude sufficient exploration of the problems, thereby leading to inaccurate assessment and irrelevant ideas for action. Also, it can be difficult to measure progress without a clear understanding of what goals are to be pursued. If no goals have been set, then why are actions being identified? What does the client hope to accomplish, and how will she know when she has accomplished it?

Client Resistance. Helpers may have to deal with client resistance when they work with clients to identify actions. In the process of setting goals, identifying actions, and then taking action, clients are asked to take increasingly greater risks— from talking about behavior change to actually implementing it. Their resistance may increase as they get closer to the point of actually taking action. As clients work to identify actions, their resistance may manifest itself in the same ways it does when they work to set goals (e.g., expressing fear of change, demonstrating a lack of readiness, and putting off change). Helpers may explore and seek to understand resistance using such skills as asking questions and confronting. They also need to consider whether anything they are doing may be causing the resistance (e.g., pressuring their clients to identify actions).

Struggling to Identify Actions. Clients might set goals but then struggle to determine how to achieve them. They may not know what actions to take, or the potential actions they think of may be unrealistic. Helpers may use such skills as asking questions and brainstorming to assist clients in identifying realistic actions.

Identifying Actions That Do Not Possess Characteristics of Effective Actions. If the actions that clients identify are nonspecific, irrelevant to their goals, unrealistic, or stated in negative terms, among other things, the clients may encounter difficulties as they attempt to take the actions. The clients may not know what they are supposed to do, the actions may be too difficult to undertake, or the actions may not promote goal achievement. Ideally, actions should possess the characteristics described earlier in this chapter so clients have the best chance of achieving their goals.

Helpers Imposing Their Own Perspectives, Needs, and Biases. It is risky for helpers to push clients to take actions that the helpers think are best. For example, suppose a client's goal is to get a divorce, and the helper strongly suggests that the client tell her husband to move out of the house immediately. This action may not be consistent with what the client wants (perhaps the divorce will be very amicable) and may cause animosity between the client and her husband if she were to do it. If actions are not consistent with client needs, interests, and desires, they may not be effective. Clients may not even be willing to pursue them.

Identifying Actions in a Manner That Is Either Too Formal or Too Casual. As with the process of setting goals, when the process of identifying actions is too formal (e.g., involving writing lengthy, complex, highly detailed action statements), actions may seem like unpleasant, impersonal tasks. Clients may not have the desire or the motivation to pursue them. If the process is too casual (e.g., involving helpers and clients briefly and generally talking about actions), clients may forget about the actions that they planned to take or they may not take the process seriously.

Skills Used in Identifying Actions

Many of the skills discussed in previous chapters are useful in the process of identifying actions. In the following section, we briefly revisit several skills that are particularly useful in this regard. We then introduce four new skills: brainstorming, advising, suggesting, and directing.

Previously Described Skills

Listening

As clients express themselves, helpers listen for clues about what actions clients might be willing to take. Listening also tells helpers what clients have already tried when attempting to manage or resolve their problems.

Asking Questions

Open questions, in particular, can encourage clients to identify actions. For example, helpers may inquire, "What are some ways that you could achieve your goal?" or "What actions do you think might help you reach your goal?"

Reflecting Feelings

Identifying actions can cause apprehension in clients, who are being asked to describe new behaviors to perform. Helpers may reflect the clients' feelings to show that they recognize and understand the clients' fears and concerns.

Focusing

This skill can be used to help clients articulate clear, specific actions. For example, if a client decides to pursue an exercise regimen as part of her plan to lose weight, the helper can use focusing to encourage the client to identify more specifically what kinds of exercises (and how much of each exercise) she would like to do. To this end, the helper might say, "Describe specifically what kinds of exercises you would do to help you lose weight."

Summarizing

Once actions have been identified and discussed, helpers can summarize them to ensure that they and the clients agree on the actions the clients will take.

Confronting

This skill can be useful to address client resistance to identifying actions (e.g., "You say you want to be different, but when we start talking about how you want to achieve your goal, you change the subject."). It is not unusual for clients to express a desire for change but then resist when the time comes to set goals, identify actions, and take action. For example, they may give reasons for why every possible action identified will not work. When such resistance is confronted, it can be discussed to gain understanding of the resistance. Helpers and clients can then decide whether they are ready to proceed with identifying actions.

Providing Information

Helpers provide information throughout the helping process. In the process of identifying actions, they can offer information to assist clients in selecting specific, realistic actions. For example, if a client plans to leave her abusive husband, the helper can provide information about public resources and shelters as a way to help the client decide which actions to take to achieve her goal of leaving.

Four New Skills

Brainstorming

Brainstorming can be especially valuable as a way to identify numerous potential actions for clients to consider (see, e.g., Egan, 2002). The initial task in brainstorming is to identify a large number of potential actions. At this point, actions are not accepted, rejected, explained, judged, or evaluated, even if they seem far-fetched. Even seemingly unrealistic actions might later be refined to be more practical. When helpers and clients avoid comments or decisions on potential actions as they are being identified, clients generally feel more free to be prolific.

Although helpers may offer potential actions for clients to consider, clients are primarily responsible for identifying potential actions (see Egan, 2002). Helpers typically facilitate brainstorming with questions and directions, such as the following:

"What are some actions that you might like to take?"
"What are some ways for you to spend more time with your wife?"
"Let's make a 'Top Ten' list of possible actions."

Helpers and clients often brainstorm verbally during sessions and write ideas in list form. Sometimes, clients prepare written lists on their own and bring them to the next meeting for discussion. The number of brainstormed actions may range from a few to dozens.

Once potential actions have been identified, helpers and clients evaluate them and select ones that will be taken in pursuit of goals. Evaluating potential actions involves considering various factors, such as how challenging the actions are, whether they will promote positive change, and whether they are relevant to client goals. In short, helpers and clients consider the characteristics of effective actions, described earlier in this chapter.

Consider the following example of brainstorming. A client sets a goal related to getting into a high-quality graduate program in biology. The helper asks him to brainstorm some potential actions to take to help him achieve that goal. The client verbally identifies several possibilities:

1. Talk to biology professors on campus about graduate study in biology.
2. Order graduate school catalogs from several universities.
3. Talk to biology graduate students about their experiences as biology graduate students.
4. Maintain good undergraduate grades.
5. Prepare for the Graduate Record Examination.
6. Visit five different graduate biology programs at universities that I might be interested in.

As this list is being prepared, no attempt is made to evaluate the potential actions. When the helper and the client feel that a sufficient number of actions have been identified, they evaluate each one. The client decides that possibilities 1 through 5 are realistic actions that he would like to take. Possibility 6 would be too time-consuming and expensive given his schedule and financial situation, so he concludes that it would not be realistic. However, he can modify it to be realistic. He decides to visit two local, high-quality graduate biology programs.

Advising

Advising occurs when helpers state what they believe their clients should do or not do in a given situation. Helpers may offer advice on their own initiative, or advice may be solicited by clients (a common occurrence). People often seek advice from professionals. They meet with teachers, doctors, financial advisers, attorneys, and spiritual leaders and expect to receive advice on how to address issues or resolve problems. Many clients have the same expectation in helping relationships. As noted earlier in this book, many clients from racial and ethnic minority groups prefer a more directive and active approach to helping. This may include helpers providing advice (as well as suggestions and directions, discussed below).

Although advising may be appropriate and widely used in many professional contexts, it can be problematic and risky when used to help people make significant personal decisions that involve their feelings, behaviors, values, and lifestyles. Consider the following risks and potential problems.

Advice Is Subjective and Prescriptive ("You should . . ."). When helpers tell clients what they believe should be done, the helpers may be imposing their own solutions and disregarding the right of clients to make their own decisions and find their own answers.

Advice May Seem Condescending. Clients may not appreciate helpers' advice, especially when it is unsolicited. Unsolicited advice may convey the impression that helpers are superior and controlling and that clients are unable to manage or resolve their own problems without someone else telling them what they should do.

Advice May Not Fit Clients' Needs and Values. A piece of advice may reflect how the helper would address a particular issue; thus, it may fit for the helper but not necessarily for the client.

Advice May Preclude Further Exploration and Understanding of Feelings and Problems. When advice is given, clients may avoid the hard work that is often required to confront problems, develop emotional awareness, find one's own answers, and learn new skills. If the root of a problem has not been addressed, the problem may continue.

Advice Shifts Responsibility for Change From Clients to Helpers. Advice provides an immediate solution; it does not help clients learn how to manage or resolve problems. Further, it can promote client dependence on helpers to provide answers. One of the goals of helping is to assist clients in learning how to make good decisions and effectively manage or resolve problems, now and in the future. The goal is not for helpers to provide all of the answers.

Advice Can Lead to Blaming. If advice is taken and does not have positive results, clients may blame helpers. In some cases, clients, seeing helpers as experts, may blame themselves for not properly following the advice. Even if the advice is helpful, clients may not learn much from it, except to seek answers from other people.

Advising is not always improper in helping, but it should be used sparingly and only in certain circumstances. As a solution-focused skill, advising can be useful as a way to help clients focus their decision-making abilities and decide what actions to take to achieve their goals. However, helpers need to consider carefully whether advising is the best option among all of the skills they could use, such as asking questions, focusing, and brainstorming. Advising may be acceptable in the following situations.

■ *When Clients Need Reinforcement for Decisions They Have Already Made or Are Considering.* Sometimes, clients are not sure of the goals they have set or the actions they are considering. Advice can be a way to offer reassurance and validation (and sometimes cautions) regarding clients' decisions and choices (Benjamin, 1987). For example, the helper may say, "I agree that as a first step you should tell your husband about the concerns you have in your marriage."

■ *When Clients Need to Resolve Crises or Appear to Be in Immediate Danger.* In emergencies, such as ongoing domestic violence or serious threats of suicide, advice can be used to help ensure client safety and well-being (see Young, 2001). An example of helper advice in such situations is, "You've said some things that are worrying me. I think you should contact the police."

■ *When Clients Need Guidance Regarding Generally Accepted Ways of Doing Things.* Helpers may provide advice when clients need guidance regarding generally accepted ways of doing things (Doyle, 1998). However, helpers need to be careful about the topics on which they provide advice. For significant personal decisions, such as where to go to college or whether to break up with a boyfriend or girlfriend, there is not a "generally accepted" way of doing things. In situations in which the ways or procedures for doing things are fairly well established, advice may be appropriate. For example: "You should follow up the job interview with a short written note thanking the interviewer for her time."

■ *When Clients Would Benefit From Helper Expertise in Particular Areas.* Helpers sometimes provide advice when they possess expert knowledge on particular topics or issues (see Doyle, 1998). For example, the helper may say, "You should consider going to Al-Anon while your husband is in treatment and going to AA. This may help you get the support you need, and it's often helpful when a couple is trying to heal their relationship."

■ *When Clients Seem to Need Direction, Guidance, or a "Push" to Take Action.* Sometimes, clients struggle to set goals and identify actions to take. In these cases, helpers may consider using such skills as reflecting feelings, confronting, and brainstorming to gain understanding of the clients' reluctance or fears and to move the action process along. However, advising may also work in these cases (e.g., "I think you should focus on your strengths rather than your weaknesses. Maybe that would help you come up with some more ideas for how to accomplish your goal.").

Advice typically is not the best choice in the following situations (Brammer & MacDonald, 2003; Doyle, 1998; Young, 2001).

■ *When Clients Expect Answers on Significant Personal Decisions.* Examples include whether to marry, what career to select, or which friends to choose. Clients sometimes ask, "What should I do?" or "What would you do if you were in my shoes?" On these matters, it is not the place of helpers to make decisions or tell clients what actions they should take. Instead, the role of helpers here is to assist clients in evaluating various choices, options, and actions. Evaluation could include a cost/benefit analysis and a discussion of the feelings and concerns associated with particular choices, options, and actions.

■ *When Helpers Lack Training or Knowledge on Particular Topics or Are Uncertain About What to Say.* In such cases, there is a greater chance that the advice will be "bad." For example, a helper with no training in drug counseling should not advise a client on how to treat a drug addiction, except to recommend that the client seek assistance from a trained professional. The helper may be able to provide a referral.

■ *When Clients Depend on Others to Make Decisions for Them.* Overreliance on other people prevents clients from taking responsibility for their own lives. When clients depend too much on others to provide answers, it is usually prudent for helpers to avoid advising.

■ *When Clients Have Not Followed Previously Given Advice.* Clients may ignore advice because they do not trust it or because they are too invested in current behaviors. If helpers have provided advice and clients have not followed it, advising may not be the best choice in the future. Additional advice may not be followed, either.

■ *When Clients Already Possess Necessary Information and Can Manage or Resolve Problems Without Advice.* When clients have the information they need to make decisions and take action, they can find their own answers and do not need advice. In these situations, helpers may assist the clients in understanding and organizing information so it can be put to good use.

When advising, helpers should consider the following points and guidelines:

■ Avoid premature advice-giving—that is, ensure sufficient understanding of client problems, needs, and goals before offering advice.
■ Ensure sufficient knowledge about the issues or topics on which advice is given.
■ Ensure that advice is relevant to client problems, needs, goals, and culture.
■ Provide advice tentatively and respectfully; advice provided in emergencies may be more direct and blunt.
■ Use clear, concrete, specific language.
■ Follow the advice with a question to determine clients' thoughts and feelings about the advice provided (e.g., "What do you think about that?" "How does that sound to you?").
■ Note client responses and discuss the advice with clients: How did clients react to it? Was the advice understood? Do clients plan to follow it? Was it helpful? Helpfulness may be assessed in the next session (Benjamin, 1987).
■ Use this skill sparingly.

Suggesting

Suggesting has been described as "a mild form of advice" (Benjamin, 1987, p. 231). Suggesting occurs when helpers identify and propose possible actions, options, or solutions for clients to consider in order to make important decisions, work through problems, and achieve goals. Examples include the following:

"You could enroll in the new study skills course as a way to help improve your grades."
"You could talk to your boss about the problems you're having with your coworker."
"If your husband is so busy right now, what about trying to discuss your finances *after* he finishes the project at work?"

Suggesting is more tentative and less directive than advising. The message is "you *could* do this" instead of "you *should* do this." Benjamin (1987) stated: "Suggestion provides the client with the therapist's considered opinions but leaves her leeway to accept, refuse, or propose ideas of her own. Indeed, its purpose may be to stimulate the client to think and plan for herself" (pp. 231–232). In short, when suggesting, helpers offer clients options and possibilities to think about; they do not impose solutions or tell clients what should be done. This skill may be useful when working with clients from many racial and ethnic minority groups. The D. Sue (1997) counseling study involving Asian international students found that the students did not want to be told what to do (that is, they did not want advice), but rather they wanted to discuss various suggestions and options so they could consider possible solutions to problems. With regard to the risks, appropriate use, and guidelines for suggesting, essentially the same considerations as described under the skill of advising apply.

Directing

Directing involves providing instructions to clients. With this skill, helpers tell clients to do something or tell them how to engage in particular actions or behaviors. Directing can occur at various points in helping and for various reasons. For example, it can be used to give clients instructions on how to take psychological tests or access desired services. It may also be used to instruct clients on their role in such activities as role-playing, breathing exercises, and relaxation exercises.

Directing can also be used to help clients get started in identifying actions. For example, a helper might say, "Let's identify some ways you can achieve your goal of getting a new job." Directing may also be helpful when discussing with clients how to take action, such as instructing clients about the order in which to take actions.

Directing is more blunt than advising or suggesting. When helpers use this skill, they tell clients what to do. The elements of "you should" or "you could" are eliminated. The benefit of directing is that it allows helpers to take the lead when needed and structure the helping process. It can also move clients to take desired action. As noted earlier, many ethnic and racial minority clients prefer a more directive approach to helping. Directing has risks, however. One risk is that helpers can appear controlling or domineering. Clients may resent instructions, feeling that helpers are dictating actions and commandeering the helping process while permitting little client input. Also, some clients become overly dependent on helpers to tell them what to do. Effective helpers are aware of these risks and do not use directing to control their clients, dominate the helping process, or make important decisions for clients. With regard to the appropriate use of and guidelines for directing, the same basic considerations as described under the skill of advising apply.

A Hypothetical Dialogue

The following hypothetical dialogue between a helper and a client demonstrates how actions may be identified. The client is a woman who is preparing to take a major examination for licensure in her profession. She is highly anxious about the exam. When she thinks about the exam, she begins to perspire and tremble, and negative thoughts and self-doubts race through her mind. She wants to reduce her anxiety and has set a goal to go into the exam in 2 months calm and prepared, without perspiring and trembling. The dialogue is from the fifth helping session. The helper and the client are working to identify actions.

Helper: Well, we've talked a little about how you want to reduce anxiety related to the exam—how you want to be more calm and prepared. You mentioned last time that sometimes you read as a way to relax. Have you tried anything else?

[The helper asks a closed question to inquire whether the client has done anything other than reading to relax and reduce anxiety. Knowing what the client has already attempted can be a good starting point. The previous efforts can be evaluated and then modified or discarded.]

Client: Not really. And reading hasn't been too effective. There's a review course that's offered in a couple of weeks. It lasts for 3 weeks. I'm registered to take it, and I've been hoping that it will help me relax a little bit by giving me some structure. But, so far, I guess I haven't really done too much to deal with the anxiety. Most of all, I tend to try to ignore it, as if that'll make it go away.

Helper: Okay. Well, the review course could be a good step. How about if we think about some other things you could do?

[The helper is inquiring about brainstorming with the client—seeing whether the client would be willing to try brainstorming.]

Client: Okay.

Helper: Let's make a list of some possible actions. I'll write things down and you talk. Just think of anything that comes to mind that you might try so you can relax and reduce anxiety, no matter how strange it might seem. After we have several items on the list, we'll talk about it.

[The helper describes the process of brainstorming. The helper places primary responsibility on the client to identify possible actions—without evaluating them for the time being. The helper will write to allow the client to focus on identifying possible actions. Note that the helper is also using the skill of directing here. The helper is providing instructions to the client on how to brainstorm.]

Client (pauses as she thinks about options): Well, I could choose not to take the exam at all; I could take the review course; I could exercise; I could kick my husband and kids out of the house—it's important to have no distractions; I could eat more—food has always been comforting; I could make a study schedule; I could find someone else who's taking the exam and study with that person; I could talk to other people who have taken the exam to see how they handled the experience. (pauses) That's all I can think of right now.

Helper: All right. This is a good list. Which of these seem like good possibilities to you?

[The helper asks the client to begin evaluating the possible actions to determine which ones are desirable and realistic.]

Client: Let me think. (pauses) Not taking the exam at all really isn't a good option. I don't get a license if I do that. Eating a lot feels good at first, but then I feel miserable. That wouldn't be a good option. Studying with other people doesn't appeal to me much. I don't know anyone else who's taking the exam, and I study best by myself anyway. Kicking everyone out won't work, but I wish I could do it! (pause). I'd say that the review course, exercising, setting a study schedule, and talking to other people are the best possibilities I can think of.

Helper: Let's go back for a moment to kicking everyone out of the house. You may not be able to do that, but you said that it's important to have no distractions. What are some ways you could arrange to avoid distractions, short of kicking everyone out?

[In the first sentence, the helper uses the skill of directing to specify the subject for discussion. Note that the helper's statement could also be an example of focusing in the sense that the helper is turning attention back to the issue of kicking everyone out of the house. The helper then asks an open question to encourage the client to think about modifying an unrealistic action (kicking everyone out of the house).]

Client: I might be able to use the den at home for studying, but even if I keep the door closed, the kids still make noise and they would come in when they want something.

Helper: What about studying somewhere other than at home? You could study at the library on campus. That would help you avoid the noise of the kids. Or maybe your husband would be able to take the kids out a couple of nights a week so you could have uninterrupted time to study.

[The helper uses the skill of suggesting to assist the client in considering other ways she could find quiet, uninterrupted study time.]

Client: Well, I don't like studying at the library—too many people around—so I don't think I would do that, but I can see what John could do with the kids. I didn't think of having him take them somewhere. That's a good idea. He's always home in the evenings.

Helper: Okay, so let's see what we've got. Some actions that you can take that might help you relax, reduce anxiety, and be prepared include taking the review course, setting a study schedule, studying at home while your husband takes the kids out, talking to other people who have taken the exam, and exercising. Are these steps that you're willing to take?

[The helper uses the skill of summarizing so both the helper and the client are clear on what actions are being considered. The helper then asks the client whether she would be willing to take these actions.]

Client: Yeah, I can do them.

Helper: All right. Let's talk about how we can make them a little more specific. What kinds of exercising would you want to do?

[The helper uses the skills of directing, focusing, and asking open questions to encourage greater specificity. "Exercising," by itself, is not a specific action. To facilitate achievement of the client's goal, the type and amount of exercise need to be identified more precisely.]

Client: Probably walking. I don't want to do anything too stressful at this point.

Helper: How much walking?

[The helper asks a closed question to encourage further specificity.]

Client: I'd say about 2 miles a day.

Helper: Okay. Before we get to the other actions, let me get some more paper so we can write this down.

[The helper and the client can get more specific with each of the other actions identified as well. Once actions have been identified specifically, they may be ordered in some way, if appropriate. The next step would be for the client to begin taking action.]

In this dialogue, the helper assisted the client in identifying several actions to be taken in pursuit of the client's goal. At the end of the dialogue, the helper decided to put the actions in writing so the client would not forget what she is going to do.

As the helper and the client continue their work together, they may identify new actions. Also, they may modify or discard actions depending on how well the actions work when the client pursues them. Although the client in this dialogue appears to be motivated to address her situation, she may need more help to take effective action. The actions identified in this dialogue, by themselves, may not be enough for the client to reduce anxiety and be calm and prepared for the exam. Thus, the helper may assist the client in developing skills to reduce anxiety. For example, the helper might teach the client some breathing exercises and relaxation techniques. Once practiced and learned, the exercises and techniques could constitute additional actions that the client would take to achieve her goal.

Summary and Concluding Remarks

Identifying actions comes after setting goals. At this point, clients identify what they will do to achieve their goals. This is an important task that is sometimes overlooked in the helping process and in everyday life. It is common for people to set goals but not articulate the actions they will take to achieve the goals. This oversight can lead to ineffective, haphazard action and can doom goals to failure.

Once actions have been identified, clients begin to take action. Typically, they do so immediately or in the near future. Sometimes, however, they need help taking action. The topic of taking action is discussed in chapter 12.

Questions for Thought

1. How would you explain to someone the importance of identifying actions in the helping process?

2. How might helpers deal with the difficulties that can arise when identifying actions (e.g., client resistance to identifying actions)?

3. Have you ever brainstormed as a way to identify options or solutions to a situation that you were facing? Was it helpful? Why or why not? How closely did your brainstorming process resemble brainstorming as described in this chapter?

4. Think of a time in your life when you received advice, suggestions, or directions. What factors or circumstances (e.g., how well you knew the person, the level of expertise of the person) made the advice, suggestions, or directions helpful or unhelpful to you?

Exercises

The following exercises cover the skills that were discussed in this chapter and the process of identifying actions. The exercises that require more than one person may be most useful as classroom exercises.

BRAINSTORMING EXERCISE

This exercise requires two people: a helper and a client. The client should select one of the following three goals to role-play: (1) to make more friends at school, (2) to find a more satisfying job in his or her field, or (3) to raise his or her college grade point average from 3.4 to 3.5 in the current semester. In a role play with the client, the helper should spend a few minutes exploring the client's concerns to gain understanding of those concerns using skills described so far in this book (e.g., listening, asking questions, paraphrasing, reflecting feelings). At some point, the goal to be achieved should be identified and set. Then, the helper should assist the client in brainstorming potential actions for achieving the goal. The helper and client should bear in mind these four points:

- Identify potential actions without evaluation.
- Primary responsibility for identifying potential actions is on the client; the helper facilitates with questions and directions.
- Write down potential actions.
- When done brainstorming, evaluate the potential actions by considering the characteristics of effective actions (e.g., How realistic is each action?) and select actions that the client would like to pursue.

After doing the role play, each person should share his or her observations. How well did the helper facilitate brainstorming? How well were potential actions initially identified without evaluating them? When it came time to evaluate, were the characteristics of effective actions considered (e.g., whether the actions will promote positive change)? After discussing the role play, the partners should switch roles and repeat the exercise.

ADVISING EXERCISE

Three client statements follow. After each statement, write a helper response that provides advice to the client. An example of a helper response to each client statement is provided at the end of this chapter.

Statement 1:

Client (just had her children removed from her home by child protective services): I don't understand what's going on. I've never hurt my kids, and I don't even know what all the allegations are. What am I supposed to do now?

Helper advice: _____

_____

_____

Statement 2:

Client (applying for a job right out of college): I've got a job search going, but I don't know who I should get letters of recommendation from.

Helper advice: _____

_____

_____

Statement 3:

Client (client's mother just passed away): My kids were pretty close to their grandmother, and they're feeling sad. They seem to be taking it pretty hard.

Helper advice: _____

_____

_____

SUGGESTING EXERCISE

Three client statements follow. After each statement, write a helper response that makes a suggestion to the client. An example of a helper response to each client statement is provided at the end of this chapter.

Statement 1:

Client (struggling with a career choice): I can't decide which one of these job offers to accept. I have no idea how to make the decision.

Helper suggestion:_____

_____

_____

Statement 2:

Client (has set a goal related to overcoming her fear of flying): I've decided to take a flight from Chicago to Nashville by myself by the end of next month. I think I can do it, but I'm struggling a little bit in preparing myself for it. I definitely need to do this step-by-step.

Helper suggestion:_____

_____

_____

Statement 3:

Client (working on improving her marriage): I'm trying to figure out some ways Bill and I could spend more time together.

Helper suggestion:_____

_____

_____

DIRECTING EXERCISE

Three client statements follow. After each statement, write a helper response that provides a direction to the client. An example of a helper response to each client statement is provided at the end of this chapter.

Statement 1:

Client (has set a goal to lose weight): Well, I wonder what I can do to lose weight. It seems like there are so many options out there—all these diet plans and exercise programs.

Helper direction: _____

_____

_____

Statement 2:

Client (helper and client are about to brainstorm possible actions to take; client needs instructions on how to brainstorm effectively): How should we do this?

Helper direction: _____

_____

_____

Statement 3:

Client (has selected actions to take related to his goal of staying sober and successfully getting treatment for alcoholism; he is going to (1) enter the treatment program at the hospital in 1 week, (2) contact a good friend for support, and (3) attend Alcoholics Anonymous meetings): Okay, sounds like a plan. Where do I start?

Helper direction: _____

_____

_____

IDENTIFYING ACTIONS EXERCISES

EXERCISE 1: Three client goals follow. For each goal, identify three possible actions that the client could take to achieve the goal. You may do this exercise on your own or in a group of three or four people. A list of possible actions for each client goal is provided at the end of this chapter.

Client 1:
The client has a fear of public speaking. Her goal is to speak for 5 minutes at the podium at the city council meeting in 4 weeks.

Possible actions: _____

_____

_____

Client 2:
The client wants to excel in a math course. Her goal is to receive an A on the mathematics final in 3 weeks.

Possible actions: _____

_____

_____

Client 3:
The client wants to gradually stop smoking. His goal is to reduce cigarette smoking to 2 cigarettes per day by the end of the month.

Possible actions: _____

_____

_____

EXERCISE 2: This exercise requires three people: a helper, a client, and an observer. A role play will be conducted in which the helper assists the client in identifying actions to achieve a goal. The client should select a topic to role-play (e.g., relationship difficulties, an academic or vocational concern). After exploring and understanding the client's concerns, the helper and the client should work together to identify a goal. Once a goal has been set, the helper and the client should identify actions to be taken to achieve the goal. The helper should keep in mind the characteristics of effective actions. The observer should take notes about how the actions are identified, the skills the helper uses, the extent to which the actions identified possess characteristics of effective actions, and any difficulties that arise in the process. After the role play is completed, each individual should share his or her observations about the role play. The following questions should be considered and discussed: How did the helper assist the client in identifying actions? What skills did the helper use? Did the actions identified possess characteristics of effective actions? Did any difficulties arise when identifying actions? If so, how well were they handled? The participants should repeat the exercise often enough for each person to play each role.

Exercise Responses

Note that these responses are examples of good responses. They are not the only correct responses.

ADVISING EXERCISE

Statement 1 helper advice: This is a pretty serious situation. I think you should contact an attorney to find out exactly what your rights are.

Statement 2 helper advice: You should consider getting letters of recommendation from people who know you well and know your abilities—maybe your college professors or your internship supervisor.

Statement 3 helper advice: This is a tough time for the kids. I think you should give them some extra attention and tell them that it's okay to talk about their grandmother's passing.

SUGGESTING EXERCISE

Statement 1 helper suggestion: You could prepare a list showing the advantages and disadvantages of each job. Weighing the good points and bad points might help you come to a decision.

Statement 2 helper suggestion: You could start by going to the airport and watching planes take off and land. That might help you get used to the environment.

Statement 3 helper suggestion: What about taking a vacation—just the two of you?

DIRECTING EXERCISE

Statement 1 helper direction: Let's brainstorm some actions that you could take. Would that be okay?

Statement 2 helper direction: Well, think of several possible steps you could take to reach your goal. You talk, and I'll write them down. Don't worry if they seem off the wall or ridiculous. We'll talk in a little while about which ones seem realistic. So, what are some steps you could take?

Statement 3 helper direction: Well, the treatment program begins in 1 week. In the meantime, contact your friend. I think his support is important. Then, start the program at the hospital.

IDENTIFYING ACTIONS: EXERCISE 1

Possible actions for Client 1:

1. Read a book on how to overcome public speaking fears.
2. Practice my speech at least twice in front of family members.
3. Do relaxation exercises each day and immediately before going to the city council meeting.

Possible actions for Client 2:

1. Study 3 hours per night, Monday through Thursday.
2. Do practice exercises and practice exams.
3. Take a brief course on effective study skills.

Possible actions for Client 3:

1. Chew nicotine gum each day.
2. Invest extra money rather than spend it on cigarettes.
3. Occupy spare time in the evenings with walking for exercise rather than with smoking.

Working for Positive Change

CHAPTER 12

Taking Action

CHAPTER OVERVIEW

This chapter focuses on taking action, the next step after identifying actions. At this point, clients begin pursuing the new course that they have charted; that is, they take the actions that they have identified to facilitate achievement of their goals. In this chapter, we describe the purposes and benefits of taking action, the process of taking action, difficulties related to taking action, and skills used in taking action. A hypothetical dialogue and an exercise are included at the end of this chapter to facilitate understanding of taking action.

What I must do is all that concerns me, not what the people think.

—Ralph Waldo Emerson
(1841/1926, p. 38)

Time for Action

For the client, it is time for what Rogers (1942) called "one of the fascinating aspects" of helping: "the initiation of minute, but highly significant, positive actions" (p. 41). Taking action is one of the most active parts of the helping process. It is the time when clients begin to work toward achieving their goals.

Purposes and Benefits of Taking Action

Clients take action to

■ put new attitudes and behaviors into effect,
■ work toward goal achievement,
■ manage or resolve problems, and
■ keep themselves from returning to previous ineffective attitudes and behaviors.

Taking Action: Easy for Some Clients, Hard for Others

For some clients, helpers are most needed to promote understanding of problems and to assist with setting goals and identifying actions. Once these clients know what to do, they have little problem taking action (see Egan, 2002). Between sessions, these clients take action, and then at the next session they report how things are going. The helpers' role is to offer encouragement and feedback, monitor progress toward goal achievement, and address any difficulties that the clients encounter.

Often, however, taking action is very challenging for clients, perhaps the toughest part of the helping process. Clients are faced with putting new attitudes and behaviors into effect, and client resistance is not unusual. As in the processes of setting goals and identifying actions, resistance may manifest itself as clients expressing fear of change, clinging to negative beliefs that problems will never be managed or resolved, putting off change, and refusing to participate, among other things.

Clients may also learn at this point, if not earlier, that they do not possess the skills or resources needed to take action (see Cormier & Nurius, 2003; Egan 2002; Hill & O'Brien, 1999). For example, consider a client who sets a goal related to improving his social life and then identifies actions he can take, such as initiating conversation with people. If the client lacks good social skills, he will not be able to perform this action in a way that will promote goal achievement. The helper may need to assist the client in developing social skills so the client can take action effectively.

In short, some clients reach an impasse at the point of taking action and need help moving forward (Egan, 2002). Helpers can assist them by showing understanding of the resistance and apprehension that the clients may be feeling, recognizing any skill or resource deficits that may exist, and discussing with clients how to address those deficits. Lauver and Harvey (1997) suggested role-playing as a way to determine client motivation and self-efficacy for taking action. Role-playing can be a good way to identify client skill levels and barriers to goal achievement. This activity may also suggest ways in which goals or actions need to be modified.

The Process of Taking Action

At the point in helping when clients take action, helpers function largely as facilitators, assisting clients in taking effective action. The following are important steps in the process of taking action.

Create and Maintain a Positive Atmosphere of Support, Confidence, and Trust While Challenging Clients to Change. Helpers push their clients to act, but they also create and maintain a safe, trusting, supportive, nonjudgmental atmosphere that encourages clients to express their feelings, try out new attitudes and behaviors, and develop the perspective that they can successfully make changes. Helpers may also motivate clients to take action through encouragement and by expressing confidence that the clients can achieve their goals. Such positive statements as, "We'll work together" and "You're doing a great job," can encourage clients to pursue their goals, persist in their efforts, and develop an expectation of success.

Proceed at a Comfortable Pace. Although limits on insurance coverage or number of sessions sometimes make it necessary for helpers and clients to try to accomplish their work together within a certain period of time, in general, clients determine the pace at which they take action. Some clients take action confidently and want to work quickly, whereas others are more cautious or hesitant and need to proceed at a slower pace. For helpers, patience is a virtue. Helpers need to recognize that learning new skills and making changes can be tough for clients.

Help Clients Develop Skills and Access Resources Needed for Positive Change. This point is discussed by Cormier and Nurius (2003), Egan (2002), and Hill and O'Brien (1999). Clients may need to develop skills and access resources to successfully achieve their goals. For example, consider a client who sets a goal to improve his social life and identifies the action of initiating conversation with people when he is in social settings, such as parties. If the client lacks social skills, the helper may use a technique such as role-playing to help the client develop these skills and build confidence. The client could play himself and the helper could play someone the client approaches for conversation. Essentially, the role-playing would serve as a form of practice that would help the client prepare for social encounters. The hypothetical dialogue at the end of this chapter demonstrates how a helper might conduct a role play with a client.

Helpers can also teach their clients such skills and techniques as meditation, relaxation, and imagery. The latter technique involves teaching clients to visualize and rehearse various scenes (such as speaking in front of a crowd) through their imagination. This technique has been shown to be helpful in promoting effective performance of the imagined event in real life (see Cormier & Nurius, 2003). In addition, helpers might assist their clients by suggesting books and videos, recommending support groups, and identifying community resources.

Help Clients Understand That Positive Change Is Not Always Steady and Consistent. Positive change may take the form of two steps forward and one step back. Often, change comes in "plateaus," with some plateaus being more difficult to achieve than others. Some clients feel excited about initial progress as they take action but then either stop working or prematurely terminate helping (J. Dagley, personal communication, May 23, 2002). To head this off, helpers can educate clients about the nature of change and encourage clients to continue working toward their goals, especially if it looks as if they might prematurely stop taking action.

Provide Constructive Feedback to Clients. As clients take action, helpers share their observations, impressions, opinions, and reactions. Helpers' constructive feedback lets clients know how they are doing, from the helper's standpoint, as they learn new skills and practice new attitudes and behaviors. The feedback reinforces effective attitudes and behaviors and identifies areas for improvement.

Think of an athletic coach who helps his players learn new techniques, skills, or moves, or a teacher who writes comments on her students' assignments. As practice and new learning take place, the learners receive information about their performance—what they are doing well and what they can improve or change. Similarly, helpers provide constructive feedback to clients about their performance and progress as the clients work toward their goals. Consider the following example. Suppose a helper and a client are role-playing how the client plans to speak to her husband about spending more time together. The helper may stop the role play at certain points to comment on the client's statements and behaviors, perhaps saying something like this:

> "You started out very well. Telling Mark that you love him and that you want your marriage to work shows how much you care for him. But when you said that he cares more about his job than you, you seemed to become hostile. You moved your arms a lot more and your voice got louder. It seemed like the tone of the conversation became aggressive. I suspect that your husband would become defensive if you actually said that to him, and then you'd both fall back into the same old pattern of arguing. Can you think of something else you might say that would not create such tension?"

After the client considers other possible statements, the role play would resume. The helper's feedback assists the client in developing more awareness of her statements and behaviors and the impact that they have. With this understanding, the client can make necessary adjustments, which will increase her chances of communicating effectively with her husband.

Promote Deeper Client Understanding. New, deeper understandings often develop as clients implement new attitudes and behaviors and witness the effects that they have. That is, clients "learn by doing," by being actively engaged in the process of change. Rogers (1942) observed that once positive actions have been attempted, there is "a development of further insight—more complete and accurate self-understanding as the individual gains courage to see more deeply into his [or her] own actions" (p. 43). Helpers must be prepared to explore these new understandings with such skills as asking questions and reflecting feelings.

Facilitate the Transfer of Learning. Helpers assist clients in applying what they learn in helping to their "real-world" lives—that is, helpers facilitate the transfer of learning. Facilitating the transfer of learning involves (1) helping clients apply new skills, attitudes, and behaviors to manage or resolve the problems that prompted them to seek help; and (2) teaching clients how to apply what they learn in helping to other challenges and problems that they may confront in the future (see Hackney & Cormier, 2001; Ward, 1984). Transfer of learning continues throughout the helping process.

The helping session can be seen as a laboratory in which clients work with helpers to test new attitudes and behaviors in a comfortable, accepting environment. Role-playing is a good example of a way in which clients can practice new skills in an environment in which they will not be rejected and their performance can be discussed and improved. However, what is learned needs to be transferred outside the helping relationship. Clients need to be able to apply new attitudes and behaviors to real-life situations. Indeed, helping clients function more effectively in the real world is the main purpose of the helping process.

Often, helpers facilitate the transfer of learning by encouraging clients to try out new skills, attitudes, and behaviors in their daily lives and then having the clients discuss their experiences (e.g., how they felt, what worked and what did not, how other people responded) during the next helping session. To facilitate discussion, helpers may encourage clients to keep a journal in which they note their feelings, thoughts, and actions as they apply new skills, attitudes, and behaviors. Helpers may also give clients other "homework" assignments, if clients are willing, such as imagery exercises, reading books and articles, or practicing new behaviors (Hutchins & Cole Vaught, 1997). For example, a helper may teach a client breathing and relaxation techniques and ask the client to practice them before the next session. Homework helps clients work on specific behaviors outside of helping and gives helpers and clients something to discuss in future sessions (Hutchins & Cole Vaught, 1997). This discussion may reveal how well clients are progressing toward their goals and whether clients are confronting any barriers to change.

Homework should not be overused, however (J. Dagley, personal communication, May 23, 2002). It is tempting, especially perhaps for novice helpers who are eager to see clients change, to assign homework in each session. However, constant homework may make helping seem like an unpleasant work or school task. Homework may also pressure clients toward progress and changes for which they are not ready. And in some cases, the movement facilitated by homework may not be what clients need. After a session, clients may need to think about the helping process—to "percolate"—in their own way rather than have the process structured for them through homework assignments.

Identify Ways That Clients Can Receive External Support and Maintain Gains. Helpers are not always available, in person, to offer support and encouragement as clients strive to achieve goals and make changes. Without consistent support, clients may feel alone in their efforts, slip back into ineffective attitudes and behaviors, or succumb to fears or lack of motivation. To minimize the chances of these negative developments, helpers may assist clients in identifying various resources and sources of support to supplement the helping process (see, e.g., Cormier & Nurius, 2003).

Examples include written materials, videotapes, family, friends, workshops, support groups, and community resources. These resources and sources of support can not only help clients achieve their goals, but they can help clients maintain their gains as well, especially after the helping process has ended. Helpers may also teach clients other ways to support their efforts. These could include self-rewards and reinforcements, such as setting aside time to go out with friends after completing a difficult work task (Carkhuff, 2000).

Monitor Progress Toward Goal Achievement. As clients take action, helpers monitor how well things are working. They consider such questions as: What challenges are clients facing? Are actions facilitating goal achievement? (Remember, successful actions do not equal goal achievement; they lead to goal achievement.) Are clients' attitudes and behaviors changing? For example, if a client agrees to do some relaxation exercises to help her achieve her goal of effectively managing stress, then at the next session, the helper and the client may talk about how well the exercises have worked. To what extent are they helping the client achieve her goal of managing stress? To monitor progress, helpers listen to clients' statements and concerns, ask questions, and take notice of clients' verbal and nonverbal messages.

Helpers may also teach clients how to monitor their attitudes, feelings, behaviors, and progress toward goal achievement (see Watson & Tharp, 2002). This self-monitoring involves clients noting and recording their thoughts, feelings, and behaviors as they take action and work toward goals. The clients may record their observations on paper or on videotape or audiotape. Then, they can review and discuss the observations with the helper.

Be Prepared to Modify Goals and Actions. In the process of taking action, it may become apparent that modifications are needed in some areas. Goals may be unrealistic; actions may not be working; clients may even change their minds about what they want. For example, a client may identify "studying 3 hours per night" as one of the actions he will take en route to the goal of raising his grades. When the client begins to take this action, he may find that he does not have this much time to commit to studying. He has too many other obligations, such as work and family. In this case, the goal or the actions identified to achieve the goal may need to be modified to be more realistic. As clients take action, they are able to see just how realistic and achievable their goals are. Flexibility and willingness to make appropriate adjustments are important.

Difficulties Related to Taking Action

The following paragraphs describe difficulties that are sometimes associated with the process of taking action.

Taking Action Prematurely. It is important for goals to be set and appropriate actions to be identified before action is taken. Positive change is more likely when goals and actions have been discussed and when goals and actions possess the characteristics that make them effective (see chapters 10 and 11). When action is taken before goals and actions have been discussed, there is a greater chance that the action will be ineffective and discouraging.

Clients' Lack of Skills or Resources. As discussed earlier, clients sometimes do not possess the skills or resources needed to accomplish their goals. Such deficits may become apparent when clients identify the actions they want to take or when they try to take action. Helpers assist clients in learning new skills and accessing resources. If this cannot be done for some reason, goals and actions may need to be modified.

Client Resistance. Client resistance to taking action may manifest itself in many of the same ways that resistance is seen when clients set goals and identify actions. These include clients expressing fear of change, demonstrating a lack of readiness, clinging to negative beliefs that problems will never be managed or resolved, putting off change, and refusing to participate, among other things. Helpers may "join," or go along with, the resistance—not fight it—as a way to explore and understand it. They may also use such skills as listening, asking questions, confronting, interpreting, and immediacy to understand the cause of the resistance. Finally, helpers need to carefully consider whether they are contributing to or causing the resistance (e.g., by pushing too quickly for change).

Setbacks and Slow Progress. Making positive changes can be difficult, uncomfortable, and frustrating. It can be a slow process, and it may involve some occasional discouraging setbacks. For example, a client might lapse into old ways or succumb to familiar sabotage strategies that have prevented change in the past. Or an action that the client takes may not work as well as hoped. Helpers may find it beneficial to discuss with their clients the possibility that setbacks may occur. This preparation may help clients maintain their motivation and accept setbacks and slow progress, should they occur, as part of the change process and not as signs that they have failed. In addition, when clients seem to be struggling, helpers can offer support and understanding of how difficult it can be to make changes. Such skills as asking questions and reflecting feelings can be helpful.

Skills Used in Taking Action

Many of the skills discussed in previous chapters are useful in helping clients take action. In the following sections, we briefly revisit several skills that are particularly useful in this regard.

Taking Notice

This skill is important when monitoring client progress toward goals. For example, helpers may note their clients' demeanor and affect to ascertain whether the clients seem frustrated or pleased with their progress. Helpers also use the skill of taking notice when helping clients learn new skills. For example, they may note client responses during role plays (e.g., how comfortable clients seem).

Asking Questions

Asking questions is another valuable skill for determining how well clients are progressing toward their goals. Helpers may ask how things are going as the clients take action. Questions may also be used to inquire about any difficulties that clients may be experiencing as they take action.

Reflecting Feelings

Helpers may reflect their clients' feelings to show that they recognize and understand client fears and concerns about making changes. When clients feel good about successes in taking action, helper reflections can reinforce these feelings.

Focusing

As noted earlier, clients often take action between sessions and then, during the next session, tell helpers how things are working. As clients describe what they have done, helpers may use the skill of focusing to address things that seem particularly important, such as feelings, thoughts, and difficulties that clients have experienced when taking action.

Providing Constructive Feedback

As has been discussed, helpers share their observations, impressions, opinions, and reactions as clients take action. Constructive feedback lets clients know how they are doing, from the helper's standpoint, as they learn new skills and practice new attitudes and behaviors. This feedback reinforces effective attitudes and behaviors and identifies areas for improvement.

Confronting

This skill can be used to address resistance (e.g., "You say you want to make changes, but in the last two sessions you've told that you haven't started to work on the steps we talked about."). When resistance is confronted, it can be discussed and understood. Helpers and clients can then determine whether they are ready to proceed with taking action.

Providing Information

Helpers may use this skill to identify helpful resources and sources of support for clients (e.g., books, community resources, support groups).

Interpreting

When taking action, clients may experience new feelings and thoughts and face difficulties that impede their progress. To assist clients in understanding the meaning of these new feelings, thoughts, and difficulties, helpers may use interpreting. For example, if a client becomes nervous and stutters during a role play in which he is practicing conversing with someone at a party, the helper might connect this behavior to social rejection that the client experienced as a teenager.

Immediacy

This skill is useful as a way to recognize and address client resistance, fears, and concerns about taking action (e.g., "It seems like our conversation has really slowed down a lot in the last few minutes since we started talking about the actions you've taken. Does it seem that way to you, too?"). In addition, positive immediacy statements can reinforce effective client action and help clients feel good about successes (e.g., "That's wonderful! I'm so glad to hear that you had a good time on your date. You worked hard to get to this point.").

Brainstorming

Like providing information, this skill can be used to help clients identify possible resources and sources of support as they take action.

Directing

This skill can be used to instruct clients when they need to learn new skills, access resources, or engage in certain activities, such as role plays. For example, a helper might say: "In this role play, you'll be yourself and I'll be someone you want to approach for conversation. Try to be natural and think about the skills we worked on earlier. Afterwards, we'll talk about it. Is that okay?"

A Hypothetical Dialogue

The following hypothetical dialogue between a helper and a client demonstrates an aspect of taking action. In the previous session, the client identified actions to help her achieve her goal of being more sociable and more assertive when interacting with people. One of the actions she identified was to invite her classmate and friend Sally to socialize with her. She is struggling somewhat to take action. The dialogue is from the sixth helping session.

Helper: Last time, I think we talked about some steps you were going to take before today. You were going to ask your friend Sally if she would like to spend some time with you. Did you do that?

[The helper summarizes what was discussed in the last session as a way to begin the current session. The helper also asks a closed question.]

Client: Actually, no. I chickened out. I figured that she was probably busy anyway. She always seems to have something to do.

Helper: Hmm. I remember that you were feeling kind of excited last week about talking to Sally. What happened that caused that to change?

[To explore and understand what happened, the helper asks an open question. Why did the client not follow through with the action that she planned to take? The helper is trying to determine the reason.]

Client: Yeah, I was excited about it. I don't know what happened. I saw Sally a few days ago, and then right before I was going to ask her if she wanted to get together, I started getting nervous and blanking out. I didn't know what to say. I thought I would fumble over my words and make a fool of myself, so rather than do that, I just decided not to ask.

Helper: What were you feeling at that point?

[By asking an open question about the client's feelings, the helper attempts to understand further the client's reason for not following through with taking action.]

Client: Frustrated, but also kind of relieved.

Helper: What do you mean?

[The helper asks a clarifying question.]

Client: Well, not asking her meant that I wouldn't embarrass myself. That's why I felt relieved.

Helper: And what about the frustration?

Client: I'm still stuck in my apartment with no plans for the weekend. This always happens because I can't figure out what to say or get up the nerve to call a friend, or something.

Helper: Sounds like you have some conflicted feelings. (pauses) I have an idea. Would you be willing to try a role play where we can practice what you might say to Sally?

[The helper notes the client's conflicted feelings. The helper also suggests role-playing, which is a form of behavior rehearsal. Doing a role play will allow the helper to see how the client tries to make social invitations. Through role-playing, the client can become aware of problems with her approach, receive feedback from the helper, and work on developing more effective social skills.]

Client (pauses momentarily): Okay. I'll try it.

Helper: All right. Maybe this will help us to better understand some of the roadblocks you're hitting when you try to socialize. You be yourself, and I'll be Sally. Let's say that you and I are in class and we have some time to talk before the instructor comes in. I'm sitting beside you, and you're considering asking me to get together with you sometime. We'll do this for a few minutes and then talk about it. (pauses) Okay, think for a moment about what you'd like to say and start whenever you're ready.

[The helper describes the purpose of the role play and the role of each person. Note that the helper is using the skill of directing when describing how to do the role play.]

Client (pauses): Hi, Sally.

Helper: Hi, Anna. How are you?

Client: Okay. A little tired today. (pauses; appears somewhat nervous) Well, Sally, do you want to do something?

Helper (takes note of client's nervousness): Sure. What did you have in mind?

Client (pauses): I don't know. (pauses further, looks frustrated, and stops the role play) I just don't know what to say at this point. I'm blanking out. I just don't know how to converse with people.

Helper: You know, you say that you blank out and get nervous in situations like this. I'm wondering if that could be because you're not considering in advance what you'd like to ask—not because you don't know how to have a conversation. (pauses) What are some activities that you and Sally like to do together?

[The helper uses a form of interpretation here to offer a reason why the client gets nervous and blanks out. This may help the client recognize and understand her own behaviors and reframe her perception about her conversational abilities. The helper then asks an open question to invite the client to think of activities. The helper's intention is to get the client to identify things she could say when she approaches Sally. This question is also an invitation to brainstorm. The helper is encouraging the client to identify options.]

Client: We usually just talk, and occasionally we go out to lunch. She usually asks me out to lunch.

Helper: Hmm. What about you asking *her* to lunch?

[The helper, seeing an opportunity for the client to ask her friend to socialize, makes a suggestion.]

Client (pauses): Yeah, I think I could do that.

Helper: Okay. What do you think you might say to her?

[The helper asks an open question to encourage the client to be specific.]

Client: Well, I could just ask if she wants to go to lunch sometime.

Helper: When? "Sometime" is a little vague. I'm concerned that you might hit another roadblock and blank out without being more specific.

[The helper encourages more specificity.]

Client: Oh, let's say Saturday.

Helper: Okay. You know, in addition to being specific about what you want, making a little small talk at first might make it easier for you to ask Sally out to lunch. It could break the ice a little bit and would seem less forward than asking her out to lunch right off the bat.

[The helper suggests small talk as a way to make the conversation go smoother.]

Client: Yeah, that's a good point.

Helper: Okay. So, let's start the role play again. This time, you know going in that you're going to ask Sally to lunch on Saturday. I'll get us started. Are you ready?

[The helper makes sure that the client feels ready to begin. The client appears to need more focus as she goes into social situations. In the last several lines of dialogue, the helper has assisted the client in achieving this focus.]

Client: Yes.

Helper (brief pause as the helper begins the role play): Hi, Anna. How's it going?

Client: Okay. (brief pause) I'm a little tired. I was cleaning my apartment all day yesterday.

Helper: Ah, did you get a lot done?

Client: Yeah, but I've still got a lot left to do. It's a big apartment.

Helper: I know how it goes. I've got some cleaning to do myself.

Client (pauses; seems a little more relaxed): Say, do you want to have lunch with me on Saturday?

Helper: Sure, okay. I have an errand to run that day that will probably take me until 11:30. What time did you have in mind?

Client (pauses; seems a little more confident): Oh, how about noon?

Helper: That sounds good. Do you want to meet somewhere or go together?

Client: I can pick you up around noon.

Helper: Great. Where do you want to go?

Client: Oh, I didn't think about that. Maybe we could decide on Saturday.

Helper: Okay. I'll see you at noon! (role play ends). How are you feeling right now?

[The helper, who has been monitoring the client's verbal and nonverbal behaviors throughout the role play, requests the client's response to the role-play experience as a way to begin discussion.]

Client: A little better.

Helper: Yes, I noticed that when you knew what you were going to ask Sally, you seemed more confident and assertive. Your words flowed smoothly. You didn't seem to get flustered or hung up on what to say.

[The helper uses the skill of providing constructive feedback to comment on the client's performance in the role play.]

Client: Yeah, I did feel a little more focused.

Helper: Good. Would you like to ask Sally to lunch before our next meeting? Next time, we can talk about how it goes, if you want.

Client: Yes, I'd like to do that.

[By asking the client if she wants to ask Sally to lunch, the helper is trying to get the process of taking action back on track. However, the action that the client will now take has been slightly modified to be even more specific—the client will not merely invite Sally to socialize with her, she will invite Sally to lunch.]

Helper: Great. Remember to have a clear idea about what you want to ask before you approach Sally—like when you want to go to lunch and maybe even where. That might help you feel more confident.

[By encouraging the client to have, in advance, a clear idea about what she wants to ask, the helper is facilitating the transfer of learning. The helper is assisting the client in applying new learning from the session and the role play to her "real-world" life.]

In this dialogue, a helper assisted a client who was struggling to take action. The role-play exercise allowed the client to practice what she might say to her friend Sally. It also helped to illuminate at least one reason why the client has had difficulty asserting herself in certain social situations, such as when making invitations: She has not considered in advance what she wants to say, which has contributed to her feeling nervous and blanking out. Of course, it is not necessary to pre-plan or script every word. Spontaneity is part of social interaction. However, as this client learned through the session and the role-play exercise, it is often helpful to have a basic idea of what one wants when making a social invitation. In short, the role-play exercise and the helper's comments helped the client develop a deeper understanding of herself and her interactional style. They also helped to increase the client's self-confidence and give her some direction as she moves forward and takes action.

Throughout the dialogue and role play, the helper maintained a positive, supportive atmosphere while encouraging the client to press forward and take action. With the helper's support and assistance, the client seems to be on her way to achieving her goal of becoming more sociable and more assertive when interacting with people.

Summary and Concluding Remarks

This chapter addressed the process of taking action to achieve goals. Taking action can be challenging. When taking action, clients need to work diligently, commit to change, and be patient. The new responsibilities and consequences of change can feel uncomfortable, overwhelming, and scary for some clients, but those who persist in their efforts usually see positive results.

Next, we focus on an activity that is sometimes ignored in the helping process: evaluation. This activity addresses such questions as: How well are clients progressing toward their goals? How well are actions working? How well are the helper's skills, interventions, and strategies working? Have goals been achieved? If the answer is yes, what evidence is there that they have been achieved? What, if anything, needs to be modified? The evaluation process is the focus of chapter 13.

Questions for Thought

1. Think about a time in your life when you took action to achieve a goal that you set. What difficulties did you face? How did you maintain your motivation to take action and pursue your goal? What did you learn from the action that you took? Did you ultimately achieve your goal?

2. In your view, what is the role of helpers in the process of taking action?

3. Several difficulties related to taking action were discussed in this chapter. What other difficulties can you identify?

Exercise

The following exercise covers the process of taking action. It may be most beneficial as a classroom exercise.

EXERCISE: This exercise is essentially a role play within a role play. It requires three people: a helper, a client, and an observer. The client selects one of the following issues to role-play: (1) asking the boss for a raise at work, (2) approaching a romantic partner about spending more time together, or (3) talking to an instructor about an academic concern (e.g., a low grade). After the client selects an issue, begin the role play. The helper should spend a few minutes exploring and gaining understanding of the issue. The helper and the client should then identify the client's goal (e.g., to achieve a $3,000 per year raise at work) and some actions that the client could take to achieve the goal.

Next, the helper should suggest a role play as a way for the client to practice taking action to achieve the goal. The helper should describe role-playing to the client and explain what each person's role will be. The helper should assume the role of the boss, the romantic partner, or the instructor, and the helper and client should role-play how the client will go about attempting to address the selected issue. The helper should monitor the client's statements and behaviors during the role play. The helper can stop the role play now and then to provide constructive feedback as it seems necessary: What is the client doing well? What could be improved?

After a few minutes, the helper and the client should stop and discuss the role play. (They should not stop the entire exercise—just the role play on how the client is going to address the issue selected.) The helper should provide constructive feedback and ask for client reactions to the role play. How well did the client ask the boss for the raise, approach his or her romantic partner, or talk to the instructor about the academic concern? What feedback does the helper have about the client's performance? How did the client feel about doing the role play? Was it helpful? The observer's role is to note how well the helper conducts the role play and the discussion afterwards: How well does the helper set up and describe role-playing to the client? How well does the helper provide constructive feedback and monitor client responses?

When the helper and the client have finished discussing their role play, the observer should share his or her comments and observations about the helper's performance. Then, the helper and the client should share their reactions. What did each participant learn from this exercise? The exercise should be repeated often enough for each person to play each role.

CHAPTER 13

Evaluation

CHAPTER OVERVIEW

This chapter focuses on evaluation, a process in which helpers and clients engage to examine progress in helping. Evaluation provides a status report, and it occurs at many points in helping, not just at the end. In this chapter, we define evaluation and describe its purposes and benefits. We also describe the process of evaluation, difficulties related to evaluation, and skills used in evaluation. A hypothetical dialogue and exercises are included at the end of this chapter to facilitate understanding of evaluation.

When you feel how depressingly / slowly you climb, / it's well to remember that / Things Take Time.

—Piet Hein (1966)

Evaluation: An Important Feature of Helping

Evaluation is sometimes overlooked in helping. However, it is important to determine how well the change process is working, and that is done through evaluation. Evaluation shows helpers and clients "where they are" in the process of making changes and working toward goals. It reveals what has been accomplished and how much more remains to be done.

What Is Evaluation?

In the helping process, evaluation involves assessing, measuring, or reviewing the nature, quality, or effectiveness of various aspects of helping. *It is a continuous, ongoing process, not merely a one-time event at the end of helping.* In this chapter, we focus largely on evaluation of client goals and actions. Basically, helpers and clients want to know how well the helping process is working and how well clients are making changes. Evaluation is a way to monitor progress.

Purposes and Benefits of Evaluation

The following are some of the reasons why evaluation is valuable in helping.

Evaluation Provides a Way for Helpers to Assess the Effectiveness of Their Skills, Interventions, and Strategies. As helpers use helping skills and other interventions and strategies, such as role plays and breathing exercises, they observe clients and ask for their responses (see Hill & O'Brien, 1999). One of the purposes of these observations and inquiries is to assess the effectiveness of the skills, interventions, and strategies used: What impact did they have? Did they have the effect that the helper hoped for, or some other effect? Do modifications need to be made in how skills, interventions, and strategies are applied? The answers to these questions give helpers a sense for what works and what does not.

Evaluation Provides a Way to Assess Client Progress. Evaluation provides a status report that offers information on how well clients are progressing in helping. It shows how far they have come and how far they have to go. Specifically, evaluation helps to identify

- the extent to which actions are promoting goal achievement and positive change,
- what clients are doing well and in what areas they need improvement,
- attitude and behavior changes and new skills developed, and
- the extent to which problems have been managed or resolved.

Evaluation Reveals Whether Goals, Actions, or Problem Definitions Need to Be Modified. By showing what is working and what is not working, evaluation assists helpers in assessing the need for modification of goals, actions, or problem definitions. It may be discovered, for example, that goals and actions are unrealistic. Evaluation also gives helpers the opportunity to reexamine their understanding of client problems. They may find that a problem was not thoroughly explored or accurately identified.

Evaluation Reveals Difficulties That Clients Confront as They Pursue Their Goals. Evaluation gives clients the opportunity to describe any difficulties they have encountered as they work toward their goals. Once such difficulties are aired, helpers can assist clients in overcoming them. For example, suppose a client wants to improve her social skills. As she begins to take action, she finds that she is struggling to get up the courage to put herself in social situations, which prevents her from effectively taking action. When the client describes the difficulty, the helper may explore the reason for the client's apprehension and apply various skills, interventions, and strategies (e.g., interpreting, role-playing, relaxation exercises) to assist the client in overcoming the difficulty. It is also possible that the helper and the client will decide to modify the client's goal and actions.

Evaluation Reveals New Issues or Changes in Client Needs and Desires. New developments may occur as clients take action toward their goals. For example, a client who is seeking a new professional job may learn that certain credentials are required before he can be hired. As the helper and the client discuss this situation, they may decide to modify the employment goal and related actions to include pursuit of the required credentials. As another example, a client may discover that she no longer has any interest in pursuing her previously stated goal and wants to set a new one. This desire could be revealed through evaluation.

Evaluation Gives Clients the Chance to Provide Feedback. Both helpers and clients participate in evaluation, with each person contributing comments and feedback. Clients have the opportunity to say how well they believe things are going. For example, they may comment on how much progress they believe they have made, how their lives have changed as a result of the actions they have taken, what they have learned from taking action, or how satisfied they have been so far with the helping process (see McClam & Woodside, 1994). Evaluation also gives clients the opportunity to express any frustrations or concerns they have. Clients often feel refreshed and motivated after having the opportunity to "clear the air."

Evaluation Promotes Client Understanding. Through evaluation, clients have the opportunity to learn more about their strengths and areas for improvement. Evaluation may help clients understand why goals and actions have succeeded or failed.

Evaluation Assesses Transfer of Learning. Evaluation helps to reveal how well clients have transferred what they have learned in helping (e.g., new skills, attitudes, and behaviors) to their real-world lives—that is, it assesses how well clients have applied their learning. Evaluation can reveal situations in which clients seem to progress well in helping sessions but struggle to put new learning into effect in the outside world.

Evaluation Motivates Clients to Persist in Their Efforts to Achieve Goals. Evaluation helps to point out and reinforce positive change. When positive change occurs, evaluation provides validation and verification and shows clients that their efforts and the helping process are working.

Evaluation Teaches Clients How to Evaluate for Themselves. The evaluation process teaches clients how to review and assess their goals and actions—a skill that may benefit them for life. Clients learn how to monitor their actions, note their progress toward goals, and make adjustments when needed.

Evaluation Gives the Helping Process Credibility. Evaluation reinforces the hard work that has been done in helping (McClam & Woodside, 1994). It shows that helping can be a beneficial process for managing or resolving problems.

Evaluation Facilitates Responsibility, Accountability, and Documentation. Two points are relevant here. First, many helpers are accountable to supervisors or employers. Evaluation aids in assessing helpers' job performance, as it indicates positive points and areas for improvement. Even if helpers do not directly report to others, evaluation gives helpers the opportunity to conduct a self-assessment: How well did they identify client problems, apply skills, interventions, and strategies, and help clients make positive changes? What difficulties did helpers encounter in the process (McClam & Woodside, 1994)? Second, in this time of managed care, helpers in many settings need to demonstrate that the services they provide actually work. They may be required to document specific, observable changes in client behavior. Continued insurance coverage for clients may be contingent upon showing that helping is making a positive difference in the clients' lives.

The Process of Evaluation

The following are some basic steps for engaging in evaluation as clients work toward their goals.

Explain Evaluation and Encourage Client Participation. In their everyday lives, clients may not be very good at evaluating their attitudes, behaviors, goals, and actions. Indeed, the process of evaluation may be new to them, and they may not fully understand its purpose. Recall the example of the Somali employee in the discussion in chapter 9 on providing constructive feedback. If the supervisor had explained the purpose of the performance review (evaluation) and what his feedback meant, the significant misunderstanding that occurred might not have happened. Clients may be more willing to participate in evaluation and see it as meaningful if they understand its purpose (McClam & Woodside, 1994). In describing evaluation, helpers may talk about some of the purposes and benefits of evaluation (discussed earlier in this chapter). When evaluation tools, such as tests or videotaping, are used, clients need to know their purpose. For example, a helper may ask the client for permission to videotape a role play and explain that videotaping will allow the two of them to review the tape and discuss the client's performance.

Specifically Identify the Goals and Actions to Be Evaluated. Helpers and clients need to specifically identify the goals and actions that will be evaluated. For example, if a client identifies three actions that he will take to achieve his goal, these three actions will be specified for evaluation. Are the actions being taken successfully? What problems have been encountered along the way? How well are the actions facilitating goal achievement?

Determine When and How Frequently to Evaluate. As noted earlier, evaluation does not occur only at the end of the helping process. It occurs at many points in helping, with helpers exercising their discretion and professional judgment to determine when evaluation would be most appropriate. Some of the factors that affect when and how frequently to evaluate include the following:

- Helper and Client Needs and Preferences: Helpers vary in their diligence in making sure the helping process is on track. Some prefer more evaluation than others. As for clients, resistant clients and clients who find taking action difficult may require more feedback and evaluation regarding their efforts and performance than other clients may require (McClam & Woodside, 1994).
- The Nature of What Is Being Evaluated: Goals and actions come in many shapes and sizes. For long-range goals, helpers and clients may evaluate progress numerous times before the goals are achieved. For short-range goals, progress may be evaluated fewer times before goal achievement. Complex goals and actions may require more periodic evaluation than simpler ones (McClam & Woodside, 1994).
- Lack of Progress: If progress is not being made toward goals, evaluation may be necessary to determine the source of the problem. Are the goals or actions unrealistic? Is the client not motivated to pursue his or her goals?
- The Completion of an Action or the Apparent Accomplishment of a Goal: Evaluation is appropriate when these aspects of helping have been completed or accomplished. Helpers may also evaluate when other aspects of helping have been completed (e.g., role plays and other interventions).
- The Length of the Helping Process: Longer helping processes offer more chances for evaluation than shorter ones.

In any case, evaluation should be done in moderation. Too much evaluation can cause clients to feel that everything they say and do is being judged and scrutinized. Too little evaluation can make it difficult to assess progress and determine whether the helping process is on track.

Determine What Evaluation Tools to Use. To assist in evaluation, helpers may use various tools in addition to such skills as taking notice, asking questions, and providing constructive feedback. Evaluation tools include questionnaires, checklists, rating scales, surveys, tests, videotapes and audiotapes, and journal exercises, all of which can be used to measure progress and change. For example, a helper and a client may create a checklist of the behaviors expected to be seen if the client is making good progress toward her goal. Suppose the goal is to increase self-confidence and participation in social situations, and the goal is to be pursued with actions that include joining a local singles club, attending an assertiveness training seminar, and inviting friends to go out with the client over the weekend. Behaviors the helper and client might write on the checklist that would indicate progress toward the goal could include (1) more speaking and less passivity in conversation; (2) more involvement in social events and activities—going out instead of staying at home alone; and (3) more positive, realistic self-talk about the client's ability to socialize and be liked by other people. At some point in the process of taking action, the helper and the client would review the checklist and check off each behavior that has been observed. If most or all of the behaviors are checked, the helper and the client may conclude that the client has made good progress toward her goal.

Note and Measure Observable Behavior Changes. Observable behavior changes serve as the basis for evaluating goals and actions, as well as for evaluating helper interventions and strategies, such as role-playing and relaxation exercises (Okun, 2002). Helpers use observable behavior changes as "evidence" to determine client progress and the extent to which the helping process is working. Of course, attitudes and feelings change, too, but such changes are manifested in behavior, such as a happy feeling being reflected in a smile (Okun, 2002). If goals and actions are put in writing, the observable behavior changes that will indicate progress may be described in writing as well. Helpers may also write these behavior changes in their case notes.

As a way to measure behavior changes, evaluation may occur on a "before, during, and after" basis, with helpers noting the frequency, duration, intensity, and occurrence of specific behaviors at each of these times (Cormier & Nurius, 2003). For example, for the client just described who wants to increase her self-confidence and participation in social situations, a count could be made of the number of times the client attends social events and activities, such as parties, at the point she first seeks help. As she proceeds through helping—setting goals, identifying actions, taking action, and engaging in interventions (e.g., role plays)—the number of times that she socializes could again be counted. Finally, near the end of helping or even in a follow-up meeting weeks or months after helping has ended, another count could be done. All of these counts could be compared to determine the extent to which the client's actions were successful and her goal was achieved.

Determine the Level of Success or Achievement. The question of whether an action has been successfully completed or a goal has been achieved can be answered affirmatively or negatively, but the issue is not always that black and white (see McClam & Woodside, 1994). One hundred percent success is not always attained, but that does not mean that failure has occurred. For that reason, helpers and clients may evaluate achievement on a continuum or a scale. For example, goals can be evaluated as "not achieved," "somewhat achieved," "substantially achieved," or "fully achieved." Suppose a client had a 3.3 grade point average and set a realistic goal of achieving a 3.5 GPA by the end of the school year. If he achieved a 3.47 GPA, he would not have met his goal, but he would have accomplished a significant increase in his GPA. Thus, his goal could be evaluated as substantially achieved.

Involve Clients in Evaluation. Evaluation is a mutual process in which both helpers and clients assess progress, performance, and success. Indeed, helpers need feedback from clients to determine how things are going. Helpers want to know: What changes have clients made? What do clients still struggle with? How satisfied are clients with their progress? What feelings do clients have as they engage in evaluation? During evaluation, helpers and clients can also discuss how clients can transfer what they have learned in helping to real-life situations, how clients can maintain gains, and how clients can use new learning to tackle future problems. Together, helpers and clients can decide what modifications to make (e.g., changes to goals or actions) and can determine what to do next.

Acknowledge and Prepare for Future Opportunities to Evaluate. Completing an evaluation does not necessarily mean that problems have been managed or resolved or that the object of the evaluation will never be discussed again. Evaluation is continuous. Progress may be evaluated on many occasions. Also, because clients sometimes lapse into old, ineffective attitudes and behaviors after making progress, subsequent evaluations are conducted to help reveal lapses and suggest ways to address them. Talking with clients about future opportunities to evaluate can help clients feel more comfortable by letting them know that important issues will be addressed again and will not be forgotten.

 Record Evaluations. Helpers often record evaluations in their case notes. This documentation helps them track client progress, and it creates a record for helping professionals who may provide assistance in the future.

Difficulties Related to Evaluation

The following paragraphs describe difficulties that are sometimes associated with the process of evaluation.

 No Opportunity to Evaluate. It is not unusual for clients to terminate helping, with little or no notice, before the process has had a chance to be completed or work as intended. The process may not be what the clients expected, or they may feel that they are not a good "fit" with their helpers. Sometimes, clients complete the process of setting goals and identifying actions, take action and experience success, and then do not feel the need to return for more helping sessions. In other instances, clients may not return because the actions they took did *not* work and they view helping as ineffective. In all of these situations, helpers may not have had an opportunity to engage in evaluation with clients (although they may have evaluated their own performance to see whether they could have done anything differently).

 Inaccurate Evaluation. It is possible for evaluation to be inaccurate. Helpers may conduct evaluation hastily and without due care, they may misinterpret what they observe, or they may fail to consider cultural variables. For example, consider this situation: A client from a culture that values emotional control says, rather calmly, that he believes he has made good progress and feels less distressed than when he entered helping. The helper, who is from a different culture and expects to see more animation and more of an emotional response (e.g., smiling, expressions of relief), concludes that the client has not made as much progress as he says he has. The helper disputes the client's assessment of his progress and encourages the client to continue pursuing his goals. The client in this case may feel confused and may even choose to terminate helping.

 Clients may contribute to inaccurate evaluation by incorrectly reporting the effectiveness of the actions they have taken between sessions. For example, if a client feels embarrassed or demoralized about an action that did not work, he or she may downplay the failure or even lie about it. This may lead to an inaccurate evaluation of the effectiveness of the client's action and his or her progress toward goal achievement. Careful, ongoing, objective, culture-sensitive evaluation and the use of numerous evaluation skills and tools help to make evaluation as accurate as possible.

 Clients Feeling Personally Judged. Many clients are uncomfortable with evaluation because they feel that they are being personally criticized or are being evaluated as individuals (see McClam & Woodside, 1994). Poorly conducted evaluation may justify this feeling. Such evaluation may feel shaming and seem like an insult. The purpose of evaluation is not to judge clients personally, but to assess helping processes, behavior changes, goals, and actions, as well as helper skills, interventions, and strategies. Helpers should avoid labeling or stigmatizing clients. They should also avoid making broad, critical overgeneralizations (e.g., "You're not very good at doing role plays.").

Strong Client Reactions to Evaluation. As has been discussed, evaluation gives clients the opportunity to discuss how well the helping process is working and how well they are progressing toward their goals. If they are not pleased or if they feel scrutinized by evaluation, they may express strong emotions, such as frustration and anger. To address the clients' feelings and concerns and to keep the helping process on track, helpers may reflect the clients' feelings and discuss what can be changed to improve the situation (e.g., modifying goals and actions). Effective helpers do not criticize clients or dwell on what clients are doing wrong. Instead, they strive to provide balanced, constructive feedback on positive points and areas for improvement.

Too Much or Too Little Evaluation. We noted earlier that evaluation should be done in moderation. Too much evaluation can create a judgmental environment and evoke defensiveness and resistance in clients. Some helpers evaluate too much because of an excessive focus on their own need to feel effective, which they measure by client change. Too little evaluation can make it difficult to assess progress. Sometimes, evaluation occurs infrequently because helpers or clients resist it. They may be trying to avoid the discomfort sometimes associated with examining attitudes and behaviors, or they may fear negative evaluations. Helpers can talk with their clients about how much evaluation is needed.

Not Knowing What to Do After Evaluation. Evaluation provides a status report on how well things are going for clients. After discussing what is going well and what could be improved or changed, clients may feel directionless and wonder what happens next. Helpers and clients can address this topic. For example, they may decide to modify goals and actions. They may plan for future evaluation. If goals have been achieved, they may decide to end the helping process.

Skills Used in Evaluation

Many of the skills discussed in previous chapters are useful in the process of evaluation. In the following sections, we briefly revisit several skills that are particularly useful in this regard.

Listening

Listening is one of the best ways to gather information about client progress. For example, helpers may evaluate the extent to which goals have been achieved by listening to clients' statements about the actions they have taken. Through listening, helpers try to answer such questions as, "What successes have clients seen?" "What difficulties have they encountered?" and "How close are clients to goal achievement?"

Taking Notice

Taking notice is also useful for gathering information about how well clients are doing. Paying attention to body language, speech patterns, and behavior patterns can give helpers clues about client progress. For example, although clients differ in how they express themselves, a client who seems energetic and upbeat may be making good progress toward his or her goals, and a client who demonstrates low emotional expression and apathy may not be doing so well.

Asking Questions

This skill is useful for inquiring about client progress as clients work to achieve their goals. Here are some examples of questions that may be asked:

"How far along do you feel you are in reaching your goal of communicating effectively with your employees?"

"How well have the relaxation exercises helped you reduce stress at work?"

"What changes have you noticed since you started eating better and exercising regularly?"

Focusing

Helpers can use this skill to zero in on relevant areas for evaluation (e.g., specific topics, statements, feelings, behaviors, goals, and actions) and address them in detail. Here are two examples of how focusing may be used in evaluation:

"Let's talk about the steps you planned to take to raise your grades. How's that been coming along since our last meeting?"

"You said earlier that you feel you have more work to do before reaching your goal. Can you say more about that?"

Summarizing

Helpers can use summarizing to review clients' accomplishments, thereby reinforcing positive change and showing clients how far they have come in managing or resolving problems. This skill is also useful for pointing out problems or patterns in client behavior. For example, if a client is struggling to achieve a goal, summarizing can be used to identify the problem and suggest corrective action, such as modifying the goal or the actions taken in pursuit of the goal. Here are two examples of summarizing:

"Well, why don't we see where we are? You made a plan to find a good job. You did some research on jobs in your field, talked to several professionals, and improved your computer skills by taking the night school course. Now, you've got two good companies making attractive offers to you. It sounds like your plan was a success."

"It seems like we're not doing too well. You were going to take some time off to spend with Amy, but you never got around to it. Then, you planned to take her out to dinner and talk about your relationship, but you said you've been too busy. I'm wondering whether you're still interested in trying to improve your relationship with Amy. Is this a goal you still want to pursue?"

Providing Constructive Feedback

This skill is particularly important in the evaluation process. It involves helpers providing their assessment of how well clients are doing: What progress is being made? What are clients doing well or not so well? With information about their behavior, clients may develop greater self-understanding and then make appropriate behavioral adjustments as they strive to live more effectively. Here are two examples of constructive feedback:

> "I hear you saying that you're frustrated with slow progress. Let's look at the actions we talked about a few weeks ago. From what you described, the only actions you've taken are the easier and more passive ones, like reading self-help books and watching videotapes on assertiveness. Those are important steps in meeting people, but by themselves, they're safe and they don't put you in contact with other people. You're taking action, and that's good—a lot of people don't do anything—but you seem apprehensive about taking the riskier steps. What do you think?"

> "You did the breathing exercise very well. You seem calmer and more relaxed. But you still appear to be a little tense. Your body looks stiff and your breathing is a bit rapid. It might help if you try breathing in and out slower. By slowing the pace, you'll probably feel more relaxed. How about if we try the exercise again? I'll count a little slower to help you slow down your breathing."

Immediacy

Clients do not always directly express how they feel about the helping process or the process of making changes. For example, if a client feels disappointed with slow progress, he or she may manifest this feeling through silence, apathy, or passive-aggressive behavior. The helper may use immediacy to point out what seems to be going on in the helping relationship at that time so it can be discussed. In short, immediacy can be used to initiate an evaluation of progress at that point in time. Immediacy can also be used to reinforce positive changes. Here is an example:

> "I think we got quite a bit done today. I'm really pleased with your enthusiasm. You've really made a lot of progress in the last few meetings."

A Hypothetical Dialogue

The following hypothetical dialogue demonstrates the process of evaluation. The client is a man who sought help because of relationship difficulties. The process of exploring and understanding his concerns revealed that he does not listen well to other people, talks a lot about himself, and tends to focus solely on his own needs in a relationship while ignoring the needs of the other person. The client wants to improve his communication with people in his relationships, including his wife. One of the goals that he set is to become a more effective listener by significantly increasing the amount of time that he listens while decreasing the amount of time that he talks when he converses with his wife. To reach this goal, the client has planned to take the following actions: (1) deliberately focus on listening to what his wife is saying without talking or interrupting; (2) ask questions about what his wife says, needs, and wants rather than talk about his own needs; and (3) attend joint marital counseling, which his wife agrees to do.

The helper and client have decided that more effective listening may be indicated by the following behavior changes: (1) less client talking during conversations with his wife; (2) more happiness and closeness and less marital stress; (3) richer, more satisfying, more frequent communication; and (4) greater understanding of his wife's needs. The helper and the client have been working together once a week for about 3 months. Recently, the client has been taking action on his goal. The following dialogue occurred when the client reported that his relationship with his wife seems to be better. The helper and the client are assessing progress toward goal achievement.

Client: Amy and I seem to be getting along better.

Helper: What's different now compared to before?

[The helper asks an open question to elicit details. A comparison between "now" and "before" can show how much change has occurred and the extent to which the client has progressed toward goal achievement.]

Client: There's less tension and stress around the house. Amy seems happier and wants to be around me more. And we talk more. Before, it seemed like whenever we talked about something, the conversation would be pretty short.

[The client's response provides some evidence that the client has made good progress toward his goal.]

Helper: What do you think are the reasons for these changes?

[The helper asks another open question to get the client to be specific about why the changes occurred. The helper listens to the response to help evaluate progress toward goal achievement.]

Client: Well, I really have tried hard to be a better listener. That role-playing thing we did last week was an eye-opener. I've always known that I like to talk about myself, but I never realized just how much I focus on myself when I talk to people. So, when I've talked to Amy lately, I've just tried to listen. I found myself having to bite my tongue a lot, but I've managed to do it and just listen—and it's worked.

[The client's response provides more evidence that the client is making good progress. He is talking less. He has improved his listening skills, and the quality of communication between his wife and himself has improved.]

Helper: You sound a little surprised.

[The helper reflects feelings.]

Client: Yeah, a little bit, I guess. You know, recently, while Amy and I were talking, she was saying that she felt like she wasn't getting anywhere with her job—she didn't like it. My first reaction was to tell her how much I hated my job, but I thought for a second, and instead I asked her what she didn't like about her job. She talked about not being able to be creative and write. I never knew she liked writing. I learned something about her that I never knew in 8 years of marriage, and it was actually kind of interesting—like getting to know her all over again.

Helper: That's great. It sounds like there's a sense of renewed vitality in your marriage.

Client: Yes. It does seem more fresh, I guess you could say. I've even found that now that she feels like I'm listening to her, she seems more interested in what I have to say.

Helper: Sure. It sounds like your relationship is more balanced. Since you're showing more interest in her needs, she'll show more interest in yours. (pauses) Let's talk for a minute about the goal you set—to become a more effective listener. From what you've just described, it sounds like you've made good progress. What's your take on it? Where do you feel you are in reaching that goal?

[The helper uses the skill of focusing to specifically address the client's goal. The helper gives an impression of the client's progress and then involves the client in evaluation by asking him for his input.]

Client: For the most part, I would say that I've reached it. It's still more challenging for me to listen than to speak, but that's something I can keep working on. I think it's not so much an issue of achieving the goal anymore as much as an issue of continuing it.

Helper: It seems to me as well that you've basically reached your goal. You seem more relaxed, you listen more, you're communicating better with your wife, and it sounds like you and your wife have become closer over the past few months—talking together more than before.

[The helper uses three skills here: taking notice, summarizing, and providing constructive feedback. The helper takes note of the client's relaxed appearance. Presenting this observation to the client is a form of feedback. The helper also summarizes earlier dialogue—more listening, better communication, and a better marital relationship. The helper's comments may help to reinforce the positive changes that the client has made.]

Client: That's true.

Helper: You said that it's still more of a challenge for you to listen than to speak but that you can work on it. Can you say more about that?

[The helper addresses an issue that could cause problems if it is not monitored—the challenge the client still experiences with listening. The helper focuses the discussion on that issue and asks a question to get the client to elaborate. Remember that the evaluation process is continuous, so although it appears that the client has largely achieved his goal, the changes that he has made will be monitored and perhaps evaluated at a later time to make sure that he is still on track.]

Client: Well, old habits die hard. I think I can just keep trying to listen and not talk too much.

Helper: You've made good progress, and it's important to maintain it. The next time you and your wife have a conversation and you feel like talking too much, how about if you focus on what's going on at that moment? What are you feeling? What are you thinking? Maybe writing down your feelings and thoughts would be helpful. We can talk about it later and maybe also talk about some ways to make sure you stay on track.

[The helper encourages the client to monitor his feelings, thoughts, and behaviors. The helper also encourages the client to engage in continued evaluation by asking him to pay attention to potentially problematic behavior (talking too much) and to prepare for further discussion.]

Client: Yeah, I'll think about those things. I'd rather not write them down, though. I'll remember what's going on.

Helper: Okay. I just don't want you to lose the good progress you've worked hard for.

In this dialogue, evaluation revealed the client's progress toward goal achievement and the extent to which the client had made changes in his life. Evaluation provided the helper with the opportunity to reinforce positive changes that the client had made. It also gave the helper and the client a chance to address and monitor a potentially problematic behavior (i.e., the fact that it is more challenging for the client to listen than to speak) that could interfere with maintaining the client's success. The client appears to have substantially achieved his goal, but he needs to work to maintain his accomplishment. He needs to keep monitoring his progress to avoid returning to ineffective behaviors.

Summary and Concluding Remarks

This chapter addressed evaluation in the helping process. Evaluation is an important and continuous part of helping. It allows helpers and clients to note progress and assess the extent to which goals have been achieved. Helpers and clients both participate by reviewing and discussing goals and actions to make sure that the helping process is on track. They address such questions as the following: What is working and not working? What difficulties are present? What changes in client attitudes and behaviors are occurring? To what extent have goals been achieved? Evaluation is a learning experience for both helpers and clients.

At the end of helping, helpers evaluate the overall helping process with their clients, focusing on client functioning, goal achievement, and the extent to which client problems have been managed or resolved. This type of evaluation was discussed in chapter 3.

We have reached the end of our discussion of the major helping activities: exploring client concerns, promoting client understanding, charting a new course, and working for positive change. It is important to bear in mind that helping is not a linear process in which each activity is methodically and sequentially completed and then the helping process ends. Each of the helping activities may occur many times and at many points throughout helping.

Questions for Thought

1. If someone were to ask you why evaluation is necessary in helping, how would you explain the importance of this aspect of the helping process?

2. Think of a time when you evaluated something in your life—an experience you had, a goal you set, or an action you took. How did you do the evaluation? What similarities and differences exist between how you evaluated and how evaluation is done in helping?

3. How does culture factor into evaluation? What can helpers do to ensure that they engage in culture-sensitive evaluation?

Exercises

The following exercises cover the process of evaluation. Exercise 2 may be most beneficial as a classroom exercise.

EXERCISE 1: Two client situations follow. For each situation, the client's goal is stated. Then, a brief description of the client's status after taking action on the goal is provided. Based on the goal and the brief description of the client's status, provide an evaluation of the extent to which the client has achieved the goal. Specifically, do the following: (1) Evaluate the client's goal on the following achievement scale: not achieved—somewhat achieved—substantially achieved—fully achieved; (2) provide evidence to support your evaluation, noting why you evaluated the client's goal as you did on the achievement scale. After providing evidence, suggest what the client might do to continue to progress toward goal achievement, if you did not evaluate the goal as fully achieved. For purposes of comparison to your evaluations, a possible evaluation of each client situation is provided at the end of this chapter.

Client Situation 1:

Goal: To improve my social life, feel more at ease in social situations, and make more friends by the end of the year.

Description of client status: At the end of the year and after taking action on his goal, the client reports that he has made two friends—people he met in his classes. He spends time with them but says that he still feels a little apprehensive around people and spends some weekends by himself (slightly more time alone than he would prefer). He says that he feels much more relaxed and confident in social situations than he did at the beginning of the helping process and is hopeful that he can continue to make improvements in his social life.

Evaluation (circle one):

not achieved   somewhat achieved   substantially achieved   fully achieved

Evidence in support of evaluation: _____

_____

_____

Client Situation 2:

Goal: To lose 8 pounds in 2 months by following the "Slim Down Now!" diet.

Description of client status: After 2 months, the client reports that she has lost 4 pounds. Though she has done some exercising, she has struggled to implement her exercise regimen. She has often "cheated" on her diet by eating fast food meals.

Evaluation (circle one):

not achieved   somewhat achieved   substantially achieved   fully achieved

Evidence in support of evaluation: _____

_____

_____

EXERCISE 2: This exercise requires three people: a helper, a client, and an observer. A role play will be conducted in which the helper assists the client in evaluating progress toward a goal. Before the start of the role play, the client should identify a goal that he or she is trying to achieve (e.g., losing weight, raising grades, finding a new job, or making more friends). The client should also identify a few actions that he or she would take to achieve the goal. The helper may assist the client in identifying the goal and the actions.

Now, begin the role play. Suppose that it has been 2 weeks since the goal and actions were identified. The client has had an opportunity to work toward the goal. Using the concepts and skills discussed in this chapter, the helper should assist the client in evaluating the client's progress toward goal achievement. The following questions should be considered: Has the client taken action? If so, what happened? What difficulties, if any, has the client encountered? How close is the client to achieving his or her goal? What evidence supports this assessment? What adjustments, if any, need to be made to the goal or the actions? The helper and client should spend about 5 minutes evaluating the client's progress.

The observer's role is to note how the helper conducts the evaluation process. What skills is the helper using? What is the helper doing well? What could the helper do differently? The observer may find it helpful to take written notes during the role play.

After the role play is completed, each person should comment on it and provide feedback: How well did the helper conduct the evaluation? How did the client feel about evaluation? Also, each person should share what he or she learned about the evaluation process from the role play. After discussing the role play, the participants should switch roles and repeat the exercise often enough for each person to play each role.

Exercise Responses

The following are examples of evaluations for the client situations presented in Exercise 1. Note that these are not the only correct evaluations possible.

Client Situation 1:

Evaluation: substantially achieved

Evidence in support of evaluation: The client seems to have substantially achieved his goal because he has made two new friends and he reports feeling much more relaxed and confident in social situations than he did at the beginning of helping. These appear to be significant gains. His goal might not be fully achieved because he continues to feel somewhat apprehensive around people and he spends a little more time alone than he would prefer. Of course, he can continue to strive to make positive changes in his social life (e.g., he can identify social activities that he can participate in on weekends).

Client Situation 2:

Evaluation: somewhat achieved

Evidence in support of evaluation: The client's goal appears to be somewhat achieved. The client has lost some weight (4 pounds), so she has not totally failed to shed pounds. However, she did not adhere very well to her diet or exercise regimen, and she did not reach her goal of losing 8 pounds in 2 months. The time frame of her goal could be extended and she could continue trying. The reasons she did not stick to her diet and exercise plans could be explored, possibly leading to a modification of the goal or the actions taken to achieve the goal.

Helping Issues, Aspects, and Topics

CHAPTER 14

Ethical and Legal Issues in Helping

CHAPTER OVERVIEW

In their work, helpers make many decisions, such as what to say and not say, whom to reveal information to, and what skills to use. These decisions are often laden with ethical and legal concerns and require familiarity with relevant ethical guidelines and laws. There are many types of helpers, and not all helpers are specifically subject to the ethical guidelines of a particular profession. Nevertheless, it behooves helpers to be aware of and follow ethical guidelines and laws. By doing so, they will increase the quality of service they provide and minimize the chance that disciplinary or legal action will be brought against them. In this chapter, we discuss ethical guidelines and laws that pertain to the helping professions. We also describe a number of issues that have ethical and legal implications, including confidentiality, record keeping, and values. We discuss how ethical complaints are handled and how helpers may become involved in legal proceedings. We also describe why ethical complaints and legal proceedings often are not initiated even if violations apparently have occurred. Finally, we discuss how helpers can manage risks and make good decisions when ethical and legal issues arise.

Integrity can be neither lost nor concealed nor faked nor quenched nor artificially come by nor outlived, nor, I believe, in the long run denied. Integrity is no greater and no less today than it was yesterday and will be tomorrow. It stands outside time.

—Eudora Welty (1987, p. 147)

Ethical Guidelines and Codes

The starting point for helpers when learning about ethical issues is to become familiar with the ethical guidelines of their profession. Ethical guidelines are the rules, principles, standards, and norms established by a profession to ensure the dignity, responsibility, and accountability of its members. They are written in professional codes, such as the American Counseling Association's (ACA) (1995) *Code of Ethics and Standards of Practice,* the American Psychological Association's (APA) (2002) *Ethical Principles of Psychologists and Code of Conduct,* and the National Association of Social Workers' (NASW) (1999) *Code of Ethics.* There are many different ethical codes in the helping professions, but they all reflect six fundamental principles (Kitchener, 1984; Meara, Schmidt, & Day, 1996):

- Beneficence: Helpers "do good"; they work to promote client well-being.
- Nonmaleficence: Helpers "do no harm" to their clients.
- Autonomy: Clients determine what they want.
- Justice: Helpers treat all clients in a fair, dignified, and nondiscriminatory manner.
- Fidelity: Helpers honor their obligations and commitments to their clients, their colleagues, and their profession.
- Veracity: Helpers are truthful with their clients.

The various ethical codes for the helping professions cover the same basic topics, including confidentiality, client rights, multiple (dual) relationships with clients, informed consent, respect for cultural and individual differences, professional competence, assessment, research, fees, record keeping, advertising, supervision, and responsibilities to other helping professionals (see, e.g., American Counseling Association, 1995; American Psychological Association, 2002; National Association of Social Workers, 1999).

Doyle (1998) stated that ethical codes serve a number of functions. Specifically, they

- clarify helper responsibilities to clients, employers, professional organizations, and society in general;
- provide guidelines for handling issues and resolving conflicts that may arise in particular situations; and
- provide standards by which members of the profession may be judged.

Ethical codes also provide protection for helpers, clients, and the public. Helpers use the guidelines in the codes to justify the decisions they make when working with their clients, and compliance with the guidelines is evidence that helpers acted properly, thus minimizing the possibility of professional discipline. Ethical codes also protect clients and the public from irresponsible or unscrupulous behavior by helpers. They let clients and the public know what standards of behavior helpers are expected to meet. They outline proper and improper behavior, and violations are deterred by the possibility of discipline.

It should be noted that ethical guidelines are just that—guidelines. To encompass a wide range of issues and situations, they are written in fairly broad and general terms. For example, the American Psychological Association's (2002) *Ethical Principles of Psychologists and Code of Conduct* often uses such words as "reasonable" or "reasonably" when describing obligations of psychologists. For example, psychologists terminate helping when it becomes "reasonably clear" that helping is no longer necessary or beneficial (Section 10.10(a)); they take "reasonable precautions" to protect confidential information (Section 4.01). What is "reasonable" is often determined by the circumstances. Because of the use of such broad and general terms, there are few situations for which ethical guidelines provide clear-cut, specific, definitive answers. Helpers often have to interpret guidelines, applying the general language to the facts of their particular situation. In so doing, helpers may find that there is more than one ethical resolution to a particular problem. When addressing ethical issues and interpreting ethical guidelines, it is a good idea for helpers to review the rules of their workplace and consult with their supervisors or colleagues.

Laws

Helpers must be familiar with laws that affect their practice. Laws are the standards and requirements that govern conduct in a society. They include, most typically, state and federal statutes and court decisions. Laws tend to be more objective and specific than ethical guidelines (Gladding, 2000).

Examples of laws that impact the helping professions include the following:

- The Family Educational Rights and Privacy Act of 1974 (often referred to as the Buckley Amendment): allows parents to inspect the educational records of their unemancipated minor children
- State statutes requiring that child abuse and neglect be reported to authorities
- State statutes that prohibit helpers from having sexual relations with their clients
- *Tarasoff v. Regents of the University of California* (1974, 1976): established the helper's duty to warn and protect a person when a client expresses a serious intention to harm that person (because this is a California case, courts in other states are not obligated to follow it, although many have; also, many states have enacted their own duty-to-warn statutes) (Woodworth, 2000)
- *Jaffee v. Redmond* (1996): a United States Supreme Court case that recognized psychotherapist privilege (protection from compelled disclosure of confidential client communications) and extended it to confidential communications made to licensed social workers during therapy; this privilege applies in federal court cases that concern issues of federal law

The subject of the *Jaffee* case—privilege—is related to confidentiality, and the two concepts are often discussed together. Confidentiality, which may be defined in ethical guidelines and laws, requires that helpers safeguard client communications and information and not reveal them to other people. Privilege is defined by law and protects confidential client communications from compelled disclosure (e.g., by sub-poena or court order) in legal proceedings (Glosoff, Herlihy, & Spence, 2000; Woodworth, 2000). Privilege belongs to clients and is asserted by helpers for their clients when helpers are asked or ordered to make disclosures.

Privilege is a complicated issue, but it is wise for helpers to become familiar with the privilege laws of their jurisdiction. Here are some basic points about privilege:

- Whether privilege is available depends on the jurisdiction and the particular help-ing profession to which the helper belongs (Reisner & Slobogin, 1990; Woodworth, 2000). For example, clients of professional counselors and clinical social workers have the protection of privilege in some states, but not in others (Woodworth, 2000). One study found that of the 45 states that license profes-sional counselors, 44 had statutes or rules of evidence that granted privilege to the counselor-client relationship (Glosoff et al., 2000). Where privilege does not apply, helpers still have to honor confidentiality and cannot reveal information whenever they feel like it, but they can be compelled to disclose information in legal proceedings.
- Even where privilege is available, not all information is necessarily protected. State laws determine the extent of the protection (B. A. Weiner & Wettstein, 1993; Woodworth, 2000).
- Some situations are typically excluded from grants of privilege. For example, in situations in which the law requires disclosure (e.g., child abuse), helpers must reveal information to authorities. Exceptions to privilege also may exist when clients raise the issue of mental condition in legal proceedings or when there is a dispute between a helper and a client (e.g., the client sues the helper) (Glosoff et al., 2000). In addition, court-ordered mental health examinations and civil com-mitment proceedings are typically excluded from grants of privilege (B. A. Weiner & Wettstein, 1993; Woodworth, 2000).
- Privilege depends on whether the legal matter is in state court or federal court. In state court, state privilege rules apply. In federal court, federal rules may control (Woodworth, 2000).
- Clients can waive privilege and consent to disclosure.

Issues With Ethical and Legal Implications

The following are 10 issues that have significant ethical and legal implications in the helping professions.

Assessment/Exploration. Helpers have an obligation to ensure that they are properly trained to use the assessment/exploration tools they employ, such as psy-chological tests. Ethical codes state that clients are entitled to know the nature and purpose of assessment/exploration. They are also entitled to see the results of this process (e.g., test results and diagnostic decisions) and to have the results explained in a way that is understandable to them (see, e.g., American Counseling Asso-ciation's [1995] *Code of Ethics and Standards of Practice,* Section E.3; American Psychological Association's [2002] *Ethical Principles of Psychologists and Code of*

Conduct, Sections 9.03 and 9.10). Helpers should ensure that their clients understand these explanations, and they should provide an opportunity for clients to ask questions. Poor training and practice in assessment/exploration can lead to ethical complaints and lawsuits.

Client Rights. As part of informed consent procedures (discussed in chapter 3), helpers address various client rights. For example, clients have the right to be the focus of the helping process, and they are entitled to their helpers' full attention and competent service. Indeed, helpers have an ethical obligation to put client needs first and to not use helping relationships to satisfy their own personal needs for attention, friendship, or financial gain. Clients also have choices regarding the interventions in which they are asked to participate. They have the right to have the interventions described and the right to agree or refuse to participate. In addition, clients have a right to privacy (see, e.g., American Counseling Association's [1995] *Code of Ethics and Standards of Practice,* Section B.1). This means that helpers must take steps to safeguard client identities and information.

Competence. Several topics fall under the heading of competence. Being competent involves having obtained proper training and education and often involves having obtained licensure or certification, where available (G. Corey et al., 2003). Helpers have an obligation to accurately represent their training, education, licensure, and certification in all situations, including advertising, informed consent statements, and verbal discussions with clients. It is unethical for helpers to misrepresent their credentials in any way. Helpers also need to know what titles they may use to describe themselves. States regulate the use of many titles. For example, "licensed psychologist" refers to a helper who has met specific licensure requirements.

Competence also involves being trained in the use of various helping skills, interventions, and strategies and being familiar with a wide range of resources to assist clients (e.g., support groups, community programs and services). Academic degree programs, internships, supervision, and continuing education enable helpers to develop and improve their techniques. Indeed, in many helping professions, helpers must obtain a certain number of continuing education credits within a specific time period to maintain their licensure (see G. Corey et al., 2003). These credits are earned through various professional development activities, such as attending lectures, conferences, and workshops. Failure to meet continuing education requirements may result in suspension or nonrenewal of licenses.

Another area of competence involves understanding and respecting cultural differences. For example, helpers must recognize the need to adapt their skills and techniques to accommodate the needs of culturally diverse clients. They must develop multicultural competence in the areas of awareness, knowledge, and skills (see chapter 2).

Competence also requires that helpers know their limitations. For example, a client may present a problem that the helper is not trained to handle. In such cases, helpers typically need to make referrals to more qualified professionals (G. Corey et al., 2003).

Finally, being a competent professional means consulting with supervisors or colleagues when questions or concerns arise. Consulting is not a sign of incompetence. It reflects a recognition that one does not know everything and sometimes needs guidance or another perspective. Consulting is often an important step when addressing ethical or legal concerns.

Confidentiality. Helpers have an ethical duty to not disclose client statements and information to other people. The purpose of confidentiality is to build trust and encourage clients to express themselves openly with the knowledge that what they say will not be shared with other people. As discussed in chapter 3, there are exceptions to confidentiality, defined by ethical guidelines and laws, that permit helpers to disclose client information in certain circumstances, such as when consulting with supervisors. Clients can also waive confidentiality and give helpers permission to release information. Ethical guidelines and laws also identify several situations in which confidentiality *must* be breached, with or without client permission. These typically include, for example, situations in which (1) a client reports the abuse or neglect of a child or a vulnerable adult, (2) a client seriously threatens to harm him- or herself, and (3) a client seriously threatens to harm another person. The requirement that helpers breach confidentiality when clients make serious threats to harm other people is commonly referred to as the "duty to warn and protect" (see the *Tarasoff* case described earlier) (G. Corey et al., 2003; Welfel, 2002). Helpers have a duty to notify the potential victims of the clients' threats and assist them in getting protection. Law enforcement officers are also typically notified (Welfel, 2002). Helpers also have a duty to protect suicidal clients (e.g., by notifying law enforcement officers).

When helpers breach confidentiality, either intentionally or unintentionally, or fail to inform clients about the exceptions to confidentiality, ethical complaints and lawsuits may be filed against them and state licensing boards may consider disciplinary action (Pope & Vasquez, 2001). Helpers must then be prepared to defend their actions (e.g., by showing that their disclosure of client information falls within one of the exceptions to confidentiality).

An ethical and legal dilemma that helpers often face regarding confidentiality is whether something must be reported (e.g., to law enforcement officers or potential victims). The issue is not always clear. How does a helper determine, for example, whether a threat of harm is serious? Is there a threat of imminent harm? These are judgment calls that are often made with the assistance of supervisors and colleagues.

Cultural Diversity. As has been discussed throughout this book, helpers need to recognize and respect their clients' cultural characteristics. Most ethical codes direct helpers to respect cultural diversity (e.g., ACA [1995] *Code of Ethics and Standards of Practice,* Section A.2; APA [2002] *Ethical Principles of Psychologists and Code of Conduct,* Principle E and Section 2.01(b); NASW [1999] *Code of Ethics,* Section 1.05). Indeed, to provide competent service and put client needs first, helpers need to consider cultural variables. Helpers can get into ethical trouble if they assist all clients in the same way and fail to recognize cultural differences. Although changes have been made to ethical codes to make them more sensitive to cultural variables and differences, the codes have still been criticized for not being sensitive enough to these factors. For example, Pedersen (1997) asserted that the ethical guidelines of the ACA possess the weaknesses of (1) not identifying their underlying philosophical principles, (2) assuming a dominant culture perspective, and (3) minimizing or trivializing the role of culture in ethical decision making.

Multiple Relationships. Multiple relationships (sometimes called dual relationships) occur when a helper assumes two or more roles with a client or has connections with a client that are in addition to the helping relationship (G. Corey et al., 2003; Kitchener & Anderson, 2000; Welfel, 2002). These roles and connections may be concurrent with the helping relationship or consecutive with it—that is, before, during, or after (Sonne, 1994; Welfel, 2002). Some examples of multiple relationships include the following (G. Corey et al., 2003; Welfel, 2002):

- Having a sexual relationship with a client
- Having a personal relationship (e.g., friendship) with a client
- Serving as a teacher or supervisor to a client
- Entering into a business venture with a client
- Providing helping services to a friend, family member, or employee
- Bartering for helping services
- Attending social events with a client

Multiple relationships can impair helper objectivity, interfere with therapeutic progress, intensify power differences between the helper and the client, lead to exploitation, and affect the client's emotional connection to the helper (Welfel, 2002). For these reasons, multiple relationships are often risky and can lead to ethical and legal problems. However, multiple relationships are not always prohibited or unethical. The type of relationship, cultural variables, and the circumstances must be considered. For example, Schank and Skovholt (1997) noted that in small, rural communities, where social and business relationships often overlap, certain types of dual relationships may be unavoidable.

One problem with multiple relationships is that they can present conflicts of interest for helpers (Pope & Vasquez, 2001). That is, in one relationship with a client, a helper may choose or be required to pursue a course of action that could compromise another relationship the helper has with the client. For example, if a helper is in business with a client and reports the client to authorities for illegal insider trading, such an action would clearly make it difficult for the helper and the client to function effectively in the helping relationship.

In the helping professions, the issue of sexual relationships with clients has been a major topic of discussion. Because of the power difference between helpers and clients, the intimate nature of sexual contact, and the potential for exploitation, sexual relations with *current* clients are always inappropriate and unethical. Some disagreement and controversy exists about the appropriateness of sexual relations with *former* clients. The NASW (1999) ethical code states that social workers should not have sexual contact with former clients (Section 1.09(c)). The ACA (1995) and APA (2002) ethical guidelines state that counselors and psychologists do not have sexual contact with former clients within a minimum of 2 years after the end of the helping relationship (ACA Section A.7.b; APA Section 10.08(a)). The APA guidelines state that psychologists do not engage in sexual contact with former clients even after the 2-year time period "except in the most unusual circumstances" (Section 10.08(b)). Psychologists who engage in sexual contact after the 2-year period must be prepared to demonstrate that there has been no exploitation of the former client (Section 10.08(b)). Many helpers believe that sexual relationships with former clients are never appropriate because the power imbalance and the potential for exploitation may still exist.

In several states, sexual contact with a current client is a criminal offense (Haspel, Jorgenson, Wincze, & Parsons, 1997). Sexual contact may also expose the helper to a civil lawsuit brought by the client (Haspel et al., 1997; Seto, 1995; Smith, 1994).

Based on Herlihy and Corey's (1997) guidelines, here are some suggestions for dealing with multiple relationships:

- Set appropriate boundaries with clients.
- Review ethical guidelines, laws, and workplace policies.
- Determine whether the multiple relationships are avoidable or unavoidable.
- Carefully evaluate motives, risks, and benefits related to entering into multiple relationships.
- Document discussions, actions, and situations.
- Consult with supervisors or colleagues.
- Consider working under supervision.
- Consider providing referrals.

Physical Contact. The issue of whether and how helpers may touch clients has significant ethical and legal implications. Ethical and legal concerns include exploitation, sexual overtones, and satisfaction of helper needs rather than client needs. The touch of another person can be a powerful gesture—it connects one human being to another. However, just as a touch can be comforting, it can also be offensive and inappropriate. Touch in the form of a handshake or a pat on the shoulder usually does not lead to ethical or legal problems, but what about a hug or an arm around the shoulder? Factors such as age, gender, cultural customs, the nature of client problems, and the quality of the helping relationship guide helpers in deciding whether to touch. For example, a hug between a female helper and a female client may be appropriate. In contrast, a hug (or many other kinds of touch) between a male helper and a female client may feel uncomfortable to the client because it may blur boundaries, feel disempowering, or be perceived as a sexual advance (Alyn, 1988). When considering whether to touch clients, helpers should be clear about their motives and their clients' needs (Pope & Vasquez, 2001; Welfel, 2002).

Certain types of touch are always inappropriate. These include sexual contact and hitting clients. These forms of touch harm clients and create mistrust of helpers.

Record Keeping. Helpers have an ethical obligation to keep complete, accurate records (Bernstein & Hartsell, 2000). Records include, for example, session notes, intake reports, signed informed consent statements, correspondence, goal statements, treatment plans, and termination reports (see Piazza & Baruth, 1990). Keeping good records allows helpers to identify treatment strategies and review client issues prior to sessions. Records are also important when clients see other helping professionals in the future, as they provide valuable information for those professionals to use. In addition, records are essential when ethical complaints and legal actions are filed. Careful, accurate documentation of client cases increases the chance that helpers will be able to mount an effective defense (Bernstein & Hartsell, 2000). Helpers can get into ethical trouble when records are inaccurate, altered, filled with irrelevant information, insufficiently detailed, or deleted (Bernstein & Hartsell, 2000). Indeed, it is hard to defend against allegations of improper conduct when documentation supporting the helper's version of what happened is lacking or inaccurate.

Most helping settings have policies and guidelines concerning record keeping, including requirements regarding form, content, and level of detail. Professional organizations, such as the American Psychological Association (1993), also provide guidelines. As a general guideline, records should be sufficiently detailed so that someone who reviews them (e.g., a supervisor, another helper, a judge) will know what transpired in helping (Bernstein & Hartsell, 2000). Records should not be overly detailed, but they also should not be too brief or cursory. As noted earlier, records may be a significant piece of evidence if ethical complaints or lawsuits occur, so they should be prepared as if they may someday be reviewed in these contexts.

Laws related to client access to records vary from state to state, but the trend is toward increasing client access (Soisson, VandeCreek, & Knapp, 1987). It is wise for helpers to assume that clients will eventually review or request copies of their records; thus, helpers should be mindful of the content they include and the language they use when preparing the records (Soisson et al., 1987).

Helpers also need to exercise care when storing and disposing of client records. They have an ethical obligation to keep records in a secure manner that preserves confidentiality and prevents viewing by people not authorized to see them—for example, using locked file cabinets and password-protected computers (American Psychological Association, 1993; Bernstein & Hartsell, 2000). When records are discarded, they should be disposed of in such a way that eliminates the possibility of recovering the information (e.g., shredding, incinerating).

Finally, helpers need to attend to the issue of how long to keep records. Laws and regulations on this point vary from state to state. Helping settings typically have policies in this regard that are consistent with laws and regulations. American Psychological Association (1993) guidelines suggest that when laws or regulations do not address the issue, complete records for adult clients should be kept for at least 3 years after the last contact with the client. Records, or a summary of the records, should be kept for an additional 12 years before disposal (American Psychological Association, 1993).

Self-Care. To assist clients effectively, helpers need to take care of themselves (see Skovholt, 2001). Self-care has ethical and legal implications because when helpers feel tired and burned out (exhausted, lacking interest in work), they can become irritable and insensitive, make mistakes, exercise poor judgment, and appear uninvolved, thus hurting their clients more than helping them. Helpers take care of themselves and combat burnout in many ways, including maintaining a manageable workload, consulting with colleagues, taking vacations, and spending time with friends and family. Self-care is discussed in more detail in chapter 15.

Values. Helping is not a value-free process. Both helpers and clients have values, and their values are not always the same. Value differences or value conflicts do not automatically mean that helpers must terminate helping and refer clients to other helpers (M. S. Corey & Corey, 2003). Indeed, it is unlikely that helpers and clients will share the same values on everything. However, referrals may be appropriate when helpers' values compromise their objectivity and openness (M. S. Corey & Corey, 2003). Often, value differences in helping become most significant and potentially problematic when they relate to sensitive and emotionally charged topics, such as religion, reproductive rights, and sexual orientation (see M. S. Corey & Corey, 2003). The risk is that helpers may force their values on clients. When this appears to be the case, making referrals or consulting with supervisors or colleagues is an appropriate step to take.

As these 10 issues show, helper conduct can have implications with regard to both ethical guidelines and laws. Thus, it is important for helpers to understand their ethical and legal obligations. Those who are uninformed and careless may someday find themselves before an ethics committee, a licensing board, *and* a judge.

Sometimes, ethical guidelines and laws conflict, creating a dilemma for helpers. How do they comply with competing obligations? Helpers should try to comply with both obligations to the extent possible. In the long run, helpers typically should make sure that they are in compliance with the law.

In any case, helpers ultimately make decisions based on their understanding of ethical guidelines and laws, consultation with supervisors and colleagues, and their personal values. Once they have made decisions, they have to be prepared to deal with any ethical or legal consequences that may result.

Ethical Complaints and Legal Proceedings

Over the past few decades, the helping professions have seen an increase in the number of ethical complaints and lawsuits filed against helpers (Bernstein & Hartsell, 2000; Smith, 1994). Among the various possible reasons for this increase, two significant reasons include (1) the litigious environment in the United States, with clients possessing more knowledge of their rights and more willingness to seek redress for perceived wrongs; and (2) the increase in the number of helping professionals and clients over the past few decades. In the next two sections, we examine ways in which ethical complaints are handled and ways in which helpers may become involved in legal proceedings.

Ethical Complaints

Bernstein and Hartsell (2000) reported that in any given year, fewer than 2% of all mental health professionals are the subjects of ethical complaints filed with licensing boards. They indicated that the unethical acts helpers commit include sexual exploitation, dual (multiple) relationships, boundary violations, breach of confidentiality and refusal to provide records, fraudulent billing, financial exploitation of clients, provision of services while impaired, violations of reporting statutes (e.g., failing to report child abuse), and miscellaneous acts (e.g., falsifying records, felony convictions).

Complaints against helpers may be filed with their employers, professional associations, or boards that license helpers within their jurisdiction. Anyone can initiate a complaint, including clients, members of the public, other helpers, and licensing boards (Bernstein & Hartsell, 2000).

Procedures for initiating and handling ethical complaints vary from helping profession to helping profession and state to state. In the following paragraphs, we do not address these procedures in detail but rather explain some general processes.

Complaints May Be Initiated and Handled Internally or Informally. Especially if rather minor offenses are at issue, complaints may be handled informally through supervisors, concerned colleagues, or employers of the helpers in question (Welfel, 2002). This step tends to be quicker than formal complaints to professional associations or licensing boards, and it gives offending helpers the chance to alter their behavior and correct their mistakes while retaining professional dignity (Welfel, 2002).

Complaints May Be Initiated and Handled Through Professional Associations. National and state professional associations, such as the American Counseling Association and the American Psychological Association, have ethics committees that hear complaints filed against members. Welfel (2002) summarized ACA and APA procedures regarding complaints, which are basically as follows: Once a complaint is filed, the ethics committee reviews it to assess its validity and determine whether the matter warrants further investigation and attention. If it does, the helper is notified and has a chance to respond to the complaint. Helpers have an ethical duty to cooperate with ethics committee investigations and proceedings. A hearing may be held. The ethics committee considers the matter and makes a determination as to whether an ethics violation occurred. If the committee determines that a violation occurred, it can impose sanctions, such as a reprimand or stripping the helper of membership in the association. The helper has the right to appeal the decision.

Complaints May Be Initiated and Handled Through State Licensing Boards. State mental health licensing boards are state agencies that regulate particular disciplines through licensure (Bernstein & Hartsell, 2000). Bernstein and Hartsell (2000) summarized the basic complaint procedure through state boards as follows: Filed complaints are reviewed by the board to determine whether a board rule, licensing act, or ethics code was violated. If it appears that a violation occurred, the helper is notified and has a chance to respond to the allegations. Based on this response, further investigation may be conducted if any doubt remains as to the existence of a violation. However, if, after the helper's response to the board, it still appears that a violation occurred, adjudication is typically the next step. Informal adjudication usually occurs with less serious violations and may result in, for example, a reprimand or additional supervision for the helper. Formal adjudication typically involves seeking revocation of the helper's license through an administrative hearing.

Legal Proceedings

In addition to ethical complaints brought in the ways just described, legal proceedings—criminal prosecution or civil actions—may be brought against helpers.

Helpers may become involved in the legal system in many ways. For example, they may assist with mediation and child custody evaluations. They may be called to testify in court cases or to serve as expert witnesses. Also, helpers may be prosecuted for alleged violations of criminal laws, and they may be sued by clients. It is these two legal proceedings that we focus on below.

As with ethical complaints, the percentage of helpers who have legal proceedings brought against them appears to be rather small—probably less than 4% (see, e.g., Otto & Schmidt, 1991; Smith, 1994). One study on malpractice found that between 1969 and 1990, 634 liability claims were filed against social workers who carried malpractice insurance through the National Association of Social Workers Insurance Trust (Reamer, 1995). This is a rather small number of claims considering the time span and the fact that the NASW Insurance Trust covers tens of thousands of social workers (Reamer, 1995).

Conduct that can result in helpers being involved in legal proceedings includes, but is not limited to, sexual relationships with clients, other types of multiple relationships, failure to obtain informed consent, breach of confidentiality, practicing outside one's area of training or beyond the level of one's competence, making improper diagnoses, abandoning clients, failure to warn and protect third parties, failure to report child abuse, failure to diagnose a client's suicidal condition, making defamatory statements, failure to supervise people under helpers' control (e.g., assistants, interns), wrongful commitment to a hospital or institution, and failure to keep adequate records (G. Corey et al., 2003; Pope & Vasquez, 2001; Smith, 1994).

We now briefly examine two types of legal proceedings in which helpers may become involved as defendants: criminal and civil proceedings.

Criminal Proceedings. A criminal proceeding against a helper occurs when a helper is charged with violating a criminal law. The helper is prosecuted by the government. Examples of helper conduct that may result in criminal charges include being an accessory to a crime, failing to report suspected child abuse, contributing to the delinquency of a minor, engaging in sexual misconduct, and engaging in fraudulent billing practices (Hopkins & Anderson, 1990, p. 49; Pope & Vasquez, 2001). If a helper is found guilty in a criminal proceeding, the punishment may include fines, restitution to victims, imprisonment, counseling, community service, and/or probation.

Civil Proceedings. Helpers may be sued for malpractice. Most malpractice suits are based on a negligence theory of liability, though sometimes the suits are based on other theories, such as intentional infliction of emotional distress or breach of contract (Smith, 1991, 1994). There are four elements to a malpractice suit based on negligence (Reisner & Slobogin, 1990; Smith, 1994):

1. *Duty.* The plaintiff (i.e., the person suing, such as a client) must show that the helper (defendant) owed a duty to the plaintiff. Showing the existence of a helping relationship is typically part of establishing a duty. A helper has a duty to render helping services with the same degree of skill as other competent professionals in the field. This is called the "standard of care." Ethical codes may be used to establish the standard of care (Bernstein & Hartsell, 2000).

2. *Breach of Duty.* The plaintiff must show that the helper failed to meet the standard of care.
3. *Injury.* The plaintiff must show that he or she has been harmed or injured. The harm or injury does not necessarily have to be physical in nature.
4. *Causation.* The plaintiff must show that the helper's conduct (breach of duty) was the cause of the harm or injury.

Plaintiffs have the burden of proving their claims by demonstrating all four of these elements. The private nature of helping, which often produces little evidence and few witnesses, can make that difficult. Indeed, plaintiffs succeed in only a small proportion of cases (Smith, 1994). If they do succeed and helpers are found liable, monetary damages may be awarded.

With regard to malpractice litigation initiated by clients against helpers, Buffone (1991) noted that "a claim usually represents the combination of patient injury and patient anger and dissatisfaction" (p. 30). He discussed several client characteristics that tend to increase the risk of malpractice litigation. Specifically, the risk of litigation may be greater with clients who

- express dissatisfaction with the helping services received;
- pay fees late or not at all;
- have a history of litigation against professionals;
- exhibit exaggerated concerns over fees;
- are critical of helpers who have assisted them previously;
- possess unrealistic expectations about treatment;
- are angry;
- are harmful to themselves or others;
- deny or transfer responsibility for care (e.g., overly dependent on helpers);
- do not follow helper recommendations or treatments.

Litigious clients may not possess every one of these characteristics. However, one or more of the characteristics usually are present in such clients (Buffone, 1991).

Buffone (1991) also described some litigation risk factors related to helpers and helping settings. According to Buffone, the following factors can increase the chance of clients initiating litigation:

- Helpers practicing beyond their level of competence
- Helpers providing a guarantee of successful treatment (or making other claims) and failing to deliver
- Helpers violating client rights
- Helpers engaging in dual (multiple) relationships
- Poor communication
- Poor office safety (e.g., physical dangers)
- Inadequate follow-up procedures
- Helpers providing impersonal treatment

Why Ethical Complaints and Legal Proceedings Often Are *Not* Initiated

So far, we have focused on reasons why helpers may be subjected to ethical complaints and legal proceedings. Most, if not all, helpers have probably committed at least one unethical, illegal, negligent, or improper act in their careers, even if only very minor. However, for all such acts that occur, only a small proportion result in ethical complaints or legal proceedings (Pope & Vasquez, 2001; Welfel, 2002). In other words, in most cases in which unethical, illegal, negligent, or improper acts have occurred, ethical complaints and legal proceedings are not initiated. The following are some possible explanations.

Lack of Awareness. Clients, and in some cases helpers, their supervisors, and their employers, may not realize that unethical, illegal, negligent, or improper acts occurred. Clients may not know what is proper or improper, and sometimes helpers do not know that their conduct violates an ethical guideline or law. Even if clients believe that something improper has occurred, they may not know their rights and options, including how to take action and where to file complaints.

Little or No Harm Done to Clients. If unethical, illegal, negligent, or improper acts are minor and relatively harmless, clients may choose not to report the acts or file lawsuits.

Lack of Willingness to Commit Time and Resources. Clients may not want to commit to the process of filing complaints and lawsuits. They may not want to take time out of their schedules to deal with the matter (e.g., filling out paperwork). Lawsuits, in particular, can be time-consuming.

Negative Views of People in Helping. Due to negative stereotypes and stigmas often attached to people who seek professional help for personal problems, clients may see themselves, or be seen by others, as less credible than people not in helping (Otto & Schmidt, 1991). Thus, they may feel that actions they take against helpers will fail.

Reluctance to Release Personal Information. Clients may be reluctant to share their personal problems and concerns with people outside the helping relationship. Thus, they may be disinclined to discuss their circumstances with ethics committees, licensing boards, law enforcement officers, or attorneys. Also, in court cases, clients will likely be questioned about the nature of their problems. In general, trials are public, so clients' problems may be exposed for all to see (Smith, 1994). To avoid spreading personal information and suffering public humiliation, many clients choose to forgo lawsuits.

The Adversarial Nature of the Legal Process. Clients may feel intimidated by the legal system to the point that the stress and discomfort involved in filing and pursuing lawsuits would be too great.

The Difficulty of Proving Allegations. Showing harm, especially emotional harm, caused by helpers is challenging (Smith, 1994). Moreover, when it comes to damages, "the law has traditionally been reluctant to recognize emotional or mental injuries, except when they relate to physical harm" (Smith, 1994, p. 241). Also, because of the difficulty of producing evidence and witnesses in such a private activity as helping, clients may find it hard to prove their claims. Thus, they may refrain from filing lawsuits, having concluded that they may not prevail.

Perceptions That Filing Ethical Complaints or Lawsuits Will Accomplish Nothing. Clients may feel that ethical complaints or lawsuits will not afford them a satisfactory remedy. For example, some clients are not interested in filing ethical complaints because they do not see how they would benefit (e.g., financially) from the process. Also, some clients feel that the "system" protects helpers, so filing ethical complaints or lawsuits would be a waste of time.

Corrective Steps Taken by Helpers. When unethical, illegal, negligent, or improper acts have occurred, helpers might take corrective steps to attempt to remedy the problem or minimize consequences (see Welfel, 2002). Depending on the circumstances, such steps could include offering an apology to the client, being more diligent about obtaining informed consent, being more attentive to client needs and concerns, and making appropriate referrals. Such steps may lessen the likelihood that ethical complaints or legal proceedings will be initiated.

The Impact of Ethical Complaints and Legal Proceedings on Clients and Helpers

An ethical complaint or a lawsuit obviously represents a breakdown of the helping relationship. Trust has been destroyed, and the helper and the client are now adversaries—a relationship that is entirely contrary to the principles of helping, which envision helpers and clients functioning as allies. Both parties suffer in some manner when the helping process ends this way. Clients may have great difficulty ever trusting helpers again and, indeed, may come to resent them. They may, therefore, choose not to seek further help for the problems with which they struggle. Also, their personal issues may have been revealed to the public (Smith, 1994), causing anger, shame, and embarrassment. For helpers, ethical complaints and legal proceedings can challenge their sense of competence, create defensiveness, anger, and emotional stress, cause fear and apprehension regarding the use of certain techniques, damage their reputations, result in professional discipline, court judgments, and/or convictions, and lead to increased malpractice insurance premiums (see Smith, 1994).

While ethical complaints and legal proceedings can hurt the parties involved, they can also have beneficial consequences. For example, injured clients who prevail in malpractice suits often receive compensation, and helpers and helping professions become more aware of serious issues that demand their attention and action. The helping process is not intended to end in front of an ethics committee or a licensing board or in a courtroom, but sometimes this result promotes justice and motivates necessary change.

Managing Risks

Helpers cannot eliminate the possibility that ethical complaints or legal proceedings will be initiated against them, but they can take several prudent steps to manage risks and minimize the chances that such actions will occur. The following list is derived from Buffone (1991), G. Corey et al. (2003), Woodworth (2000), and our own observations:

- Know ethical guidelines, laws, and workplace policies, and avoid violations.
- Have in place a decision-making plan for how to handle ethical and legal issues.
- Obtain informed consent (e.g., make sure clients understand policies and the helping process).
- Promote realistic expectations about helping, and do not make promises that cannot be kept.
- Identify and screen clients at high risk for filing ethical complaints and lawsuits.
- Strive to provide personalized care and build positive relationships with clients.
- Treat clients with respect, observe their rights, and recognize cultural characteristics.
- Maintain confidentiality, but make sure that clients understand the exceptions.
- Fulfill "duty to warn and protect" obligations as well as obligations to report certain information to authorities (e.g., child abuse).
- Practice within one's education, training, and level of competence.
- Increase self-awareness and be able to articulate one's approach to helping.
- Carefully prepare treatment plans for clients.
- Keep good, accurate records and carefully document treatment.
- Consult with supervisors and colleagues.
- Know when to refer clients to other professionals.
- Do not abandon clients.
- Do not ignore client dissatisfaction or complaints.
- Practice addressing and resolving ethical and legal issues (e.g., through role plays with colleagues).
- Engage in continuing education activities (e.g., attend seminars and workshops, read journal articles).
- Engage in self-care activities.
- Carry malpractice insurance.
- Be prepared to contact an attorney.

A Decision-Making Process for Ethical and Legal Issues

Helpers need to develop a personal decision-making method that will enable them to make good, justifiable decisions when they face situations that must be handled in careful compliance with ethical guidelines and laws. Helpers may not know with 100% certainty whether the decisions they make are correct, but a sound, well-reasoned, well-documented course of action can reduce the stress of making important decisions and maximize the chances of a favorable outcome.

All helpers encounter ethical and legal issues, and thus all helpers need to apply decision-making processes at some point. A suggested approach is presented here. It is based in part on decision-making models proposed by G. Corey et al. (2003) and Kottler and Brown (2000).

1. *Determine That an Ethical and/or Legal Issue Exists.* Reading ethical guidelines and laws and consulting with clients, supervisors, and colleagues can assist helpers in identifying potential problems and issues.

2. *Frame the Issue.* What is the nature of the issue? Is it ethical or legal or both? What are the potential risks involved? What are the rights and responsibilities of the client and the helper? How do cultural variables factor into the situation?

3. *Review Ethical Guidelines, Laws, Policies of the Work Setting, and Helping Literature.* Helpers need to understand which guidelines, laws, or policies apply. Reading relevant journal articles can offer additional information and possible ways to resolve the issue.

4. *Consult With Supervisors, Colleagues, and/or Other Professionals.* It is wise for helpers to talk to supervisors and colleagues about the situation to receive guidance and make sure that they have considered all important issues and perspectives. Depending on the circumstances, helpers may also choose to consult with other professionals, such as attorneys.

5. *Consider Personal Values.* Decision-making on ethical and legal issues is rarely a clear-cut process. Ethical guidelines, laws, and policies of the work setting do not always give precise, definitive answers. So, helpers also consider their own sense of what is right. They consider their personal values, instincts, intuitions, and feelings.

6. *Identify and Consider Various Options for Resolution.* Helpers identify the choices they have for resolving the situation. They weigh the risks, costs, and benefits of different options.

7. *Make a Decision and Act on It.* At some point, helpers must decide what to do and then take action. This should be done after going through the preceding steps.

8. *Accurately and Fully Document the Issue, Including All Steps and Actions Taken.* This step is critical. Documentation is essential if ethical complaints or legal proceedings are subsequently initiated. Documentation may be the most important and compelling piece of evidence in support of the helper's actions.

9. *Process the Experience With Supervisors or Colleagues.* Helpers can use this ethical and legal decision-making experience to debrief and reflect on what they have learned. Talking with supervisors or colleagues may aid helpers in solidifying their decision-making processes, identifying difficulties in their decision making, and considering other ways of handling ethical and legal issues in the future.

Summary and Concluding Remarks

This chapter focused on ethical and legal issues in helping. Ethical guidelines, ethical codes, and laws were discussed, as were several issues that have ethical and legal implications. Ethical complaints and lawsuits involving helpers have increased in number over the past few decades. As a result, helpers now possess a greater awareness of the threat of ethical complaints and legal proceedings and are paying more attention to risk management. Helpers are encouraged to develop a personal decision-making process so that they will be prepared to make decisions on ethical and legal issues. Decision making on ethical and legal issues is a developmental, flexible, career-long process.

We end this chapter with the following point. G. Corey et al. (2003) contrasted lower-level ethical functioning (that is, "mandatory ethics," or basic compliance with minimal ethical standards) with higher-level ethical functioning (that is, "aspirational ethics," or living up to the spirit of ethical guidelines and reflecting on the effects of interventions with clients). Helpers can basically comply with ethical guidelines and laws and probably avoid criminal prosecution, civil liability, and sanctions imposed by professional associations and licensing boards. However, this does not necessarily make them exceptional helpers. Virtuous, high-quality, effective helping cannot be imposed by ethical guidelines and laws. Helpers must find within themselves the motivation to practice in this way (see, e.g., Cohen & Cohen, 1999).

Questions for Thought

1. If you were a helper, which of the 10 issues with ethical and legal implications, discussed in this chapter, would be the most challenging for you to manage? Why?

2. If you were a helper and one of your clients expressed dissatisfaction and an intention to pursue an ethical complaint or legal action against you, what would you do?

3. We listed several steps that helpers can take to manage risks and minimize the chances that ethical complaints or legal proceedings will be initiated against them. What additional steps might helpers take?

CHAPTER 15

The Helper's Professional Journey

CHAPTER OVERVIEW

This chapter focuses on the helper's professional journey. What is it like to be a helper? How do helpers develop and evolve as professionals? What are the challenges and rewards of helping? These are some of the questions addressed in this chapter. Specifically, the chapter discusses helper development, challenges in helping, motives for and rewards of being a helper, and helper self-care. The chapter concludes with several suggestions for those who plan to pursue further studies and work in the helping professions.

The journey, not the arrival, matters; the voyage, not the landing.

—Paul Theroux
(1979, p. 5)

The Helper's Professional Journey

For many helpers, their adventures begin when they are 20-something graduate students in helper training programs. They may have had some experience in helping settings in the past—perhaps as camp counselors, youth leaders, or bachelor's degree–level intake workers. But their formal, in-depth training in helping begins in graduate school. After some years of course work, practicum experiences, and internships, they embark on their careers as helpers, putting their knowledge, skills, and training to work. This professional journey may continue for decades.

Of course, not all helpers follow this career pattern. Some decide to pursue a career in helping as a mid-life career change. Others may decide that a career in helping is not for them, leave the profession, and pursue other work. The point, however, is that for most helpers, being a helper is a long-term commitment that spans many years. In that time, helpers grow as professionals and as people. They confront many challenges and experience many rewards.

Helper Development

Helper development is a career-long activity that has many facets, including pursuing education and training, identifying professional interests, engaging in personal reflection, developing self-awareness, gaining work experience, and maintaining competence through continuing education activities, such as attending workshops and reviewing research. Development can be conceptualized as a process, with helpers progressing through several stages as they learn, grow, and gain experience. Numerous stage models have been proposed. The following discussion describes the model constructed by Skovholt and Rønnestad (1995).

Stages in Helper Development

Using a qualitative research methodology to identify stages in helper development, Skovholt and Rønnestad (1995) interviewed 100 helpers (50 males and 50 females) who ranged in education and experience from first-year graduate students to helpers who were 40 years beyond graduate school. Eight stages in development were identified. They reflect the progression of professional development throughout the helper's career—a lifespan approach that extends from before helpers begin formal training to the end of their careers. How rapidly helpers progress through these stages depends on a number of variables, such as age, maturity, and openness to learning.

Conventional Stage. According to Skovholt and Rønnestad (1995), "the key here is being untrained in [helping] yet engaged in the process of trying to help another person feel better, make decisions, understand self or improve relationships" (p. 17). "Helpers" at this stage often take on the role of a sympathetic friend. They are curious about human behavior and very interested in people. When helping others, they rely on common sense, their own experiences, and what they know. They tend to give advice. They are often inclined to assist in resolving problems by using a strongly directive style that involves self-disclosure and suggestions (e.g., "This is what I did" or "Try harder next time"). They are not typically concerned with measuring the success of their efforts, but they may believe that they are effective when they feel the emotional closeness of friendship.

Transition to Professional Training Stage. This stage begins with the decision to pursue formal training as a helper and continues through the first year of training. People possess various motives for pursuing helper training, such as a desire to help other people, a need to further develop and refine skills for helping positions that they are already in, a desire to become licensed professionals, and a desire to work through their own personal problems. Individuals at this stage can be quite different from one another if they vary significantly on such variables as age and previous professional work experience. The stage description that follows pertains most to the younger, less experienced student.

At this stage, individuals enter helping programs and begin to assimilate massive amounts of information through classes and practicum experiences. This assimilation of information is a challenging task that can be both exciting and scary at the same time. Individuals experience enthusiasm as well as insecurity as they learn new concepts. They worry about how well they will be able to apply what they learn. They also psychologize a lot, striving to understand themselves and other people.

Individuals at this stage are heavily influenced by theories, professors, supervisors, the social/cultural environment, other students, and their own personal lives as they seek support and guidance. They begin to search for models, frameworks, or approaches to make sense of all the information they are learning. This stage can be confusing as students feel caught between the "sympathetic friend" role of the conventional stage and the "professional helper" role about which they are just beginning to learn. They feel highly invested in their first clients—they want to be effective. They tend to define success by visible client improvement, client comments, supervisor feedback, and comparisons to fellow students.

Imitation of Experts Stage. This stage occurs in the second or third year of graduate school. Some people in this stage may have just completed a master's degree and are newly employed. Helpers at this point have a more sophisticated view of human behavior and begin to recognize helping as a complex and difficult process that involves more than providing sympathy or emotional support. The central task associated with this stage is to maintain an openness to information and theory while also engaging in the "closing off" process of selecting theories and techniques to use. Individuals at this stage want to become competent like experts in the field. However, that process will take years. So, to achieve more immediate success in helping, they seek out experts to model. Modeling provides a sense of structure and security; it is a way to reduce complexity and confusion.

Introspection and self-understanding are important in this stage. Helpers may feel uncertain about their role: Who are they? If not a friend, then what? What skills should they use? Helpers begin to search for and develop conceptual maps to answer such questions as: What is normal and abnormal human development? What causes normal and abnormal human development? What reduces problematic behavior, emotions, and thinking? As they evaluate their skills and progress, helpers may experience some anger toward faculty or supervisors because they do not feel adequately prepared to be helpers. Helpers in this stage define success largely by feedback from clients and supervisors, but gradually they become less dependent on constant positive feedback to maintain their sense of professional competence.

Conditional Autonomy Stage. For many individuals, this stage begins with (or during) a supervised internship at the end of the training program. The central task of people in this stage is to function at a professional level. Helpers use the skill level of experienced practitioners as their criterion for judging their own competence. They also compare themselves to other interns and expect to function at a higher professional level than practicum students. They typically feel variable confidence at this stage. At times, they feel capable as a result of becoming increasingly skilled, but at other times, they feel less competent as they struggle to master tasks and responsibilities and satisfy the demands of their supervisors and their work settings. They have a strong need for validation and feedback from supervisors.

Interns tend to feel a lot of pressure to do their jobs correctly, and their approach to helping is often serious, thorough, conforming, and conservative. Their focus on high professional functioning can create within them the belief that they should be able to help most people. They may feel that they have to take on every client, and they may find it difficult to refer clients or end helping at the appropriate time. They often feel excessively responsible for client progress. At this stage, interns refine the modeling they began in the previous stage and begin to shape their own conceptual systems, extending beyond their models. They also increasingly focus on how their personalities influence their work. Supervisor evaluations are an important measure of success.

Exploration Stage. At this stage, which tends to last from 2 to 5 years, individuals have graduated from their training programs and are now working as helpers. To develop as professionals, they begin to explore beyond the imitation of models. They have found that the complexity of helping requires new learning, so they develop new concepts and techniques while shedding some of the less helpful aspects of what they have learned. Theoretical concepts blend with professional experience to inform their perspectives on helping. They feel an increased sense of freedom, but many individuals also struggle with feelings of inadequacy. Helpers at this stage desire to test the quality of their training and want to be able to defend the programs in which they were trained. Yet, they also often feel some disillusionment, realizing that their training was not as adequate as they had hoped. They tend to feel confident as their competence increases, but they also feel anxiety about not being able to adequately address the complexity of their work.

Supervisors tend to be a less prominent influence than in the previous stage, as there is less of an evaluative atmosphere than existed in the training program. Peers and colleagues tend to be important sources of influence. Helpers also have a more mature perspective on responsibility for their clients. They realize that they are not totally responsible for client success or failure. They are better able to distinguish between their professional responsibilities as helpers and the personal responsibility that clients have for their own lives. They also begin to understand how their personalities impact the helping process. They shed some of the seriousness of the previous stage and begin to develop a more natural and relaxed style. Their essential learning process is by reflection, as they search for theory and techniques and ponder meaning in their work. They measure their effectiveness by client improvement but also by other criteria, including reflection and discussions with colleagues.

Integration Stage. This stage typically occurs a few years into professional practice and may last for 2 to 5 years. The main task associated with this stage is to develop a "professional authenticity," a genuine working style. Professional skills and personality combine to accomplish this, as more "inauthentic" elements are shed. Helpers tend to feel more satisfaction at this stage than in previous stages as they achieve experience, credentials, and financial rewards. They develop helping styles that are less rigid and more natural, flexible, and creative. Their approach to helping tends to be more integrative or eclectic as they gain experience, work with a variety of clients, and try out techniques. They are more tolerant of the ambiguities of helping—the frequent lack of clear answers—and they have developed excellent relationship skills.

Helpers at this stage also realize that while they influence their clients, they are not as powerful or as responsible for client change as they had previously thought— a humbling, yet liberating realization. They have a more realistic, less grandiose notion about their ability to change people. They are still influenced by supervisors and colleagues; however, some may actually be supervisors themselves at this point and thus have a different perspective on supervision. They measure their effectiveness by listening to client feedback, but they also rely on their own assessments of client problems and improvement.

Individuation Stage. This stage tends to occur several years after graduate school and may continue for 10 to 30 years. Helpers at this stage continue to develop "authentic" learning and working styles that are unique, idiosyncratic, and personal. Having a vision for the future and having deeply satisfying work are key to success at this task. Helpers settle into comfortable working styles while continuously exploring ways to grow as professionals. Learning is very self-directed. Helpers often experience great satisfaction and excitement, which come from feeling creative as professionals. However, if their work environment is unsupportive or their work tasks are uninteresting, distress, stagnation, and boredom may occur. The challenge for helpers at this stage is to avoid burnout.

Peers and colleagues are major sources of influence, as are clients, who are a significant source of learning for helpers at this stage. In fact, experience with clients is now the epistemological center of the helper's work. Helpers at this stage are senior members of the profession and may be looked to for guidance and support by more junior members. Their techniques become more personalized, and they use them less mechanically than in previous stages. While these helpers develop deep relationships with their clients, they are able to maintain professional distance and not over-involve themselves. They are better able to accept the complexity of the helping process and feel less of a need to rigidly categorize clients and problems. Measures of effectiveness are unique to the helper. Client feedback can be important, but helpers at this stage are clear that clients are ultimately responsible for their own change. By this stage, helpers are able to see that some positive change, even if not dramatic, is an indicator of success.

Integrity Stage. At this stage, helpers have practiced for 25 to 35 years and are close to retirement. This stage may last from 1 to 10 years. Personality, experience, and accumulated wisdom guide these helpers in their work. The main task associated with this stage is to maintain the fullness of one's individuality while preparing for retirement. This stage is typically marked by a profound acceptance of oneself as a helper—acceptance of one's strengths, abilities, successes, failures, and limitations. Feelings of humility, security, serenity, satisfaction, and confidence are common. Sometimes, helpers at this stage experience regret as they ponder missed opportunities and the realities of a career winding down. Anxiety is minimal because they have done the work for so long.

These helpers focus less on experimenting with new techniques and focus more on sticking with what works. More so than in previous stages, they feel free to be who they want in their roles and working styles. Clients, especially ones with profound life experiences, can be a source of learning. Some helpers at this point have become professors or supervisors and find working with students and supervisees rewarding. Even students and supervisees can be a source of new learning, which is valued by helpers in this stage but with less of a sense of urgency than is often seen in younger helpers. For helpers in the integrity stage, measures of effectiveness do not depend so much on client feedback. They have found that witnessing client improvement is a measure of their effectiveness, and they have developed an acceptance that success often comes in small increments.

Themes in Helper Development

Skovholt and Rønnestad (1995) observed 20 themes in helper development:

1. Professional development is growth toward professional individuation.
2. An external and rigid orientation in role, working style, and conceptualization of issues increases throughout training and then declines continuously.
3. As the professional matures, continuous professional reflection becomes the central developmental process.
4. Beginning practitioners rely on external expertise (e.g., instruction, supervisor feedback); senior practitioners rely on internal expertise (e.g., accumulated wisdom).
5. Conceptual system and working style become increasingly congruent with the helper's personality and cognitive schema.
6. There is movement from received knowledge (e.g., formal schooling) toward constructed knowledge (choosing how to continue the learning process).
7. Development is impacted by multiple sources (e.g., supervisors, professors, colleagues, clients, helpers' own personal lives), which are experienced in both common and unique ways.
8. Optimal professional development is a long, slow, and erratic process.
9. Post-training years are critical for optimal development.
10. As the professional develops, he or she experiences a decrease in pervasive anxiety.
11. Interpersonal encounters are more influential than impersonal data.

12. Personal life is a central component of professional functioning (i.e., personal themes and experiences, such as helpers' own personal problems or intense cross-cultural experiences, influence helpers' professional practice).
13. Clients are a continuous major source of influence and serve as primary teachers.
14. Newer members of the field view professional elders and graduate training with strong affective reactions (e.g., idealization).
15. External support is most important at the beginning of one's career and at transition points.
16. Professional isolation becomes an important issue with increased experience and age.
17. Modeling/imitation is a powerful learning method that is preferred early in the helper's professional development, but not later.
18. There is a movement toward increased boundary clarity and responsibility differentiation.
19. For the practitioner, there is a realignment from a narcissistic position to a therapeutic position (e.g., to a more realistic, less grandiose notion about one's ability to bring about client change).
20. Extensive experience with suffering produces heightened tolerance and acceptance of human variability.

Optimal Development Versus Stagnation and Pseudodevelopment

Skovholt and Rønnestad (1995) addressed the issue of optimal development versus stagnation and pseudodevelopment. *Optimal development* requires maintaining an awareness of and openness to the complexity of the helping process, a desire to learn, and a reflective approach to personal and professional experiences and development. *Stagnation* occurs when helpers become self-protective and defensive, avoid experiencing anxiety related to the complexities and challenges of helping and helper development, and do not engage in continuous reflection—all of which close helpers off to further professional development and may cause helpers to leave the profession. *Pseudodevelopment* connotes apparent development but refers to changes in professional behavior that result from premature closure. Helpers engaged in pseudodevelopment do not engage in reflection or try to develop an individualized helping style, but rather rely on the work of others. Their behavior is defensively motivated and largely repetitive (Rønnestad & Skovholt, 1991). By engaging in continuous professional reflection, helpers may be able to get back onto the developmental track.

Sometimes, helpers enter "moratorium," which Skovholt and Rønnestad (1995) defined as a "psychological sanctuary and a temporary retreat" (p. 135). Moratorium can be thought of as a largely conscious move into some other nonprofessional activity, such as volunteer work or a hobby. It gives helpers some "psychological space"—a temporary retreat from development before they reenter a more active learning process.

Some factors that influence whether helpers will pursue the developmental track or the stagnation/pseudodevelopment track include the intensity of their motives to enter and stay in the profession, their awareness of complexity, their attitudes toward complexity and challenge (e.g., do they embrace or fear them?), their ability to tolerate and modulate negative affect, and the degree to which they can gradually attain higher levels of integration between techniques, theory, values, and their own personalities as they develop their helping style.

Challenges in Helping

Helping is a complex process. Helpers face formidable professional and personal challenges, many of which have been discussed throughout this book, including the challenges of suppressing personal problems and needs to focus on clients, deciding how and when to use particular skills, respecting individual and cultural differences, and handling ethical and legal issues. The following are several additional challenges.

Enduring Loneliness and Isolation. Helpers do much of their work quietly and behind closed doors. Because of the confidential nature of the helping process, they cannot reveal what they learn in helping to other people (with some exceptions, as discussed in chapters 3 and 14). Further, they do not enjoy the public recognition that may come in many other occupations, such as business, politics, journalism, and professional sports, and they do not have as much freedom to discuss or share their work with family and friends (see Skovholt, 2001). The helping professions, therefore, can be somewhat lonely.

Constantly Beginning, Building, Maintaining, and Ending Helping Relationships. As discussed in chapter 4, with each client, helpers engage in a "cycle of caring" that consists of empathic attachment, active involvement, and felt separation (Skovholt, 2001). The cycle of caring describes the process of building, maintaining, and eventually ending helping relationships with clients—a process that helpers engage in repeatedly throughout their careers. For each new client gained, another may end helping and never return. Think back to the times in your life when you made new friends and said good-bye to others. The feelings of excitement and loss in those situations are ones that helpers confront throughout their careers.

Dealing With Emotional Fatigue and Trauma. Helping is an intense performance skill—like acting or public speaking. It can be a very emotionally draining process (see Kottler, 1993). As noted earlier in this book, helping relationships are "one-way"; that is, helpers focus on clients' needs and problems. Clients do not reciprocate and assist helpers with problems. Helpers are constantly giving of themselves. Also, helpers do not merely converse with their clients; they spend their careers listening to intense personal problems and accepting some degree of responsibility for helping clients work through those problems. In their role as helpers, they bear the brunt of their clients' pain and anger. They hear powerful accounts of abuse, failures, and relationship turmoil, among other issues. Some of these concerns may remind helpers of their own personal issues, which they must suppress in the helping relationship if they are to effectively assist their clients. In some cases, spending years listening to painful client experiences produces "vicarious traumatization," in which helpers, to some extent, take on client pain as their own and experience changes in their beliefs and expectations about themselves and the world (McCann

& Pearlman, 1990; Pearlman & Mac Ian, 1995; Sussman, 1995). Even if helpers do not experience this phenomenon, the helping process can leave helpers feeling exhausted. They sometimes have very little energy left to commit to family, friends, and themselves (Kottler, 1993).

Always Setting a Good Example. Effective helpers serve as role models for their clients by consistently demonstrating good relationship skills, responsibility, and healthy, functional behavior. Responding to clients with defensiveness, anger, or irresponsible behavior can seriously damage helpers' credibility. Moreover, to some extent, helpers are on display in their everyday lives as well as in helping relationships (Kottler, 1993). If they do not "practice" in life what they "preach" in helping, their credibility may be damaged in the eyes of anyone who knows. It is important for helpers not to take this point to a perfectionist extreme—"I *must* be the epitome of mental health!"—however, they should continuously work on their professional and personal development and strive to live by the principles they espouse.

Engaging in Honest Reflection and Self-Exploration. Helpers who understand themselves well are in a better position to understand and help their clients. Reflection and self-exploration can lead to self-awareness and professional and personal growth if they are done honestly. Examining one's beliefs, values, motives, strengths, and limitations can be a challenging exercise. Helpers may discover many positive things about themselves, but they may also have to grapple with feelings and attitudes that they would rather ignore. It is natural for individuals to want to avoid aspects of themselves that are negative, uncomfortable, or unflattering, such as biases or prejudices. They may distort their statements and thoughts to make their behaviors and motives seem more acceptable. But how well can helpers encourage their clients to honestly explore ineffective attitudes and behaviors if they themselves are not willing to make this journey? Honest reflection and self-exploration may involve such activities as meditating, consulting with supervisors and colleagues, confiding in close friends, attending workshops, and seeking personal counseling.

Accepting Ambiguity. Ambiguity is part of the helping process (see G. Corey, 2001; Kottler & Brown, 2000). Ambiguity in helping refers to the variability, uncertainty, and unpredictability that come with helping people work through challenging personal problems. Some sources of this ambiguity include the strong affective component of helping (feelings are strong motivators that are often unpredictable and quick to change), human differences, the existence of many possible resolutions to a problem, and disagreements among practitioners about the best way to help people. Helpers must learn to accept and appreciate ambiguity. It cannot be eliminated. Those with low tolerance for ambiguity may impose rigid, simplistic solutions that ignore the dynamics, complexities, and nuances of problems. Helpers who learn to accept ambiguity will gain a deeper understanding of themselves, their clients, and the helping process. This leads to richer, more productive helping relationships.

Establishing Healthy Boundaries. This point was discussed by G. Corey (2001). Many helpers, especially beginners, have difficulty leaving their work at the office. All helpers think about their clients to some extent outside of sessions, but dwelling on or obsessing about client cases is unhelpful. It creates stress and can increase the risk of burnout. Effective helpers are good at balancing work time and personal time. Establishing healthy boundaries also involves managing sessions effectively— starting and ending on time, insisting that clients not come to sessions under the influence of drugs or alcohol, and being clear about unacceptable behavior, such as physical violence and verbal abuse. Finally, establishing healthy boundaries means being able to say no to clients—something that can be difficult to do: "No, I do not wish to be called at home." "No, we cannot extend our time by 15 minutes each session." When clients respond to "no" answers with anger or frustration, helpers may feel like they are not helping and thus not doing their job. However, not establishing healthy boundaries sets a bad example for clients by showing that they can do as they please in relationships without consideration for rules or other people. Nevertheless, it is a challenge to establish healthy boundaries and then deal with the negative client responses that sometimes result.

Managing Difficult Clients. It is common for helpers to encounter demanding, resistant, uncommitted, uncooperative, and highly agitated clients. These clients tend to demonstrate the behaviors that induce the most stress for helpers, such as suicidal statements, anger directed toward helpers, challenges to helpers' competence, apathy, high anxiety, severe depression, physical violence toward helpers, and premature termination of helping (see, e.g., Deutsch, 1984; Kottler, 1993).

In many cases, these clients are simply communicating in the ways they have learned—the ways that are familiar to them. Helpers try not to succumb to manipulative or intimidating behavior or to react defensively to the distance-producing interpersonal style of these clients. Rather, they strive to respond in a therapeutically valuable way. The behavior that makes these clients "difficult" may be the behavior that prevents them from developing healthy relationships, communicating effectively, and obtaining the things they want in life. In other words, this behavior is one of the reasons they need help. If helpers respond angrily or defensively, they set themselves up as being no different from the other people in these clients' lives and, consequently, unable to help. Helpers need to provide a different, fresher, healthier response. They assist these clients in recognizing ineffective behavior and making positive changes. In some cases, however, helpers have to take specific steps first, such as reporting serious threats of harm to authorities or ensuring their own safety if they feel endangered or threatened by a client.

An example of difficult client behavior is resistance, which often represents ambivalence about or opposition to change (Pipes & Davenport, 1999; Young, 2001). Some degree of resistance is normal when clients contemplate significant changes in their lives. Resistance becomes problematic when it prevents clients from making changes. In helping, resistance can arise at any point and has many possible causes, including discomfort, fear of the helping process, fear of change, lack of readiness or motivation, and being forced to seek help (e.g., by a court) (see Young, 2001). Helpers can contribute to client resistance by imposing goals or solutions on clients, pushing clients to make changes, or applying interventions inappropriately. Clients may demonstrate resistance in many ways, including intellectualizing, coming late for sessions, being silent, changing the subject, making excuses, and blaming

(Brammer & MacDonald, 2003; Pipes & Davenport, 1999). Some suggestions for dealing with resistance include the following:

- Recognize that resistance is a typical feature of helping, and expect it (Young, 2001).
- Follow, accept, join, or "travel with" client resistance (Young, 2001). If the world of clients is represented by the ocean (see chapter 5), this might be like riding the current. Helpers strive to understand resistance rather than fight it. They may even learn that something *they* are doing is causing the resistance (e.g., imposing inappropriate solutions on clients, disrespecting the client's culture). In helping, resistance is often viewed as the client's problem—an ineffective behavior that the client needs to overcome. Often this is the case, but helpers should not be too quick to rule out the possibility that they are the cause of the client's resistance. Striving to understand resistance rather than fighting it aids helpers in this assessment. "Traveling with" client resistance often involves responding with empathy, listening, and patience (see Young, 2001). These responses reduce anxiety, are nonthreatening, and may encourage clients to lower their defenses—the need for the defenses is taken away (Martin, 2000). Arguing or power struggling usually just reinforces and entrenches resistance.

Dealing With Countertransference. In chapter 8, we described "transference," which occurs when clients project feelings and attitudes onto helpers. "Countertransference" is the opposite of transference: Helpers project feelings and attitudes onto their clients. There is no uniform definition of countertransference. It has been defined narrowly as the helper's transference to the client's transference and has been defined broadly to include virtually all of the emotional reactions that helpers have toward their clients (Gelso & Fretz, 2001). As suggested by Gelso and Fretz (2001), a middle-ground definition is probably most useful. They defined countertransference as "the [helper's] transference to the client's material—to the transference and nontransference communications presented by the client" (p. 240).

Countertransference typically emanates from helpers' own issues, problems, and needs. Examples of countertransference include (1) having a sexual relationship with a client (which involves putting helper needs ahead of client needs), and (2) a helper feeling anger toward his wife and then later in the day angrily confronting a client (Pipes & Davenport, 1999).

Countertransference is often revealed in helper behavior. G. Corey et al. (2003, pp. 50–53) identified the following ways in which it may be manifested:

- Being overprotective with clients
- Treating clients in benign ways due to fears of client anger
- Rejecting clients
- Needing constant reinforcement and approval from clients
- Seeing oneself in clients
- Developing sexual or romantic feelings toward clients
- Giving advice compulsively
- Desiring social relationships with clients

Extreme helper emotions, repeatedly making the same mistakes, lack of client progress, and certain client statements (e.g., "You seem angry with me.") can also be signs of countertransference (Pipes & Davenport, 1999).

Countertransference can at times be beneficial in that helpers' reactions to clients may provide insight into the kinds of reactions that clients tend to evoke in other people (Pipes & Davenport, 1999). Helpers can then work with clients to recognize and change unproductive client behaviors and interactional patterns. The negative aspects of countertransference, however, are typically given the most attention. Countertransference is destructive and becomes an ethical issue "when a [helper's] own needs or unresolved personal conflicts become entangled in the therapeutic relationship, obstructing or destroying a sense of objectivity" (G. Corey et al., 2003, p. 49).

Countertransference is a challenging issue for helpers. Because of their role as "relationship experts" who help *other* people with problems, helpers may have difficulty recognizing or acknowledging the existence of countertransference. Countertransference can cloud helpers' judgment, distort their thinking, and cause their personal needs to become more important than client needs. Helpers who put their own needs ahead of those of their clients are behaving unethically (G. Corey et al., 2003). The challenge for helpers is to recognize, acknowledge, and understand countertransference, being as honest as possible about their feelings, attitudes, and reactions. Personal reflection, supervision, and consultation with colleagues are good ways for helpers to do this.

Managing Multiple Obligations. Helpers have to accommodate the needs and demands of many people and entities, such as supervisors, employers, clients, licensing boards, and themselves. Many helpers have to meet the demands of managed care as well. Satisfying all of these obligations and commitments can be quite challenging, especially when they conflict. For example, what a helper thinks is best for a client may not be what a supervisor thinks is best. As helpers gain experience, they become more adept at accommodating multiple obligations and finding work environments in which they can function comfortably.

Defining and Measuring Success. Consider the following challenges that helpers face in defining and measuring success in helping. First, helpers do not generate a tangible product in their work. The helping process contains few concrete rewards for helpers. Writers, carpenters, and artists can all look at the finished products of their work and say, "I did that!" What can helpers point to? How do they show that they have been working hard and have accomplished something?

Second, the difficulty of the change process can make it hard to determine how well clients are progressing in managing or resolving their problems. A client who one week seems to be making positive changes and expresses appreciation for the helper's assistance may feel angry and hopeless the next week. How do helpers determine whether they are making a positive difference in their clients' lives?

Third, helpers must deal with "ambiguous professional loss," which refers to the lack of closure that helpers may experience in their relationships with clients (Skovholt, 2001). Clients may terminate helping prematurely and helpers may never know why. Even if clients terminate at the agreed-upon time, they may never follow up with their helpers. In both situations, helpers are left wondering, "Did I make a positive difference in this person's life?" "Has the client gotten better or worse?" Helpers have to accept that they may never know what happens to their clients after termination. They may not be able to answer the question, "Was I effective?"

Accepting Normative Failure. The concept of normative failure was described by Skovholt (2001). Helpers will not always be successful in their work. They will have some clients who do not show improvement, who get worse, or who terminate prematurely. Some failure (normative failure) is to be expected, but failure can be difficult to accept, especially for novice helpers. Failure creates anxiety and may cause helpers to question their competence. Even though helpers understand intellectually that professionals are not perfect (e.g., even the best doctors lose patients), a profound understanding of the reality of success and failure does not always penetrate the helper's professional self-concept. Helpers want to believe that they can successfully promote client change. They enter helping professions with an intense desire to have a significant impact, relieve pain, and make a positive difference in their clients' lives. Gradually, as helpers gain experience, their expectations about their ability to promote client change become more realistic. Helpers become better able to accept lack of success and effectively distinguish between normative failure and excessive failure.

This description of challenges is not exhaustive; however, it should be sufficient to demonstrate that effective helping requires a great deal of maturity, patience, self-awareness, sacrifice, and training. These demands can make the helping process a taxing experience for helpers.

Motives and Rewards: Why Choose to Help People?

With all of the formidable challenges that helpers face, why would anyone want to spend a career helping people?

Motives

Individuals who pursue studies and work in the helping professions have their own motives for doing so. The following are some of the common motives:

- To obtain formal training after being told that one is a good listener or would make a good helper or because one is accustomed to being a caregiver (e.g., within one's family)
- To learn about oneself and/or to address one's own problems
- To pursue an altruistic, empathetic desire to assist people who are struggling or hurting
- To pursue a desire to "give back"; after being helped once, one wants to become a helper
- To work in the helping professions because one had a positive personal experience as a client
- To indulge a passion for understanding human nature and behavior

338   *Helping Skills and Strategies*   **Part Eight**

- To indulge curiosity and peer into other people's personal lives
- To avail oneself of the rewards of helping (see next section)
- To be in a relationship in which one has more control and influence than the other person
- To meet one's own need for close relationships
- To avoid loneliness
- To feel important, needed, liked, or loved
- To facilitate a desire to be a change agent in society (see chapter 2)

As this list shows, some motives are positive and beneficial, whereas others seem more selfish and may even be detrimental to the helping process. In many cases, people entering the helping professions can identify both types of motives (Kottler, 1993). Sometimes, even apparently selfish motives can have positive effects. For example, a helper's passion to understand human nature and behavior may help him or her thoroughly explore client concerns and understand the client's world. The important point here is that, whatever their motives, helpers must be careful not to put their own needs ahead of their clients' needs. Part of self-exploration and professional development involves helpers identifying their motives for wanting to help people. Helpers' motives shape their attitudes toward clients and shape the approach they take to helping (see Kottler, 1993).

Rewards

Although helping has many challenges for helpers, it also has many rewards. Indeed, the "helper therapy principle" recognizes that the giver in a human exchange gets a lot from giving—that is, helping is therapeutic or beneficial for the helper (Riessman, 1965; Skovholt, 1974, 2001). Here are some of the rewards that may come from helping:

- Energy from interacting with clients
- Learning from clients' experiences
- Positive, satisfying feelings of being able to successfully assist people who need help
- Seeing clients make positive changes (Witnessing such changes and playing a part in the process reinforce helpers' sense of professional and personal competence.)
- Establishing close relationships—getting to know clients on a deeply personal level
- A sense of identity
- Positive client feedback and referrals from clients
- Personal development and growth and enhanced self-awareness
- Development of interpersonal skills that are transferable to other types of relationships
- Species immortality (Helping connects helpers to the growth of human beings; it can provide enormous meaning by allowing helpers to positively contribute to the gradual evolutionary development of the species [Skovholt, 2001].)

■ Money (People rarely enter helping professions solely for the money. Indeed, in many settings, there is not much of it! But to get paid for doing something that one enjoys makes the deal that much sweeter.)

Most of the rewards that helpers receive emanate from countless hours of giving. Indeed, it is often true that in order to receive, you must give.

Self-Care: Avoiding Burnout and Sustaining the Self

Self-care, which involves avoiding burnout and sustaining the self, could easily fall under the topic of challenges in helping. Helpers spend their careers giving of themselves to assist other people. The stress involved in helping can lead to burnout, which we describe in detail before discussing burnout prevention and self-care strategies. There is no uniform definition of burnout. The term was first applied to helpers by Freudenberger (1974) and referred to the loss of will and motivation among practitioners. The term has been used generally to describe exhaustion, fatigue, weariness, depletion, and frustration at work. In mild forms, burnout may be manifested as slight fatigue. When burnout is extreme, helpers may be incapacitated to the point of not being able to function as helpers. Most helpers experiencing burnout fall somewhere in between.

A distinction has been made between two types of burnout that helpers may experience: meaning burnout and caring burnout (Skovholt, 2001). Meaning burnout occurs when helpers find that helping people no longer feels like a purposeful activity. The existential purpose—the meaning—of their work has disappeared. The "calling" to be a helper is no longer very powerful (Skovholt, 2001). Caring burnout refers to the drain that helpers feel from the process of repeatedly building, maintaining, and ending relationships with their clients. This process was described in chapter 4 as the cycle of caring, which involves empathic attachment, active involvement, and felt separation. Helpers may feel depleted and disengaged after so many cycles and may have difficulty attaching (building new relationships) again. This is the essence of caring burnout (Skovholt, 2001).

Both types of burnout can lead to impairment, or decreased professional functioning by helpers (see Kottler, 1993; Stadler, 1990). When helpers are impaired, they can make mistakes, exercise poor judgment, and appear uninvolved or indifferent, thus hurting their clients more than helping them. Impairment increases the risk of ethical complaints and legal proceedings against helpers.

Factors That Can Lead to Burnout

M. S. Corey and Corey (2003) noted that there is no single cause of burnout—it is caused by a combination of factors—and that burnout develops over time as opposed to being a sudden event. The challenges described earlier in this chapter can lead to burnout. The following list describes some additional causes. This list is derived from our own observations and from M. S. Corey and Corey (2003), Kottler (1993),

Maslach and Leiter (1997), Skovholt (2001), and Söderfeldt, Söderfeldt, and Warg (1995).

- Clients not making positive changes
- Inflexible, monotonous, unchanging routines
- Mundane, uncreative, unstimulating, unchallenging work
- The one-way nature of helping relationships—helpers constantly giving with no reciprocation
- Perfectionist attitudes
- Strong need for approval
- Lack of appreciation and feedback (or receiving negative feedback) from clients, supervisors, or employers
- Using feedback from clients and supervisors as the sole measure of success
- Low salary
- Working with challenging or difficult populations
- Unrealistic expectations about how much helpers can affect and change people
- Strong need to control people and situations
- Problems in the workplace (e.g., discrimination, disrespect, disputes with colleagues)
- Too much work
- Pressure from employers or supervisors (e.g., to achieve success with a client; to take more cases)
- Poor boundaries (e.g., taking work home at night)
- Personal problems that have not been effectively dealt with (e.g., poor social life)

Indicators of Burnout

Because of their role as helpers to others, some helpers have difficulty recognizing burnout in themselves and acknowledging their own problems and needs—"I'm the helper, not the client!" They may deny their own problems, perhaps even feeling that they should not have any. Helpers often feel intense pressure (much of it self-imposed) to be and appear mentally healthy. They may fear that their acknowledgment of problems, such as burnout, may be interpreted as a sign of weakness, incompetence, or lack of professionalism. The challenge is for helpers to recognize burnout. The following is a list of some common indicators of burnout; it is derived from our own observations and from Freudenberger (1974), Kottler (1993), Maslach and Leiter (1997), and Skovholt (2001).

- Boredom and fatigue
- Irritability, crying, anger, and frustration
- Pessimism, negativity, and cynicism
- Inflexibility and rigidity
- Hopelessness
- Emotional exhaustion
- Depression
- Anxiety
- Substance abuse

- Lack of positive feelings toward work
- Lack of enthusiasm or interest in work; apathy
- Preoccupation with things unrelated to work; distraction and lack of concentration
- Lower work output; getting behind in work; showing up late for work
- A "just getting by" attitude—a desire to do only the bare minimum at work
- Exercising poor judgment and taking irresponsible risks
- Lying, making excuses, and rationalizing
- A "clock-punching" attitude toward work—always watching the time and leaving precisely when the schedule or shift is over
- Withdrawal from family and friends
- A sense of meaninglessness and futility
- Low energy; feeling physically tired
- Physical illness

Burnout Prevention and Self-Care Strategies

To serve as role models and effectively help clients (other-care), helpers themselves must stay healthy (self-care). The greatest and primary asset of helpers is the self. Just as the singer must take care of the voice and the baseball pitcher must take care of the arm, the helper must take care of the self. It is up to helpers to take steps to avoid burnout, to do whatever helps them refresh, rejuvenate, and revitalize the self. Even in environments in which helpers have little control over policies and work tasks, they choose how to respond to the challenges and pressures of their situation—from engaging in their own self-care rituals (such as taking a walk), to pushing for change, to finding another job (Skovholt, 2001). The following list enumerates some ways that helpers can avoid burnout and care for themselves, professionally and personally. These strategies are also useful for helpers who are currently experiencing burnout and are trying to "heal" themselves. This list is derived from M. S. Corey and Corey (2003) and Skovholt (2001).

- Pursue hobbies and leisure activities, such as gardening, reading, biking, taking vacations, and listening to music.
- Engage in physical exercise and follow a good diet.
- Engage in spiritual pursuits.
- Spend time with friends, family, and partners.
- Maintain a manageable workload.
- Manage time effectively and assertively.
- Establish healthy boundaries.
- Be flexible, adaptive, and open to change.
- Maintain a sense of humor.
- Increase variety and novelty at work.
- Clean the office.
- Schedule breaks and free time.
- Attend to professional and personal development, such as self-reflection and continuing education.
- Take a proactive approach to making changes and accept what cannot be changed.

- Relish small victories and avoid grandiosity and perfectionism.
- Consult with colleagues and supervisors.
- Vent with colleagues and peers—let go of distressing emotions.
- Join support groups or seek personal counseling.
- Change jobs.

One of the greatest challenges that helpers face is balancing other-care and self-care (Skovholt, 2001). Helpers are trained to immerse themselves in the world of their clients and to put clients' needs ahead of their own. Yet, like all other individuals, helpers have the instinct of self-preservation, the drive to focus on and address their own needs and well-being (Skovholt, 2001). Part of helpers' professional development involves finding the right balance between caring for others and caring for self. Too much of one at the expense of the other can harm helping relationships and result in diminished professional functioning.

Finishing the Book, Beginning the Journey: Suggestions for Students and Novice Helpers

We have reached the end of this book, but for those of you who plan to continue your studies and become helpers, the journey is just beginning. Where you go from here in your studies and work is up to you. We conclude this book with several suggestions to help you on your way.

Recognize That There Is Still Much More to Learn. Reading a single book or taking a course in helping is not enough for you to become a skilled, effective helper. Even an entire graduate training program is not enough. The learning and professional development process will continue throughout your career. As you take this journey, continuously strive to increase your self-awareness, talk with your fellow students and colleagues, become culturally knowledgeable and skilled, keep up with research, and develop and refine your own personal helping theory. Be advised, however, that many students and helpers find that the learning and development process tends to lead to more questions than answers.

Identify Helping Professions, Areas of Practice, and Training Programs That Interest You. As you consider what type of work to pursue, you will be confronted with many choices. There are many helping professions from which to choose. For example, are you interested in social work or counseling? Do you know the differences between these two professions? You also need to consider which areas of practice interest you, such as drug and alcohol counseling, school counseling, and career counseling. Once you identify the type of work you wish to pursue, you can select a program of study that is compatible with your needs and interests.

To make informed decisions, you may need to do some research on the various helping professions, areas of practice, training programs, and licensure and certification requirements. Speak with students, professors, and helpers, and learn from their experiences. Read college catalogs that describe the available training programs. They will tell you program requirements (e.g., prerequisites, course work) and the careers for which the programs can prepare you. Finally, do some soul-searching. What are your values and interests? With which populations do you want to work (e.g., students, at-risk youth, the elderly)? Although you will need to make decisions and commitments at some point, recognize that you can change your mind as your interests develop.

Maximize Your Educational Experience. You must take the initiative to make your education fulfilling. Attending classes, doing homework, and satisfying practicum requirements are important, of course, but they are only part of the educational experience. Numerous opportunities exist for you to supplement these activities. Consider these possibilities:

- Assist in teaching courses—talk to your professors about teaching assistantship opportunities.
- Assist in research—professors often hire student research assistants to collect data and conduct research; authoring or coauthoring journal articles is even a possibility.
- Identify helping topics that interest you, and read books and journal articles on the topics.
- Attend workshops, lectures, and conferences.
- Take advantage of the time you have with your professors, advisors, and supervisors—consider setting up meetings with them to discuss concepts or issues about which you are confused or want to learn more; request their feedback about your performance and development as a helper; ask them about their own experiences in the profession.
- Join professional associations—the American Counseling Association and the American Psychological Association, for example, both allow students to join; professional affiliation allows you to stay current in the profession (e.g., through reading publications sent to you).

You will probably find your educational experience more fulfilling if you actively seek out opportunities, such as those just listed. Also, you can beef up your résumé with many of these activities, thereby increasing your chances of obtaining satisfying employment or getting into academic programs.

Seek Guidance and Support From Positive Mentors. As you learn about helping and begin to help clients yourself, you will probably find it beneficial to have someone to turn to for guidance and support (see Skovholt, 2001). Indeed, novice helpers, who often feel vulnerable and uncertain, typically have an acute need for supportive relationships with seasoned practitioners (Skovholt, 2001). A professor, a supervisor, an advisor, or a helper who is willing to spend some time with you can be a valuable resource. That person can serve not only as a role model but also as a source of guidance and support when you have concerns or questions or when you are struggling with some of the challenges of helping. He or she has "been there" and can offer the benefit of experience.

Engage in Honest Self-Exploration. Effective helpers are very reflective people who value developing a deep understanding of themselves. Honest self-exploration may involve seeking personal counseling for yourself, engaging in continuous reflection, and requesting feedback from colleagues, fellow students, family members, friends, professors, advisors, and supervisors. Be open to multiple perspectives, and reflect on the material that you encounter in your studies. Develop an understanding of your worldview and reality filters. Continue to honestly assess your values, biases, needs, desires, strengths, and limitations. Helpers who honestly examine who they are, how they see the world, what they want, and what they can do tend to function more effectively and be happier in their work. Thus, honest self-exploration benefits not only them, but also their clients.

Try to Avoid Grandiosity and Perfectionism. Individuals who want to become helpers should work constantly to improve their abilities and better themselves professionally and personally; however, this effort should not be taken to an extreme. Effective helpers realize that their ability to influence other people is limited. Regardless of how skilled they are, helpers cannot force people to change. Furthermore, they cannot help everyone, and like all people, they make mistakes now and then. Perhaps the biggest mistake that students and helpers can make is *failing to learn* from their mistakes.

Be Patient. Becoming a skilled, effective helper is a developmental process that requires a great deal of time and a strong commitment (Skovholt & Rønnestad, 1995). Developing expertise in helping takes several years of professional experience (perhaps as many as 15) and thousands of hours of practice (Skovholt, Rønnestad, & Jennings, 1997). At this point, according to Skovholt et al. (1997), "the practitioner has internalized theory and research, found a comfortable working style, developed a method for judging success, and shed elements of the professional role which are incongruent with the self" (p. 364). Over time, helping skills blend with personal characteristics to create a helping style that is more flexible, relaxed, genuine, spontaneous, and natural.

Summary and Concluding Remarks

This chapter focused on the helper's professional journey. It addressed helper development, challenges in helping, helper motives and rewards, and helper self-care. Several suggestions were offered for those who plan to continue their studies and work in the helping professions.

Becoming an effective helper requires motivation, training, and commitment. It is not easy to help people, and while the professional journey as a helper contains many rewards, it also contains many challenges. Think about where you are in your own professional journey. How would you describe the journey so far?

As we wrap up, take a few minutes to reflect on the material covered in this book and on what you have learned. Consider the following questions, and, if you wish, discuss your responses with your classmates or colleagues:

■ What thoughts, feelings, and reactions did you have as you read this book, answered the Questions for Thought, and did the exercises?
■ Were there any concepts, skills, procedures, topics, or statements that you had a particularly strong reaction to—either positive or negative? If so, what do you believe is the reason for your strong reaction?

- What concepts or statements did you agree with? Disagree with?
- What do you see as the most important thing that you learned about helping from this book?
- How has your view of helping changed, if at all, since you started reading this book?
- What have you learned about yourself since starting to read this book?
- What do you want to learn more about? What topics or issues interest you?

We hope that you found the material in this book informative and useful. We wish you well in your studies and work. Enjoy the journey!

Questions for Thought

1. What factors might promote development and movement through the stages of helper development? What factors might hinder development and movement?

2. Several challenges in helping were identified in this chapter. If you were a helper, how would you handle these challenges? What other challenges in helping can you identify, and how would you handle them?

3. If you plan to pursue a career as a helper, what are your motives for wanting to become a helper? What rewards do you anticipate receiving from helping people?

4. Have you ever experienced burnout? If so, when? What caused it, and how did you recognize it? How did you handle it? In general, what self-care activities do you engage in to refresh, rejuvenate, and revitalize your "self"?

5. How might helpers find the right balance between other-care and self-care?

6. We offered several suggestions for those who plan to continue their studies and become helpers. What additional suggestions would you offer?

Abramson, L. Y., Seligman, M. E. P., & Teasdale, J. D. (1978). Learned helplessness in humans: Critique and reformulation. *Journal of Abnormal Psychology, 87,* 49–74.

Adler, A. (1958). *What life should mean to you.* New York: Capricorn. (Original work published 1931)

Adler, R. B., Rosenfeld, L. B., & Towne, N. (1980). *Interplay: The process of interpersonal communication.* New York: Holt, Rinehart and Winston.

Albert, G. (1997). What are the characteristics of effective psychotherapists? The experts speak. *Journal of Practical Psychiatry and Behavioral Health, 3,* 36–44.

Allport, G. W. (1954). *The nature of prejudice.* Reading, MA: Addison-Wesley.

Alyn, J. H. (1988). The politics of touch in therapy: A response to Willison and Masson. *Journal of Counseling and Development, 66,* 432–433.

American Counseling Association. (1995). *Code of ethics and standards of practice.* Alexandria, VA: Author.

American Psychiatric Association. (1994). *Diagnostic and statistical manual of mental disorders* (4th ed.). Washington, DC: Author.

American Psychological Association. (1993). Record keeping guidelines. *American Psychologist, 48,* 984–986.

American Psychological Association. (2002). *Ethical principles of psychologists and code of conduct.* Washington, DC: Author.

Arbona, C. (2000). The development of academic achievement in school-aged children: Precursors to career development. In S. D. Brown & R. W. Lent (Eds.), *Handbook of counseling psychology* (3rd ed., pp. 270–309). New York: Wiley.

Argyle, M. (1994). *The psychology of social class.* London: Routledge and Kegan Paul.

Arredondo, P., Toporek, R., Brown, S. P., Jones, J., Locke, D. C., Sanchez, J., et al. (1996). Operationalization of the multicultural counseling competencies. *Journal of Multicultural Counseling and Development, 24,* 42–78.

Atkinson, D. R., & Hackett, G. (1998). *Counseling diverse populations* (2nd ed.). Boston: McGraw-Hill.

Atkinson, D. R., & Lowe, S. M. (1995). The role of ethnicity, cultural knowledge, and conventional techniques in counseling and psychotherapy. In J. G. Ponterotto, J. M. Casas, L. A. Suzuki, & C. M. Alexander (Eds.), *Handbook of multicultural counseling* (pp. 387–414). Thousand Oaks, CA: Sage.

Axelson, J. A. (1999). *Counseling and development in a multicultural society* (3rd ed.). Pacific Grove, CA: Brooks/Cole.

Bachelor, A., & Horvath, A. (1999). The therapeutic relationship. In M. A. Hubble, B. L. Duncan, & S. D. Miller (Eds.), *The heart & soul of change: What works in therapy* (pp. 133–178). Washington, DC: American Psychological Association.

Bandura, A. (1982). Self-efficacy mechanism in human agency. *American Psychologist, 37,* 122–147.

Bandura, A. (1997). *Self-efficacy: The exercise of control.* New York: W. H. Freeman.

Bankart, C. P. (1997). *Talking cures: A history of Western and Eastern psychotherapies.* Pacific Grove, CA: Brooks/Cole.

Baruth, L. G., & Manning, M. L. (1999). *Multicultural counseling and psychotherapy: A lifespan perspective* (2nd ed.). Upper Saddle River, NJ: Prentice-Hall.

Belkin, G. S. (1988). *Introduction to counseling* (3rd ed.). Dubuque, IA: Wm. C. Brown.

Benjamin, A. (1987). *The helping interview.* Boston: Houghton Mifflin.

Bernal, M. E., Knight, G. P., Ocampo, K. A., Garza, C. A., & Côté, M. K. (1993). Development of Mexican-American identity. In M. E. Bernal & G. P. Knight (Eds.), *Ethnic identity: Formation and transmission among Hispanics and other minorities* (pp. 31–46). Albany, NY: SUNY.

Bernstein, B. E., & Hartsell, T. L., Jr. (2000). *The portable ethicist for mental health professionals: An A–Z guide to responsible practice.* New York: Wiley.

Bieri, J. (1955). Cognitive complexity-simplicity and predictive behavior. *Journal of Abnormal and Social Psychology, 51,* 263–268.

Bolton, R. (1979). *People skills: How to assert yourself, listen to others, and resolve conflicts.* New York: Simon and Schuster.

Bordin, E. S. (1975). The generalizability of the psychoanalytic concept of the working alliance. *Psychotherapy: Theory, Research, and Practice, 16,* 252–260.

Bowen, M. (1978). *Family therapy in clinical practice.* New York: Aronson.

Bowlby, J. (1988). *A secure base: Parent-child attachment and healthy human development.* New York: BasicBooks.

Brammer, L. M., & MacDonald, G. (2003). *The helping relationship: Process and skills* (8th ed.). Boston: Allyn and Bacon.

Brown, L. S. (1992). A feminist critique of the personality disorders. In L. S. Brown & M. Ballou (Eds.), *Personality and psychopathology: Feminist reappraisals* (pp. 206–228). New York: Guilford Press.

Brownell, K. D., Marlatt, G. A., Lichtenstein, E., & Wilson, G. T. (1986). Understanding and preventing relapse. *American Psychologist, 41,* 765–782.

Budman, S. H., & Gurman, A. S. (1988). *Theory and practice of brief therapy.* New York: Guilford Press.

Buffone, G. W. (1991). Understanding and managing the litigious patient. *Psychotherapy in Private Practice, 9,* 27–45.

Carkhuff, R. R. (1969). *Helping and human relations* (Vols. 1–2). New York: Holt, Rinehart and Winston.

Carkhuff, R. R. (1983). *The art of helping* (5th ed.). Amherst, MA: Human Resource Development Press.

Carkhuff, R. R. (1984). *Helping and human relations* (Vols. 1–2). Amherst, MA: Human Resource Development Press.

Carkhuff, R. R. (2000). *The art of helping in the 21st century* (8th ed.). Amherst, MA: Human Resource Development Press.

Cavanagh, M. E., & Levitov, J. E. (2002). *The counseling experience: A theoretical and practical approach* (2nd ed.). Prospect Heights, IL: Waveland Press.

Claiborn, C. D., Ward, S. R., & Strong, S. R. (1981). Effects of congruence between counselor interpretations and client beliefs. *Journal of Counseling Psychology, 28,* 101–109.

Cohen, E. D., & Cohen, G. S. (1999). *The virtuous therapist: Ethical practice of counseling & psychotherapy.* Pacific Grove, CA: Brooks/Cole.

Coleman, H. L. K., Wampold, B. E., & Casali, S. L. (1995). Ethnic minorities' ratings of ethnically similar and European American counselors: A meta-analysis. *Journal of Counseling Psychology, 42,* 55–64.

Corey, G. (2001). *Theory and practice of counseling and psychotherapy* (6th ed.). Pacific Grove, CA: Brooks/Cole.

Corey, G., Corey, M. S., & Callanan, P. (2003). *Issues and ethics in the helping professions* (6th ed.). Pacific Grove, CA: Brooks/Cole.

Corey, M. S., & Corey, G. (2003). *Becoming a helper* (4th ed.). Pacific Grove, CA: Brooks/Cole.

Cormier, S., & Hackney, H. (1999). *Counseling strategies and interventions* (5th ed.). Boston: Allyn and Bacon.

Cormier, S., & Nurius, P. S. (2003). *Interviewing and change strategies for helpers: Fundamental skills and cognitive behavioral interventions* (5th ed.). Pacific Grove, CA: Brooks/Cole.

Cross, W. E., Jr. (1971). The Negro-to-black conversion experience: Toward a psychology of black liberation. *Black World, 20*(9), 13–27.

D'Andrea, M., Daniels, J., & Heck, R. (1991). Evaluating the impact of multicultural counseling training. *Journal of Counseling and Development, 70,* 143–150.

Das, A. K. (1995). Rethinking multicultural counseling: Implications for counselor education. *Journal of Counseling and Development, 74,* 45–52.

DeJong, P., & Berg, I. K. (1998). *Interviewing for solutions.* Pacific Grove, CA: Brooks/Cole.

Deutsch, C. J. (1984). Self-reported sources of stress among psychotherapists. *Professional Psychology: Research and Practice, 15,* 833–845.

Dixon, D. N., & Glover, J. A. (1984). *Counseling: A problem-solving approach.* New York: Wiley.

Donley, R. J., Horan, J. J., & DeShong, R. L. (1989). The effect of several self-disclosure permutations on counseling process and outcome. *Journal of Counseling and Development, 67,* 408–412.

Doyle, R. E. (1998). *Essential skills and strategies in the helping process* (2nd ed.). Pacific Grove, CA: Brooks/Cole.

Draguns, J. G. (2002). Universal and cultural aspects of counseling and psychotherapy. In P. B. Pedersen, J. G. Draguns, W. L. Lonner, & J. E. Trimble (Eds.), *Counseling across cultures* (5th ed., pp. 29–50). Thousand Oaks, CA: Sage.

Eaton, T. T., Abeles, N., & Gutfreund, M. J. (1988). Therapeutic alliance and outcome: Impact of treatment length and pretreatment symptomatology. *Psychotherapy, 25,* 536–542.

Edwards, C. E., & Murdock, N. L. (1994). Characteristics of therapist self-disclosure in the counseling process. *Journal of Counseling and Development, 72,* 384–389.

Egan, G. (2002). *The skilled helper: A problem-management and opportunity-development approach to helping* (7th ed.). Pacific Grove, CA: Brooks/Cole.

Ehrenreich, B. (1991, April 8). Teach diversity—with a smile. *Time, 137,* 84.

Eliot, G. (1956). *Middlemarch* (G. S. Haight, Ed.). Boston: Houghton Mifflin. (Original work published 1871–1872)

Eliot, T. S. (1943). Little Gidding, V. *Four Quartets.* New York: Harcourt Brace.

Elkind, S. N. (1992). *Resolving impasses in therapeutic relationships.* New York: Guilford Press.

Emerson, R. W. (1926). Self-reliance. *Emerson's essays.* New York: Thomas Y. Crowell. (Original work published 1841)

England, J. (1992, September). *Pluralism and community.* Speech given at the national conference of the Association for Counselor Education and Supervision, San Antonio, TX.

Erikson, E. H. (1950). *Childhood and society.* New York: Norton.

Evans, D. R., Hearn, M. T., Uhlemann, M. R., & Ivey, A. E. (1998). *Essential interviewing: A programmed approach to effective communication* (5th ed.). Pacific Grove, CA: Brooks/Cole.

Exum, H. A., & Lau, E. Y.-W. (1988). Counseling style preference of Chinese college students. *Journal of Multicultural Counseling and Development, 16,* 84–92.

Family Educational Rights and Privacy Act of 1974, 20 U.S.C.A. § 1232g (West 2000).

Fischer, A. R., Jome, L. M., & Atkinson, D. R. (1998). Reconceptualizing multicultural counseling: Universal healing conditions in a culturally specific context. *The Counseling Psychologist, 26,* 525–588.

Fiske, S. T., & Taylor, S. F. (1991). *Social cognition* (2nd ed.). New York: McGraw-Hill.

Fouad, N. A., & Brown, M. T. (2000). Role of race and social class in development: Implications for counseling psychology. In S. D. Brown & R. W. Lent (Eds.), *Handbook of counseling psychology* (3rd ed., pp. 379–408). New York: Wiley.

Frank, J. D., & Frank, J. B. (1991). *Persuasion and healing: A comparative study of psychotherapy* (3rd ed.). Baltimore: Johns Hopkins University Press.

Frankl, V. E. (1963). *Man's search for meaning: An introduction to logotherapy.* New York: Washington Square Press.

Freudenberger, H. J. (1974). Staff burn-out. *Journal of Social Issues, 30,* 159–165.

Fukuyama, M. A., & Sevig, T. D. (2002). Spirituality in counseling across cultures: Many rivers to the sea. In P. B. Pedersen, J. G. Draguns, W. L. Lonner, & J. E. Trimble (Eds.), *Counseling across cultures* (5th ed., pp. 273–295). Thousand Oaks, CA: Sage.

Gama, E. M. P. (1991, August). *Multiculturalism as a basic assumption of psychology.* Paper presented at the Minnesota International Counseling Institute, University of Minnesota, Minneapolis.

Garfield, S. L. (1994). Research on client variables in psychotherapy. In A. E. Bergin & S. L. Garfield (Eds.), *Handbook of psychotherapy and behavior change* (4th ed., pp. 190–228). New York: Wiley.

Garfield, S. L. (1995). *Psychotherapy: An eclectic-integrative approach* (2nd ed.). New York: Wiley.

Gelso, C., & Fretz, B. (2001). *Counseling psychology* (2nd ed.). Fort Worth, TX: Harcourt College Publishers.

Gelso, C. J., & Carter, J. A. (1985). The relationship in counseling and psychotherapy: Components, consequences, and theoretical antecedents. *The Counseling Psychologist, 13,* 155–243.

Gilligan, C. (1982). *In a different voice: Psychological theory and women's development.* Cambridge, MA: Harvard University Press.

Gladding, S. T. (2000). *Counseling: A comprehensive profession* (4th ed.). Upper Saddle River, NJ: Prentice-Hall.

Glosoff, H. L., Herlihy, B., & Spence, E. B. (2000). Privileged communication in the counselor-client relationship. *Journal of Counseling and Development, 78,* 454–462.

Goleman, D. (1995). *Emotional intelligence.* New York: Bantam Books.

Goodyear, R. K. (1981). Termination as a loss experience for the counselor. *Personnel and Guidance Journal, 59,* 347–350.

Gordon, T. (1977). *Leader effectiveness training (L. E. T.): The no-lose way to release the productive potential of people.* New York: Bantam Books.

Graham, S. (1991). A review of attribution theory in achievement contexts. *Educational Psychology Review, 3,* 5–39.

Graham, S., & Brown, J. (1988). Attributional mediators of expectancy, evaluation, and affect: A response time analysis. *Journal of Personality and Social Psychology, 55,* 873–881.

Greenberg, L. S., & Safran, J. D. (1987). *Emotion in psychotherapy: Affect, cognition, and the process of change.* New York: Guilford Press.

Greenfield, P. M. (1994). Independence and interdependence as developmental scripts: Implications for theory, research, and practice. In P. M. Greenfield & R. R. Cocking (Eds.), *Cross-cultural roots of minority child development* (pp. 1–37). Hillsdale, NJ: Erlbaum.

Greenson, R. R. (1965). The working alliance and the transference neurosis. *The Psychoanalytic Quarterly, 34,* 155–181.

Guerin, P. J., & Chabot, D. R. (1992). Development of family systems theory. In D. K. Freedheim (Ed.), *History of psychotherapy: A century of change* (pp. 225–260). Washington, DC: American Psychological Association.

Hackney, H. L., & Cormier, L. S. (2001). *The professional counselor: A process guide to helping* (4th ed.). Boston: Allyn and Bacon.

Hall, G. C. N., Lopez, I. R., & Bansal, A. (2001). Academic acculturation: Race, gender, and class issues. In D. B. Pope-Davis & H. L. K. Coleman (Eds.), *The intersection of race, class, and gender in multicultural counseling* (pp. 171–188). Thousand Oaks, CA: Sage.

Hanna, F. J., & Ritchie, M. H. (1995). Seeking the active ingredients of psychotherapeutic change: Within and outside the context of therapy. *Professional Psychology: Research and Practice, 26,* 176–183.

Hanna, F. J., Talley, W. B., & Guindon, M. H. (2000). The power of perception: Toward a model of cultural oppression and liberation. *Journal of Counseling and Development, 78,* 430–441.

Hansen, L. S. (1997). *Integrative life planning: Critical tasks for career development and changing life patterns.* San Francisco: Jossey-Bass.

Harris, S. M., & Busby, D. M. (1998). Therapist physical attractiveness: An unexplored influence on client disclosure. *Journal of Marital and Family Therapy, 24,* 251–257.

Haspel, K. C., Jorgenson, L. M., Wincze, J. P., & Parsons, J. P. (1997). Legislative intervention regarding therapist sexual misconduct: An overview. *Professional Psychology: Research and Practice, 28,* 63–72.

Hein, P. (1966). T.T.T. In *Grooks.* Cambridge, MA: MIT Press.

Hendrick, S. S. (1988). Counselor self-disclosure. *Journal of Counseling and Development, 66,* 419–424.

Herlihy, B., & Corey, G. (1997). *Boundary issues in counseling: Multiple roles and responsibilities.* Alexandria, VA: American Counseling Association.

Hill, C. E. (1985). *Manual for the Hill counselor verbal response modes category system* (Rev.). Unpublished manuscript, University of Maryland, College Park.

Hill, C. E. (1989). *Therapist techniques and client outcomes: Eight cases of brief psychotherapy.* Newbury Park, CA: Sage.

Hill, C. E., & O'Brien, K. M. (1999). *Helping skills: Facilitating exploration, insight, and action.* Washington, DC: American Psychological Association.

Hillerbrand, E. T., & Claiborn, C. D. (1988). Ethical knowledge exhibited by clients and non-clients. *Professional Psychology: Research and Practice, 19,* 527–531.

Ho, M. K. (1987). *Family therapy with ethnic minorities.* Newbury Park, CA: Sage.

Holland, J. L. (1997). *Making vocational choices* (3rd ed.). Odessa, FL: Psychological Assessment Resources.

Hopkins, B. R., & Anderson, B. S. (1990). *The counselor and the law* (3rd ed.). Alexandria, VA: American Association for Counseling and Development.

Horvath, A. O., & Symonds, B. D. (1991). Relation between working alliance and outcome in psychotherapy: A meta-analysis. *Journal of Counseling Psychology, 38,* 139–149.

Hutchins, D. E., & Cole Vaught, C. (1997). *Helping relationships and strategies* (3rd ed.). Pacific Grove, CA: Brooks/Cole.

Ibrahim, F. A., & Kahn, H. (1984). Scale to Assess World View (SAWV). Unpublished instrument, Storrs, CT.

Ibrahim, F. A., & Kahn, H. (1987). Assessment of world views. *Psychological Reports, 60,* 163–176.

Ibrahim, F. A., & Owen, S. V. (1994). Factor analytic structure of the Scale to Assess World View. *Current Psychology: Developmental, Learning, Personality, Social, 13,* 201–209.

Ingersoll, R. E. (1994). Spirituality, religion, and counseling: Dimensions and relationships. *Counseling and Values, 38,* 98–111.

Ivey, A. E., & Authier, J. (1978). *Microcounseling: Innovations in interviewing, counseling, psychotherapy, and psychoeducation.* Springfield, IL: Charles C Thomas.

Ivey, A. E., & Ivey, M. B. (1999). *Intentional interviewing and counseling: Facilitating client development in a multicultural society* (4th ed.). Pacific Grove, CA: Brooks/Cole.

Jacobs, D. H. (1994). Environmental failure: Oppression is the only cause of psychopathology. *Journal of Mind and Behavior, 15*(1–2), 1–18.

Jaffee v. Redmond, 518 U.S. 1 (1996).

Jennings, L., & Skovholt, T. M. (1999). The cognitive, emotional, and relational characteristics of master therapists. *Journal of Counseling Psychology, 46,* 3–11.

Johnson, S. D., Jr. (1990). Toward clarifying culture, race, and ethnicity in the context of multicultural counseling. *Journal of Multicultural Counseling and Development, 18,* 41–50.

Josselson, R. (1987). *Finding herself: Pathways to identity development in women.* San Francisco: Jossey-Bass.

Jourard, S. M. (1971). *The transparent self.* New York: Van Nostrand Reinhold.

Kitchener, K. S. (1984). Intuition, critical evaluation and ethical principles: The foundation for ethical decisions in counseling psychology. *The Counseling Psychologist, 12*(3), 43–55.

Kitchener, K. S., & Anderson, S. K. (2000). Ethical issues in counseling psychology: Old themes—new problems. In S. D. Brown & R. W. Lent (Eds.), *Handbook of counseling psychology* (3rd ed., pp. 50–82). New York: Wiley.

Kluckhohn, F. R., & Strodtbeck, F. L. (1961). *Variations in value orientations.* Evanston, IL: Row, Peterson.

Kohlberg, L. (1984). *The psychology of moral development: The nature and validity of moral stages.* San Francisco: Harper and Row.

Kottler, J. A. (1993). *On being a therapist* (Rev. ed.). San Francisco: Jossey-Bass.

Kottler, J. A., & Brown, R. W. (2000). *Introduction to therapeutic counseling: Voices from the field* (4th ed.). Pacific Grove, CA: Brooks/Cole.

Kottler, J. A., Brown, R. W., & Collins, P. L. (2000). Assessment, testing, and the diagnostic process. In J. A. Kottler & R. W. Brown, *Introduction to therapeutic counseling: Voices from the field* (4th ed., pp. 186–214). Pacific Grove, CA: Brooks/Cole.

Kottler, J. A., Sexton, T. L., & Whiston, S. C. (1994). *The heart of healing: Relationships in therapy.* San Francisco: Jossey-Bass.

Kramer, S. A. (1986). The termination process in open-ended psychotherapy: Guidelines for clinical practice. *Psychotherapy, 23,* 526–531.

Kramer, S. A. (1990). *Positive endings in psychotherapy: Bringing meaningful closure to therapeutic relationships.* San Francisco: Jossey-Bass.

LaFromboise, T. D., Coleman, H. L. K., & Hernandez, A. (1991). Development and factor structure of the Cross-Cultural Counseling Inventory—Revised. *Professional Psychology: Research and Practice, 22,* 380–388.

Lambert, M. J., & Bergin, A. E. (1994). The effectiveness of psychotherapy. In A. E. Bergin & S. L. Garfield (Eds.), *Handbook of psychotherapy and behavior change* (4th ed., pp. 143–189). New York: Wiley.

Lambert, M. J., & Hill, C. E. (1994). Assessing psychotherapy outcomes and processes. In A. E. Bergin & S. L. Garfield (Eds.), *Handbook of psychotherapy and behavior change* (4th ed., pp. 72–113). New York: Wiley.

Lauver, P., & Harvey, D. R. (1997). *The practical counselor: Elements of effective helping.* Pacific Grove, CA: Brooks/Cole.

Lee, C. C. (1991). Cultural dynamics: Their importance in multicultural counseling. In C. C. Lee & B. L. Richardson (Eds.), *Multicultural issues in counseling: New approaches to diversity* (pp. 11–17). Alexandria, VA: American Association for Counseling and Development.

Lee, C. C., & Richardson, B. L. (1991). Promise and pitfalls of multicultural counseling. In C. C. Lee & B. L. Richardson (Eds.), *Multicultural issues in counseling: New approaches to diversity* (pp. 3–9). Alexandria, VA: American Association for Counseling and Development.

Leong, F. T. L. (1996). Toward an integrative model for cross-cultural counseling and psychotherapy. *Applied and Preventative Psychology, 5,* 189–209.

Leong, F. T. L., & Bhagwat, A. (2001). Challenges in "unpacking" the universal, group, and individual dimensions of cross-cultural counseling and psychotherapy: Openness to experience as a critical dimension. In D. B. Pope-Davis & H. L. K. Coleman (Eds.), *The intersection of race, class, and gender in multicultural counseling* (pp. 241–266). Thousand Oaks, CA: Sage.

Levinson, D. J., Darrow, C. N., Klein, E. B., Levinson, M. H., & McKee, B. (1978). *The seasons of a man's life.* New York: Ballantine Books.

Levinson, D. J., & Levinson, J. D. (1997). *The seasons of a woman's life.* New York: Ballantine Books.

Lewis, J. A., Lewis, M. D., Daniels, J. A., & D'Andrea, M. J. (1998). *Community counseling.* Pacific Grove, CA: Brooks/Cole.

Liu, W. M. (2001). Expanding our understanding of multiculturalism: Developing a social class worldview model. In D. B. Pope-Davis & H. L. K. Coleman (Eds.), *The intersection of race, class, and gender in multicultural counseling* (pp. 127–170). Thousand Oaks, CA: Sage.

Locke, E. A., & Latham, G. P. (1984). *Goal setting: A motivational technique that works!* Englewood Cliffs, NJ: Prentice-Hall.

Long, V. O. (1996). *Communication skills in helping relationships: A framework for facilitating personal growth.* Pacific Grove, CA: Brooks/Cole.

Lonner, W. J., & Ibrahim, F. A. (2002). Appraisal and assessment in cross-cultural counseling. In P. B. Pedersen, J. G. Draguns, W. L. Lonner, & J. E. Trimble (Eds.), *Counseling across cultures* (5th ed., pp. 355–379). Thousand Oaks, CA: Sage.

Mack, M. L. (1994). Understanding spirituality in counseling psychology: Considerations for research, training, and practice. *Counseling and Values, 39,* 15–31.

Maehr, M. L., & Nicholls, J. (1980). Culture and achievement motivation: A second look. In N. Warren (Ed.), *Studies in cross-cultural psychology* (pp. 192–216). New York: Academic Press.

Maholick, L. T., & Turner, D. W. (1979). Termination: That difficult farewell. *American Journal of Psychotherapy, 33,* 583–591.

Mahoney, M. J. (2000). Training future psychotherapists. In C. R. Snyder & R. E. Ingram (Eds.), *Handbook of psychological change: Psychotherapy processes and practices for the 21st century* (pp. 727–735). New York: Wiley.

Maier, S. F., & Seligman, M. E. P. (1976). Learned helplessness theory and evidence. *Journal of Experimental Psychology, 105,* 3–46.

Martin, D. G. (2000). *Counseling and therapy skills* (2nd ed.). Prospect Heights, IL: Waveland Press.

Maslach, C., & Leiter, M. P. (1997). *The truth about burnout: How organizations cause personal stress and what to do about it.* San Francisco: Jossey-Bass.

Maslow, A. H. (1954). *Motivation and personality.* New York: Harper and Brothers.

McCann, I. L., & Pearlman, L. A. (1990). Vicarious traumatization: A framework for understanding the psychological effects of working with victims. *Journal of Traumatic Stress, 3,* 131–149.

McClam, T., & Woodside, M. (1994). *Problem solving in the helping professions.* Pacific Grove, CA: Brooks/Cole.

McGee, T. F., Schuman, B. N., & Racusen, F. (1972). Termination in group psychotherapy. *American Journal of Psychotherapy, 26,* 521–532.

McGoldrick, M., Giordano, J., & Pearce, J. K. (Eds.). (1996). *Ethnicity and family therapy* (2nd ed.). New York: Guilford Press.

McIntosh, P. (1989, July/August). White privilege: Unpacking the invisible knapsack. *Peace and Freedom,* 10–12.

Meara, N. M., Schmidt, L. D., & Day, J. D. (1996). Principles and virtues: A foundation for ethical decisions, policies, and character. *The Counseling Psychologist, 24,* 4–77.

Mehrabian, A. (1972). *Nonverbal communication.* Chicago: Aldine/Atherton.

Mesquita, B., & Frijda, N. H. (1992). Cultural variations in emotions: A review. *Psychological Bulletin, 112,* 179–204.

Miller, D. J., & Thelen, M. H. (1986). Knowledge and beliefs about confidentiality in psychotherapy. *Professional Psychology: Research and Practice, 17,* 15–19.

Miller, J. B. (1986). *Toward a new psychology of women.* Boston: Beacon Press.

Montaigne, M. de (1925). Of idleness. *The essays of Montaigne: Vol. 1* (G. B. Ives, Trans.). Cambridge, MA: Harvard University Press. (Original work published 1580)

Morley, J. (1910). *On compromise.* London: Macmillan.

Moursund, J., & Kenny, M. C. (2002). *The process of counseling and therapy* (4th ed.). Upper Saddle River, NJ: Prentice-Hall.

Mullen, B., Atkins, J. L., Champion, D. S., Edwards, C., Hardy, D., Story, J. E., et al. (1985). The false consensus effect: A meta-analysis of 115 hypothesis tests. *Journal of Experimental Social Psychology, 21,* 262–283.

Nash, J. (1972). I can see clearly now. On *I can see clearly now* [record]. New York: Sony Music.

National Association of Social Workers. (1999). *Code of ethics.* Washington, DC: Author.

Nelson-Jones, R. (1993). *Lifeskills helping: Helping others through a systematic people-centered approach.* Pacific Grove, CA: Brooks/Cole.

Nishio, K., & Bilmes, M. (1987). Psychotherapy with Southeast Asian American clients. *Professional Psychology: Research and Practice, 18,* 342–346.

Nugent, F. A. (2000). *Introduction to the profession of counseling* (3rd ed.). Upper Saddle River, NJ: Prentice-Hall.

Okun, B. F. (2002). *Effective helping: Interviewing and counseling techniques* (6th ed.). Pacific Grove, CA: Brooks/Cole.

Otto, R. K., & Schmidt, W. C. (1991). Malpractice in verbal psychotherapy: Problems and potential solutions. *Forensic Reports, 4,* 309–336.

Passons, W. R. (1975). *Gestalt approaches in counseling.* New York: Holt, Rinehart and Winston.

Patterson, L. E., & Welfel, E. R. (1994). *The counseling process* (4th ed.). Pacific Grove, CA: Brooks/Cole.

Pearlman, L. A., & Mac Ian, P. S. (1995). Vicarious traumatization: An empirical study of the effects of trauma work on trauma therapists. *Professional Psychology: Research and Practice, 26,* 558–565.

Peck, M. S. (1978). *The road less traveled: A new psychology of love, traditional values and spiritual growth.* New York: Simon and Schuster.

Pedersen, P. (1996). The importance of both similarities and differences in multicultural counseling: Reaction to C. H. Patterson. *Journal of Counseling and Development, 74,* 236–237.

Pedersen, P. (1999). Culture-centered interventions as a fourth dimension of psychology. In P. Pedersen (Ed.)., *Multiculturalism as a fourth force* (pp. 3–18). Philadelphia: Taylor and Francis.

Pedersen, P. B. (1991). Multiculturalism as a generic approach to counseling. *Journal of Counseling and Development, 70,* 6–12.

Pedersen, P. B. (1997). *Culture-centered counseling interventions: Striving for accuracy.* Thousand Oaks, CA: Sage.

Pedersen, P. B. (2000). *Hidden messages in culture-centered counseling: A triad training model.* Thousand Oaks, CA: Sage.

Pedersen, P. B. (2002). Ethics, competence, and other professional issues in culture-centered counseling. In P. B. Pedersen, J. G. Draguns, W. L. Lonner, & J. E. Trimble (Eds.), *Counseling across cultures* (5th ed., pp. 3–27). Thousand Oaks, CA: Sage.

Pedersen, P. B., & Ivey, A. (1993). *Culture-centered counseling and interviewing skills: A practical guide.* Westport, CT: Praeger.

Piazza, N. J., & Baruth, N. E. (1990). Client record guidelines. *Journal of Counseling and Development, 68,* 313–316.

Pipes, R. B., & Davenport, D. S. (1999). *Introduction to psychotherapy: Common clinical wisdom* (2nd ed.). Boston: Allyn and Bacon.

Pistole, M. C. (1999). Caregiving in attachment relationships: A perspective for counselors. *Journal of Counseling and Development, 77,* 437–446.

Ponterotto, J. G. (1991). The nature of prejudice revisited: Implications for counseling intervention. *Journal of Counseling and Development, 70,* 216–224.

Ponterotto, J. G., Fuertes, J. N., & Chen, E. C. (2000). Models of multicultural counseling.

In S. D. Brown & R. W. Lent (Eds.), *Handbook of counseling psychology* (3rd ed., pp. 639–669). New York: Wiley.

Ponterotto, J. G., & Pedersen, P. B. (1993). *Preventing prejudice: A guide for counselors and educators.* Newbury Park, CA: Sage.

Ponterotto, J. G., Rieger, B. P., Barrett, A., & Sparks, R. (1994). Assessing multicultural counseling competence: A review of instrumentation. *Journal of Counseling and Development, 72,* 316–322.

Poortinga, Y. H. (1990). Towards a conceptualization of culture for psychology. *Cross-Cultural Psychology Bulletin, 24*(3), 2–10.

Pope, K. S., & Bajt, T. R. (1988). When laws and values conflict: A dilemma for psychologists. *American Psychologist, 43,* 828–829.

Pope, K. S., & Vasquez, M. J. T. (2001). *Ethics in psychotherapy and counseling: A practical guide* (2nd ed.). San Francisco: Jossey-Bass.

Pope-Davis, D. B., & Coleman, H. L. K. (Eds.). (1997). *Multicultural counseling competencies: Assessment, education and training, and supervision.* Thousand Oaks, CA: Sage.

Pope-Davis, D. B., & Dings, J. G. (1995). The assessment of multicultural counseling competencies. In J. G. Ponterotto, J. M. Casas, L. A. Suzuki, & C. M. Alexander (Eds.), *Handbook of multicultural counseling* (pp. 287–311). Thousand Oaks, CA: Sage.

Pope-Davis, D. B., Toporek, R. L., Ortega-Villalobos, L., Ligiéro, D. P., Brittain-Powell, C. S., Liu, W. M., et al. (2002). Client perspectives of multicultural counseling competence: A qualitative examination. *The Counseling Psychologist, 30,* 355–393.

Prieto, L. R., McNeill, B. W., Walls, R. G., & Gómez, S. P. (2001). Chicanas/os and mental health services: An overview of utilization, counselor preference, and assessment issues. *The Counseling Psychologist, 29,* 18–54.

Prochaska, J. O. (2000). Change at differing stages. In C. R. Snyder & R. E. Ingram (Eds.), *Handbook of psychological change: Psychotherapy processes and practices for the 21st century* (pp. 109–127). New York: Wiley.

Prochaska, J. O., DiClemente, C. C., & Norcross, J. C. (1992). In search of how people change: Applications to addictive behaviors. *American Psychologist, 47,* 1102–1114.

Pronin, E., Lin, D. Y., & Ross, L. (2002). The bias blind spot: Perceptions of bias in self versus others. *Personality and Social Psychology Bulletin, 28,* 369–381.

Reamer, F. G. (1995). Malpractice claims against social workers: First facts. *Social Work, 40,* 595–601.

Reisner, R., & Slobogin, C. (1990). *Law and the mental health system: Civil and criminal aspects* (2nd ed.). St. Paul, MN: West.

Ridley, C. R. (1989). Racism in counseling as an adversive behavioral process. In P. B. Pedersen, J. G. Draguns, W. J. Lonner, & J. E. Trimble (Eds.), *Counseling across cultures* (3rd ed., pp. 55–77). Honolulu: University of Hawaii Press.

Ridley, C. R. (1995). *Overcoming unintentional racism in counseling and therapy: A practitioner's guide to intentional intervention.* Thousand Oaks, CA: Sage.

Riessman, F. (1965). The "helper" therapy principle. *Social Work, 10*(2), 27–32.

Robertson, J., & Fitzgerald, L. F. (1990). The (mis)treatment of men: Effects of client gender role and life-style on diagnosis and attribution of pathology. *Journal of Counseling Psychology, 37,* 3–9.

Robinson, R. J., Keltner, D., Ward, A., & Ross, L. (1995). Actual versus assumed differences in construal: "Naive realism" in intergroup perception and conflict. *Journal of Personality and Social Psychology, 68,* 404–417.

Rockwell, N. (1960, April 2). My adventures as an illustrator: I paint the President. *Saturday Evening Post,* pp. 31, 81, 83, 86–87.

Rogers, C. R. (1942). *Counseling and psychotherapy: Newer concepts in practice.* Boston: Houghton Mifflin.

Rogers, C. R. (1951). *Client-centered therapy: Its current practice, implications, and theory.* Boston: Houghton Mifflin.

Rogers, C. R. (1957). The necessary and sufficient conditions of therapeutic personality change. *Journal of Consulting Psychology, 21,* 95–103.

Rogers, C. R. (1961). *On becoming a person: A therapist's view of psychotherapy.* Boston: Houghton Mifflin.

Rogers, C. R. (1962). The characteristics of a helping relationship. In J. F. McGowan & L. D. Schmidt (Eds.), *Counseling: Readings in theory and practice* (pp. 215–227). New York: Holt, Rinehart and Winston.

Rønnestad, M. H., & Skovholt, T. M. (1991). En modell for profesjonell utvikling og stagnasjon hos terapeuter og radgivere [A model of the professional development and stagnation of therapists and counselors]. *Tidsskrift for Norsk Psykologforening [Journal of the Norwegian Psychological Association], 28,* 555–567.

Ross, L., Greene, D., & House, P. (1977). The "false consensus effect": An egocentric bias in social perception and attribution processes. *Journal of Experimental Social Psychology, 13,* 279–301.

Rubanowitz, D. E. (1987). Public attitudes toward psychotherapist-client confidentiality. *Professional Psychology: Research and Practice, 18,* 613–618.

Schank, J. A., & Skovholt, T. M. (1997). Dual-relationship dilemmas of rural and small-community psychologists. *Professional Psychology: Research and Practice, 28,* 44–49.

Scherer, K. R., & Ekman, P. (Eds.). (1982). *Handbook of methods in nonverbal behavior research.* Cambridge: Cambridge University Press.

Schneider, B. H., Karcher, M. J., & Schlapkohl, W. (1999). Relationship counseling across cultures: Cultural sensitivity and beyond. In P. Pedersen (Ed.), *Multiculturalism as a fourth force* (pp. 167–190). Philadelphia: Taylor and Francis.

Segall, M. H. (1979). *Cross-cultural psychology.* Monterey, CA: Brooks/Cole.

Seligman, M. E. P. (1975). *Helplessness: On depression, development, and death.* San Francisco: Freeman.

Seto, M. C. (1995). Sex with therapy clients: Its prevalence, potential consequences, and implications for psychology training. *Canadian Psychology/Psychologie Canadienne, 36,* 70–86.

Sexton, T. L., & Whiston, S. C. (1991). A review of the empirical basis for counseling: Implications for practice and training. *Counselor Education and Supervision, 30,* 330–354.

Sexton, T. L., & Whiston, S. C. (1994). The status of the counseling relationship: An empirical review, theoretical implications, and research directions. *The Counseling Psychologist, 22,* 6–78.

Shulman, L. (1999). *The skills of helping individuals, families, groups, and communities* (4th ed.). Itasca, IL: Peacock.

Simone, D. H., McCarthy, P., & Skay, C. L. (1998). An investigation of client and counselor variables that influence likelihood of counselor self-disclosure. *Journal of Counseling and Development, 76,* 174–182.

Skovholt, T. M. (1974). The client as helper: A means to promote psychological growth. *The Counseling Psychologist, 4*(3), 58–64.

Skovholt, T. M. (2001). *The resilient practitioner: Burnout prevention and self-care strategies for counselors, therapists, teachers, and health professionals.* Boston: Allyn and Bacon.

Skovholt, T. M., & Jennings, L. (Eds.). (2004). *Master therapists: Exploring expertise in therapy and counseling.* Boston: Allyn and Bacon.

Skovholt, T. M., Jennings, L., & Mullenbach, M. (2004). Portrait of the master therapist: Developmental model of the highly functioning self. In T. M. Skovholt & L. Jennings (Eds.), *Master therapists: Exploring expertise in therapy and counseling* (pp. 125–146). Boston: Allyn and Bacon.

Skovholt, T. M., & Rønnestad, M. H. (1995). *The evolving professional self: Stages and themes in therapist and counselor development.* Chichester: Wiley.

Skovholt, T. M., Rønnestad, M. H., & Jennings, L. (1997). Searching for expertise in counseling, psychotherapy, and professional psychology. *Educational Psychology Review, 9,* 361–369.

Smith, S. R. (1991). Mental health malpractice in the 1990s. *Houston Law Review, 28,* 209–283.

Smith, S. R. (1994). Liability and mental health services. *American Journal of Orthopsychiatry, 64,* 235–251.

Snyder, C. R., Ilardi, S., Michael, S. T., & Cheavens, J. (2000). Hope theory: Updating a common process for psychological change. In C. R. Snyder & R. E. Ingram (Eds.), *Handbook of psychological change: Psychotherapy processes and practices for the 21st century* (pp. 128–153). New York: Wiley.

Snyder, M. (1981). Seek, and ye shall find: Testing hypotheses about other people. In E. T. Higgins, C. P. Herman, & M. P. Zanna (Eds.), *Social cognition: The Ontario Symposium* (Vol. 1, pp. 277–303). Hillsdale, NJ: Erlbaum.

Snyder, M., & Campbell, B. H. (1980). Testing hypotheses about other people: The role of the hypothesis. *Personality and Social Psychology Bulletin, 6,* 421–426.

Söderfeldt, M., Söderfeldt, B., & Warg, L. E. (1995). Burnout in social work. *Social Work, 40,* 638–646.

Sodowsky, G. R., Kwan, K. K., & Pannu, R. (1995). Ethnic identity of Asians in the United States. In J. G. Ponterotto, J. M. Casas, L. A. Suzuki, & C. M. Alexander (Eds.), *Handbook of multicultural counseling* (pp. 123–154). Thousand Oaks, CA: Sage.

Sodowsky, G. R., Taffe, R. C., Gutkin, T. B., & Wise, S. L. (1994). Development of the

Multicultural Counseling Inventory: A self-report measure of multicultural competencies. *Journal of Counseling Psychology, 41,* 137–148.

Soisson, E. L., VandeCreek, L., & Knapp, S. (1987). Thorough record keeping: A good defense in a litigious era. *Professional Psychology: Research and Practice, 18,* 498–502.

Sommers-Flanagan, R., & Sommers-Flanagan, J. (1999). *Clinical interviewing* (2nd ed.). New York: Wiley.

Sonne, J. L. (1994). Multiple relationships: Does the new ethics code answer the right questions? *Professional Psychology: Research and Practice, 25,* 336–343.

Spengler, P. M., & Strohmer, D. C. (1994). Clinical judgment biases: The moderating roles of counselor cognitive complexity and counselor client preferences. *Journal of Counseling Psychology, 41,* 8–17.

Stadler, H. A. (1990). Counselor impairment. In B. Herlihy & L. B. Golden (Eds.), *Ethical standards casebook* (4th ed., pp. 177–187). Alexandria, VA: American Association for Counseling and Development.

Strohmer, D. C., & Shivy, V. A. (1994). Bias in counselor hypothesis testing: Testing the robustness of counselor confirmatory bias. *Journal of Counseling and Development, 73,* 191–197.

Strohmer, D. C., Shivy, V. A., & Chiodo, A. L. (1990). Information processing strategies in counselor hypothesis testing: The role of selective memory and expectancy. *Journal of Counseling Psychology, 37,* 465–472.

Strong, S. R. (1968). Counseling: An interpersonal influence process. *Journal of Counseling Psychology, 15,* 215–224.

Strong, S. R., & Claiborn, C. D. (1982). *Change through interaction: Social psychological processes of counseling and psychotherapy.* New York: Wiley.

Strong, S. R., & Schmidt, L. D. (1970). Expertness and influence in counseling. *Journal of Counseling Psychology, 17,* 81–87.

Sue, D. (1997). Multicultural training. *International Journal of Intercultural Relations, 21,* 175–193.

Sue, D. W., Arredondo, P., & McDavis, R. J. (1992). Multicultural counseling competencies and standards: A call to the profession. *Journal of Counseling and Development, 70,* 477–486.

Sue, D. W., Bernier, J. E., Durran, A., Feinberg, L., Pedersen, P., Smith, E. J., et al. (1982). Position paper: Cross-cultural counseling competencies. *The Counseling Psychologist, 10*(2), 45–52.

Sue, D. W., Carter, R. T., Casas, J. M., Fouad, N. A., Ivey, A. E., Jensen, M., et al. (1998). *Multicultural counseling competencies: Individual and organizational development.* Thousand Oaks, CA: Sage.

Sue, D. W., Ivey, A. E., & Pedersen, P. B. (1996). *A theory of multicultural counseling and therapy.* Pacific Grove, CA: Brooks/Cole.

Sue, D. W., & Sue, D. (1990). *Counseling the culturally different: Theory and practice* (2nd ed.). New York: Wiley.

Sue, D. W., & Sue, D. (2003). *Counseling the culturally diverse: Theory and practice* (4th ed.). New York: Wiley.

Sullivan, T., Martin, W. L., Jr., & Handelsman, M. M. (1993). Practical benefits of an informed–consent procedure: An empirical investigation. *Professional Psychology: Research and Practice, 24,* 160–163.

Sussman, M. B. (Ed.). (1995). *A perilous calling: The hazards of psychotherapy practice.* New York: Wiley.

Tallman, K., & Bohart, A. C. (1999). The client as a common factor: Clients as self-healers. In M. A. Hubble, B. L. Duncan, & S. D. Miller (Eds.), *The heart & soul of change: What works in therapy* (pp. 91–131). Washington, DC: American Psychological Association.

Tannen, D. (1990). *You just don't understand: Women and men in conversation.* New York: Ballantine Books.

Tarasoff v. Regents of the University of California, 118 Cal. Rptr. 129, 529 P.2d 533 (1974).

Tarasoff v. Regents of the University of California, 131 Cal. Rptr. 14, 551 P.2d 334 (1976).

Teyber, E. (2000). *Interpersonal process in psychotherapy: A relational approach* (4th ed.). Pacific Grove, CA: Brooks/Cole.

Theroux, P. (1979). *The old Patagonian Express: By train through the Americas.* Boston: Houghton Mifflin.

Triandis, H. C. (1995). *Individualism and collectivism.* Boulder, CO: Westview Press.

Triandis, H. C. (1996). The psychological measurement of cultural syndromes. *American Psychologist, 51,* 407–415.

Turock, A. (1980). Immediacy in counseling: Recognizing clients' unspoken messages. *Personnel and Guidance Journal, 59,* 168–172.

VandeCreek, L., Miars, R., & Herzog, C. (1987). Client anticipations and preferences for confidentiality of records. *Journal of Counseling Psychology, 34,* 62–67.

Vargas, A. M., & Borkowski, J. G. (1982). Physical attractiveness and counseling skills. *Journal of Counseling Psychology, 29*, 246–255.

Wampold, B. E. (2001). *The great psychotherapy debate: Models, methods, and findings.* Mahwah, NJ: Erlbaum.

Ward, D. E. (1984). Termination of individual counseling: Concepts and strategies. *Journal of Counseling and Development, 63*, 21–25.

Watkins, C. E., Jr. (1983). Transference phenomena in the counseling situation. *Personnel and Guidance Journal, 62*, 206–210.

Watkins, C. E., Jr. (1990). The effects of counselor self-disclosure: A research review. *The Counseling Psychologist, 18*, 477–500.

Watson, D. L., & Tharp, R. G. (2002). *Self-directed behavior* (8th ed.). Pacific Grove, CA: Brooks/Cole.

Weber, J. G. (1994). The nature of ethnocentric attribution bias: Ingroup protection or enhancement. *Journal of Experimental Social Psychology, 30*, 482–504.

Weiner, B. (1985). An attributional theory of achievement motivation and emotion. *Psychological Review, 92*, 548–573.

Weiner, B. A., & Wettstein, R. M. (1993). *Legal issues in mental health care.* New York: Plenum.

Welfel, E. R. (2002). *Ethics in counseling and psychotherapy: Standards, research, and emerging issues* (2nd ed.). Pacific Grove, CA: Brooks/Cole.

Welty, E. (1987). *The eye of the story: Selected essays and reviews.* London: Virago.

Woodworth, C. B. (2000). Legal issues in counseling practice. In H. Hackney (Ed.), *Practice issues for the beginning counselor* (pp. 119–136). Boston: Allyn and Bacon.

Worthington, E. L., Jr. (1989). Religious faith across the life span: Implications for counseling and research. *The Counseling Psychologist, 17*, 555–612.

Wrenn, C. G. (1962). The culturally encapsulated counselor. *Harvard Educational Review, 32*, 444–449.

Yalom, I. D. (1989). *Love's executioner and other tales of psychotherapy.* New York: Harper Perennial.

Young, M. E. (2001). *Learning the art of helping: Building blocks and techniques* (2nd ed.). Upper Saddle River, NJ: Prentice-Hall.